WASHINGTON WINES AND WINERIES

WASHINGTON WINES AND WINERIES

The Essential Guide

Second Edition, Completely Revised and Expanded

Paul Gregutt

UNIVERSITY OF CALIFORNIA PRESS

Berkeley   Los Angeles   London

University of California Press, one of the most distinguished university presses in the United States, enriches lives around the world by advancing scholarship in the humanities, social sciences, and natural sciences. Its activities are supported by the UC Press Foundation and by philanthropic contributions from individuals and institutions. For more information, visit www.ucpress.edu.

University of California Press
Berkeley and Los Angeles, California

University of California Press, Ltd.
London, England

Library of Congress Cataloging-in-Publication Data

Gregutt, Paul.
    Washington wines and wineries: the essential guide / Paul Gregutt.
—2nd ed., completely rev. and expanded.
        p. cm.
    Includes index.
    ISBN 978-0-520-26138-9 (cloth : alk. paper)
    1. Wine and wine making—Washington (State)   2. Wineries—Washington (State)—Guidebooks.   3. Vineyards—Washington (State)   I. Title.
TP557.G745 2010
641.2'209797—dc22   2010010389

Manufactured in the United States of America.
16   15   14   13   12   11   10
10   9   8   7   6   5   4   3   2   1

The paper used in this publication meets the minimum requirements of ANSI/NISO Z39.48-1992 (R 1997) (*Permanence of Paper*).

For Karen Stanton Gregutt—Mrs. G—my love, my partner, my Muse. Far more than my better half, you are my better three quarters. Without your unfailing support, this book would not exist.

Wine the good and bland, thou blessing
Of the good, the bad's distressing,
Sweet of taste by all confessing,
    Hail, thou world's felicity!
Hail thy hue, life's gloom dispelling;
Hail thy taste, all tastes excelling;
By thy power, in this thy dwelling
    Deign to make us drunk with thee!

Oh, how blest for bounteous uses
Is the birth of pure vine-juices!
Safe's the table which produces
    Wine in goodly quality.
Oh, in color how auspicious!
Oh, in odor how delicious!
In the mouth how sweet, propitious
    To the tongue enthralled by thee!

Blest the man who first thee planted,
Called thee by thy name enchanted!
He whose cups have ne'er been scanted
    Dreads no danger that may be.
Blest the belly where thou bidest!
Blest the tongue where thou residest!
Blest the mouth through which thou glidest,
    And the lips thrice blest by thee!

Translation of twelfth-century
"Latin Song of Wandering Students"

CONTENTS

LIST OF WINERIES

RISING STARS

PREFACE

It may seem as if I have jumped the gun updating the first edition of this book so quickly. What's the hurry? you might legitimately wonder. The simple answer, to quote Bob Dylan, is because "things have changed." A tidal wave of change has rolled over the Washington wine industry in just the past few years. Essentially, this is far more than a revised edition; it's almost a whole new book.

Washington State wines have made their entrance upon the world stage, and no longer need to stand shyly in the corner while some marquee player from California hogs the spotlight. Those who most closely follow developments in the wine world—bloggers, sommeliers, distributors, retailers, and even (gasp!) the press—have been keeping their eyes on the nation's second-largest wine-producing state. And they like what they see.

In the midst of a global recession, with many of the world's wine and spirits conglomerates reeling, Ste. Michelle Wine Estates, now the seventh-largest wine company in America, is posting record growth. In the Nielsen data for the sales year ending in July 2009, national sales of Washington State wines increased 9.1 percent by value and 6.8 percent by volume—figures well above national averages. The official number of bonded wineries in Washington has passed 650 and may well top 700 by the time this book reaches print.

The 2009 wine grape harvest—predicated to be the largest ever—is unofficially pegged at 155,000 tons. Statewide, there are 36,000 acres of vineyard. Better still, Washington has seen five straight exceptional vintages following the freeze of 2004, and these are the wines that form the basis for the reviews and winery classifications in this new edition. Two new AVAs (American Viticultural Areas) are profiled—Snipes Mountain and Lake Chelan—both approved in 2009. At least two more are already in the application phase.

The North American Wine Bloggers' Conference has chosen Walla Walla as the site of its June 2010 gathering. *Santé,* a national trade magazine for restaurant professionals, wrote in its May 2009 issue that "only recently has Washington wine become a must-have item in restaurants across the country." Eastern Washington is also becoming, often to the astonishment of the locals, a major wine-tourism magnet. Though these statistics are now a few years out of date, an economic impact study done by MKF Research estimated that tourists who visited Washington wineries in 2006 spent more than $237 million, up from just $18.9 million in 2000. In that same period, the number of visitors increased fivefold, from 350,000 to more than 1.7 million.

The quality of Washington wines, and the interest in these wines from around the world, has reached an all-time high. And that dramatically changes the purpose and creative focus of this book. The original edition was intended to make the case, as critically as possible, for Washington State to be considered a world-class winemaking region.

This time around, I'm starting with that as a given. The goal here is to give you a handle on the grapes, the AVAs, the vineyards, the wines, the winemakers, and the wineries that represent the best the state has to offer. Since my first wine column appeared in 1984, I have continually tasted and tracked the industry's growth, all the while benchmarking it against the wines of the Old World and the New World. I've made repeated visits to France, Spain, Italy, Germany, Argentina, and Australia, as well as up and down the West Coast and into British Columbia, and I've tasted tens of thousands of wines.

The conclusion I reached in the original edition of this book still stands. It's not often that a brand-new wine region with world-class capabilities comes along. I've been privileged to see this one grow from a tiny cutting into a major vine. Washington has moved out of the shadow of California. My sincere hope is that this book will help you to understand what makes this state and its wines unique and memorable, so that you can make your own delicious discoveries.

To Washington wine!

ACKNOWLEDGMENTS

Though I hold an Advanced Certificate from the London-based Wine & Spirit Education Trust, I owe my wine education less to any particular course of study than to the thousands of individuals who have taken the time to sit with me over the years and taste and discuss wine. They come from all sides of the business—growers and winemakers, importers and distributors, retail shop owners and sommeliers, journalists and marketers. All share a wonderful passion for this inexhaustible subject.

My Boar's Head brothers—Henry Stoll, Richard Hinds, and Ed Amyot—introduced me to the pleasures of wine drinking in college and have kept plying me with fine old wines ever since. The members of the two long-running tasting groups to which I belong, many of them winemakers and wine sellers themselves, have sparked memorable debates and kept my palate polished.

My ability to write about wine both enthusiastically and critically has been honed by the talented and supportive editors with whom I have been privileged to work. My deep appreciation goes to Harvey Steiman, who first published my work for a national readership; to David Brewster, who supported my wine column in the *Seattle Weekly* for more than a decade; to Adam Strum and the editors at the *Wine Enthusiast,* who have recognized the importance of Washington State viticulture and given me many opportunities to write about it; to Tom Stevenson, whose books have provided a model for wine criticism to which I can only aspire; and to the publisher and editors at the *Seattle Times* and its family of newspapers, who for the past nine years have allowed me the privilege of covering this most fascinating subject for the hometown crowd.

I deeply appreciate the support of University of California Press acquisitions editor Blake Edgar, who first tracked me down, doggedly insisted that I was the person he most wanted to write a definitive book on Washington State wine, shrugged off my objections, tolerated my dithering, welcomed my first manuscript with genuine enthusiasm, and eagerly approved this new edition. His patient, long-term efforts on my behalf have been invaluable, as have the contributions of many other individuals at this most prestigious publisher.

The staff, past and present, at both the Washington Wine Commission and the Walla Walla Wine Alliance have been enormously helpful in arranging numerous tastings and compiling current statistics on the industry. And to all those who grow the grapes and make the wines, I offer my most sincere thanks. You have enriched my life beyond words.

Paul Gregutt
Waitsburg, Washington
January 2010

INTRODUCTION

As in the original edition of this book, I have attempted once again to thoroughly cover the history, grapes, AVAs, essential vineyards, and most important wineries in Washington. Reading this book should feel like a tour through the state with an old friend who happens to be a local and who knows it well. I am that friend.

I have lived in Washington since 1972. A Seattleite ("wet-sider" as we're called) for most of that time, I saw my life change dramatically in 2005 when Mrs. G and I purchased a run-down, all-but-abandoned farmhouse in the city of Waitsburg—population 1,212. Founded in the 1860s by Sylvester Wait, it is located in Washington's southeast corner, just 18 miles north of Walla Walla. We loved Waitsburg immediately, for the natural beauty of the surrounding landscape, for the easy cordiality of the townspeople, for the peacefulness that we felt whenever we could escape from the big city and come work on our little cottage.

Since then, we've spent about half of every month living in eastern Washington. Rather than blasting through for a brief tour and tasting, as most wine writers do, I am now seeing the wine country through the eyes of a resident. This has deeply enriched my appreciation for, and knowledge of, the wines I review.

I remain a critic, not a cheerleader. Any region whose aspirations are to become world-class must have its wines evaluated in the context of the global competition. When I write about a winery making an exciting riesling or merlot or syrah, it goes without saying that I mean the compliment globally. These are not just good wines for the region; they are good wines for the world.

More fervently than ever, I believe that Washington State is well on its way to becoming one of the greatest wine regions in the world. This despite (or perhaps because of) its fringe location, its reliance on irrigation, its desert heat and arctic blasts, its frequent separation of growers and winemakers, its preponderance of tiny, underfunded start-ups, and the persistent myth that it is too cold, too wet, and too far north to make great wine. In other words, despite the fact that Washington is not, and never will be, California. When it comes to exploring unknown viticultural territory and crafting stylistically original, world-class wines, Washington has come as far or further, in less time, than California. Without California's vast advantages, little Washington has plugged along, driven by dreamers and doers who believed that there was something magical in the land.

People such as John Williams and Jim Holmes, who bought some barren acreage on a desolate hill called Red Mountain back in 1975 and decided to grow cabernet there. People such as Dr. William McAndrew, who planted gewürztraminer and a variety of other grapes in an old apple orchard high above the Columbia Gorge in 1972, dubbed it Celilo, and waited to see what, if anything, would survive. People such as Christophe Baron, a native Champenois who made wine in half a dozen places around the world before circling for a landing in Walla Walla, then doggedly searched for land to plant until he found the rockiest, least likely, most difficult and labor-intensive soil in the region and hand-planted his Cailloux vineyard to syrah.

Newcomers continue to flock to Washington, often abandoning careers in midlife, pulling up stakes and following their winemaking dreams. In these pages you'll find dozens of new wineries, with names such as Cadaretta, Doubleback, Gramercy Cellars, Hard Row To Hoe, Maison Bleue, Rasa, Tranche, and Trust—all ventures begun by folks who had already built successful lives, but were consumed with a desire to make wine in Washington.

Today Ciel du Cheval and Klipsun cabernet, Champoux merlot and cabernet franc, Celilo gewürztraminer, and Cailloux syrah (to name just a few) can stake a legitimate claim to greatness. They have all passed the test of time, and also the test of timelessness. These vineyards express that elusive, often abused (and misspelled) term *terroir*. Washington's vignerons are beginning to find it, and in the pages of this book you will learn specifically who and what and where.

There *is* something magical in this land. The pioneers were right about that, as are those who continue to explore and expand viticulture in Washington today. It's true that the eleven AVAs now officially recognized include millions of acres of land that is not, and will never be, dedicated to wine grape growing. But tucked away here and there are the sites that work, that have the potential, if properly managed, to create exceptional wines. Finding those places is what has obsessed those who have pioneered winemaking during the first few decades of Washington's modern wine era.

The exploration continues, in previously untapped regions such as Lake Chelan, a new AVA that may hold the key to great Washington pinot noir, if such is ever to exist;

in potential future AVAs such as the Ancient Lakes, where vineyards barely a decade old are producing grapes with astonishing complexity, minerality, and verve; and in the outer reaches of well-established AVAs such as Walla Walla, where the newest vineyards are reaching higher into the mountains and pushing deeper into wheat country than ever before.

For a wine lover, Washington is experiencing a delicious moment in time. How many people in the history of the world have witnessed the flowering of a brand-new, world-class wine region? Who among us has tasted, in each new vintage, wines that push the envelope a bit further than it has previously been pushed, that reveal unknown or unsuspected layers of flavor and bouquet, nuances previously locked away in a piece of scrub desert, or a rocky riverbed, or a mountainside blanketed in volcanic dust?

The dust of exploration has not entirely settled, to be sure, but it continues to be mapped, studied, ripped, planted, trellised, irrigated, fertilized, chronicled, and delineated into more and more meaningful subregions. The wineries and vineyards that survived the mistakes and trials of Washington's early years have learned some hard-won lessons, making it easier for those who follow in their footsteps to craft excellent wines (though competing for customers in such a crowded marketplace has never been more difficult).

Honest feedback from a well-informed, widely traveled wine journalist can be quite valuable to any winery willing to listen to what is being said. In an effort to ensure that my words of praise ring true to readers, I must be carefully selective. The first edition of this book included only about one quarter of the state's wineries. This edition expands that to a third—roughly double the previous number of winery entries. That is both to acknowledge the industry's rampant growth and to recognize that improvement in quality is ongoing and pervasive.

Nonetheless, I'm still leaving out two-thirds of those who make wine for a living in Washington, and believe me, they are not likely to be selling my book in their tasting rooms or singing its praises to their customers. But I am writing this for you consumers, who don't need another guidebook that simply lists every winery and salutes its wines as if all were created equal. You know, and I know, they are not.

My methodology and palate preferences, as I explain on my website (www.paulgregutt. com), are as follows. I prefer to taste wines for review when they are finished and bottled rather than in barrel, and just ahead of their official release dates. I taste in controlled settings, using proper stemware, and I give the wines as much time and attention as they deserve, often returning to them over a period of days. Several times each month I sit down at one-on-one tastings with winemakers, distributors, or importers. I also attend trade events and participate in two long-established tasting groups whose members include winemakers, wine distributors, wine retailers, and knowledgeable consumers.

I seek out those wines that best demonstrate typicity, specificity, clarity, elegance, polish, depth, and balance. If the wine is varietal, I want it to taste like the varietal. If it is from a specific place, I want to taste something unique that is derived from that place. If a wine is designated by vineyard, clone, or block; if it is labeled "old vine" or "winemaker's select" or "reserve," I think it should justify that verbiage by showing me something specific and special. It's OK by me if a wine is light, as long as it is not thin; elegant, but not wimpy; powerful, but not brutal; dense, but not monolithic. Obviously the qualities I seek are more easily found at higher price points, but when I recommend an inexpensive wine, you may be certain it stands out well above its peers.

In the first edition of this book, I embarked upon a rather quixotic quest to recalibrate the nearly ubiquitous 100-point scoring system. I decided to do this because, as I explained, the purported 100-point scale, in actual practice, is not a 100-point scale at all, nor even close. For all practical purposes, it has become a 10-point scale. Wines rated under 85 are ignored completely. Wines rated 85 to 89 must be marketed as value wines—those numbers work only for wines priced at the low end of the scale. If your wine is going to sell for $15 or more, it must hit 90 points at least. Once a wine moves up the ladder from there, it becomes increasingly rare and expensive. As a result, wines scoring 95 or above are virtually unobtainable.

I felt it made more sense to use at least half of the 100-point scale—allotting scores between 50 and 100—and to score wineries rather than individual wines. With that in mind, I awarded up to 30 points each for style, consistency, and value, and up to 10 points for the winery's contribution to the development and improvement of the Washington wine industry. And just to be very clear, I emphasized that every winery included in the book was, in my view, well above average. Every score, even one in the 50s or 60s, was a good score in this radically revised 100-point system.

This new edition does not use numerical ratings. I made my point, and most readers and reviewers appreciate what I was trying to do. This time, I've adopted a much simpler star rating. The exact same standards are being applied; it's just the scoring system that is simplified. As before, wineries are being evaluated for a combination of strengths, particularly style, consistency, and value, displayed over a period of time.

In terms of style, I am looking for wineries with a unique, clearly defined, technically flawless style. When I taste a Leonetti Cellar wine, for example, I recognize a particular combination of superb fruit, layering of barrel flavors, and satiny, impactful, seductive mouthfeel that is unique and that has been a hallmark of the winery for three decades. That's what a five-star winery does in terms of style. Every winery in this book is making strides toward establishing its own style. It's not easy to do. There are thousands upon thousands of great guitar players, but how many can you identify on the basis of, say, two or three well-struck notes? It's not easy to be really good, but it's much harder to be unique.

Consistency is simply a measure of experience. Young wineries are experimenting, changing blends, changing vineyard sources, working hard to define themselves. The best will eventually settle into a style and stay there consistently, but that takes time. Wineries that have succeeded in making excellent wines over many vintages naturally deserve a higher rating than those just getting started.

Value is not the same as cheap. There are plenty of $6 and $8 wines in the world that are not good values. And there are a few $50 or even $100 wines that are exceptional values, given the quality. My Top 100 lists, published on pages 303–313, are a good indication of which wines offer both exceptional quality and outstanding value. You will find twenty wineries singled out as five-star wineries, forty-five four-star wineries, sixty three-star wineries, and in the "Rising Stars" chapter, dozens of Washington's newest wineries, their careers just taking off, that have already caught my attention with outstanding wines.

If you already have your own list of favorite Washington wineries, you may find one or two missing from my own selections. Please do not take offense. Some are simply too new to evaluate. Some do not choose to take advantage of the many opportunities to submit their wines for review. Some simply do not suit my personal tastes.

There are many sources, both in print and online, that offer opinions and ratings about wines. Even the most educated palates frequently disagree. I belong to two long-established tasting groups that count among their members winemakers, distributors, retailers, and salespeople, many of them with impressive credentials and decades of experience. The roundtable discussions that our blind tastings ignite are never dull, usually hilarious, and frequently combative. They certainly sharpen my thinking and my palate, and I thank my fellow tasters (you know who you are) for sharing your time and talents so generously.

I think there is value in such group discussions, but when you read of medals awarded or points given to individual wines by tasting/judging panels, no matter how well credentialed, you may be certain that compromise was involved. When wines are reviewed and scored by a single individual, one person's palate is involved, not the decision of a committee. You can agree or disagree, but at least you have a compass and an orientation.

I taste roughly six thousand to eight thousand wines annually, mostly at home, in peer group flights. I supplement these tastings with numerous trips to wineries throughout Washington, along the West Coast, and overseas. As I live half of the time in Seattle and the other half in Walla Walla County, I travel regularly throughout the length and breadth of Washington wine country. As often as time permits, I taste new releases with winemakers, believing that the information gleaned from our conversations outweighs any chance that my impressions will be overly influenced by their presence.

I do not like hit-and-run wine judging. There are snapshots and there are movies; I think wines are movies that should be observed in motion. With that in mind, I taste wines slowly, over many hours, with and without food, and sometimes over several days. I believe that there are times when we must extend ourselves to a wine and give it a decent chance to show its stuff.

One reason that massive, jammy, oaky, fruit-bomb wines tend to win high scores and gold medals is that they stand out quickly during rapid-fire wine tastings. If a wine is one of 150 or 200 bottles being sampled in a single day (this is standard practice at wine judgings!), is it any wonder that only the biggest, brawniest, most forward and ripe will be noticed? I have lost count of the times that a young wine, just opened, failed to perform. Wines submitted for review are new releases; many have just recently been blended and bottled. They have had little time to settle down and may be a bit "shocked." But give these wines a few hours or even days, and they may open up beautifully. Which is the more accurate impression—the instant snapshot or the film clip?

Of course, there are many wines whose simplistic structure or generic character are instantly apparent. Retasting after some hours have passed merely serves to confirm the original opinion. Flawed wines with TCA, microbial taint, oxidation, volatile acidity, and so forth are also easily and quickly chronicled. But often it is the very wines that best demonstrate terroir—whose innate structure, balance, clarity, precision, and depth portend ageworthiness—that are wrapped up tight as mummies when first opened. These are the gems that will benefit from extra hours of breathing and decanting. These are the wines that are easiest to miss in a hit-and-run evaluation.

I especially value wines that do not obliterate nuance in favor of the crowd-pleasing flavors of new oak. Wines built upon grapes ripened to appropriate levels for their particular vineyard site. Wines with complex and detailed aromas, with well-defined fruit, and with balancing acids and tannins that are harmoniously integrated into the whole. The wines that I most enjoy and constantly search for are those that have a focus. They taste like something specific—a particular grape variety or well-defined varietal blend, grown and made into wine in a special place.

The best wines reflect the soil, climate, and vintage conditions of the vineyard. The French word *terroir,* which has no English equivalent, describes a wine that expresses the grape, the soil, the site, and the climate through its complex scents and flavors. Excessive ripeness, super-extraction, alcohol topping 15, 16, or even 17 percent (in unfortified dry wines!), and the ham-handed application of expensive new oak—the formula for many so-called cult wines—will obliterate terroir (if it is there to begin with).

Such jammy, flashy, high-octane, hedonistic wines are rarely fit companions at mealtime. Their very bigness—Port-like levels of fruit and alcohol, smelling like a lumber yard—makes it difficult to down a second glass. Many vintners in this state recognize that bigger is not necessarily better. Washington's unique geography gives them the opportunity, the potential, to ripen grapes to physiological maturity while retaining high natural acid levels and keeping sugars and pH in balance. If the vineyard is sited well, the vines are managed well, the picking is done at the right time, and the winemaking is noninterventionist, there is a real chance to find that elusive terroir.

Terroir-driven wines have the best chance of aging over the long term. Throughout both editions of this book, I have noted vertical tastings of Washington wines, from vintages going back as many as 30 years. They prove that this state has the ability to produce wines with the structure and character not only to last but to improve. Among the white wines, it is riesling that will last the longest, as a ten-year retrospective of Eroica recently demonstrated (they all had many years of life still ahead). Washington merlots can improve for at least a decade and continue to provide drinking pleasure for another decade. Some cabernets and Bordeaux blends may last even longer.

On average, I would recommend drinking most white wines within three years of their release, though rieslings (and perhaps other aromatic whites, such as gewürztraminer) can be held far longer. Washington syrahs are a bit of a mystery; they are almost always peak performers when very young, and I have had little opportunity to taste extensively of well-aged versions.

Merlots should generally be consumed within six to eight years; cabernets within ten to twelve. Wines that are especially high in alcohol (more than 15 percent) and unusually low in acid (or high in pH), that display powerful barrel aromas and flavors, along with raisin or prune, or that show early hints of oxidation or browning are not likely to cellar well.

Back in the 1970s a typical bottle of Washington cabernet would have between 12 and 12.5 percent alcohol. Today the average is at least two percentage points higher. The interesting thing is that some of those older wines have aged beautifully. They may have been underripe by today's standards, but with the passing of time they have evolved flavors that are closer to European wines than most others made in America. These occasional early successes clearly point the way to a Washington winemaking style that straddles the border between the massive, fruit-powered wines of California and the more acidic, austere, herbal, mineral-laced, terroir-driven wines of Europe.

A number of wineries in Washington are actively exploring this borderline, crafting superb wines that suit the twenty-first-century palate, that beautifully accompany the foods we most enjoy—wines that will not only persist but evolve over time. These wines are the beacons that show us where to find true terroir in these brand-new New World vineyards. They are the wineries that often draw my highest praise in these pages.

AUTHOR'S NOTE: For ongoing, up-to-the-minute information on Washington wines, wineries, vineyards, events, and tourism, as well as lively discussions of wine industry topics, please visit www.paulgregutt.com.

PART I

HISTORY AND *TERROIR*

1

WHICH SIDE OF THE POTOMAC?

A Brief History of Washington Wines

For many years Bob Betz, a Master of Wine (MW) who now has his own Betz Family winery, traveled the globe speaking to audiences on behalf of Stimson Lane (the corporate parent of Columbia Crest and Chateau Ste. Michelle, among others). His standard spiel neatly encapsulated the story of the wineries, their vineyards, and the growth of winemaking in Washington. Nonetheless, he found that a certain amount of confusion persisted among a significant percentage of his audiences. At one particular East Coast appearance, he recalls, his audience seemed to be paying close attention, following his every word, carefully studying the charts and photographs, and showing keen interest in his subject. Wrapping up his presentation, Betz asked if there were any questions. A hand shot up. "Just one question, Bob. Which side of the Potomac did you say the grapes were grown on?"

For most consumers who do not live on the West Coast of the United States, the name Washington is most closely identified with the District of Columbia, the nation's capital. In other countries, most wine drinkers know that the Napa Valley is in California, somewhere north of Disneyland. Beyond that, things get pretty vague. Washington State? It's up there a ways, pretty close to Alaska.

Compounding the confusion caused by this state's name is its schizophrenic geography. In terms of climate, precipitation, and the overall look and feel of the landscape, it splits neatly into two completely different halves, which may conveniently be labeled the wet side and the dry side. If you hold out your left hand, palm facing you, fingers folded, thumb spread, you have a perfect map of Washington state. Your thumb is the Olympic

Peninsula, with the Pacific Ocean on the left and Puget Sound on the right. Follow the line between your index and middle fingers on down to your wrist; there you have the Cascade Mountains, a relatively young and still active range of volcanoes best known for Mount Baker, Mount Rainier, Mount St. Helens, and across the Oregon border, Mount Hood. Pretty much everything from the bottom of the other three fingers to the wrist is desert or, as the locals like to think of it, wine country.

On the wet side, the Olympic Mountains, which would run down the center of your thumb, parallel to the Cascades, are the first shield against the massive storms that blow in from the Pacific. They turn Puget Sound into a perpetual convergence zone, with weather systems coming up from the south or down from the north and colliding, usually somewhere right around Seattle. Though not as wet or cold as its reputation would have it, the climate in western Washington allows only cool-climate wine grapes (and hybrids) to ripen.

The Cascades act as the second barrier to the moisture-laden Pacific fronts and pretty much soak up the lion's share of the rain and snow that those storms bring. Once across the mountain passes, you descend through alpine forests into dryer and dryer meadows and valleys that ultimately open onto the great deserts of eastern Washington.

Eastern Washington had nonmilitary white settlements before the western side did, and wine grapes were being grown in the Walla Walla Valley by the 1860s. More than a half century of growth and experimentation, on both sides of the state, came to an abrupt end with Prohibition. I thought there were no commercially viable pre-Prohibition vines left in Washington, until I toured Snipes Mountain with Todd Newhouse and saw muscat vines the size of trees, which he believes were planted right around 1917.

It would be misleading to say that the modern era of winemaking in Washington began with Repeal, as it did in California. Although it is true that many new wineries were bonded at that time, they made no varietal wines and only occasionally and haphazardly used vinifera grapes. In western Washington, most wines were produced from Island Belle grapes, grown on Stretch Island in south Puget Sound. In the vineyards of eastern Washington, field blends might have included anything and everything, from Concord and Campbell Early (another name for Island Belle) to zinfandel, muscat, and alicanté bouschet.

These grapes were harvested all together, tossed into fermenters together, and made into unfortified sweet wines. Many of the best-selling wines were produced by a so-called high fermentation technique that added bags of sugar to the fermenting grapes and used special yeasts to boost alcohol levels to 17 percent, the maximum allowed by the state. Labeled Burgundy, Rhine Riesling, Sauternes, and so on, these wines accounted for the lion's share of Washington wine sales right through the 1960s. A thirsty public, freed from the restrictions of Prohibition and beginning to recover from the Great Depression, wanted a good buzz, not terroir.

In retrospect, post-Prohibition liquor laws in Washington seem to have been designed, purposely or not, to block meaningful attempts to make European-style dry table wines and to create a protected market for sweet, high-fermentation wines. In 1934, the Washington State Liquor Act was passed, which created the Liquor Control Board. The Washington State Liquor Control Board regulates and controls the sales of all hard liquor to this day. Initially, it allowed only beer and wine to be sold by the glass, in licensed restaurants and taverns. Wine, according to the WSLCB, was anything fermented that contained no more than 17 percent alcohol.

Ironically, this created the incentive to manufacture wines with unnaturally high levels of both sugar and alcohol, to satisfy the desires of consumers who couldn't get served a cocktail or glass of whiskey. Part and parcel of these laws were trade restrictions that taxed out-of-state wineries heavily but allowed Washington wineries to sell directly to retail accounts. The price advantages, designed to foster the local industry, also meant that few quality wines from California or anywhere else could find much of a market in Washington.

By 1937, forty-two wineries were licensed in the state, mostly small and devoted to making fruit wines rather than grape wines. The local products were the mainstay alcoholic beverages of the taverns, while the California brands were offered (at substantially higher prices) in the state liquor stores and some restaurants. The Washington wineries banded together to push their advantage, and taxes on California wines were repeatedly raised. By the end of 1942, notes author Ron Irvine in *The Wine Project: Washington State's Winemaking History* (now out of print), there were just twenty-four Washington wineries, but they controlled almost two-thirds of the total wine sales in the state.

Legally permissible alcohol levels continued to rise, and fortified wines replaced the sugar-enhanced, 17-percenters of the prewar years. By 1948, Irvine reports, 85 percent of all Washington wines were fortified. But the Washington wine industry was again in decline, and the number of wineries in the state began dropping steadily.

The legislative tug-of-war between competing interests, and the conflicted attempts by the state legislature to support the Washington wine industry with tax breaks and other measures while its own Liquor Control Board promoted the sales of California wines, has been well chronicled elsewhere. It delayed for two decades the birth of the modern-day Washington wine industry.

In the late 1960s, two startling events brought revolutionary change virtually overnight. The first was a chance encounter between *Wines of America* author Leon Adams, making a visit to the Yakima Valley in 1966, and Victor Allison, the manager for American Wine Growers. Allison had taken notice of the growing interest in California varietal wines and begun experimenting with a few of his own. Adams happened across just a single memorable Washington wine on that trip, a rosé of grenache, made by Associated Vintners (A/V), a group of amateur winemakers from the University of Washington.

The founding members of A/V had banded together in the 1950s, intending to make dry varietal wines for their own consumption. They incorporated in 1962 and a year later purchased and planted a small vineyard, Harrison Hill, in the heart of the Yakima

Valley. Dr. Cornelius Peck, one of the ten who started the enterprise, recalled in an interview a few years ago that so little was known about growing vinifera grapes in Washington that A/V's members planted nine different varieties on their five acres to see which grapes, if any, might survive.

Apparently, grenache was an early survivor, and was made into the epiphany-producing rosé that so impressed Leon Adams. He suggested to Victor Allison that a good California winemaker might be able to make something even better with Washington grapes, and mentioned the name of André Tchelistcheff, the man behind the great wines of Beaulieu Vineyards. Allison brought Tchelistcheff to Washington the following year, and, after plowing through a selection of dismal offerings, he tasted another Associated Vintners wine, this one a gewürztraminer, and was immediately convinced that the potential existed to make great wine from Washington grapes.

Encouraged by the praise of Adams and Tchelistcheff, the Associated Vintners decided to sell their wines commercially. Tchelistcheff was hired as a consultant for American Wine Growers. His first wines were produced in 1967 and included a cabernet, a pinot noir, a sémillon, and a grenache. The second paradigm-shifting event occurred in March 1969, when the so-called California Wine Bill was passed. It eliminated the trade barriers that had propped up the Washington wine industry since Repeal and, for the first time, legalized retail wine sales off-premises. The Washington wine industry had finally entered the twentieth century.

THE 1970s

In 1970, no more than a half dozen commercial wineries were operating in Washington State. The two of lasting importance, Associated Vintners and AWG's Ste. Michelle brand, were making varietal wines from a number of different grapes, and they quickly began attracting the attention of wine lovers from out of state.

A group called the San Francisco Wine Sampling Club tasted a number of Ste. Michelle wines in 1970 and pronounced them "a serious challenge" to California varietal wines. The influential California wine writer Robert Balzer conducted a riesling competition a few years later and announced that a 1972 Johannisberg riesling from Ste. Michelle had bested entries from California, Germany, and Australia.

Spurred by the growing interest in varietal wines, Ste. Michelle, which was acquired by conglomerate U.S. Tobacco in 1974, began planting extensive vineyards in eastern Washington. Others were conducting their own experiments in far-flung corners of the state. The Associated Vintners continued to cultivate their vines in the Yakima Valley, near Sunnyside. Jim Holmes and John Williams began their exploration of Red Mountain. Gary Figgins tended an acre or two in Walla Walla. Charles Henderson planted riesling, gewürztraminer, pinot noir, and other grapes in the Bingen–White Salmon area of the Columbia Gorge, and in 1972, Dr. William McAndrew followed suit at his Celilo vineyard. A few miles farther west, Lincoln and Joan Wolverton planted pinot noir, chardonnay, and riesling at La Center, somewhat whimsically calling their vineyard the northernmost extension of the Willamette Valley.

This was the first great wave of Washington viticulture, boosted along by more and more visionaries, such as Mike Wallace, Bill Preston, Maury Balcom, Don Mercer, Mike Sauer, and Jerry Bookwalter, among many others. Ste. Michelle Vintners became Ste. Michelle Vineyards and planted cabernet and riesling at their Cold Creek site. But the most far-reaching event was the purchase of the Ste. Michelle brand, vineyards, and winemaking facilities by U.S. Tobacco (UST) in 1974. From then on, the company controlled the vast majority of Washington State's varietal wine vineyards and production.

By the end of the decade, Washington had roughly a dozen wineries and 2,600 acres of vinifera vineyard. Despite a severe freeze in the winter of 1979, the future, as a very young Bill Gates might have said, was so bright you needed sunglasses.

THE 1980s

Washington had shown that it could make competitive varietal wines. But the state's reputation for periodic arctic blasts seemed intact. If its vines were constantly being frozen back to the roots, it seemed a gamble to look beyond winter-hardy, northern European grapes and even hardier hybrids.

Somehow, a critical number of growers were not deterred. Many were farmers, whose view of wine grapes was that they were just another crop to be added to the mix of hops, potatoes, mint, asparagus, apples, cherries, Concords, and so on that was already in the ground. They were used to the weather problems. Grapes were planted, as a general rule, in the most fertile soils, watered heavily, and harvested early. Getting the crop in, rather than maximizing wine quality, was paramount.

The Yakima Valley, a fertile crescent extending from the city of Yakima in the west almost to the Tri-Cities in the east (Richland, Kennewick, and Pasco), attracted the most attention. It had plenty of water, supported well-established agricultural enterprises, and was already planted to some of Washington's oldest, most proven vineyards. Other significant vineyard developments were concentrated in the Columbia Basin, north of the Tri-Cities, and south of Prosser, in the Horse Heaven Hills above the Columbia River.

As the decade began, Ste. Michelle and Associated Vintners (renamed Columbia Winery) were the state's big players, along with a few smaller, family-owned vineyard and winery operations (Kiona, Hinzerling, Mont Elise, Preston, Yakima River) and a handful of boutiques (Leonetti Cellar, Neuharth, Quilceda Creek, Worden's). But as the '80s swung into full stride, more and more large-scale, family-run, and cooperative enterprises appeared: Hogue Cellars, Hyatt Vineyards, Gordon Brothers, Mercer Ranch Vineyards, Quail Run, Quarry Lake Vintners, and Tagaris among them. A wave of smaller mom-and-pop wineries, many without vineyards of their own, followed quickly: Arbor Crest, Barnard Griffin, Bonair, Bookwalter, Chinook, Latah Creek, L'Ecole No 41, Pontin del Roza, Portteus, Salishan, Tucker Cellars, Woodward Canyon, and dozens more.

When it opened in 1982, Chateau Ste. Michelle's Paterson Winery, as Columbia Crest was first known, represented an extraordinary $25 million commitment to the future of Washington wine. Along with the state-of-the-art winemaking facility (capacity 2 million gallons) came almost 2,000 acres of new vineyard—an instant 50 percent increase for the state.

Perhaps the most important development of the decade, even more important than the wine industry's steady growth, was national acclaim for some of Washington's red wines. Though Ste. Michelle and Columbia were certainly doing a very good job, especially with their single-vineyard cabernets, much of the interest from out of state was focused on a few of the new boutiques, notably Leonetti Cellar, Quilceda Creek, Woodward Canyon, L'Ecole No 41, and Hogue Cellars.

Hogue's 1983 Reserve cabernet sauvignon dazzled the judges at the Atlanta Wine Festival, who named the wine Best of Show. Made by Rob Griffin (his Barnard Griffin winery was begun that same year), it revealed a combination of silky elegance and pure fruit-driven power that few outside the state had ever witnessed in a Washington red. Leonetti's 1978 cabernet sauvignon (the winery's first commercial release) made the cover of a long-gone wine publication (*Wine and Spirits Buying Guide*) and was touted as the best cab in the country. Quilceda Creek's first vintage, a 1979 cabernet sauvignon, brought home the Grand Prize from the prestigious Enological Society. L'Ecole's 1983 merlot (also its first commercial vintage) won a gold medal from the Enological Society a few years later. Latah Creek's 1983 merlot was given a gold medal at the Sixteenth International Wine and Spirits Competition in Bristol, England. And the fledgling Washington Wine Writers' Association voted the 1984 Woodward Canyon Dedication Series cabernet sauvignon the wine of the year in 1986.

Throughout the decade, vineyard-designated wines began to appear, first as a trickle and then with increasing regularity. The state's first AVAs were named in quick succession: Yakima Valley, Walla Walla Valley, and the all-encompassing Columbia Valley. The first significant European investment in Washington's wine industry was made when Germany's F. W. Langguth family, along with a group of Washington investors, planted the 265-acre Weinbau vineyard and built an ultramodern, 35,000-square-foot winery in the desolate sagebrush desert outside Mattawa. Langguth's commitment to producing Germanic rieslings was decades ahead of its time, as was its foresight in developing the region that would later become known as the Wahluke Slope, Washington's eighth AVA and home to some of its most important vineyards.

The number of wineries tripled, from fewer than twenty at the beginning of the decade to sixty by 1989. Vineyard acreage grew more slowly, from 7,742 acres in 1981 (more than half of them newly planted and nonbearing) to 9,000 bearing acres in 1989. But although Washington's total wine production lacked the sheer quantity to command much of a presence outside the state, trends were appearing that would set the stage for vast changes in the decade ahead.

In the mid-1980s, the Washington Wine Commission and its companion Washington Wine Institute were funded and began their efforts to promote and legislate for

Washington vintners. The commission's first World Vinifera Conference, held in Seattle in the summer of 1989, brought winemakers from around the world to Washington State and matched Washington's rieslings with the best from elsewhere. *Wine Country* magazine named Chateau Ste. Michelle "Best American Winery" in 1988. *Wine Spectator* magazine included five Washington wines in its Top 100 list for 1989.

Meanwhile, Columbia winemaker David Lake and grower Mike Sauer were quietly laying the foundation for some of the most exciting Washington red wines of the next decade. At Sauer's Red Willow vineyard, just east of the Cascades, syrah cuttings from Joseph Phelps went into the ground in 1986, and the first varietal Washington syrah was produced by Columbia in 1988. As the decade drew to a close, syrah was still an experiment, but merlot was about to become the ticket to Washington's red wine stardom.

THE 1990s

When television's *60 Minutes* broadcast the legendary "French Paradox" segment in November 1991, little did the producers realize that it would ignite a revolution in wine drinking and that tiny Washington state would benefit hugely as a result. At the time, most wine drinkers in America were sticking to white wines and sweet pink versions of red grapes. The very notion of wine as a beverage of moderation was under attack from a neo-Prohibitionist movement that seemed to be gaining strength from month to month. In the eyes of that powerful lobby, wine was just another addictive drug, no different than heroin. The "French Paradox" story suggested otherwise. Not only was wine an essential part of a meal, it said, but red wine was a beverage that actually had proven health benefits. Voilà! Suddenly, drinking red wine was a certifiably Good Thing. Given permission to enjoy their red wines guilt-free, consumers embraced them. And merlot, which until then had been a rather listless player on the world stage, became the red wine of choice.

As luck would have it, the Washington Wine Commission's second World Vinifera Conference, held in July 1991, had chosen merlot as its focus. In a *Wine Spectator* interview some years later, Simon Siegl, executive director of the Washington Wine Commission from 1988 to 1996, recalled that the topic was selected for marketing reasons more than anything else. California already "owned" cabernet, but merlot remained unclaimed; there was far less competition in the category. Furthermore, Stimson Lane (the umbrella company for all of the UST wineries) had planted a lot of merlot, particularly at its Columbia Crest winery and vineyard. The company was eager to back any event that would promote Washington merlot to the rest of the world. And finally, merlot enjoyed the same general advantages as chardonnay: it was French, and it was a lot easier to pronounce than, say, gewürztraminer.

The merlot conference clicked, and along with the *60 Minutes* story it resulted in a perfect marketing storm, propelling the image of merlot. Washington, many were coming to believe, was making better merlots than any place outside of France, and not just the limited, expensive boutique bottlings; Columbia Crest was the state's (and later the country's) leading producer of value merlot, priced for supermarket shelves. Early in the decade, Washington's merlot vineyard acreage had overtaken plantings of cabernet to become the state's most widely planted red wine grape. During the next eight years, that acreage increased by a factor of five, to 5,600 acres in 1999.

By the mid-1990s it seemed that Washington merlot was everywhere. Merlot specialists such as Leonetti Cellar began to command Bordeaux-like prices for wines that sold out months before being released. Merlot was both trendy and spendy. National publications that had scorned Washington as the land of cheap riesling were falling all over themselves to honor the state's reds, especially its merlots, as the most Bordeaux-like in the land.

Columbia introduced the Milestone merlot from the Red Willow vineyard. DeLille Cellars' D2 blend featured merlot in the starring role. Andrew Will made as many as six different merlots annually, including four vineyard-designated bottlings, a blended Washington version, and a few cases of an R reserve. Chateau Ste. Michelle expanded its own program of single-vineyard merlots to include bottlings from Cold Creek, Canoe Ridge, and Indian Wells, plus its Columbia Valley and reserve merlots. And parent company Stimson Lane built an entire brand—and later a Walla Walla winery—dedicated exclusively to merlot. Introduced in 1994, Northstar, guided by consulting winemaker Jed Steele, was promoted as Washington's answer to France's famed Chateau Pétrus.

Meanwhile, a second red wine revolution was quietly gaining strength. The syrahs that the Columbia winery had been turning out since 1988 were beginning to attract attention. McCrea Cellars made its first varietal syrah in 1994, with fruit from vines planted in 1990 at a site above the Columbia Gorge. Ripe, rich, and seductive, McCrea's wine proved that Red Willow was not the only site where the grape could thrive.

Another arctic blast struck in 1996, severely reducing vineyard yields and wiping out much of the state's prime merlot for that vintage. But Red Willow's syrah vines survived the freeze just fine, as did other, younger syrah vineyards in the Columbia Valley and on Red Mountain. Once its winter-hardiness had been tested, more growers began to get interested in trying syrah, spurred on by winemakers' eagerness to work with the grape. "I spent two years in Australia immersed in shiraz," recalled Rusty Figgins. "I came back home and I fell in love with the variety. I knew the conditions were right, especially in Walla Walla." For several years, Figgins made three different syrahs for Glen Fiona, the first Washington winery to position itself as a syrah specialist, and the first to coferment syrah with viognier.

Vigneron Christophe Baron also saw the syrah potential of Walla Walla and settled in the area in the mid-1990s to plant his vineyards on the stony soil of an ancient, dry riverbed. When his first crop appeared, in the autumn of 1999, there were only 290 bearing acres of syrah in the entire state, though four times that amount was already in the ground. Despite its limited availability, syrah was already on the way to claiming its place as the signature wine for Walla Walla.

As the century drew to a close, Washington could claim 144 commercial wineries and almost 25,000 acres of vinifera vineyard. In addition to the Yakima Valley, Columbia

Valley, and Walla Walla Valley AVAs, a fourth—the Puget Sound—had been recognized in 1995. Though white wines were still the majority, red wine production was growing steadily, accounting for 42 percent of the state's total. The commercial and critical success of the early "cult" reds—Andrew Will, Leonetti Cellar, Quilceda Creek, and Woodward Canyon—had inspired a new generation of garagistes, wineries such as Cadence, Cayuse, DeLille Cellars, Dunham, Matthews Estate, McCrea, and Soos Creek. But the real growth was just about to begin.

2000 TO THE PRESENT

In March of 2001, the Washington Wine Commission rolled out an exhaustive study (by Motto Kryla & Fisher) on the economic impact of the Washington State wine and wine grape industries. The report's most quoted statistic was its estimate of the full economic impact of the wine industry on the state. This included the sum total of revenues generated by vineyards, wineries, and their allied industries, the wages paid to more than 11,000 full-time employees in wine-related jobs, and even taxes and charitable contributions. The report concluded that the industry was generating $2.4 billion annually.

Washington, though perhaps best known for its software, coffee, and airplane companies, is very much an agricultural state. Eastern Washington is farm country, and by pointing out the enormous value of the wine industry, the commission was saying to politicians, power brokers, and the state's citizens that this wine thing was not just some insignificant hobby business for rich guys. Wine grapes, the study noted, were already the fourth–most important fruit crop in the state, behind apples, pears, and cherries (all of which were losing sales while wine grapes were gaining).

Not long after this report appeared, then–executive director Steve Burns issued his famous dictum (a sort of Moore's law for wineries) that a new winery was bonded in Washington every 10 days. That is one of those great statistical sleight-of-mind statements that sounds more impressive than it really is. That translates to 36 new wineries a year—not bad, but nothing to beat a drum about. However, the actual growth has been significantly higher. The 155 wineries counted in the 2001 report have jumped to 655 by mid-2009. That is a new winery every six days for almost a decade.

The first decade of the new century has also brought a dramatic increase in the number of Washington AVAs sanctioned by the Alcohol and Tobacco Tax and Trade Bureau (TTB). Red Mountain, Columbia Gorge, Horse Heaven Hills, Wahluke Slope, Rattlesnake Hills, Snipes Mountain, and Lake Chelan have all been added, each with distinctive soil, climate, and ripening profiles.

Just 20 years ago, merlot was considered cutting-edge in Washington. Now it is difficult to name any varietal grape grown anywhere in North America that is not being cultivated somewhere in this state. Wine tourism is also on the rise, and not only in established centers such as the Yakima Valley and Walla Walla. The warehouse district of Woodinville, just north of Seattle, is home to more than four dozen start-ups, and many eastern Washington wineries are opening second tasting rooms there. Visitors seem to love the opportunity to experience the excitement and youthful vigor of an industry that is really hitting its stride.

The Vintner's Village in Prosser, the Columbia Gorge, and Lake Chelan are newly popular wine-touring destinations. The faux-Bavarian hamlet of Leavenworth has more than a dozen tasting rooms. Even south Seattle has its own winery association. Most of the major islands in Puget Sound have their own wineries, and welcome visitors. Spokane, Yakima, the Tri-Cities, Wenatchee, Bellingham, Olympia, Bellevue, and of course, Seattle are fairly bursting with wine shops, wine bars, and winery tasting rooms.

As we move into the century's second decade, I'd like to see the industry take more of a leadership role in using ecofriendly packaging and instituting green practices throughout the entire winemaking, shipping, and retailing environment, not just in the vineyard. Recycling corks, eliminating excessively heavy glass bottles, exploring nonglass packaging options more aggressively, and banning the use of Styrofoam shippers would all be steps in the right direction. At the moment, California and Oregon wineries seem to be much more proactive in managing their carbon footprints.

Washington's reputation will be built upon more than just good, or even great, wines. As the state's wineries and their marketing associations continue to reach out to the rest of the world, it will be increasingly important to be perceived as sensitive stewards of the land, committed to recycling and repurposing all possible materials; thoughtful and creative not only in the making of wines but also in the making of lives.

The days that a "signature" wine or grape, a clever name or label, a three-dollar price tag, or a 90-point review could somehow catapult a winery or wine region to instant fame and fortune are, I believe, at an end. To succeed in the twenty-first century, any wine region, old or new, must consistently demonstrate quality and value across the full spectrum of its products. Washington can and must continue to do so.

2

THE AVAs

The American Viticultural Area (AVA) system was instituted by the Bureau of Alcohol, Tobacco, and Firearms (ATF) in the late 1970s in order to regulate the use of place-names on wine labels. Though widely viewed as an American version of the tightly controlled appellation systems in place in Europe, it is really nothing of the sort.

In Europe the granting of an appellation generally brings with it specific rules regarding the grapes that may be planted, the sugar levels (and sometimes the actual picking dates) at harvest, prescribed (and outlawed) viticultural and winemaking practices, and other quality controls. In the United States, by contrast, there are few such requirements. Rather, the TTB (acronym of the Alcohol and Tobacco Tax and Trade Bureau, which took over from the ATF in 2004) wants to know your proposed boundaries, some soil and weather analysis, what you are planning to name your AVA, and how that name has historical significance for your area.

Apart from prescribed limits on chemical additions to wines, actual wine quality is the least of TTB's concerns. Its agents are label approvers who want to regulate the verbiage on wine labels. Yet even that simple task sometimes proves to be a challenge. Such basics as varietal names can occasionally be found misspelled on wine labels that have been fully vetted—in recent weeks I've seen both Rousanne (*sic*) and Reisling (*sic*) in big bold type on approved wine labels. Spell-check anyone? Dire warnings about the dangers of pregnant women driving heavy machinery after drinking a glass of wine are clearly a higher priority than meaningful quality guidelines. There are no legal definitions of such terms as *reserve* or *old vines,* for example; they are unregulated and hence meaningless.

The TTB does expect an AVA to be "a delimited grape-growing region distinguishable by geographical features [in order to] allow vintners and consumers to attribute a given quality, reputation, or other characteristic of a wine made from grapes grown in an area to its geographical origin." To qualify its role still further, the TTB explains that its goal in designating viticultural areas is "to allow vintners to better describe the origin of their wines, and to allow consumers to better identify wines they may purchase. Establishment of a viticultural area is neither an approval nor an endorsement of the wine produced in that area."

Allow consumers to better identify wines they may purchase?! How many consumers can be expected to know that Red Hill Douglas County (an Oregon AVA) is completely different from the well-known Red Hills of Dundee, which has been the center of great Oregon pinots for decades? For that matter, Red Hill Douglas County might well be confused with Red Mountain (in Washington) or Red Hills Lake County (in California), both existing, approved AVAs.

In its official posting for the Red Hill Douglas County AVA, the TTB went so far as to say that "the regulations pertaining to the establishment of viticultural areas do not require the existence of a substantial viticultural history, a production of unique wines, or a demand for wines originating in the proposed viticultural area. Therefore, in evaluating a petition, TTB does not consider as determining factors the questions of whether the viticulture of the proposed area is new or established, whether the area is producing unique wines, or whether wine from the area is in demand in the marketplace." Any sane person might wonder exactly what the TTB does consider or require or, more important, what an AVA, once granted, actually signifies. This issue is especially relevant to Washington State, which has only recently begun to parse its mammoth Columbia Valley AVA into smaller, more crisply defined subappellations.

In purely legal terms, that a wine is AVA designated tells you that the named area was approved by the TTB under current regulations, that at least 85 percent of the grapes used to make the wine were grown in the named AVA, and that the wine was made ("fully finished") within the AVA. But even that is not as straightforward as it seems. A recently passed Washington State regulation stipulates more stringent requirements. If a winery claims only "Washington" as the appellation of origin, the wine needs to contain at least 95 percent Washington grapes under this new state law. Which leads to another question: exactly what are Washington grapes? Well, they could be from (a) an AVA located entirely in Washington, (b) an AVA located partly in Washington (there are three that spill over into Oregon), or (c) a non-AVA location in Washington. Now, here is where it gets really dicey.

For purposes of the new Washington law, grapes grown in Oregon but within a cross-border AVA—for example, the Columbia Valley, Columbia Gorge, or Walla Walla Valley AVAs—would count toward the 95 percent Washington content requirement. However, under federal law, to use the name Washington, the wine would need to contain at least 75 percent Washington grapes, and cross-border AVA grapes would not qualify for that purpose. So, for example, to use only the name Washington as the appellation of origin, a wine could not be made from 95 percent Walla Walla AVA grapes grown in the Oregon portion of that AVA. Cayuse, for example, can be a Walla Walla wine, but not a Washington wine.

If a winery claims both Washington and a specific AVA such as Walla Walla as the appellations of origin, the wine needs to contain at least 95 percent Washington grapes for state law purposes, and 85 percent Walla Walla AVA grapes and 75 percent Washington grapes for federal purposes. So if a wine contains 85 percent Walla Walla AVA grapes, then in order to satisfy the new Washington law requirement, an additional 10 percent of the wine must be from (a), (b), or (c) above. However, again, the winery would be required to comply with the federal law mandating 75 percent state content in order to use just "Washington" on the label. Are you with me? Clear as mud, huh?

Finally, if a winery claims only an AVA (such as Walla Walla) as the appellation of origin, it would be required to satisfy only the 85 percent AVA content requirement under federal law.

The task of creating AVAs whose value extends beyond such arcane guidelines falls, inevitably, to the wineries and growers whose land lies within the proposed boundaries. In Washington as elsewhere, the AVAs whose cachet has value beyond the official legalese have created that value by producing exceptionally good wines and promoting them with the name of the AVA. If all the great wines sourced from Red Mountain vineyards were labeled Yakima Valley or Columbia Valley or Washington (all quite legal), who would know or care what Red Mountain stands for?

If your vineyard does grow good grapes and make good wines over a reasonable time frame, formal certification that locates it within a more focused AVA makes good marketing sense. Most recently approved Washington AVAs have followed this path. A notable exception is the Lake Chelan AVA, which has been fashioned more in the Walla Walla Valley mode: first establish some wineries, then get your AVA and let the wines from local vineyards prove themselves down the road.

Wineries choose which AVA names to put on the labels according to their individual marketing goals and philosophy. For many years, Columbia Valley was used rather than Yakima Valley by most wineries; now, with so many high-profile boutiques sourcing Yakima Valley fruit, the decisions are more likely to center on whether to use Yakima Valley or one of its new sub-AVAs. As smaller, more concisely defined AVAs such as Snipes Mountain continue to emerge, the notion of an identifiable stylistic terroir associated with an AVA becomes more and more viable.

In the early decades of industry growth, Washington vintners avoided wholesale petitioning for new AVAs. The all-at-once parsing of Oregon's Willamette Valley to include a half-dozen, soil-based sub-AVAs may ultimately prove worthwhile, but so far it has been more a source of confusion than of enlightenment, at least for consumers. As of this writing, there are just eleven Washington AVAs, apart from the generic

"Washington." They have been developed rather methodically, and in a reasonably logical and meaningful progression.

When considered individually, they make sense; when taken collectively, they do a pretty good job (so far) of defining the emerging contours of the state's wine industry. It seems reasonable to expect that future, smaller, more narrowly defined AVAs will contribute to an understanding of what differentiates their particular slice of "perfect climate" from the larger region(s) around them. They should not only show you where the grapes are grown but also convey some sense of the conditions of soil and climate that made them a candidate for AVA status. Most important, you should be able to taste something in their wines that unites them; a common thread, a stylistic imprint that can be traced to the land rather than to the hand of the winemaker.

WASHINGTON: "THE PERFECT CLIMATE FOR WINE"

In 2005, the Washington Wine Commission launched an ambitious advertising campaign with the tagline "Washington State—The Perfect Climate for Wine." Is it really? And if so, how so?

The search for answers to those questions begins with the research done by Alan Busacca. Retired from a teaching post at Washington State University (WSU) and now a principal at Vinitas, a vineyard consulting firm, Busacca is a certified professional soil scientist and licensed geologist with a PhD in soil science from the University of California at Davis. His pioneering research with Larry Meinert, who also taught at WSU, compiled exhaustive studies of soils and geology in eastern Washington. From these studies, a list of the most important and singular aspects of Washington's geology, soils, and climate has begun to emerge, an important step on the road to defining a distinctive Washington style. The work has proven to be especially useful because it is based on solid science rather than on poetic descriptions gleaned from winemakers' (and wine writers') tasting notes.

It is now an accepted fact that the Washington wine story began with a series of cataclysmic floods that inundated the region at the end of the last ice age. Much of eastern Washington owes its present-day landscape and soils to these extraordinary events. To sum up briefly: Some 18,000 years ago, the Pacific northwestern part of the North American continent was on the edge of a vast glacial sheet of ice. In a complicated series of events that took place over centuries, the ice repeatedly dammed and completely blocked the Clark Fork River, which drains a large part of what is now Montana.

This created an immense lake—Lake Missoula—containing something on the order of 500 cubic miles of water. Periodically, the water overcame the blockage, unleashing the largest floods ever recorded on the planet. These cataclysmic Lake Missoula floods sent some 2,500 cubic kilometers of water (think Lake Erie and Lake Ontario combined) rushing across the Columbia Plateau, 500 feet high and traveling at 60 miles an hour. The waters inundated a vast area of central Washington that corresponds, more or less, to what is now the Columbia Valley AVA.

Another lake briefly formed as the waters reached the Horse Heaven Hills and backed up, reaching as far west as Yakima and east into Idaho. Then, rushing through the Wallula Gap, a narrow canyon where the Columbia River breaches the Horse Heaven Hills, the floodwaters continued down the Columbia Gorge to present-day Portland, flooding the Willamette Valley before ultimately emptying into the Pacific Ocean.

A practiced eye can still see the scars and scabs left by these floods in the brutal, jagged landscapes of eastern Washington, with its profusion of coulees (huge channels eroded in the basalt rock), dry waterfalls, gravel bars, and massive boulders scattered across the desert. More important, the residue of the floods—the gravels, silts, and sands deposited by the receding waters or, later, windblown over the land—constitute the basic soils that contribute to the distinctive flavors of Washington State wines. Busacca goes so far as to say that the floods and their aftermath are what created the potential for all agriculture in eastern Washington.

The soils that typically characterize Washington vineyards are derived from mixtures of glacial and postglacial materials. The base soils are the gravels carried down by the floodwaters and deposited over basalt bedrock. These are layered over with windblown sand from the post-flood era and finished with up to several feet of loess, a mix of fine silt and volcanic dust.

LATITUDE

The next important piece of Washington's "perfect climate" assertion can be found in the state's climatic characteristics. Eastern Washington is largely sagebrush desert. It begins in the rain shadow of the Cascade Mountains, a volcanic chain that is anchored by Mount Baker near the Canadian border and runs south to include Mount Rainier (the highest, at 14,411 feet) and the well-known, still-active Mount St. Helens.

The majority of Washington's vineyards lie between latitude 46 degrees (the Oregon border) and latitude 47 degrees (just north of the Wahluke Slope). Thus, they are roughly comparable to Bordeaux and Burgundy. Much has been made of this by marketers, but it doesn't really tell you a great deal about the state's aptitude for ripening grapes. Those same latitudes cross Mongolia and Minnesota, but don't look for Ulan Bator or Fargo to become the next Beaune anytime soon. It's also fun to point out that parts of California are on a parallel with Algeria, but that doesn't really speak to the quality of either region's wines.

What is significant is that Washington's relatively high latitudes mean that the growing season is edgier and more prone to extremes than the long, relatively smooth conditions that apply to much of California. There are four quite distinct seasons here, and the temperature ranges in eastern Washington are far wider than those west of the Cascades. A hard freeze can occur as late as Mother's Day and as early as mid-October.

On the plus side, eastern Washington summers and falls are virtually guaranteed to be dry. The combination of that desert dryness and the deep winter chill means that many insect pests, mold, and rot are rarely significant problems for eastern Washington vineyards. Even phylloxera has not been able (so far) to establish a foothold in the state. Consequently, wine grapes are almost always planted on their own rootstock, though some forward-thinking vintners (among them, Chris Figgins at Figgins Family Wine Estates and Christophe Baron at Cayuse) have been experimenting with grafted vines, just in case.

The higher latitude also means that Washington vineyards receive as much as 17.4 hours of sunlight daily during the growing season, well above the California average. The extra hours compensate for the rather late start to bloom in the spring; while the predictably dry, warm September and early October weather encourages picking grapes at their optimal physiological ripeness, different for each varietal and each site. It's not unusual for a vineyard such as Klipsun on Red Mountain to begin picking its sauvignon blanc in late August and to finish up its cabernet toward the end of October.

During harvest, diurnal temperature variations of 40–50 degrees (daytime highs in the low 90s and nighttime lows in the mid-40s) are common. So *hang time* is not just a buzzword in Washington; it is something that can be relied on to ripen pips and sweeten tannins, without the grapes reaching absurd sugar levels or sacrificing acids.

IRRIGATION

The average eastern Washington vineyard receives just eight inches of precipitation annually (many get even less). It falls almost entirely during nongrowing months, from November through April. A few dry-farmed vineyards exist in locations that are close either to the Cascades (the western edge of the Columbia Gorge AVA) or to the Blue Mountains (the eastern edge of the Walla Walla Valley AVA). But these are the exceptions; by and large, Washington vineyards are irrigated.

The use of irrigation, which is disparaged (and prohibited) throughout much of the wine-growing world, is not something that must be overcome to grow quality grapes in Washington. On the contrary, research has demonstrated the positive impact of timely and specific applications of water to the vines. In recent years, the proper management of irrigation has become an essential component of the quest for quality.

The improvement and refinement of viticultural irrigation practices has evolved over several decades. The first significant commercial plantings of vinifera were in place by the late 1970s at widely scattered locations around the state. These early growers were mostly farmers interested in adding wine grapes to their other crops, which might include apples and cherries, hops, mint, and row crops. At first, traditional irrigation techniques were employed, generally either ditch-furrow (rill) irrigation or solid-set (permanent overhead) sprinklers. The largest of these vineyards, at Columbia Crest, used center-pivot irrigation, a circle sprinkler system that was also used at Mercer Ranch, now Champoux. But by the early 1990s, growers had begun to replace sprayed water systems with drip irrigation.

It offered numerous advantages, not the least of which was a substantial (50 percent or more) reduction in water usage. Rich Wheeler, vice president of vineyards at Ste. Michelle Wine Estates, estimates that 95 percent of all the vinifera acreage in Washington (about 36,000 acres in all) is now under drip irrigation. Along with much more efficient water conservation, Wheeler points out, drip irrigation offers precise control. "You can spoon-feed the plant to create the stress you want. By controlling the canopy, which in part controls the cluster exposure, it's a great quality enhancer," he adds; "the vine is putting the majority of its energy into the fruit, not vegetation." Watering at precisely the right time also allows some control over berry size. "Usually we want a smaller berry," says Wheeler, "so we run them pretty close to stress over the whole season." Another plus with drip is that it allows the grower to irrigate at lower water volumes, so it costs less to pump. The only real disadvantage, Wheeler concludes, is when a vintner wants a particular kind of cover crop that isn't drought tolerant.

By the end of the past century, experiments at WSU and Columbia Crest had demonstrated that deficit irrigation—intentionally withholding all water during the first weeks of growth—would stress the vines and help control vigor. Controlling vigor early and then applying water to help ripen the fruit brought dramatic reductions in the vegetative aromas and flavors of the Bordeaux varietals. Growing less canopy also saved money: costly leaf-stripping, sucker-pruning, and mildew treatments were eliminated or reduced. Properly irrigated grapes ripened earlier and more fully, with no reduction in overall quantity.

Another breakthrough was the discovery that giving the vines a good soaking right after harvest, so the soil stays moist down to a depth of two feet, helps protect the roots from severe damage (or death) during one of the brief but brutal arctic blasts that strike the state every few winters. As early as the 1950s, some pioneering growers, many under the tutelage of WSU's Walter Clore, had begun trying test plantings of vinifera vines. But every six years or so, along would come a particularly severe freeze that would kill the vines down to their roots and sometimes eradicate them completely.

Winter-hardiness is somewhat variable, according to the age of the vines, the particular varietal, and the duration of the cold snap. Most vines can survive temperatures as low as −5 to −8 degrees Fahrenheit. But should it slip just a degree or two lower, damage begins to occur. At −15 degrees the vine will die to the ground. A prolonged period of such extreme cold can freeze the ground itself to a depth of several feet, killing the roots.

A post-harvest irrigation affords an extra measure of insulation and root protection should a dry winter and deep freeze occur. In some locations, wind machines can also be used to raise temperatures by as much as 4 degrees, which can be a critical difference.

The occasional incidents of extreme cold will continue. The worst in recent years was during January 2004. It hit the Walla Walla Valley especially hard and wiped out most of that year's harvest. But with each episode, something valuable is learned, and better vineyard sites are developed. In much of Washington, and Walla Walla especially, most new vineyard plantings are moving to higher ground.

Despite the occasional setbacks, the once-common belief that Washington winters are simply too cold for vinifera grapes to thrive long-term has been proven wrong. With proper site selection, post-harvest irrigation, and practices such as burying canes, much cold damage can be avoided. And there is a plus side to Washington's cold winters. In all years, the vines go into full and complete winter dormancy, a rarity in warmer regions and a factor in vine health and the development of fruit flavor.

In an often-repeated anecdote that may or may not be apocryphal, the late André Tchelistcheff is quoted as having proclaimed, while touring a Washington vineyard planted with roses at the end of the vine rows, that the roses smelled more fragrant than those in his California garden. He believed it was because his roses never really went dormant.

FLAVORS

None of the foregoing would mean much if the particular influences that impact grape growing in eastern Washington didn't deliver unique, desirable, and identifiable flavors in the wines. Washington's rather bold claim to being "perfect" should not be taken to mean that other places are not as good. There are great wine-producing regions scattered across the globe. But those who live in Washington, grow grapes there, make wine there, and have spent decades, as I have, tasting thousands upon thousands of Washington wines have come to believe, with good cause, that Washington has earned a seat at the table with the rest of the world's great wine-producing regions.

In the range and overall quality of its wines, it is the equal of California, though the wines differ stylistically. Washington vintners long ago stopped trying to make California wine from Columbia Valley fruit. They want to make great Washington wines, and in many instances they are succeeding. The present challenge is to build on that success, to identify what works and why and how, and to focus on developing the potential that has been demonstrated but not yet deeply explored. One important part of that process is to identify and delineate newer, more specific, and more meaningful AVAs.

The TTB may insist that AVAs are geographic, soil-based entities, but in truth the most important American AVAs are flavor based. Napa Valley has a flavor, and Dry Creek Valley has a flavor, just as Walla Walla and Red Mountain, the Rattlesnake Hills and Wahluke Slope have flavors. Those new to Washington wines will discover that the baseline wine flavors of all these regions are built on vivid fruit, bright acids, and ripe, compact tannins. The defining character is intensity married to purity of varietal fruit. It is most identifiable in pure varietal wines and particularly in single-vineyard, single-varietal wines. This clarity, intensity, and focus can frequently be found in aromatic white wines, especially riesling, gewürztraminer, and viognier. It is less distinctive but still applicable for chardonnay, sauvignon blanc, sémillon, pinot gris, and roussanne.

Among red wines, there is little argument that Washington makes some of the world's finest merlots, thick and dense and substantial. Washington cabernet sauvignon—especially old-vine juice from one of the state's dozen or so 30+-year-old vineyards—straddles the line between the herbal elegance of Bordeaux and the sweet lushness of Napa. Syrah ripens beautifully all over the state and creates a wide variety of pleasing flavors, retaining enough acid and peppery character to stand up as a legitimate (though different) peer to wines from Australia and the Rhône. Some impressive varietal wines (in very small quantities) are also being made from barbera, cabernet franc, carmenère, counoise, malbec, mourvèdre, petite sirah, petit verdot, sangiovese, tempranillo, and zinfandel.

THE WASHINGTON AVAS

Doug Gore, who oversees all winemaking and vineyards for Ste. Michelle Wine Estates, describes the baseline signature of the Columbia Valley as "its fruit intensity and varietally correct wines, first in the nose, then in the palate. Whether it is blueberry in cabernet franc, black cherry in cabernet sauvignon, raspberry in merlot, pear in chardonnay, melon in sauvignon blanc, or peaches and apricots in riesling," he says, "we seem to have it in spades."

That's as good a broad-brush overview as any, but it just begins to hint at the complexity and detail that can be found in the state's best wines. As those wines increasingly show, the exploration of specific vineyard sites has evolved rapidly, with dramatic quality improvements in a very short time. Now Washington vintners are embarking on the difficult, expensive, and time-consuming process of delineating meaningful subappellations.

COLUMBIA VALLEY

The subappellations nestled within the vast Columbia Valley AVA are profiled individually. The most important Columbia Valley vineyard areas not yet officially designated as AVAs lie north and northeast of the Yakima Valley, separated by long ridges of east-west hills—the Rattlesnake Hills, the Yakima Ridge, the Umptanum Ridge, the Saddle Mountains, and the Frenchman Hills. Much of this sparsely populated midsection is rugged, isolated scrubland consisting of vast stretches of desert, occasionally irrigated for hops or stone fruits or vineyards. The Columbia River meanders through the region on its way south and east, ultimately cutting through the Wallula Gap and abruptly jogging due west, defining the border between Washington and Oregon as it flows into the Pacific Ocean.

A few miles north of the Wallula Gap, the Columbia, Yakima, and Snake rivers meet at the Tri-Cities. North of the Tri-Cities the ridges flatten out into the broad Columbia Basin, where some of the state's oldest and largest vineyards are situated. Major vineyard developments first went in during the 1970s, when the Sagemoor vineyard (and its Dionysus and Bacchus neighbors) were established. Today Sagemoor Farms is still among the most prolific suppliers of grapes to Washington wineries. But based on the significant number of vineyard-designates that are appearing, winemakers' interest seems to be shifting farther west, to newer vineyard plantings in the Wahluke Slope, the Royal Slope, and the Ancient Lakes.

Apart from these areas, there are other, smaller subsections of the Columbia Valley still being explored, some of which may yet become AVAs unto themselves. Cold Creek is among the most important, a single-vineyard site owned and used almost exclusively by Ste. Michelle Wine Estates. And in the Cascade foothills along the Columbia Valley's western edge, and the lower slopes of the Blue Mountains in Walla Walla, new plantings continue to reach farther out past the established edges of viable vineyard land, poking into corners of the state that had previously been considered unsuitable for grape growing.

Some failures will inevitably occur. But the many successes in the past four decades surely have permanently boosted Washington viticulture into the proven category, after more than a century of being considered marginal at best. In this new century, with global climate change posing difficult challenges for proven wine regions and opening up new opportunities for wine grape growing in what were formerly fringe areas, it is inevitable that within the 11 million acres of the Columbia Valley lie as-yet-undiscovered vineyard locations that may well produce Washington's Hermitage or Pétrus.

YAKIMA VALLEY

Washington's first officially designated AVA, and its third-largest overall, is the Yakima Valley AVA. It encircles the Yakima River as it winds from the Cascade foothills east toward the Tri-Cities. Established in 1983, the Yakima Valley includes roughly 12,000 acres of bearing vineyards, just over a third of the state's total. Long before it was officially designated, the Yakima Valley was well established as a winegrowing region. The Otis vineyard (planted in 1957) and Harrison Hill (planted in 1962) were—and still are—home to this state's oldest cabernet vines. But other pioneers had also begun putting in substantial acreage: Mike Sauer (at Red Willow), Stan Clark (at Quail, now Covey, Run), Gail Puryear (at Bonair), Mike Hogue, Dick Boushey, and the Holmes and Williams families up on dusty, scrub-covered Red Mountain.

In 25 years—a blink of an eye in the wine industry—a lot has changed. As is generally the rule in rapidly growing wine regions, the larger appellation has been subdivided. Three subappellations are located entirely within the Yakima Valley. At the eastern edge is the state's most prominent AVA, Red Mountain; along the central northern rim is the higher-elevation Rattlesnake Hills AVA, with some of the region's best vineyard sites; and smack dab in the middle is the tiny Snipes Mountain AVA, home to some of the oldest vines in the state. These smaller areas are more tightly defined and in some ways have stolen some thunder from the rest of the valley.

At the same time, they have raised the bar for all growers and wineries in the region and attracted some of this state's best winemakers. Chardonnay, merlot, and cabernet sauvignon are the most-planted varieties, but in recent years it is riesling and syrah that have proven to be the most site specific and terroir-driven. Pinot gris and viognier also do quite well, and Yakima Valley reds are impressive, both from old-vine sites such as Otis and Harrison Hill and from newer plantings at Boushey, DuBrul, and Red Willow.

During the 1980s and early 1990s, Yakima Valley wines were often prone to vegetative smells and flavors. Ascribe it to overcropping, valley floor locations, or simply unsophisticated winemaking, but it slowed down the appreciation—among both consumers and critics—for the many assets and strengths of the region. But with newer vineyards going in at higher elevations, and the widespread introduction of progressive viticultural practices such as drip irrigation, tighter vine spacing, and lower yields, the problems of underripe, vegetative aromas and flavors are rarely found today, even in cooler vintages. If anything, the more moderate climate throughout much of the valley is becoming a treasured asset, allowing longer hang times and better physiological ripeness than in warmer sites, especially in warm years such as 2005 and 2007.

The cooler sites in the western half of the Yakima Valley are at their best in such vintages. At the extreme western edge, on a high plateau in the Cascade foothills, sits the Red Willow vineyard, which was for many years a sort of viticultural laboratory for grower Mike Sauer and Columbia winemaker (now deceased) David Lake. Among many, many innovations, they were the first to plant syrah in Washington, back in 1985, with cuttings from Joseph Phelps.

At the time it was just one more experimental block, but it has succeeded beyond anyone's expectations. Today there are more than 2,800 acres of syrah in Washington, and at least a third of the state's wineries make one or more versions of the grape. Some of the best syrah is grown in the Yakima Valley, at vineyards such as Boushey, Lewis, and Red Willow. The cabernet and merlot are exceptional also; look for vineyard designates from Dineen, DuBrul, Elerding, Harrison Hill, Otis, Two Blondes, and Sheridan. Pinot gris has been a success at Minick, and riesling does well at many sites.

The first wave of Yakima Valley vintners seemed at times to resent the success enjoyed by vintners in other parts of the state, but that is no longer true. Amateurish and flawed wines are rare now, and the influx of new talent, often with globally savvy palates and winemaking experience, has changed the landscape almost overnight.

"We're playing catch-up here," Sheridan's Scott Greer admits, "but at a very rapid pace. I had people tell me, 'Don't put *Yakima Valley* on your label.' But I did put it there. We're very proud of where we're located. It's happening." Owen Roe's David O'Reilly recently purchased Yakima Valley vineyard land and leased a new winery in Sunnyside, specifically to take full advantage of the region's fruit. "I remember the first year I made wine from here," he recalls. "I was told by several distributors not to put *Yakima Valley* on the label. That's why it's so important for winemakers to make that stand. To say I'm working with some of the best vineyards in the U.S., a growing area that makes great, distinctive wines, with great acid, and varietal character."

"The good, experienced winemakers are coming here right now, buying fruit here," adds grower Dick Boushey. "To me that means they like the results. There is more planting and discovery here than anywhere in the state. Maybe they are not promoting or exploiting that, but there's a rediscovery going on."

The same things that have boosted quality elsewhere in Washington are just as effective now that they are being widely practiced in the Yakima Valley. Plant the right grapes in the right place. Don't overcrop; don't overwater. Get outside input from qualified experts who can give you honest feedback. Beware of tunnel palate, and don't expect the comments of friends and visitors to your tasting room to be taken seriously by critics and retailers outside the state.

It is heartening to see Yakima Valley growers and winemakers working together to promote their many strengths. They are successfully building a regional reputation that can compete effectively in the global marketplace.

WALLA WALLA VALLEY

In the southeastern corner of Washington, spilling over the border into Oregon, is the Walla Walla Valley. The area includes some of the earliest settlements in the Northwest. Lewis and Clark camped a few miles north of Walla Walla, near the present-day town of Waitsburg, as they followed the Touchet River on their way back home in 1806. Clark noted in his journal that "three young men arrived from the Wallah wallah Village, bringing with them a steel trap belonging to one of our party." No mention of any wineries in the area.

The name Walla Walla purportedly translates as "many waters." Records indicate that vineyards were thriving as early as the 1850s and that a commercial wine industry was being explored during the 1870s. But the modern era of Walla Walla winemaking didn't begin until 1977, when Leonetti Cellar was bonded and became the first local winery dedicated to producing varietal vinifera wines. Seven years later, with just four wineries and 60 acres of vineyard, the Walla Walla Valley was certified as the second official Washington State AVA.

It is shaped much like a cut diamond laid on its side, with the short, straight edge forming the western border. The AVA fans out as it follows the Walla Walla River east. A long ridge of windmill-topped hills runs along its jagged southern edge, which crosses the border into Oregon; the straight-line northern edge leads northeast into the green and tawny hills of the Palouse wheat country. The jagged eastern perimeter of the cut diamond runs along various waterways and ridges heading up into the Blue Mountains, which wrap dramatically around the town's eastern border.

Recognition as a premier red wine–producing appellation came quickly to Walla Walla, because the early releases of Leonetti, Woodward Canyon, L'Ecole No 41, and a handful of others enjoyed remarkable success, winning gold medals and accolades from the press. The funny thing was that few wines were actually made with Walla Walla fruit; the grapes came from Columbia Valley and Yakima Valley vineyards.

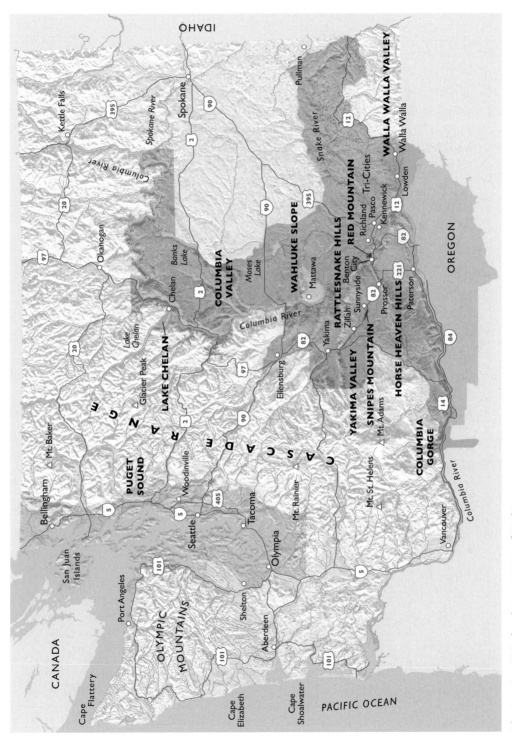

The American Viticultural Areas (AVAs) of Washington state

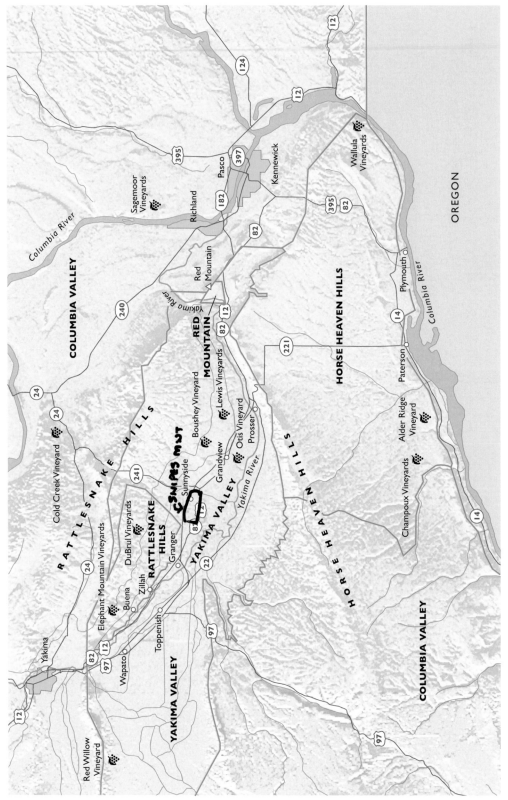

The Horse Heaven Hills, Yakima Valley, Rattlesnake Hills, and Red Mountain AVAs, the latter two situated within Yakima Valley

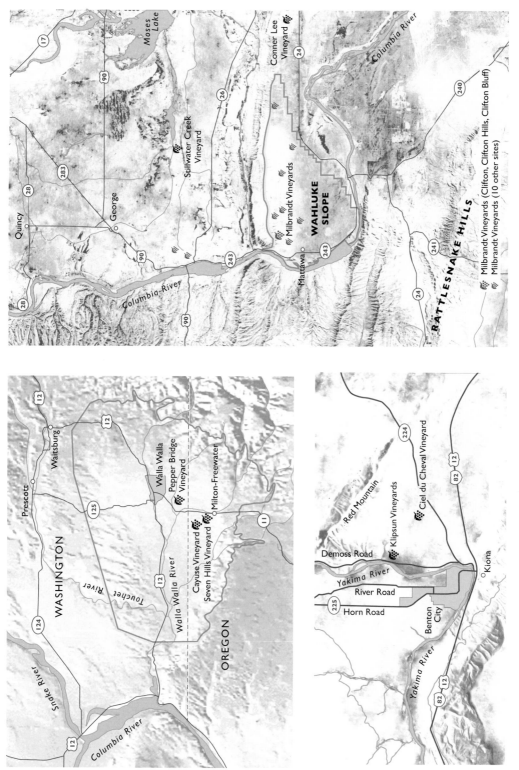

Walla Walla Valley (upper left), Red Mountain (lower left), and Wahluke Slope (right) AVAs

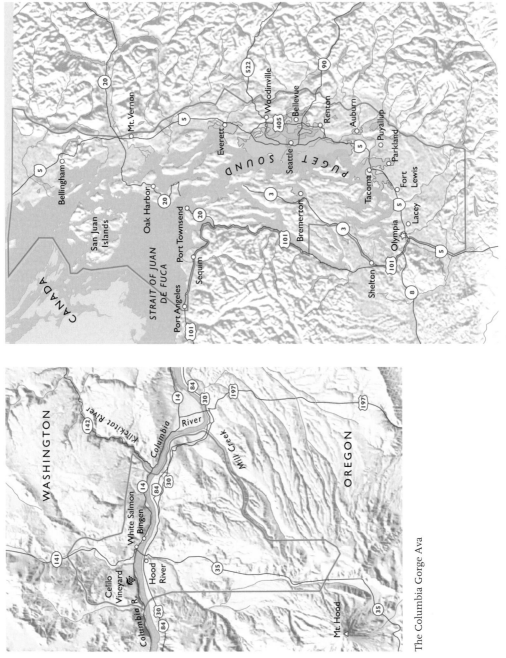

The Puget Sound Ava

The Columbia Gorge Ava

Leonetti had planted a trial acre of cabernet in 1974, but the first significant planting in the valley was at Seven Hills in 1981. Though legally part of the AVA, Seven Hills was rather inconveniently located in Oregon. That matters not at all today, for vineyards are scattered all over the region. But in the early days it drove a marketing wedge squarely down the middle of the AVA. The Seven Hills winery, then headquartered in Milton-Freewater, found itself isolated. Oregon was busy promoting the Willamette Valley pinot producers, while Washington was not about to include an Oregon winery in its marketing efforts.

Such shortsightedness may have contributed to the region's stalled growth. Despite its quick start, by the mid-1990s fewer than a dozen wineries called Walla Walla home. In an interview in the spring of 2000, Leonetti's Gary Figgins told me he had "always envisioned that Walla Walla would happen at some point. But it was just going so slow. There were only four or five of us, and we were doing well; but I had just about given up that it would happen within my lifetime. And about that time, it just went nuts!"

There were 10 wineries by 1995, when the real growth accelerated. As of this writing, there are about 110, and more on the way. Most begin as micro-wineries making a few barrels of wine and renting a little space in an existing facility or at Artifex, a winery incubator that opened in 2007. Finding industrial space out at the Walla Walla airport, where once-cheap, World War II–vintage buildings could be easily leased from the Port, has become highly competitive. Five new incubators constructed in 2007 were leased almost immediately, and one new winery has set up shop in an abandoned ammunition bunker!

After a whirlwind 15-year growth spurt, there are signs that things may be slowing down. Walla Walla is not immune to the nation's economic woes, and tourism, the lifeblood of the local wine economy, shuts down for about three months of the year. In 2008 and 2009 dozens of new wineries made their debut; they may be the last gasp of the boom times. But the region's stunning physical beauty and the infusion of winemaking talent—from France, from celebrity winemaker projects such as Long Shadows, and from the starry-eyed annual graduating class at the community college— ensure continued long-term growth.

Impressive vineyard projects continue to pop up, many in higher-altitude locations above Seven Hills, some scattered throughout the old riverbed informally known as the Rocks, others located east of town in the foothills, where it is possible to grow grapes without irrigation—a rarity in Washington. Vineyard growth first took off in 1991, when Norm McKibben and his business partner Bob Rupar put in the first 10 acres of cabernet and merlot at Pepper Bridge. A few years later, they purchased 200 acres at Seven Hills and developed (with Leonetti and L'Ecole) Seven Hills east, an additional 170 acres. The most ambitious venture yet for McKibben and his partners is SeVein, a contiguous, 2,000-acre block of steep, north-facing land on the southern border of the AVA. Elevations at the site range from just under 1,200 to 1,450 feet; when completed, its 1,600 plantable acres will double the total acreage in the Walla Walla AVA. Much of the expensive infrastructure work (power, roads, wells, pumps, ponds, soil sensors, weather stations, etc.) is done, and the first 350 acres on the SeVein property have been planted, with more acreage being developed each year.

Along with sizable new vineyards for partners Leonetti, L'Ecole, and Pepper Bridge, blocks of SeVein land have been reserved by Figgins Family (for FIGGINS, Chris Figgins's new project), JM Cellars, Cadaretta, Waters, and Doubleback (retired NFL quarterback Drew Bledsoe's project). Another prime slice, named Octave, belongs to a different group of partners including Jean-Francois Pellet (winemaker at Amavi and Pepper Bridge) and Tony Rynders (formerly at Domaine Serene). Plans are underway for several of the properties to include wineries on site.

As more and more new vineyards scattered throughout the AVA begin bearing fruit, different Walla Walla flavor profiles are appearing in the region's wines. There is enough meaningful variation in soil types, rainfall, altitude, and aspect to add at least four or five new subappellations over the next decade or so. In the December 2000 issue of *Geoscience Canada,* geologists Larry Meinert and Alan Busacca identified four quite different soil profiles: slackwater terrace, loess, river gravel, and floodplain silt. Good examples of each can be found in the wines of Pepper Bridge, Leonetti, Cayuse, and Spring Valley, respectively. Most Walla Walla vineyards currently are planted on slack-water deposits (residue of the great floods), loess (silty, wind-borne soils), or some combination of the two.

Pepper Bridge is one of the coolest sites, planted on loess over slack-water deposits. In some parts of the vineyard are big pockets of volcanic ash from the eruption of Mount Mazama, which formed Oregon's Crater Lake. "It's a totally different soil," McKibben explains. "We either pull the grapes or farm it differently." From Pepper Bridge fruit come broad flavors of strawberry preserves and black cherry. In cooler years it can show distinct herbal notes, but as the vines have matured, these have diminished. The vineyard is more prone than most to frost and freeze damage.

The area known locally as the Rocks, located in Oregon west of Milton-Freewater and just north of Seven Hills, was first planted to wine grapes in the late 1990s. Beresan's Tom Waliser and Christophe Baron of Cayuse independently converted orchards to grapes, and unintentionally set off a land rush. The ancient, dry riverbed is extremely rocky, with large, round cobblestones that recall the vineyards of Châteauneuf-du-Pape. Difficult to establish, labor- and time-intensive, and low yielding, they reward the patient vintner with complex mineral, meat, truffle, and forest-floor flavors.

Leonetti's father-son team of Gary and Chris Figgins began planning to make all of their wines from 100 percent Walla Walla fruit almost two decades ago; that dream became a reality as of the 2007 vintage. In addition to their Seven Hills and SeVein properties, they have 16 acres (11 cabernet, 3 merlot, 1 each petit verdot and sangiovese) at Mill Creek Upland, planted in 1997; the 28-acre Loess vineyard (same grapes plus a bit of malbec and viognier), planted in 2001; and a 55-acre C. S. Figgins estate vineyard (also out Mill Creek) that began bearing in 2008. Some of that fruit is destined for a new

Figgins Estate wine—a blend of cabernet, merlot, and petit verdot—due for release in the fall of 2011.

The Mill Creek Upland vineyard has extremely deep (70 feet) loess soils and sits on a fairly steep hillside close to the Blue Mountains. It is frost free and gets up to 25 inches of rainfall annually, triple the precipitation of most Walla Walla vineyards. Therefore it can be dry-farmed, though some irrigation has been used to get it established. At sunset the temperature drops rapidly; Chris Figgins notes that it can quickly fall from 90 degrees to 50. The grapes mature with deep colors, high acids, concentrated flavors, and firm tannins. Three 20-acre parcels adjacent to Mill Creek Upland are now in production, belonging to àMaurice, Walla Walla Vintners, and the Chan family of Seattle.

Spring Valley winery, located 12 miles northeast of town, is surrounded by the rolling, wheat-covered hills of the Palouse. A trial two-acre block of merlot was planted in 1993 and immediately produced positive results. After selling grapes for a few years, the owners established their winery in 1999, and the wines, all red, immediately drew rave reviews. Soils are extremely deep and rich, and more vines were planted, on moderately steep south-facing slopes between 1,100 and 1,400 feet. Since purchasing the winery in 2006, Ste. Michelle Wine Estates has expanded the original 40-acre vineyard to 115 acres (all leased, not owned): a mix of merlot, cabernet franc, syrah, cabernet sauvignon, petit verdot, and malbec. Spring Valley wines are deep and powerful, very high in alcohol, but carry unique and fragrant aromas of grain, light herb, and explosive, jammy fruits. A few other projects have been proposed for sites nearby, but several obstacles (besides the stagnant economy) intervene. First, the land is controlled by multigeneration wheat-farming families that are reluctant to sell and must offer very large parcels when they do. Second, there are severe limitations on water rights and usage. And last but not least, siting a vineyard in the midst of wheat fields almost guarantees issues of pesticide drift, unless you also own (or control) the surrounding acreage.

These four widely scattered and quite different vineyard sites demonstrate that what currently falls under the umbrella Walla Walla AVA should ultimately be divided into several subregions. This may not happen anytime soon, but what has been proven is that many Walla Walla vineyards are capable of ripening outstanding merlot, cabernet, and syrah. Much smaller plantings of sangiovese, cabernet franc, tempranillo, and other red grapes also show promise, and what few Walla Walla viogniers are produced have been quite good. The future remains extremely bright for this corner of the state.

RED MOUNTAIN

If you are looking for Red Mountain—Washington State's smallest (and most exclusive) AVA—don't expect to find something either red or particularly mountainous. Red Mountain rises like a brownish lump of unbaked bread at the eastern end of the Yakima Valley, just past the point where the Yakima River turns abruptly north at Benton City.

Red Mountain was awarded AVA status in 2001. Hedges Cellars (now Hedges Family Estates) was a leader in that effort. Founder Tom Hedges describes Red Mountain as "essentially a southwestern-facing slope of homogenous soil types, with very high heat units and low-vigor, low-nutrient soils." What makes it unique, he believes, is the elevation, the slope, the way the winds are channeled from the north, and other factors that lend a dense minerality to its grapes, particularly the classic Bordeaux grape varieties. "Red Mountain produces a distinctive wine," says Hedges, "alcoholic, tannic, tight, very ageworthy, dark, dense, and lightly aromatic."

Viewed from a distance, on a hot and dusty summer day, Red Mountain hardly seems the sort of place that can grow grapes for many of Washington's greatest red wines. A few green squares of vineyard adorn the slopes nearest the highway, but nothing that would suggest that you are approaching the most prized vineyard land in the state. What does underscore that point is the impressive who's who list of wineries using Red Mountain grapes to make vineyard-designated wines. The majority come from two of the region's founding vineyards, Ciel du Cheval and Klipsun. Between them they ripen around 280 acres of (mostly) red grapes: merlot and cabernet sauvignon, syrah and cab franc, and smatterings of such exotica as counoise and mourvèdre.

Neither has a winery of its own, though the Klipsun owners' daughter may release a wine shortly and Ciel's owner periodically floats the notion of bottling some wines under his own label. But the cachet that these vineyards have acquired arises from their grapes being featured in wines from A-list producers such as Andrew Will, Betz Family, Boudreaux, Cadence, DeLille, Grand Rêve, Januik, Mark Ryan, McCrea, O•S, Quilceda Creek, Seven Hills, Soos Creek, and Woodward Canyon. Quilceda Creek and DeLille became so enamored of their Ciel du Cheval grapes that each now owns an adjacent vineyard, joint ventures with Ciel's owner, Jim Holmes.

Scattered across the mountain are about fifteen wineries, the biggest being Hedges and Kiona. Both use estate-grown fruit for their best wines and sell grapes to other wineries also. Kiona's Scott Williams owns three large vineyards on Red Mountain. The original 65 acres, first planted in 1975, still grows some old-vine riesling and chenin blanc; the 25-acre Ranch at the End of the Road, planted in 1995, is mostly syrah, with some sangiovese as well; and the newest, named Heart of the Hill, totals almost 150 acres, 44 of it planted so far. Located right between Ciel du Cheval and Ste. Michelle's Col Solare winery and vineyard, Heart of the Hill seems likely to become equally as important, given Williams's proven talent for farming wine grapes.

Small but impressive boutiques such as Tapteil Estate, Fidélitas, Hightower, and Cadence have also set up shop on Red Mountain. A new venture called Red Mountain Vineyards, part of a trio of wineries that includes Corliss Estates and Tranche, began production in 2009 after purchasing 40 acres of prime vineyard land and retooling the former Sandhill winery. Another 100-acre site (near Tapteil) will be planted in the future. Though total planted Red Mountain vineyard acreage remains low (around 800 acres), the Col Solare project (a partnership between Ste. Michelle Wines Estates and Tuscany's

Antinori family) is bringing further expansion and attention to the region, as is an additional 600 acres of previously undeveloped Department of Natural Resources land recently leased (with water rights) to a variety of wine industry veterans.

The land was first developed in 1972, when Jim Holmes and partner John Williams (Scott's father) bought 80 acres of what Holmes laughingly calls "worthless desert" and decided to plant 10 acres of riesling, chardonnay, and cab. "We paid two hundred an acre," Holmes recalls, grinning, "but the crook who sold it to us had paid only one hundred!" To say it was desolate country does not do justice to the leap of faith that the initial purchase required. "It was like the frontier," says Holmes: "no roads, no water, no power, no people. Just sagebrush." There was no wine industry to rely on as potential customers: 35 years ago there were fewer than a dozen wineries in the whole state, and their mainstay grape was riesling. Holmes and Williams forged ahead and planted cabernet, despite the fact that "everybody knew you couldn't grow red grapes here in Washington."

As the Washington wine industry has grown to include more than 650 wineries and 35,000 acres of vineyard, Red Mountain grapes have been a big part of the reason that the state's shiniest calling cards are its red wines, particularly its Bordeaux blends and syrah. It was Kiona cabernet, for example, that Alex Golitzin used exclusively in his Quilceda Creek wines in the mid-1980s. Red Mountain grapes—from some mix of Kiona, Klipsun, Ciel du Cheval, and the Tapteil vineyards—were important components of every Quilceda Creek cabernet for over two decades.

In 2001 and 2002, Alex Golitzin and his son Paul planted their own 17 acres (all cabernet sauvignon) on Red Mountain. The first full crop from the Galitzine vineyard was harvested in 2004; the initial plan was to include those grapes in the flagship wine. It didn't fit, say the Golitzins—"The blends are never as good as the single vineyards," Alex explains—so a Galitzine cab has become one of two vineyard-designates added to the Quilceda lineup in recent years.

Red Mountain has been sculpted by repeated glacial floods ("a hydraulic massacre" is how Ciel's Jim Holmes describes it) that deposited massive granite boulders and layered its thin soils with an unusual mix of rock, clay, and mineral. Strong winds funnel through a gap in the surrounding hills, slamming into west-facing vineyards, thickening skins. Cabernet and merlot grapes ripen at smaller sizes than elsewhere, creating concentrated, tannic wines. "Our berry size is just 50 to 60 percent of standard berry size," says Holmes. "Where Napa berries might weigh about 1.3 grams, ours weigh about 0.88."

The resulting tannins are perfectly ripe, not harsh or green; but upon release Red Mountain wines can be hard, tough, tarry, and wrapped up tight. Another distinguishing factor is the high pH of the soils, which keeps nutrients tied up as insoluble minerals, so the vines must struggle. They don't grow big, unwieldy canopies. In late summer and early autumn, the mountain's diurnal temperatures vary by 40 degrees or more, keeping acids up while sugars accumulate. In general, red wines from Red Mountain have a firm cherry core to the fruit, and they often show distinct mineral notes, with scents of graphite and iron ore.

Most of the mountain's total vineyard is planted to cabernet sauvignon and merlot, but here and there are numerous small experimental plots of a couple of dozen other grapes. Keeping the Bordeaux focus, there are blocks of cabernet franc, malbec, and petit verdot. Syrah is another popular red, with the majority planted at Terra Blanca, Klipsun, Ciel, Ranch, and DeLille's Grand Ciel vineyard. With prodding from Doug McCrea (McCrea Cellars), mourvèdre, counoise, and grenache are also planted at Ciel and turn up in blends and occasionally as limited-edition varietal wines.

Though considerably less white wine acreage is planted, those wines are also well structured, with steely spines and semitropical fruit. Kiona grows the appellation's only chenin blanc and riesling, often used to make racy, densely concentrated late-harvest wines and the occasional ice wine. Owner Scott Williams has planted a smidge of gewürztraminer at Ranch at the End of the Road. Klipsun and Artz have useful plantings of sauvignon blanc and sémillon. Small plots of roussanne, pinot gris, viognier, and chardonnay are scattered about the mountain, making up the rest of the whites.

Along with a doubling of vineyard acreage, the near future holds more sweeping changes for Red Mountain. A master plan is being developed by a group of vintners (organized as the Red Mountain Agricultural District), with the goal of setting strict guidelines governing the construction of tourist amenities such as restaurants, retail shops, lodging, and walking trails on the mountain. Ciel's Jim Holmes insists that the key to Red Mountain is and always should be its wines. "There's no reason for anyone to visit unless we make great wine here," he says. "If you do that, people will knock down your door. If you don't, what's there? Why would anyone come? It's just a wild spot in the desert." At Hedges Family Estate, second-generation winegrower Christophe Hedges is another strong advocate for retaining the mountain's agricultural focus. "It's always been viticulturally focused up here," he says; "never was tourism a factor at all. What we're trying to do now is preserve that sense of agricultural community."

That may prove difficult. More than 400 acres of state land just across the road from Col Solare have been leased to a partnership that proposes to develop the Piazza Project, described as "a modern hillside village or 'villeggiatura' reminiscent of the great walled cities of Italy." A document prepared for the project's backers by Boxwood Architects waxes euphoric: "At the heart of the villeggiatura is a piazza or town square. Here as many as a dozen winemakers artfully make small lots of wine from a variety of high-end estate-grown Red Mountain grapes. Their wineries line the piazza offering glasses of wine in charming tasting rooms with views of barrels and the wonderful smell of aging wine, or outdoors under brightly colored umbrellas with fountains and shade provided by 32 trees. Winemaker residences can be found above each winery where owners and guests can enjoy spectacular views . . ." Stay tuned; the battle for Red Mountain may just be getting started.

Washington State gained its seventh appellation with the official certification of the Horse Heaven Hills on August 1, 2005. Its borders lie entirely within the established Columbia Valley appellation but do not cross over into Oregon as do the Walla Walla and Columbia Gorge AVAs. It is bounded on the north by the ridge of the hills that form the southern border of the Yakima Valley and on the south by the Columbia River. Most vineyards are planted on south-sloping hills with sandy, well-drained soils.

Currently, the AVA is home to just six wineries, but its twenty-five-plus vineyards, with 8,400 acres of wine grapes planted, provide roughly a quarter of Washington's total grape production. By some estimates as much as two-thirds of the region, which totals 570,000 acres, has wine grape–growing potential. The first important vineyards to be established were Champoux (then Mercer Ranch), started in 1972, and Columbia Crest, which went into the ground in the late 1970s. Further growth came a decade or so later, when California's Chalone Group and Ste. Michelle Wine Estates both planted vineyards named Canoe Ridge. Canoe Ridge Vineyard, now owned by Diageo, has a winery headquartered in Walla Walla. Canoe Ridge Estate, still owned by Ste. Michelle, remains a vineyard-designate for some of the winery's chardonnays, merlots, and cabernet sauvignons, as well as a production facility for red wines.

Another important site is Alder Ridge, first planted in 1997, now totaling 812 acres and growing twenty-eight different grape varieties. Owned by the Baty family, Alder Ridge provides grapes for the company's own brands and also sells to more than thirty independent vintners, including Andrew Rich, Betz Family, Forgeron, Hightower, Januik, L'Ecole, Long Shadows, Maryhill, Owen Roe, Rulo, and Syncline. Across the road from nearby Champoux (profiled elsewhere) is Phinny Hill Vineyards, a well-regarded site whose premier tenants include Buty, Reininger, and Robert Karl. Quilceda Creek's new Palengat vineyard is also close at hand. The Crimson Wine Group (owners of Napa's Pine Ridge and Oregon's Archery Summit) owns Double Canyon Vineyards, a 600-acre site just up from Phinny Hill. With 85 acres of grapes already in the ground, Crimson halted plans for a dedicated winery when the recession hit.

Continuing north, away from the river and farther up into the hills, are two more substantial vineyards: 243-acre Destiny Ridge, the estate vineyard for Alexandria Nicole Cellars; and 1,100-acre Coyote Canyon. Founded in 1994, Coyote Canyon grows twenty-five varieties of wine grapes, including rare blocks of albariño, graciano, Juan Garcia, nebbiolo, and primitivo. Ste. Michelle Wine Estates is the principal client, but owners Bob, Mike, and Jeff Andrews sell grapes to more than two dozen wineries in Washington and Oregon, many brand-new, and offer a broad lineup of estate-grown wines under their own label.

Without a doubt, one of the most interesting recent additions to the region is the vast, steep, terraced Wallula vineyard (also profiled elsewhere). This 1,300-acre site, originally developed by the Den Hoed family, is now principally owned by Allen Shoup (Long Shadows) and his partners in the Premier Vineyard Estates LLC. First planted in 1998, Wallula incorporates a stunning variety of microterroirs, set on a series of small plateaus that rise from 300 to 1,350 feet above the water. Roughly 145 acres are farmed biodynamically, primarily growing riesling for Randall Grahm's Pacific Rim winery. Another 500 acres are in production, and new blocks—many quite small and experimental—are being added annually.

Most Horse Heaven Hills vineyards benefit from the moderating effect of the Columbia River. Bud break begins early and is fairly warm, but those vineyards in close proximity to the river rarely suffer the heat spikes (100 degrees or more) that can shut down vines in other parts of the state. The river also helps to protect them from winter freeze damage. Without question, this AVA is where the most experimentation in varietal trials is occurring, but proven successes at this point are the more established plantings of chardonnay, riesling, sauvignon blanc, merlot, cabernet sauvignon, syrah, and zinfandel.

The Horse Heaven Hills AVA is subject to stiff, steady winds throughout the growing season. On the plus side, these winds, which funnel through the Columbia Gorge, keep canopies dry and help control disease while moderating temperatures throughout the growing season. That said, growers must be wary of too much berry exposure to winds; this can toughen skins and thicken tannins, yielding wines that are hard and chewy. There is no doubt that when managed properly, Horse Heaven Hills vineyards produce some of Washington's best merlots and cabernets.

Why the odd name? An oft-quoted local legend asserts that a rancher, camping in the hills many years ago, tracked his horses to an upland meadow and found them happily chewing on bunch grass. "Surely this is horse heaven," he supposedly remarked. A more credible story is told by Ken Lewis, the octogenarian owner of a Yakima Valley vineyard. "My father walked from Ketchum [Idaho] to Prosser," Lewis told me, "barefoot beside a covered wagon when he was just six years old in 1901. His father—my grandfather George J. Lewis—had missed the covered wagon days, and he wanted that adventure, so they did it. They call it the Horse Heaven Hills because you can't get a horse across it alive without water."

COLUMBIA GORGE

On July 9, 2004, the TTB gave its blessing to the Columbia Gorge Viticultural Area, a two-state AVA that occupies an especially scenic, 15-mile stretch along both sides of the Columbia River. It is for all intents and purposes a further extension of the western edge of the Columbia Valley AVA, though not technically included within it.

As legally defined, the Columbia Gorge AVA comprises a total of 191,000 acres, with just 500 currently under vine. Though vineyards are small and most are relatively new, the quality of the grapes being grown has caught the attention of winemakers from both states. On the Washington side, south-facing vineyards occupy plateaus and slopes perched high above the river. Some are buffeted by fierce winds, yet protected from desert extremes of heat and cold by the rain shadow of the Cascade Mountains. Among them are a handful of Washington vineyards that can be dry-farmed.

The Cascade Mountain foothills occupy the western border, bisected by the Columbia River as it runs through a very narrow passage and framed by snowcapped Mount Hood and Mount Adams. Cool marine air rushes through, creating a wind tunnel effect. Depending on its proximity to the mountains and its elevation above the river, a vineyard may receive as much as 30 or as little as 18 inches of rainfall annually.

The landscape shifts quickly and dramatically, moving from the cool, heavily treed slopes of Underwood Mountain to the hot, dusty, continental high desert of the Columbia Valley AVA to the east. The climate is more modulated on the Oregon side of the Gorge; here orchards abound, and growing conditions overall are less extreme. Though the AVA's vineyards are small, the varied climate affords site-specific opportunities for both cool-climate whites, particularly gewürztraminer and pinot gris, and hot-climate reds such as syrah and tempranillo. Such novelties (for Washington) as grüner veltliner and pinot noir are also being tried here.

"It's not a big AVA," notes Peter Rosback of Sineann. He purchases grapes from vineyards on both sides of the river and sees firsthand the sudden changes in temperature and elevation. "You shed a lot of moisture as you travel across the AVA," he points out, "an inch less rain per year per mile as you go east, from the Cascade Locks at 60 inches per year to The Dalles at 12 inches per year."

Columbia Gorge is the third Pacific Northwest AVA (along with Columbia Valley and Walla Walla Valley) to straddle the Oregon-Washington border. Some confusion exists regarding the use of the term Columbia Gorge, because another steeply canyoned stretch of the same river, much farther north and well inland, is also home to a number of vineyards and a famous outdoor amphitheater known as The Gorge. But as far as the legally approved Columbia Gorge AVA is concerned, it refers only to the region straddling the Oregon border.

WAHLUKE SLOPE

On January 6, 2006, the 81,000-acre Wahluke Slope became Washington's eighth certified AVA, just 14 months after the application was submitted to the TTB. The name supposedly means "watering place," an odd choice for this amazingly dry stretch of rather scrubby desert. It lies in the dead center of the Columbia Valley AVA, bounded on the west and south by the Columbia River, on the north by the Saddle Mountains, and on the east by the Hanford Reach National Monument.

Geographically isolated, it has nonetheless proven an excellent grape-growing region, thanks to its uniform sand-and-gravel soils, its consistently smooth, south-facing slope, and its virtually rainless, reliably sunny, and quite warm climate—perhaps the hottest in the state. Vineyard elevations range from 425 feet along the Columbia River up to 1,475 feet at the irrigated high point of the slope. The soils are coarse and well drained, and grapes ripen evenly and predictably well. "No other AVA in Washington State is contained on a single landform with large areas of uniform sandy and gravelly soils over a large area," notes Alan Busacca, a certified professional soil scientist and registered geologist who wrote the AVA petition in partnership with the Wahluke Slope Wine Grape Growers Association. Grower Butch Milbrandt describes it as "one big plateau that lays on a southerly plain."

Currently the 81,000-acre region encompasses more than twenty vineyards, two wineries, and three wine production facilities, notably the Wahluke Wine Company and Coventry Vale. Despite its isolation and lack of tourist amenities—the taco truck in Mattawa is about the only highlight—this is a region that any wine tourist should at least drive through, if only to see the sprawling Milbrandt vineyards, whose ten Wahluke properties include Sundance, Clifton, Talcott, Pheasant, and Katherine Leone, names frequently cited as vineyard-designates from a host of wineries.

With nearly 6,000 bearing acres, Wahluke Slope accounts for a sixth of the total wine grape acreage in Washington. More important, it is in many ways the heart of the state's red wine production. Although Red Mountain and Walla Walla have more notoriety, neither region actually grows significant tonnage. Wahluke Slope does.

The first important vineyard and winery development in the region was also the first investment by a foreign firm in the post-Prohibition Washington wine industry. In 1981, Germany's F. W. Langguth Winery, with financial backing from two of the founding partners in the Sagemoor vineyard, planted the original 221 acres of the Weinbau vineyard (*weinbau* means "vineyard" in German). It was truly in the middle of nowhere, a few miles east of Mattawa. Sixty percent of the vines were riesling, 20 percent gewürztraminer, and 20 percent chardonnay, and the wines were made nearby at a huge, state-of-the-art, high-tech production facility—the best by far in the state at the time. The wines were actually quite good, especially the late-harvest rieslings. But with clunky, Germanic labels and virtually no on-site sales, Langguth never found a market, and after just four or five vintages the Germans sold out.

For a brief time following, the winery was the headquarters of the second-largest wine company in the state, producing Snoqualmie, Langguth, and Saddle Mountain wines, with a young Mike Januik as winemaker. Januik remembers making a late-harvest Langguth in '87 and possibly '88, but that was the end of the brand. Following a series of legal battles and further changes of ownership, the winery became what it is today, strictly a custom crush facility. The Weinbau vineyard, however, remains part of the Sagemoor group and still includes 67 acres of the original riesling and 40 acres of the original chardonnay plantings. More riesling, chardonnay, and later plantings of cabernet sauvignon, cab franc, and merlot have bumped up the total to 265 acres. Since 2004, Weinbau fruit has been available to a number of smaller wineries (previously it all went to Ste. Michelle) and is considered one of the best sites in the AVA.

Apart from Weinbau, red wine grapes, especially merlot, cabernet franc, cabernet sauvignon, and syrah, make up 80 percent of the total Wahluke Slope production. Among the largest vineyard holdings are Wyckoff Farms (925 acres), Milbrandt (746 acres), Jones (626 acres), Desert Wind (540 acres), Shaw (464 acres), and Stone Tree (450 acres). Indian Wells is a vineyard-designate on several Ste. Michelle wines.

RATTLESNAKE HILLS

The Rattlesnake Hills, Washington's ninth AVA, was officially certified on March 20, 2006, and is entirely contained within the Yakima Valley. The initial goal may or may not have been to establish a tourist trail that would lure cars off the interstate and into winery tasting rooms—the cover of the first Rattlesnake Hills Wine Trail touring and tasting brochure proudly reads "Come Tread on Me!"—but more importantly, the confirmation of the AVA, though controversial, marks an important turning point in the evolution of Yakima Valley wines.

Gail and Shirley Puryear (owners of Bonair Winery) were among the first to explore the wine potential of the region, purchasing five acres just outside Zillah in 1979 and planting wine grapes the following spring. They spearheaded research and provided documentation regarding the unique topography of the Rattlesnake Hills and successfully fought for its status as a separate AVA.

The 68,500-acre AVA encompasses an east-west ridge of hills along the northern border of the Yakima Valley. It begins at an elevation of 850 feet (demarcated by the Sunnyside Canal) and tops out at about 3,100, placing it significantly higher than much of the Yakima Valley. Temperatures are moderate to warm, matching Red Mountain heat units in the westernmost vineyards. Winters average 8–10 degrees warmer than Red Mountain and Walla Walla; the sheltering hills help protect the vines from freeze damage by blocking the winter blasts that come down from Canada.

"Climate is what really differentiates the Rattlesnake Hills AVA," writes Gail Puryear. "The Yakima Valley AVA encompasses Regions I (pinot noir country) through III (zinfandel country). The boundaries of the Rattlesnake Hills AVA were drawn along climatic lines to make it a solid Region II. Red Mountain is a solid Region III. Cabernet sauvignon should not be grown in region I, but does quite well in Regions II and III. So, if [you are] trying to find a common thread in the wines of the Yakima Valley AVA, it will be very difficult when you are comparing cabernet sauvignon from Regions I, II, and III and trying to draw a generalization." Puryear goes on to say that wines from the Rattlesnake Hills have longer hang times than Red Mountain, hence softer tannins; and because the region is warmer than the lower parts of the Yakima Valley, the Bordeaux reds do not have the vegetal (bell pepper, green bean, or asparagus) character. These claims seem to me to be quite legitimate.

The most recent tally names seventeen wineries and thirty vineyards (with 1,246 planted acres) within the AVA, though it excludes some wineries (Sheridan, Côte

Bonneville) that do not belong to the vintners' association or use the name Rattlesnake Hills on their labels. Lest you wonder about that name, Gail Puryear offers the following guidance on the AVA website: "Our mascot, *Crotalis viridis oreganus*, a.k.a. the Northern Pacific Rattlesnake, is seldom longer than 30 inches and is very shy. He prefers to avoid contact with people. He will rapidly slither off unless cornered or surprised. He is seldom spotted in land suitable for grape growing, preferring rocky outcroppings at higher elevations and the north slopes of the Rattlesnake Hills where there are fewer people and less intensive agriculture." OK then! How about those wines?

There is no question that some excellent wines are made or sourced from the region. Winemakers from around the state seek out grapes from a number of vineyards within its borders, notably Dineen, DuBrul, Elephant Mountain, Portteus, and Sheridan. Andrew Will's Two Blondes vineyard and Owen Roe's Outlook vineyard are also located here. Still, it is much more common to see wines from these vineyards designated with a specific vineyard name and Yakima Valley rather than the more localized AVA. Why is that? I'll give Puryear the last word: "Our biggest challenge is to get our growers and wineries to express this excellence. Much to my dismay, some mediocre wines have already been labeled Rattlesnake Hills. We at Bonair are working hard to produce estate-grown fruit that expresses the excellence of the terroir, but avoids the overripe, high-alcohol, semisweet, jammy 'New World' syndrome. We can do that also in the Rattlesnake Hills should we choose."

SNIPES MOUNTAIN

The Snipes Mountain AVA became Washington's tenth on February 20, 2009. Like the Rattlesnake Hills AVA, its neighbor to the north, and Red Mountain a few miles east, it is a subdivision of the much larger Yakima Valley AVA. Its boundaries are based on altitude as well as the usual criteria of history, soil, and topography. Snipes Mountain rises rather abruptly just south of Interstate 82 in midvalley. On its northern slopes the AVA begins above 820 feet; on its much steeper and warmer southern side the line is drawn at 750 feet. The altitude at the top, where new vineyards continue to be developed, climbs to 1,300 feet.

The AVA boundaries reach across the freeway to include Harrison Hill, a smaller lump that is home to the vineyard of the same name. Originally planted in 1963 by the founders of Associated Vintners (now Columbia winery), the Harrison Hill vineyard is currently owned by the Newhouse family. Its grapes go into a vineyard-designate from DeLille Cellars.

The total area included in the new AVA measures 4,145 acres—roughly 100 acres more than Red Mountain—but the bearing acreage is just around 800. Snipes Mountain got its name from Benjamin Snipes, once known as the Northwest Cattle King. In the mid-1800s, Snipes had up to 125,000 head of cattle roaming Yakima Valley range land, and the mountain named for him was their winter home, sheltering them from harsh north winds. W. B. Bridgman liked the area also and established the Upland Winery and vineyards in the early 1900s. The original Upland Winery closed in 1972. But some of Bridgman's original vines—Muscat of Alexandria dating from around 1917—are still bearing. When the winery closed, his vineyards were acquired by the Newhouse family, an already well-established orchard grower on the mountain.

Almost immediately the Newhouses began renovating the neglected vineyards and planting new ones. Todd Newhouse estimates that the family currently has more than 700 acres planted to vinifera (not all bearing). Four other growers contribute small amounts to the AVA totals. The Newhouse holdings include six different varieties of muscat vines and more than thirty-five different varietals in all, many experimental. Chardonnay, pinot gris, merlot, and cabernet sauvignon—sold primarily to Hogue, Milbrandt, and Ste. Michelle—constitute the bulk of the tonnage.

It is not yet possible to pin down specific flavors for Snipes Mountain fruit. Vineyard designates (other than Harrison Hill) have not yet appeared; most grapes are tossed into the big hoppers at the big wineries. But even a casual survey of the terrain is revelatory. It's a microcosm of almost everything possible in eastern Washington, with every conceivable aspect, a mix of elevations, and vines ranging in age from just planted to almost a century old.

Where the mountain has been cut away on its south side, there are deep veins of compressed river sediment, smooth river rock, basalt, and gravel—side by side in a jumble that makes even trained geologists gasp. These are ancient Columbia River soils thrust up by the fault activity that shaped the land eons ago, pushing it above the massive floods that deposited most Columbia Valley soils. It is ancient river sediments that are more common here—surprising for the top of a mountain. These unique soils alone provide justification for AVA status.

LAKE CHELAN

The Lake Chelan AVA, officially certified on May 29, 2009, is Washington's eleventh and the state's second-smallest in terms of total vineyard land under cultivation—about 265 acres. Located at the far northwestern corner of the overriding Columbia Valley AVA, Lake Chelan currently includes just fifteen wineries. Historically, the bench lands surrounding the lake—the largest natural lake in the entire Cascade Range—have been covered with apple, pear, and cherry orchards. But as the apple business became less and less profitable in the late 1990s, a few adventurous growers decided to try wine grapes. The first of these new vineyards went into the ground in 1998, and within a few years, a mini-land rush had gobbled up many more old orchards and replaced them with vines.

The AVA application (also prepared by Alan Busacca) explains that the Lake Chelan wine valley includes unique soils built up with layers of glacial debris, sediment from stream erosion, and airborne volcanic loess. The so-called lake effect moderates temperatures year-round, so that the incidence of summer days over 95 degrees (the temperature at which photosynthesis shuts down) and the severity of deep winter freezes (which can kill vines) are significantly less than in most other eastern Washington AVAs.

The region has other assets as well, including (relatively) abundant water and a remarkable range of microclimates. But its biggest advantage, from a business standpoint, is tourism. "The Wine, The Lake, The Life" boasts the Lake Chelan Wine Valley brochure. New condo developments line both shores, and during the brief but hectic summer vacation season, many tasting rooms are open seven days a week. Most of the wineries sell the bulk of their production right out of their cellar doors, and there are gorgeous views, picnic areas, well-stocked gift shops, full-on restaurants, music events, and other inducements at many of them.

The AVA includes only about one-fifth of the lake, focusing on the narrow strip of benches and hummocks that ring the southernmost portion. In many respects it resembles a smaller version of Canada's Okanagan wine region. At its southern end the lake runs approximately east-west rather than north-south, so there is a north shore and a south shore, with different slopes and exposures. The north shore benefits from south- and west-facing vineyards and is perhaps a bit more suitable for red grapes, though white grapes are grown there also. The south shore, with its vineyards facing more to the north and east, seems better for white wine grapes and cool-climate reds (pinot noir), though here again, at this early stage, there are plenty of red grapes being tried.

There is very little that isn't planted somewhere in this new AVA; vintners are caught up in the excitement of experimentation, and they are happy to try a few rows of almost anything. Surprisingly, pinot noir has been a bit of a slow starter. Bob Broderick, whose south-shore Chelan Estate winery planted most of its seven acres to pinot noir in 2000, has determined that three clones are needed to make a complete wine. Some clones, he and others have noted, do not work at all. After much experimentation, Broderick has settled on clone 115 ("ripens early and has the aromatics"), clone 113 ("has the big center fruit core"), and clone 13 ("needs the heat, ripens last, and adds structure and color").

Though pinot has been problematic, syrahs have fared well at several locations. But the aromatic white wines—riesling, gewürztraminer, and viognier—are the real stars here. If asked to characterize the Lake Chelan terroir at this early date, I would point to the elegance and purity of the fruit flavors, the floral, complex aromatics, the bright natural acids, and the lack of heavy oak in almost all of the wines.

PUGET SOUND

Though Puget Sound was given AVA status in 1995, it remains Washington's odd man out. It covers a big chunk of western Washington that includes Puget Sound and the San Juan Islands, parts of the Olympic Peninsula, and a wide swath of the mainland's western edge. Yet fewer than 100 acres of this vast area are actually planted to wine grapes.

Most of the wineries that fall within the appellation purchase their grapes from eastern Washington, and only about a dozen or so make any Puget Sound wines at all. But cool-climate white varietals are successfully grown in a number of locations, the focus predominantly on chasselas, Madeleine angevine, siegerrebe, and Müller-Thurgau. Experiments with chardonnay, pinot gris, and pinot noir are ongoing. Vintners frequently point to statistics that show that west-side rainfall is quite low during the growing season, and they are correct. Rain is not the problem with ripening grapes here; it's temperature. Western Washington temperatures rarely climb into the mid-80s, let alone higher. The growing season is relatively brief, and problems brought on by humidity, which don't exist in eastern Washington, can occur here.

Some excellent berry wines are produced, and the Puget Sound wineries as a group go out of their way to welcome visitors and make wine touring on the islands and the Olympic Peninsula great fun. As new clones and vineyard sites are explored, wines made from Puget Sound AVA vineyards are becoming a bit more diverse and occasionally quite interesting. In particular, look for homegrown varietals from these island wineries—Vashon Winery, Bainbridge Island Vineyards, Whidbey Island Vineyards, Lopez Island Vineyards, and San Juan Vineyards.

ANCIENT LAKES NEXT?

As this book goes to press, rumors abound concerning a purported application for an Ancient Lakes AVA in Washington State. No such application exists as of now, nor does anyone I have spoken to—winemakers, vineyard owners, or experts often involved in the preparation of such applications—know of one being prepared. Theoretically, an Ancient Lakes region would cover land east of the Columbia River in central Washington, with Highway 28 (Quincy to Moses Lake) as a rough northern border and Highway 26, just north of the Wahluke Slope AVA, marking the southern edge. Some of this area is also known as the Royal Slope, and certainly the vineyards located there and to the north— top sites such as Evergreen, Stillwater, and Stoneridge—suggest that this area is worthy of AVA status. Cooler than the Wahluke Slope to the south, Ancient Lakes is already a proven location for high acid, intensely fruity riesling, viognier, chardonnay, and pinot gris.

3

THE GRAPES

There is no simple answer to the question, What is Washington's signature grape? But that question—a natural for those trying to get their arms around an unfamiliar wine region—makes a good entrance point for an overview of what does grow best here.

The focus on identifying wines by their grape varietals is largely an American invention. The standard European model for classifying wines has relied almost exclusively on place names—the exception being varietally labeled wines destined for American supermarkets, usually from appellations with little or no cachet. This American penchant for varietal labeling was a reaction to the jug wines that ruled the marketplace in the decades following the repeal of Prohibition. The wines were simply bottled as Burgundy, Chablis, and Rhine (supposedly a nod to their imagined European antecedents), such terms rather vaguely indicating whether a wine was "hearty," sweet (Rhine), or dry (Chablis). *Sauternes, Sherry, Port,* and especially *Champagne* were also terms widely appropriated and abused, with the result that American consumers, who were just beginning to explore and learn about wine in the 1960s and '70s, were often left more confused than ever.

Most jug wines included little or no vinifera grapes in their blends. With varietal labeling, farsighted vintners attempted to differentiate their wines of higher quality— those made exclusively from vinifera grapes—from the jug wine pack. An early Robert Mondavi label for his California White Table Wine carefully distinguished itself from the generic chablis of the day by noting it was "a wine for everyday use made entirely of varietal wine grapes." Washington produced its share of jug wines, but as early as the

1940s, reports Leon Adams, W. B. Bridgman was bottling varietal Johannisberg riesling and cabernet sauvignon in this state. The first wines released by Associated Vintners were varietally labeled, and André Tchelistcheff's early experiments in Washington, in the late 1960s, were with batches of cabernet sauvignon, pinot noir, sémillon, and grenache.

It's interesting to note that more than 40 years later, sémillon remains mysteriously unpopular with consumers, and grenache has only recently begun to be planted here again after virtually disappearing. Pinot noir is a curiosity at best, being tried in just a handful of growing regions—most notably Puget Sound, the eastern foothills of the Cascade Mountains, the Okanogan Valley, and the borders of Lake Chelan. Among those grapes originally investigated by Tchelistcheff, only cabernet sauvignon has secured a place for itself at the top of the Washington vinifera hierarchy.

In Europe, once you dig past the geographical names on the wine labels, you find that the great wine-growing regions always have a signature grape or blend, backed by legal restrictions. You can't grow just anything anywhere, unless you are content to call it simply table wine or country wine. If you want to call it Chablis, it had better be chardonnay. Barolo is going to be nebbiolo and nothing else. In emerging New World viticultural regions, vintners enjoy definite marketing advantages if they can point to one particular wine they do better than anyone else and compare it to the Old World standard-bearer. This is how Oregon has made its reputation with pinot noir, Argentina with malbec, and New Zealand with sauvignon blanc. Even in California, the land where everything grows ("Plant a nail and you'll grow a crowbar" one old-timer told me), many leading wine regions have grabbed onto something to call their own. Napa has its cabernets, Dry Creek its zinfandels, Russian River its pinot noirs, and so on.

Like California, Washington does many things well. But unlike California, this state has not yet succeeded in establishing distinct regional identities. In some of the more tightly defined Washington AVAs, the outlines of particular local strengths are beginning to emerge. Red Mountain is certainly cabernet country first and foremost. The Yakima Valley can lay claim to aromatic whites—riesling and gewürztraminer and pinot gris. The Wahluke Slope does especially well with Rhône varietals, both white and red. The Horse Heaven Hills arguably grows the country's best merlot. And some sites in Walla Walla produce exceptional syrahs remarkably like those of the northern Rhône.

But let's face the truth head on: there is little chance that any single grape, white or red, will ever become the icon for the state's wine industry. Is that a weakness? From a marketing viewpoint, this versatility can be perceived as a lack of strength. This state may appear to be what baseball managers call a utility player, the can-do, hustling newcomer who can play anywhere, fill any gap, step in and substitute for the stricken star. But everyone is looking for the star. Americans love star power.

Name almost any frontline grape or wine region, and Washington can put up a very good version of the same wine, one that offers exceptional quality and often at a better price than California. Is that a curse or a blessing? Time will be the final judge. I've picked my candidates for the top four white and top four red grapes and given them extended profiles below. But even these "proven" winners are still being significantly improved upon.

Grower Dick Boushey, who has done more than his fair share of experimenting over the years, notes that "we are still in a bit of an age of discovery in Washington. Sure we know that merlot, syrah, riesling, and cabernet do quite well here, but why not find out what other varieties might excel in Washington? Yes, there is some risk in a new variety, but the rewards in the long run can be worth the risk. If you guess right, you can ride the wave for a while until everyone else catches up with you."

The most recent surveys confirm that Washington's bearing wine grape acreage is officially up to 34,000, a modest increase over the past few years. What that does not show, however, is the nonbearing acreage or the nondeclared bearing acreage; so that total seems likely to rise significantly in the near future. Tracking the official figures over the past seven years, the bearing acreage has risen only from 27,000 to 34,000—roughly 25 percent—yet the number of bonded wineries has gone from 240 to more than 650, and production at the largest wineries has climbed dramatically. Something doesn't quite add up.

On the upswing are chardonnay (up 19 percent from 2008 to 2009) and riesling (up almost 13 percent in the same year). White varieties hold a significant edge over reds (54 versus 46 percent) in terms of total tonnage. Riesling and chardonnay are fighting for first place, with pinot gris, sauvignon blanc, gewürztraminer, viognier, sémillon, and chenin blanc completing the top eight. On the red side, cabernet sauvignon and merlot account for almost three-quarters of the total crop, with syrah, cabernet franc, malbec, pinot noir, and sangiovese filling in most of the rest. Four grapes account for three quarters of the total harvest: riesling (20 percent), chardonnay (21 percent), cabernet sauvignon (18 percent), and merlot (16 percent).

As old vineyards are replanted or expanded, and new vineyards developed, growers are drawing upon a much wider variety of clones. Row orientation is being fine-tuned, and tighter spacing and higher densities are being tried. It's not uncommon in new locations, especially in wheat country, for cover crops to be planted to revitalize dead soils before the first grapevines are put into the ground. Sustainable viticultural practices are promoted by organizations such as Walla Walla's Vinea—the Winegrowers' Sustainable Trust—and the wide-ranging experimental programs of Washington State University and other educational institutions. At Ciel du Cheval for example, WSU is conducting experiments with previously untried native plant species, planting them as between-row cover crops, both to preserve biodiversity and to fix nitrogen in the soil. The Washington Association of Wine Grape Growers (www.wawgg.org) is focusing substantial efforts on research and education in the areas of integrated pest management, insect and mildew control, and the use of cover crops—often a challenge in Washington's dry, sandy soils.

Technological innovations in soil mapping and improved techniques for measuring soil moisture retention aid in the fine-tuning of irrigation, even in a single row. How important is that? Rich Wheeler, Ste. Michelle's vice president of vineyards, points out that "drip irrigation really gives us precise control. By controlling the canopy, which in part controls the cluster exposure, it's a great quality enhancer. The vine is putting the majority of its energy into the fruit, not vegetation. Watering at precisely the right time gives some control over berry size. Usually we want a smaller berry so we run them pretty close to stress over the whole season."

As a result, the quality and uniformity of the fruit, and the range of clone-specific characteristics available to winemakers for blending, have never been better. And the thirst to try even newer varietals has never been greater. Winemakers often have a mad scientist gene. They want to try something they have never done before, and if no one else has done it, so much the better. It's only in the past dozen years that high-quality French clones of grenache blanc, grenache, syrah, counoise, marsanne, mourvèdre, viognier, roussanne, and picpoul, for example, have been available to growers anywhere in the country, thanks largely to the pioneering efforts of the Haas family at Tablas Creek. All of these varieties are now planted in Washington, and being tried both in blends and as stand-alone varietals. Similar trials of Iberian grapes—albariño, tempranillo, and various Portuguese varietals—are also in vogue currently.

With so many new wines becoming available, a grape-by-grape survey of this state's extraordinary depth and breadth remains the best way to really understand what Washington wines are all about. Here are my candidates for the state's top four white and top four red grapes—in terms of both production and proven quality—followed by a comprehensive listing of everything being made as a varietal wine. I've listed my favorite producers for each grape and added separate listings for non-varietally labeled Bordeaux and Rhône blends.

WASHINGTON'S BEST: THE TOP EIGHT WINE GRAPES

CHARDONNAY

Chardonnay is grown in almost every corner of Washington—on close to 7,000 acres in all, placing it right behind resurgent riesling in the competition for the state's most planted grape. Washington chardonnays have always shown fresh green-apple flavors and crisp acidity, a clean, food-favoring style that is roaring back into popularity in place of the buttery, tropical, banana and mango bombs of yesteryear. The most distinctive examples bring a mix of tree fruit, tropical fruit, and moderately toasty barrel flavors, always with refreshing acids and sometimes a mineral cut to the finish. There are many chardonnays being done exclusively in stainless steel, and others, including widely available brands such as Snoqualmie, emphasizing organically grown grapes.

àMaurice	Goose Ridge
Abeja	Gordon Brothers
Arbor Crest	Gorman Big Sissy
Baer Shard	Hogue (Reserve)
Barnard Griffin	Januik (esp. Cold Creek)
Bonair Chateau Puryear	JM Cellars
Boudreaux	L'Ecole No 41
Buty	Mark Ryan
Cadaretta	Milbrandt
Caterina	Novelty Hill
Chateau Ste. Michelle (Ethos, Cold Creek, Canoe Ridge, and Reserve)	Olsen Estates
	Owen Roe DuBrul
Coeur d'Alene Cellars	RiverAerie
Columbia Crest (esp. Reserve)	Rulo
Columbia Wyckoff	Saviah
Côte Bonneville	Sparkman Lumière
Dunham Shirley Mays	Tamarack
Dusted Valley Old Vine	Waterbrook (Reserve)
Forgeron	Woodward Canyon

RIESLING

When asked to name the greatest white wine grape in the world, most wine professionals will unhesitatingly say riesling. With consumers, the grape's reputation rises and falls, sometimes precipitously. In recent years, it has clearly been on the rise, especially here in Washington. Riesling is now the state's most planted grape, white or red, and Ste. Michelle is all by itself the largest riesling producer in the world—before adding its Columbia Crest and Snoqualmie brands to the total.

So it's déjà vu all over again; in the early years of the industry, riesling was suggested as a good starter grape for Washington growers. They had no hope, it was believed, of ripening much else here in the frigid north. And riesling did do well here, so well that in the early 1980s a prestigious German company, Langguth, invested millions of dollars planting vineyards and building a magnificent winery in the stark, dusty middle of nowhere just outside Mattawa, strictly dedicated to riesling.

The Langguth winery didn't last long, but time has proven its founders right about Washington riesling. The grape thrives here, and not just as a basic, off-dry, fruit-driven slurp. It can be bone dry yet retain amazing concentration and depth of flavor. It can be juicy, vibrantly off-dry, and tart, packed with ripe citrus fruits, as is perfectly expressed in the nation's best-selling version, Chateau Ste. Michelle's Johannisberg riesling. And it can make arguably the most dense, luscious, decadent, yet gloriously structured TBA-style wine in the country, the Single Berry Select from Ste. Michelle and Dr. Loosen.

Dr. Ernst (Ernie) Loosen, whose decade-long partnership with Ste. Michelle has brought great improvements to riesling in both vineyard and winery, remembers, "It was in 1998 that a friend in Portland first showed me some of Chateau Ste. Michelle's rieslings. They were much better than I expected," he admits. "Not great wines, and definitely not built for aging, but well made and showing a hint of what I thought could be called a real 'Washington' taste. They immediately made me think that there was a chance to do something really interesting with riesling in Washington."

He made his first visit to the vineyards of eastern Washington in July 1999. "I learned that it's really a cold-climate wine area," he says, "with very warm days and cool nights. I like wines from this kind of climate—and from the mineral soils they have in Washington. They have more delicacy and are more European than wines from hot climates, like most of California."

Loosen quickly discovered that he was working in a totally different environment than the Mosel he was accustomed to: perhaps a bit like the Pfalz, he now says, because of the warm days and similar soils. But irrigation is outlawed in Germany and in most of Europe, and growing grapes in a desert climate is one of the unique aspects of Washington viticulture. "All of the vineyard management techniques are totally different," Loosen explains. "But the collaboration has been very interesting, and we've all learned quite a lot about growing riesling in such a climate. Some of the things we've learned go against the conventional wisdom, but that is based mostly on European traditions, which don't necessarily apply in the New World. The main thing we've discovered is that to get concentrated flavors and elegance in the wine, you have to extend the ripening time as long as possible without the grapes getting overripe. But we also found that, with riesling, you can't withhold water to control growth, as they do with red wines in Washington. So it's been a continual process of working out the best ways to irrigate, to manage the canopy, and to control growth so we get the taste in the wine that we think best represents the true terroir of Washington."

Following his lead, other prestige rieslings have emerged: Poet's Leap, crafted by Armin Diel for Long Shadows, and the exciting lineup of single-vineyard, organic, and biodynamic rieslings from Pacific Rim, Randall Grahm's Washington project. But at the inexpensive end, quality is also superb, and wines such as Charles Smith's Kungfu Girl put a packaging face on riesling that is the other side of the galaxy from its stodgy Germanic origins.

Many Washington vintners release the new vintage in the spring, when the young wines are steely and fresh and still showing a bit of spritz. Pleasantly frizzante, they tickle the tongue on the way down and send up aromas loaded with the scents of spring blossoms and sweet citrus. The fruit-driven flavors mix oranges, tangerines, apricots, apples, peaches, and pears. Some of the very best dry rieslings also weave in textures of wet stone or light hints of herb, such as cilantro or fennel.

What ties them together stylistically is their vivacious mix of bright fruit, high acids, and the perception of sweetness (except in the raciest dry versions). The dozens of rieslings that fall somewhere in between bone dry and the sweet, late-harvest dessert wines are often the best choices to match with food. But how sweet are they? One of the frustrations of all domestic riesling is that the labels rarely indicate the residual sugar, making it guesswork to match them with food. Here Washington's predictable levels of ripeness make it relatively simple to figure it out for yourself, by looking at the percentage of alcohol.

With rare exceptions, any Washington riesling with alcohol over 13 percent is bone dry; 12–13 percent is dry; 10.5–12 percent will be off-dry; under 10.5 percent will be quite sweet. Basically the lower the alcohol, the sweeter the wine. The very sweetest late-harvest rieslings may have alcohol levels of 8 percent or even less. These excellent late-harvest wines, which are sometimes but not always botrytis affected, maintain significant acidity, despite their high sugars, and are never cloying or syrupy. From time to time genuine ice wines are also made (none of this cryogenic stuff) and offered at remarkably affordable prices.

Best Bottles Dry to Off-dry Riesling

Airfield Estates

Arbor Crest

Barnard Griffin

Bonair

Boudreaux

Canoe Ridge

Chateau Ste. Michelle (esp. Eroica and
    Cold Creek)

Columbia Cellarmaster's

Columbia Crest Grand Estates

Covey Run

Dunham Four Legged White

Efesté

Gamache

Gård Vintners

Hogue

J. Bookwalter

Kiona

Kungfu Girl

Mercer Estates

Milbrandt

Nefarious

O•S Winery

Owen Roe

Pacific Rim

Poet's Leap

Seven Hills

Smasne Cellars

Snoqualmie Naked and Winemaker's
    Select

Southard

Trio Lewis

Trust

Vin du Lac (esp. LEHM estate)

Whitman Cellars

Woodward Canyon

Zero One

Chateau Ste. Michelle Single Berry
    Select and Ethos Late Harvest

Covey Run

Dunham

Kiona

Pacific Rim

Washington Hills Summit Reserve

SAUVIGNON BLANC AND FUMÉ BLANC

Sauvignon blanc is grown all over the world, yet it seems to be one of those wines that does everything possible to confuse people. First is the name. In France, the best sauvignon blanc–based wines are named for a place (Sancerre); in Italy they may be called fumé sauvignon or just plain sauvignon; in the United States it is sometimes labeled fumé blanc, a marketing gimmick that has outlived its usefulness. Wine writers often love sauvignon blanc, yet by using terms such as gooseberry, crushed nettle, and even *pipi du chat* to describe the stuff, they do little to convince consumers that it's worth trying.

Winemakers don't help much either. They often overripen, occasionally underripen the grape. Too ripe, and the flavors turn soft and tropical; underripe, and grassiness quickly turns to canned asparagus. Overcrop, and the grape just gets sour and watery. But troubles don't end when the grapes are picked. Sauvignon blanc expresses itself best when made in stainless steel, but many winemakers, apparently imitating the seductive flavors of chardonnay, insist on barrel fermentation (sometimes in new oak) and a secondary (malolactic) fermentation, guaranteed to strip away any trace of varietal character.

Here in Washington, sauvignon blanc acreage has been steadily climbing, and it ranks fourth among white wine grapes in terms of tonnage. Some very good versions are made, with the snap, the zip, the assertive flavors of (here we go) cut grass, lime, citrus peel, and a dozen different herbs and green fruits. These are sauvignon blancs that resonate with varietal character; they penetrate the palate and liven up the tongue. That's why they are so perfectly matched to food, especially goat cheeses, shellfish, and other light seafood and poultry.

Best Bottles Varietally Labeled Sauvignon Blanc

Arbor Crest	Efesté
Balboa	Gordon Brothers
Barnard Griffin	Guardian Cellars
Barrister	JM Cellars
Cadaretta	Lone Canary
Chateau Ste. Michelle (esp. Horse Heaven)	Merry Cellars
	Milbrandt
Chinook	Novelty Hill

Page Cellars	Vin du Lac LEHM estate
Rulo	Waterbrook
Sineann	Woodinville Wine Cellars
Upland Estates	Woodward Canyon

SÉMILLON

Like sauvignon blanc, with which it is often blended, sémillon can be made into a lightly grassy, dry white table wine, or it can be late-harvested, shriveled with botrytis, and turned into a sweetly honeyed dessert wine. Washington State does very well with the grape, and one producer (L'Ecole No 41) makes several different versions each year. Best drunk young, sémillons taste of figs and melons, adding leafy notes as they age.

Sémillon has enjoyed a long and successful history in Washington, and if critics ruled the world, I suspect it would become a genuine calling card for the state. It doesn't make truly distinctive wines in many places in the world, but it does in Washington. And it has a history there as well: sémillon was one of a handful of varietal wines to be released from the watershed 1967 vintage—the first commercial vintage for both Ste. Michelle Vineyards (now Chateau Ste. Michelle) and Associated Vintners (now Columbia).

Sémillon has a lot going for it. The name is not impossible to pronounce, as is *gewürz-traminer*. It's got a good French pedigree. It's a grape that can be used as part of a high-end Bordeaux blend (notably the Chaleur Estate Blanc, the Buty Semillon/Sauvignon Blanc, and the L'Ecole No 41 Luminesce). It can be mixed with chardonnay, as the Australians do, to make a very nice warm-weather quaffing wine. What's not to like?

The best way to appreciate the flavors that varietal sémillon brings to the table is to drink wines labeled as such, which means that even if blended, they must be at least three-quarters sémillon. The addition of sauvignon blanc may give the finished wine more acid backbone and lift and a pleasant whiff of grassy herb. When it is blended, barrel fermented, and aged in new oak, sémillon is usually aiming for the Bordeaux blanc model. But some of my favorite Washington versions are unblended, a few are done in stainless steel, and others see more used than new oak, yet still deliver stand-up flavors.

Best Bottles Varietally Labeled Sémillon

Airfield Estates	Columbia
Amavi Cellars	Columbia Crest
Andrew Will Cuvée Lucia	Fidélitas
Ardenvoir	Hestia
Barnard Griffin	L'Ecole No 41
Beresan	Merry Cellars
Chateau Ste. Michelle	Novelty Hill
Chinook	

Best Bottles White Meritage Blends

Buty Semillon/Sauvignon/Muscadelle
Cadaretta
DeLille Chaleur Estate
L'Ecole No 41 Seven Hills Vineyard
Luminesce
Woodward Canyon Charbonneau

Best Bottles Sémillon Late-Harvest and Ice Wines

Chateau Ste. Michelle
Columbia Crest
JM Cellars
L'Ecole No 41
Owen Roe
Trust Cellars

CABERNET FRANC

The first cabernet franc plantings in the state were part of Washington State University's experimental blocks established in the mid-1970s. In 1985, Red Willow put in a small block suitable for commercial use (in a red blend). A varietal cabernet franc was introduced by Columbia (the first in Washington) in 1991, followed by Ste. Michelle's Cold Creek vineyard bottling in 1992. Today cabernet franc is widely grown and generally admired, although at least one veteran winemaker refers to it half jokingly as a "generally noxious weed." Alder Ridge has a particularly large block of 100 acres.

Good Washington cabernet franc displays appealing scents of fresh-ground coffee and ripe, tangy, berry-flavored fruit, packed with berries, particularly blueberries. In all other respects, it sits squarely alongside cabernet sauvignon, showing pretty floral and herbal nuances. Such light-olive, cut leaf, or forest floor aromas are fine in cabernet franc when balanced against some riper fruit flavors.

Washington did not have cabernet franc planted in sufficient quantities to be statistically relevant until 1993, when a few wineries began using it in their Bordeaux blends. Slowly plantings increased (though they appear to be leveling off), and today it ranks a distant fourth for red grape production behind cabernet sauvignon, merlot, and syrah.

Despite its popularity with winemakers and consumers, cabernet franc tonnage peaked at 3,300 tons in 2001 and has actually come down quite a bit since then. So if you are looking for these wines in the marketplace, you'll find that, although overall quality is very good, quantities are low. Most often it is blended in modest percentages into varietal merlots and cabernet sauvignons, to boost the color or add some interesting aromas.

A few of these red blends (those listed below) contain a high proportion of cabernet franc and clearly reflect its varietal character, and some dedicated winemakers produce pure varietal cabernet franc, as noted below by the (v). As a rosé the grape excels also; Chinook gets credit for making it into a modest cult wine; Trust makes a very good version also.

Andrew Rich

Barrister (v)

Beresan (v)

Camaraderie

Chandler Reach

Chateau Ste. Michelle Cold Creek
    Vineyard

Chatter Creek

Chinook (v)

Corvidae

Dusted Valley

Fielding Hills

Gamache (v)

GraEagle (v)

Hard Row To Hoe (v)

Nefarious Cellars

Northstar

O•S Winery

Owen Roe

Saviah Cellars

Sheridan

Sineann

Spring Valley

Stevens

Substance

Tamarack Cellars (v)

Tildio

Walla Walla Vintners

Willow Crest

Best Bottles Franc-Friendly Bordeaux Blends

Basel Cellars Inspired

Buty Merlot/Cabernet Franc

Cadence Bel Canto

Mark Ryan Long Haul

O•S Winery Ulysses

CABERNET SAUVIGNON

Because it has remained phylloxera free, Washington now has some of the oldest cabernet sauvignon vines in North America (see profiles of the Champoux, Cold Creek, and Otis vineyards in chapter 4). Better still, since they are planted on their own rootstock, the roots of these old vines go deep, and their flavors follow, deep and long.

Washington cabernets have been the signature wines of many of the state's most successful wineries, from Leonetti and Woodward Canyon to Abeja, Andrew Will, Betz Family, Boudreaux Cellars, DeLille Cellars, Dunham Cellars, Ste. Michelle, and Quilceda Creek. More than any other varietal, Washington cabernet sauvignon seems to capture the best of France and California in a single wine. Though they come in a range of styles, these cabs share an ability to walk the line between precision and opulence. They balance their bright, polished fruit with vibrant acid; they integrate their new oak slowly but surely, creating complete wines that are more than the sum of their components. Best of all, they make wines that are delicious young and yet have the capacity to age gracefully over decades.

Pure, 100 percent varietal cabernet sauvignon is relatively rare. More often, some percentage of merlot is included, and increasingly the other Bordeaux red grapes (cabernet franc, petit verdot, malbec, and even carmenère) are tossed into the blend. A developing trend is to mix cabernet, merlot, and syrah, a Washington take on a super-Tuscan.

Cabernet sauvignon is grown in every Washington AVA except for Puget Sound, but it does particularly well on Red Mountain, in the Horse Heaven Hills, on the Wahluke Slope, and in parts of the Walla Walla Valley. Rattlesnake Hills cabernet can be thrilling, especially in warmer vintages when its herbaceous tendencies are in check. The old-vine, vineyard-designated bottlings from Champoux, Cold Creek, Harrison Hill, Otis, and Sagemoor are especially noteworthy. Other vineyard-designates to look for include Ciel du Cheval, DuBrul, Klipsun, and Seven Hills.

Best Bottles Varietally Labeled Cabernet Sauvignon

Abeja

Alder Ridge

Amavi Cellars

Arbor Crest Klipsun

Balboa Mirage

Barnard Griffin Reserve

Barrister

Beresan

Betz Family Père de Famille

Boudreaux Cellars

Browne Family

Bunchgrass

Canoe Ridge Vineyard (esp. Block 1 Reserve)

Caterina

Cayuse The Widowmaker

Champoux Vineyard (all producers)

Chandler Reach Parris Estate Reserve

Chateau Rollat Edouard

Chateau Ste. Michelle Cold Creek and Ethos

Columbia Otis and Red Willow

Columbia Crest Reserve

Corliss Estates

Côte Bonneville

Couvillion Sagemoor

DeLille Cellars Harrison Hill and Chaleur Estate Grand Ciel

Den Hoed Andreas

Donedéi

Doubleback

Dunham Cellars

Dusted Valley

Efesté Big Papa

Fall Line

Feather

Fidélitas

Fielding Hills

Forgeron Cellars

Gamache

Gordon Brothers

Gorman The Bully

Gramercy Cellars

Isenhower Cellars

Januik

J. Bookwalter

JM Cellars

L'Ecole No 41

Leonetti Cellar

Milbrandt Vineyards The Estates

Novelty Hill

Owen Roe DuBrul

Pepper Bridge

Powers Coyote Vineyard Reserve

Quilceda Creek

Reininger

Robert Karl

Ross Andrew

Rulo

Saviah Cellars

Seven Hills Seven Hills Vineyard and Klipsun

Sheridan Vineyard Reserve

Sineann Baby Poux and Block One

Soos Creek

Southard

Sparkman Kingpin

Spring Valley Derby

Stephenson Cellars

Stevens XY Reserve

Substance

SYZYGY

Tamarack Cellars

Tertulia Cellars

Tulpen Cellars

Upland Estates Old Vine

Va Piano Estate

Walla Walla Vintners

Woodward Canyon Old Vines and Artist Series

Best Bottles Cabernet-Dominated Bordeaux Blends

àMaurice Artist Label

Andrew Will Sorella and Ciel du Cheval

Baer Arctos

Balboa Mith

Basel Cellars Merriment

Bergevin Lane Intuition

Betz Family Clos du Betz

Brian Carter Cellars L'Etalon

Cadence

Cayuse Camespelo

Col Solare

Columbia Crest Walter Clore

Côte Bonneville DuBrul Vineyard Red and Carriage House

DeLille Cellars Chaleur Estate and D2

Dunham Cellars Trutina

Fall Line

Fidélitas Meritage

Grand Rêve Collaboration Series I

J. Bookwalter Chapter One

JM Cellars Tre Fanciulli

L'Ecole No 41 Perigee

Leonetti Cellar Reserve

Mark Ryan Dead Horse

Nicholas Cole Camille, Michele, and Reserve

:Nota Bene Miscela

Robert Karl Inspiration

Saviah Cellars Une Vallée

Soos Creek Artist Series

Spring Valley Frederick and Uriah

Woodinville Wine Cellars Indomitable

Woodward Canyon Estate and Special Selection

Poor old merlot got knocked sideways by the movie of the same name, yet it can be argued that worse damage to the grape's reputation has been done by the vast amounts of cheap junk labeled merlot that is being pumped out by wineries around the world. Plonk, thy name is merlot! And yet merlot, as much or more than any other grape, is what put Washington State viticulture on the map. Until merlot proved otherwise, Washington was stuck with a "too cold to make serious red wine" reputation. Stick with lemberger was the advice from the experts.

Fortunately, winemakers don't always follow such advice. The state's first superstar winery, Leonetti Cellar, began as a merlot specialist. Andrew Will's Chris Camarda made his mark in the early 1990s by producing up to six different vineyard-designated merlots each vintage. And Columbia Crest, the state's biggest winery, still sets the standard for the country for supple, succulent, budget-priced merlots.

Alas, despite all it's done for the state, merlot still finds itself struggling to regain its former credibility. It is, say the critics, the chardonnay of reds: easy to pronounce, pleasant, and versatile but lacking any substantive character of its own. (The great exception, of course, is Bordeaux's Chateau Pétrus, where it comprises 95 percent of the blend.) I say it's time for Washington to reclaim the grape as its own. Especially in the Horse Heaven Hills, but absolutely across the entire state, merlot ripens beautifully and creates fleshy, powerful wines that can age for a decade or more.

Washington merlots start where most others leave off, with ripe flavors of sweet cherries, and then reach well beyond simple and fruity, adding plush, packed, textured flavors of mixed red and black fruits and berries. The best of them play out broadly across the palate, with smooth, supple tannins and plenty of lively natural acid. They happily embrace the flavors of new oak (toast, espresso, vanilla, and chocolate), but first and foremost they taste of rich, ripe fruit. Why does merlot seem to ripen better in Washington than almost anywhere else? Marty Clubb (L'Ecole No 41) believes that "the key to doing merlot right is that it's the thinner-skin varietal, and like sémillon, it tends to plump up with rain at harvest. We don't have that problem; we control the water."

Recently, merlot slid from first– to second–most planted red wine grape in the state, but overall tonnage continues to grow, up almost 25 percent in the most recently documented four-year period. Rather than using merlot as a simple blending grape to soften their cabernets, Washington winemakers are just as likely to do the reverse. In his tasting note for Ste. Michelle's 2006 Cold Creek vineyard merlot, Bob Bertheau writes, "We added 22 percent Cold Creek cabernet to soften the tannins." I doubt you'll find such notes on any California merlots.

Any list of the best Washington merlot vineyards must begin with Ciel du Cheval, Klipsun, and Kiona (on Red Mountain); Pepper Bridge, Spring Valley, and Seven Hills (in Walla Walla); both Canoe Ridges and Champoux (in the Horse Heaven Hills); DuBrul, Sheridan, and Boushey (in the Yakima Valley); and Ste. Michelle's Cold Creek.

It's true that Washington merlots won't age quite as long as the state's top cabs. But the more muscular, dense vintages can certainly go for a good decade and will acquire soft, lush flavors of dried fruits, toast, honey, caramel, and cinnamon. By and large they are best consumed during the first four to eight years after bottling.

Best Bottles Varietally Labeled Merlot

Abeja

Alexandria Nicole

Barnard Griffin

Barrister

Basel Cellars Pheasant Run

Beresan

Boudreaux Cellars

Canoe Ridge Vineyard (esp. Block 13
    Reserve)

Chandler Reach

Chateau Ste. Michelle vineyard
    designates and Ethos

Chinook

Columbia Crest Grand Estates and
    Reserve

Dunham Lewis

Fidélitas

Fielding Hills

Forgeron

Gordon Brothers

Helix by Reininger

Hightower Cellars

Hogue Reserve

Januik

J. Bookwalter

JM Cellars

Kestrel

Leonetti Cellar

L'Ecole No 41 (esp. Seven Hills)

Milbrandt Vineyards

Nelms Road

Novelty Hill

Northstar

Otis Kenyon

Owen Roe DuBrul

Pedestal

Pepper Bridge

Quilceda Creek

Reininger

Robert Karl

Seven Hills (esp. Klipsun and Seven
    Hills)

Sineann

Soos Creek

Sparkman Outlaw

Spring Valley Muleskinner

Stevens

Tamarack Cellars

Tulpen Cellars

Walla Walla Vintners

Waterbrook Reserve

Woodward Canyon

SYRAH

At the beginning of this century, eighteen Washington wineries were making syrah, which seemed at the time to be an explosion of interest in such an obscure grape.

Bearing acreage was up tenfold and on track to double again within a year. At 12 years of age, the first commercial syrah ever made in Washington (from Columbia winery in 1988) was alive and still drinking well.

As I write these words, almost a decade later, I would guesstimate that at least three hundred Washington wineries are making syrah, and most of them make more than one. There could easily be seven hundred different bottlings annually from this state alone. Syrah is a solid third among red grapes grown in Washington. It ripens differently throughout the state, showing a chameleon-like ability to reflect the specific growing conditions. Winemakers such as Bob Betz, Doug McCrea, Christophe Baron (Cayuse), and Charles Smith (K Vintners) use this to their particular advantage, offering different bottlings that seem genuinely distinct from one another.

In the vineyard, syrah behaves differently from Bordeaux grapes. A Bordeaux vine will do everything it can for the fruit to survive, including drop its leaves. Syrah will do the opposite. It will drop its fruit to save its leaves. The skins start to soften up, and the grapes do a kind of raisining. "Once those grapes start to shrivel up significantly, that's it for sugar," McCrea explains. "What you have to do is deficit irrigation. That's why we can make these wonderful wines; you can water and back off, and when the plants begin to fade a little, you give them a little more water, and it's kind of a dance really."

In the winery, syrah does not need to be soaked in oak to perform well; in fact, it shows more character when the oak is kept in check. Whether or not it is co-fermented with viognier (some wines are, others not), Washington syrah often shows a distinct citrus flavor, a streak of lemon-lime zest that adds lift and life to the wine. From other sites, notably Boushey in the Yakima Valley and the vineyards down in the rocks in Walla Walla, syrah becomes smoky, meaty, more tannic, with scents and flavors distinctly Rhône-ish.

In my annual Top 100 lists I find that syrahs account for a surprisingly high percentage of the total. Clearly winemakers and many critics—this one included—like the stuff. And yet . . . somehow syrah has become the poster child for the "too expensive" crowd. Dozens of winemakers, distributors, and retailers confirm that it is a tough sell these days. There is a disconnect between winemakers' estimation of the most promising red grape in the state and consumers' perception of quality-to-value.

That will have to be addressed, but I remain convinced that the quality is proven. In just the past couple of years, some thrilling new wineries have debuted with syrah as their passion and focus. Not all are making pure-blooded syrah; the trend is to blend, especially with cabernet sauvignon and merlot. But blended or not, Washington's leading syrahs light up the palate with a mix of highlighted flavors that California (and for that matter Australia) can only dream of. These are wines that dance, that capture the bright, fresh, tangy berry fruit, the nuances of citrus and spice, and the sharp acids that provide the nerve structure, the definition, and the sheer vitality of this state's wines.

Abeja	Grand Rêve
Alexandria Nicole	Guardian Cellars
AlmaTerra	Helix by Reininger
Amavi Cellars	Hestia Cellars
Andrew Rich	Isenhower Cellars
Andrew Will	Januik
Barnard Griffin	JM Cellars
Barrister	K Vintners
Beresan	Kestrel
Bergevin Lane	L'Ecole No 41
Betz Family	Mark Ryan Wild Eyed
Bunnell Family	McCrea Cellars
Cayuse	Morrison Lane
Charles Smith	Nefarious Cellars
Chateau Ste. Michelle	Nicholas Cole Dauphiné
Coeur d'Alene Cellars	:Nota Bene
Columbia Crest	Novelty Hill
Corliss Estates	O•S Winery Dineen
Côte Bonneville	Olsen Estates
DaMa	Otis Kenyon
Darby	Owen Roe Lady Rosa and Ex Umbris
Des Voigne Montreux	Rasa Vineyards
Doyenne	Reininger
Dumas Station	Reynvaan Family Vineyards
Dunham Cellars Lewis	Robert Karl
Dusted Valley	Ross Andrew
Efesté Ceidleigh	Rôtie
Fidélitas	Rulo
Fielding Hills	Sapolil Cellars
Forgeron	Saviah Cellars
Gamache Vintners	Sequel
Gordon Brothers	Seven Hills
Gorman The Pixie	Sheridan Vineyard
Gramercy Cellars	Sparkman

Spring Valley Nina Lee

Stephenson Cellars

Stevens Black Tongue

Syncline

SYZYGY

Tamarack Cellars

Tertulia Cellars

Tulpen

Upland Estates

Va Piano

Walter Dacon

Waterbrook Reserve

Watermill

Waters

Woodward Canyon

WASHINGTON'S WHITE WINE GRAPES

ALBARIÑO

Credit must absolutely be given to Earl and Hilda Jones at Oregon's Abacela winery for igniting the first sparks of interest in Iberian grapes in the Pacific Northwest. They first planted tempranillo in 1995 on a hilltop in the Umpqua Valley, and 15 years later, they have found exceptional success not only with that grape but with their other signature wines, which include albariño. TAPAS—an advocacy group for producers of these wines modeled after successful efforts such as ZAP (for zinfandel) and P.S. I Love You (for petite sirah)—now has more than sixty members, but just a single Washington winery (Brian Carter Cellars) is listed on its site (Texas has four, and Arizona two!). So things are ramping up slowly here in Washington. But a little albariño is going into the ground here and there across the state, and Shady Grove has released what I believe to be the first Washington version. Adamant, Maison Bleue, and O•S are among the growing list of wineries that have said they intend to make albariño in the future.

ALIGOTÉ

Burgundy's "other" white grape is widely planted in eastern Europe but is virtually unknown in the United States. The Newhouse vineyard on Snipes Mountain grows a couple of acres that date back to the 1970s. Once a popular wine for Quail (now Covey) Run winery, the Newhouse vineyard fruit currently goes to Jed Steele (for his Shooting Star aligoté), to FairWinds winery in Port Townsend, and to La Bête in Oregon. Steele barrel-ferments his aligoté in neutral oak, making a high-acid, fruity wine that tastes of green apples, much like a pinot blanc.

CHASSELAS DORÉ

Chasselas Doré grapes were planted in 1950 on Vashon Island, in the Puget Sound AVA just west of Seattle. A mainstay in Switzerland, Chasselas makes a dry, floral, fruity wine. Vashon Island winery has experimented with both barrel-fermented and stainless steel–fermented versions; the stainless is fresh, lively, and lightly peppery, a bit like grüner veltliner.

CHENIN BLANC

Few Washington producers make much of an effort with their chenin blanc. Most knowledgeable consumers have moved on to more fashionable grapes, relegating chenin to the tasting rooms, where they are offered off-dry from the most recent vintage at bargain prices. Nothing wrong with these wines, and a handful of producers—notably L'Ecole No 41—have proven that you can make an off-dry chenin that shows a bit more complexity than is typically assumed. Still, there is no question in my mind that if market economics permitted vintners the luxury of treating their chenin with the care given to their other white wines, these old vines could produce wines of superb character. Washington could and should make world-class, bone-dry chenins, wines that show the complex, floral aromas and flavors of the dry chenins from the Loire. But as things stand, other than the occasional brilliant chenin-based late-harvest or ice wine, most Washington chenins are destined to be fruity, off-dry, and rather forgettable.

Best Bottles Dry or Off-dry Chenin Blanc

Cedergreen Cellars

Covey Run

L'Ecole No 41 Walla Voila

Tagaris

Best Bottles Late-Harvest or Ice Wine Chenin Blanc

Kiona

Syncline

GEWÜRZTRAMINER

As author Leon Adams recounts in his *Wines of America,* it was a taste of a homemade Washington gewürztraminer in the mid-1960s that inspired visiting Beaulieu Vineyards winemaker André Tchelistcheff to proclaim it "the best in America." That bottle, and Tchelistcheff's timely comment, may well have sparked the modern-day Washington wine industry, which sprang to life shortly thereafter. The first commercially produced, vintage-dated varietal Washington wines (from Associated Vintners) included gewürztraminer. Tasted some years ago (at 35 years of age), the oldest, from 1967, was still showing (delicate) signs of life.

Gewürztraminer plantings are on the rise, and acreage has tripled in the past decade. These wines do surprisingly well with consumers, who happily stumble over the name and find many excellent and generally inexpensive versions made in a range of styles from dry to late harvest (or occasionally ice wine). Most typically, they will have a bit of residual sugar, nicely balanced against refreshing acids, and sport citrus flavors of grapefruit and lime. Occasionally the more distinctive, pungently floral Alsatian aromatics can be found, with whiffs of blossom and fresh-cut fruit, hints of spice and honey—you get the picture.

Some have shown the ability to improve with a few years of bottle age, taking on flavors of fruit candy and softening the racy acids just a bit. But in general, you're safest seeking out gewürztraminers from the most recent vintage. Cooler regions—Columbia Gorge, Lake Chelan, and parts of the Yakima Valley—do especially well with the grape. The best gewürztraminer vineyard in Washington is Celilo, and several vintners make wines from those grapes. Very good late-harvest gewürztraminer is also made by Kiona, from estate fruit.

Best Bottles Dry or Off-dry Gewürztraminer

Bonair	Covey Run
Canoe Ridge Snipes Vineyard	Dowsett Family
Celilo Vineyard (all producers)	Hogue
Chateau Ste. Michelle	Pacific Rim
Columbia Crest Two Vines	Upland Estates
Columbia	

Best Bottles Sweet Gewürztraminer

Bonair Port

Kiona

GRÜNER VELTLINER

Just now coming to the Pacific Northwest, grüner veltliner should find a good home in places such as the Columbia Gorge. From grapes planted there at Underwood Mountain, Syncline and Viento have made wines that brim with potential. Searingly tart, with sharp lime, barely ripe pineapple, and green-apple flavors, and a hint of white pepper in the nose, Syncline's bottling is an encouraging start, displaying some youthful varietal character at moderate alcohols.

MADELEINE ANGEVINE

This northern French grape is one of the more successful to be grown in western Washington (Puget Sound AVA) vineyards. When done well, it mixes dry, crisp citrus fruit flavors with herbal, spicy overtones—quite nice when served chilled with picnic foods.

Lopez Island Vineyards
Mount Baker Vineyards
Whidbey Island Vineyards

MARSANNE

The most important white wine grape of the northern Rhône, marsanne has recently begun to be planted in Washington. All cuttings are from Tablas Creek material, so it may not be propagated. It's often blended with roussanne or viognier, or both, though a handful of varietal versions are made (notably McCrea and Alexandria Nicole), usually for mailing list customers, and show ripe, round flavors of white peaches and lightly spiced pears.

MÜLLER-THURGAU

Müller-Thurgau is another grape whose adaptability to cool-climate conditions makes it a natural for western Washington. It's best characterized by its aroma, which is both floral and musky. The flavors can be very fruity and refreshing when the wine is cleanly made. Bainbridge Island Vineyards makes both a dry and an off-dry ("traditional") version.

Best Bottles Varietally Labeled Müller Thurgau

Bainbridge Island Vineyards
Mount Baker Vineyards
Whidbey Island Winery

MUSCAT

Washington muscats labeled black, orange, or Canelli turn up at a surprising number of tasting rooms. The grape was often planted in the early days, at scattered locations around the state. The oldest vines still bearing are at Upland Estates on Snipes Mountain and date back to the end of World War I. (Morio muscat, which you may also encounter, is a different critter entirely, according to Oz Clarke's *Encyclopedia of Grapes*.) Distinctly marked by a penetrating aroma of oranges, Washington muscats can be made in a range of styles from dry to ultrasweet, but most convey a definite hint of sweetness. Both Ste. Michelle (Moscato Frizzante) and Latah Creek (Moscato d'Latah) produce light sparkling muscats reminiscent of the Moscato d'Asti of northern Italy.

Best Bottles Off-dry Muscat

Chateau Ste. Michelle

Covey Run

Latah Creek

Best Bottles Late-Harvest Muscat

Kiona

Thurston Wolfe Sweet Rebecca

Upland Estates

PINOT GRIS AND PINOT GRIGIO

Despite its growing popularity, pinot gris is not easily turned into fine wine. If planted in a place too warm, its naturally low acidity becomes a liability, making fat, clumsy wines. If planted in a place too cool, it can be tart and tasteless. It's a varietal, one grower thoughtfully notes, "that dances or sags based on acidity."

Oregon's David Lett was the first to make pinot gris commercially in the United States, from cuttings that he hand-carried from Alsace in the late 1960s. Oregon vintners grabbed onto the grape in earnest in the 1990s, making rich, often buttery, oaky wines that seemed at times to have a yearning to be chardonnay. Then, dramatically, consumer tastes jumped on the Italian pinot grigio bandwagon, and that brisk, light, food-friendly, high-acid style became the new template.

Washington only recently began to grow pinot gris in any significant quantities, but in just the past few years it has jumped up to third place among all white grapes in total production, and both quantity and quality are on the rise. Though not as concentrated or fleshy as many Oregon bottlings, Washington's pinot gris and grigios (no difference—the name is just a marketing choice) are lively, fruit-forward wines, showing a zesty mix of tart green apple and Japanese pear flavors.

Best Bottles Varietally Labeled Pinot Gris or Pinot Grigio

Alexandria Nicole	Maryhill
Andrew Will (Cuvée Lucia)	Mercer Estates
Benson Vineyards	RiverAerie
Boomtown	Seven Hills
Chateau Ste. Michelle	Stella Fino
Chatter Creek	Tsillan Cellars
Columbia Crest	Vin du Lac LEHM Estate
Hogue	Willow Crest
Hyatt Vineyards	

ROUSSANNE

Roussanne, an aromatic white wine grape from the Rhône Valley of France, is one of a number of Rhône-inspired varietals being explored here in Washington. Wine writer Oz Clarke pegs roussanne as "a tricky, finicky, inconsistent beast of a vine," but for all that, he likes it, at least when it is not ripened past 14 percent alcohol. Although the classic comparables are from France—notably Beaucastel, Clos des Papes, Domaine de la Janasse, and Chave—roussanne is still too new and too rare in Washington to have fully defined itself.

What exactly should Washington roussanne taste like? "Intense . . . elusive and intriguing," says Clarke in his *Encyclopedia of Grapes*, "reminiscent of pears or aromatic herbal tea." But he's speaking of French wines, and New World wine flavors are almost always bigger, rounder, and more fruity than the European classics. Winemaker Doug McCrea says that "typical descriptors would include apricot, honeyed white peach, blanched almond, crisp apple and a distinct minerality."

I would agree. Full-bodied and fleshy, roussanne in Washington can taste like a real fruit salad mix, everything from apples, citrus, and lime to peaches, honey, and cream. Roussanne often complements marsanne or viognier in many Rhône-influenced white blends, and even when it is bottled as a varietal, there will usually be a bit of viognier mixed in. There is not much planted: five acres at Ciel du Cheval, four at Alder Ridge, a few more at Stillwater Creek, Destiny Ridge, Wallula, and Boushey; and recently, a little showing up in Walla Walla.

Roussanne has a reputation for being flabby and can be prone to early oxidation. But Doug McCrea believes that Washington roussanne, when grown properly and picked with sufficient acid levels, has very good potential for bottle aging. The producers listed below have a firm grip on it and do an excellent job.

Best Bottles Varietally Labeled Roussanne

Andrew Rich

Brian Carter Oriana (roussanne/
    viognier/riesling)

Darby Le Deuce (roussanne/viognier)

Doyenne

Forgeron

Isenhower Snapdragon

Maison Bleue

McCrea Cellars

Novelty Hill

SuLei Cellars

Syncline

Tranche

SIEGERREBE

A cross between gewürztraminer and Madeleine Angevine, siegerrebe grabs the grape-fruity spice of the former and some of the lemony acid of the latter. It ripens well in the Puget Sound (western Washington) AVA, and you'll find some excellent, crisp, fresh versions being sold in the island and North Sound winery tasting rooms.

Best Bottles Varietally Labeled Siegerrebe

    Bainbridge Island Vineyards

    Lopez Island Vineyards

    Whidbey Island Vineyards

VIOGNIER

Washington's viognier acreage seems to have hit a plateau, though on average it remains the most expensive white grape in the state. First planted at Mike Sauer's Red Willow vineyard back in 1983, it really didn't take off here until the Rhône Ranger movement took hold in Washington in the early 2000s. The wine clearly has cachet, both with winemakers who love the challenge and with consumers who thirst for something new. And yet there are plenty of skeptics still. One important grower flatly told me, "Viognier? That was supposed to be a big hit, and a lot of people planted it. But it just didn't move in the marketplace."

As is usually the case when new varietals are being tried, viognier has not settled comfortably into a typical style. That may account for some consumer resistance—they don't know what to expect. It presents unusual challenges for winemakers also; it ripens quickly and must be picked in a very tight window of optimal ripeness. Pick too soon, and it's tart and bitter; too late, and it's fat, oily, and alcoholic. Pick it exactly right, ferment and age it in stainless steel, and your viognier will strike a neat flavor chord composed of citrus blossom, zest of lime and grapefruit, vivid peach and apricot stone fruit, and a tangy, sometimes creamy, textured elegance. When it works, viognier really works.

Best Bottles Varietally Labeled Viognier

àMaurice	Kestrel
Abeja	Mark Ryan
Alexandria Nicole	McCrea
AlmaTerra	McKinley Springs
Bergevin Lane	Nefarious Cellars
Bunnell Family	Novelty Hill Stillwater Creek
Caterina	Rulo
Cayuse	Seven Hills
Chatter Creek	Stephenson Cellars
Coeur d'Alene Cellars	Stevens
Dusted Valley	Syncline
JM Cellars	Walter Dacon
K Vintners	

BARBERA

Barbera has begun appearing in very small quantities as a surprising number of vineyards and wineries begin to explore the potential of Italian varietals in Washington State (and Oregon as well). Small plantings are being tried at Cascade Cliffs, Ciel du Cheval, Morrison Lane, Sagemoor, Wallula, and Woodward Canyon, with a bit more at Alder Ridge and in the Columbia Gorge. Varietal bottlings come up occasionally, and a few move beyond fresh and fruity, with a strawberry tang. It's still too soon to judge the long-term viability of barbera in Washington, but it's off to a better (more expressive of varietal character) start than nebbiolo, though not as surefire as sangiovese.

Best Bottles Varietally Labeled Barbera

Barnard Griffin Gunkel Vineyards

Cascade Cliffs

CAVU Cellars

Hard Row To Hoe

Morrison Lane

RiverAerie

Ryan Patrick

Stella Fino

Viento

Woodward Canyon

BORDEAUX RED BLENDS

Here I've listed some of the best Bordeaux blends not dominated by a single grape. Please note that blends can change drastically from vintage to vintage; these are wines that are excellent no matter what the blend turns out to be. Also, though I'm calling them Bordeaux blends, it's not uncommon for a little syrah to be added, to punch up the fruit and give a young wine more accessibility.

Best Bottles Bordeaux Blends

Andrew Will (esp. Sorella and Ciel du Cheval)

Betz Family Clos du Betz

Buty Merlot/Cabernet Franc

Cadence Bel Canto

Cayuse Camespelo

Col Solare

Columbia Crest Walter Clore

DeLille Chaleur Estate

Fidélitas Meritage

J. Bookwalter Chapter One

L'Ecole No 41 Perigee

Leonetti Cellar Reserve

Mark Ryan Dead Horse and Long Haul

Nicholas Cole (Camille, Michele, and Reserve)

:Nota Bene

O•S Winery Ulysses

Soos Creek Artist Series

Spring Valley Frederick and Uriah

Three Rivers Meritage

Woodward Canyon Estate

CARMENÈRE

Leonetti's Chris Figgins believes that he and his father secured the first carmenère plants to arrive in Washington. They were acquired in 1997 from Guenoc winery in California, in the form of bud wood from a newly planted vineyard that was, apparently, the first in California.

Those vines went in at Leonetti's Mill Creek Upland vineyard, mixed in with some petit verdot. Figgins remembers referring to the whole adventure, tongue in cheek, as "Operation ABV, short for 'Ancient Bordeaux Varietal'!" The following year a larger amount of wood was purchased and planted to five acres at Seven Hills East. Some of those cuttings were shared with Mark Colvin and planted separately at Seven Hills and Morrison Lane. Colvin (now out of business) was the first Washington winery to make varietal carmenère.

Small amounts are being grown at scattered sites elsewhere, including Alder Ridge, Minnick Hills, and Phinny Hill. It is generally introduced into Bordeaux blends as a grace note. The rare varietal carmenères have been a mixed bag. I've had a handful that seemed to hint at long-term potential in a lead role, but apart from these excellent bottles, Washington carmenère may remain a curiosity and a minor blending grape.

Best Bottles Varietally Labeled Carmenère

Beresan	Seven Hills
Morrison Lane	Smasne Cellars
Otis Kenyon	Tertulia Cellars
Reininger	

CINSAULT

Morrison Lane grows a small amount, as do Minnick Hills and Alder Ridge; it's generally used sparingly in Rhône blends. Morrison Lane and Syncline do cinsault as a varietal; Syncline's is pretty, pale purple-rose, bright, peppery, and rather delicate. It shows excellent floral aspects, like a good Beaujolais—it's somewhere between pinot noir and gamay; big fat grapes and heavy clusters that somehow produce a real finesse wine. The acids keep it lively, the peppery notes add a lot of spice, and the floral qualities turn the tart cranberry fruit into something special.

COUNOISE

A very few wineries are making varietal counoise, from grapes grown at Ciel du Cheval on Red Mountain and at Morrison Lane in the Walla Walla Valley. Ciel owner Jim Holmes, who planted counoise at the request of Doug McCrea, recalls that he "took a wild shot with counoise, never having tasted it. But I read the Beaucastel webpage, and they used it, they said, for its special qualities. It has a strange color—it doesn't match up with anything. But it's part of the evolution ongoing in the state. If we're going to make top wine, we have to be top blenders."

McCrea has made varietal counoise (blended with 10–12 percent syrah) since 2002. Morrison Lane also grows a small amount and does a fine job with its (very) limited bottling. A tiny bit is planted at Alder Ridge also; vineyard manager John Farmer (now deceased) was one of the first to plant Rhône varietals in the Horse Heaven Hills.

Who knows what its future might be, but the existing examples are unique and fascinating. It makes quite a fragrant wine, scented and then flavored with blue plum, tart pie cherry, and blackberry. It shows the bracing acidity of sangiovese, with added notes of spice, cinnamon, and light chocolate and exotic suggestions of soy, cumin, and curry.

DOLCETTO

Though most fly well under the critics' radar, several grower-producers are experimenting with Italian varietals (other than sangiovese, which is fairly common) in Washington. Very tart, leafy, pie-cherry flavors seem to characterize the few-and-far-between releases of Dolcetto. Best versions so far are at Cascade Cliffs, Morrison Lane, and Woodward Canyon.

GAMAY NOIR

What little gamay noir is still grown in Washington winds up in blush wines with sweet, simple strawberry, raspberry, and cherry candy flavors.

GRENACHE

Grenache was one of the first successful vinifera grapes to be planted in the eastern Washington desert. Wine historian Leon Adams reported in his seminal *Wines of America* that on a trip to the Yakima Valley in 1966 "the only fine wine I tasted . . . was a Grenache Rosé made by a home winemaker in Seattle."

Yet despite its head start, grenache for decades stayed a bit player in the region's viticulture, for it is not especially winter-hardy. Doug McCrea made a superb varietal bottling from 1989 until the mid-1990s, sourced from vines planted above the Columbia Gorge in 1965. That vineyard was wiped out in the 1996 freeze. McCrea also made a grenache-syrah blend called Tierra del Sol, a pioneering effort that presaged the Rhône Ranger movement in the state.

The freeze of 1996 seemed for a while to have marked the end of the road for grenache in Washington. But recently it has staged a remarkable comeback. Elerding vineyard was the first to replant grenache, in 1999, and since 2001, McCrea has gone back to making a spicy, brightly fruited varietal bottling. He also uses grenache in his southern Rhône blend called Sirocco. Some old grenache vines remain at Cold Creek and Columbia Crest, destined for wine club offerings. Additional new grenache plantings—from better clones than before—have gone in at Alder Ridge, Cayuse, Destiny Ridge, and Ciel du Cheval and are now bearing. The quality they see already is inspiring winemakers such as Bob Betz (Betz Family), Charles Smith (K Vintners), and Gordy Rawson (Chatter Creek) to work with the grape. Consumers who manage to find one of the rare bottles are quickly converted.

It's easy to see why. Sappy, grapey, bursting with fruit, and nicely spiced, grenache is more approachable and purely fruity than syrah. These young vines do not (so far at least) show the kind of concentrated power that you find in old-vine grenache from Spain, France, and Australia. Those vines have six or eight extra decades under their belts. With just a fraction of that much time, this grape could become a real showstopper in Washington.

Best Bottles Varietally Labeled Grenache

Andrew Rich	Dusted Valley
Betz Family Bésoleil	K Vintners The Boy
Bunnell Family	McCrea Cellars
Cayuse God Only Knows	Novelty Hill
Chatter Creek	Syncline

LEMBERGER

Austria's Blaufränkisch, which translates as "the blue grape from France," goes by a number of names elsewhere, the least user-friendly being *limberger*. Here in Washington it is known as lemberger. When Washington vineyards were first being planted in the 1960s and 1970s, the grape was heavily endorsed by Walter Clore, the scientist and researcher who pioneered much of Washington's viticulture at the time. As a result, lemberger gained considerable appeal throughout Washington. At one time it could easily be found in a wide variety of styles, from grapey, rustic table wines to elegant, claret-style reserves to zinfandel wannabes to lemberger "ports."

The classic Washington lemberger is a blood-red, lightly peppery picnic wine, bursting with the scents and flavors of ripe berries. When there was no Washington syrah or zinfandel to be had, it was the stand-in; good to guzzle by the glassful with thick cuts of greasy lamb or grilled sausage. These days, lemberger is, quite fränkly, passé, perhaps feeling just a bit, well, blau. It's down to a couple of hundred acres and relegated mostly to being an everyday tasting-room red or tossed into mutt wine blends. Jed Steele's Blue Franc, which he makes as a joint venture with Ste. Michelle, is a more serious attempt to elevate its profile. Kiona and Champoux vineyards have some excellent old vines, and the classiest bottles are sourced there.

Alexandria Nicole

Covey Run

Hogue

Kiona

Shooting Star Blue Franc

Thurston Wolfe

MALBEC

Outside Argentina, where it makes spicy, tart red wines that take well to aging in new oak, varietal malbec remains a minor figure on the world stage. However, a number of growers are betting that it will become a bona fide player in this state in the coming decades. Malbec is easy to grow, they point out, ripens conveniently in between merlot and cabernet sauvignon, and adds dark colors and flavors to Bordeaux blends.

Casey McClellan planted some of the first malbec in the Walla Walla Valley, at the Windrow vineyard in the late 1990s. His Seven Hills winery began producing 100 percent varietal malbec in the 2001 vintage, and these days it is becoming fairly common for Walla Walla wineries to produce a bit of it. In fact, more than four dozen Washington wineries are making varietal malbecs, with more new versions appearing each vintage, often as mailing list exclusives.

Even so, most of it ends up in Bordeaux blends. The best expressions of varietal Washington malbec capture the dark notes and peppery herbal qualities of the grape.

Best Bottles Varietally Labeled Malbec

àMaurice

Alexandria Nicole Cellars

Arbor Crest

Barnard Griffin

Beresan

Bunchgrass

Buty

Camaraderie

Canoe Ridge

Dusted Valley

Flying Trout

Milbrandt The Estates

Nefarious Cellars

:Nota Bene Cellars

Otis Kenyon

Patterson Cellars

Reininger

Saviah

Seven Hills

Stevens Timley

Substance

Tertulia Cellars

Three Rivers

Upland Estates

Walla Walla Vintners

Watermill

William Church

MOURVÈDRE

Mediterranean-influenced mourvèdre (from France and Spain, where it is known as monastrell) makes medium-bodied, lightly spicy wines with pretty, cherry-flavored fruit and occasionally a distinctive, gravelly minerality. Mourvèdre is found in the red and rosé wines of Bandol and blended into many Côtes du Rhône, Châteauneuf-du-Pape, and Côtes de Provence wines. In Washington the grape was first planted in 1983 at Mike Sauer's Red Willow vineyard. More recent plantings have gone in at Alder Ridge, Ciel du Cheval, Coyote Canyon, Destiny Ridge, Elephant Mountain, Northridge, and elsewhere. Most of the grapes go into Rhône-inspired blends such as Brian Carter's Byzance, Doyenne's Métier, and Bunnell Family's vif. David Minick at Willow Crest and Doug McCrea at McCrea Cellars both began producing varietal mourvèdre at about the same time in 2001–2; more wineries join them each vintage. McCrea's is a big, smoky, meaty, gamy, chewy mouthful, enhanced with the addition of syrah. Other excellent versions are Bunnell's Northridge Vineyard, Trio Vintners' Den Hoed Vineyard, and Mark Ryan's Crazy Mary.

NEBBIOLO

The principal grape of Barolo, Barbaresco, and Gattinara (all made in the Piedmont region of Italy), nebbiolo unquestionably belongs with the great red wines of the world. Yet it remains, far more stubbornly than any other significant red vinifera grape, almost impossible to ripen with genuine varietal character anywhere outside northern Italy.

A handful of Washington vintners are giving it a try, along with barbera and Dolcetto, its Italian stablemates. Nebbiolo has been planted at Red Willow since 1985 and was first made as a varietal bottling (by Cavatappi) in 1987. Cascade Cliffs is also growing a bit of nebbiolo, as are Klipsun and Morrison Lane. Chatter Creek's Clifton Vineyard bottling, with its graceful aromas of rose petal and tobacco leaf, is among the best Washington nebbiolos I've tasted to date. Unfortunately, the Clifton vines, which were just planted in 2002, have already been ripped out. Some new efforts to plant nebbiolo in Walla Walla, where sangiovese and barbera have already had some success, should be interesting to watch.

Best Bottles Varietally Labeled Nebbiolo

Cascade Cliffs	Morrison Lane
Chatter Creek	Wilridge

PETITE SIRAH

Petite sirah remains very much a California grape, one of the original "mixed blacks" as Ravenswood's Joel Peterson characterizes it, planted in field blends more than a century ago. It has no such history that I am aware of in Washington, nor do any of my older reference books mention the grape being grown here. But there is no reason it should not thrive in the eastern Washington climate, especially at warmer locations, and a handful of varietal bottlings, from Alexandria Nicole, Animale, Arbor Crest, Bunnell Family, Cascade Cliffs, Corvidae, Milbrandt, Palouse, Portteus, and Thurston Wolfe, have appeared in recent years. It's planted in a few widely scattered locations; among them are Northridge on the Wahluke Slope, Destiny Ridge in the Horse Heaven Hills, Portteus in the Rattlesnake Hills, Dusted Valley in Walla Walla, and Cascade Cliffs in the Columbia Gorge.

Best Bottles Varietally Labeled Petite Sirah

Alexandria Nicole Cellars Mr. Big

Arbor Crest

Bunnell Family

Corvidae

Thurston Wolfe

PETIT VERDOT

Longtime Columbia winemaker (recently deceased) David Lake once recalled that in the early 1970s the agricultural research division of Washington State University established small experimental vineyard blocks in a number of locations around the state. These consisted of three or four vines each of fifteen or twenty different varietals, but the project ran short of funding and was abandoned. However, one such block, at Mike Sauer's Red Willow vineyard, was kept up, and in 1985, at Lake's urging, Sauer planted small commercial-sized blocks of cabernet franc and petit verdot. Unfortunately, the petit verdot was UCD 1, a clone that failed to set a crop and had to be replanted (to cabernet franc) in 1991.

Different petit verdot cuttings from the University of California, Davis, were brought to Walla Walla by Gary and Rusty Figgins in 1990 and planted at Spring Valley Vineyard in 1991. Additional plants went in at Mill Creek Upland vineyard in 1997 and Destiny Ridge a few years later. Petit verdot is a significant part (as much as 13 percent) of Leonetti's Reserve, and the 3.5 acres planted at Ciel du Cheval find their way into many of the state's best Bordeaux blends. The grape usually works best in small amounts (3 percent or less), beefing up the color and the tannins and adding some pretty violet aromas to the top end. A handful of varietal petit verdots are made, but most seem more like a blend component than a completely satisfying wine. Here are the ones that best make the case for petit verdot as a stand-alone grape.

Best Bottles Varietally Labeled Petit Verdot

Andrew Rich

Gifford Hirlinger

Januik

O•S Winery

Olsen Estates

Saviah

Thurston Wolfe

Watermill

Zerba Cellars

PINOT NOIR

Of all the red grapes grown successfully on the West Coast, pinot noir is among the last to have grabbed a toehold in Washington. Ironically, it was also one of the first. Experimental vineyards scattered around the Yakima Valley in the 1960s and '70s often included a few rows of pinot noir. Salishan Vineyards, situated west of the Cascades in southern Washington, began making a pinot from its own grapes in 1976. Columbia (then Associated Vintners) also made pinots as far back as 1967, its first commercial vintage.

But despite occasional successes, the grape did not find a good home in Washington, a place where it could ripen reliably yet retain its natural elegance and feminine charm. That is changing as new viticultural regions are opening up in the state. Good early returns from new plantings in the Columbia Gorge and Lake Chelan AVAs are especially encouraging.

Lake Chelan winery started its vineyard in 1998 with pinot noir; Bob Broderick at Chelan Estate began making his estate-grown version in 2002. Benson, Wapato Point Cellars, and Tunnel Hill also produce interesting examples from Chelan vineyards.

The Celilo vineyard has pinot vines dating back to the early 1970s, and Syncline makes a delicate, high-acid wine from them. Pinot noir is also being planted in the Puget Sound AVA, and on the northern fringes of the state, in Washington's Okanogan. It is a principal component of Domaine Ste. Michelle's Blanc de Noirs and of the nonvintage sparkling rosé from Mountain Dome.

Best Bottles Varietally Labeled Pinot Noir

Benson Vineyards	Syncline
Chelan Estate	Wapato Point Cellars
Lake Chelan Winery	Tunnel Hill

SANGIOVESE

Tuscany's mainstay grape has struggled in California, where it was barely a blip on the radar until recently. Washington may be better suited to grow sangio that can express more typical varietal character; parts of eastern Washington could visually pass for the heart of Brunello country.

Sangiovese, it turns out, is well suited for making dry rosés; they come and go quickly in the late spring and are rarely sold outside the state. As a blend component, sangiovese may be mixed with just about anything, but most efforts seem to be someone's take on a super-Tuscan, with some combination of cabernet, merlot, and syrah in the blend. Nicholas Cole Juliet, Reininger Cima, and Long Shadows Saggi are excellent examples.

When it's not overloaded with new-barrel flavors, fully ripened Washington sangiovese shows clear varietal notes of spicy cranberry, red currant, tart cherry, anise, and fresh-cut tobacco leaf. If the oak becomes more prominent, the more subtle, lightly herbal side of the grape disappears.

There is no denying that sangiovese does take well to the warm, butterscotch flavors of new oak barrels, and its natural acids give a nice lift to the midpalate. Some especially rich versions are being made in the Walla Walla Valley. Leonetti Cellar, though best known for its Bordeaux reds, makes smaller amounts of an exceptional sangiovese and prices it somewhat below its other wines. Recently, the Figgins family decided to give its sangiovese an extra year of bottle age before releasing it—a testament to the increased depth and power of the wines.

Best Bottles Varietally Labeled Sangiovese

Andrew Will Cuvée Lucia	Mannina Cellars
Arbor Crest	Morrison Lane
Chandler Reach Parris Estate	Trio Vintners
Des Voigne Cellars San Remo	Tulpen Cellars
Helix by Reininger	Walla Walla Vintners
Leonetti Cellar	Walter Dacon

TEMPRANILLO

Tempranillo is slowly finding a place for itself in Washington. The first attempts at growing and vinifying the classic Rioja grape, inspired by the pioneering work of Abacela Vineyards in southern Oregon, are already yielding wines that bring more than a trace of varietal character.

In Walla Walla it's planted at Dunham's Double River Ranch vineyard, at Cayuse's Armada and En Chamberlin vineyards, and at Spofford Station, Seven Hills, and Les Collines. Tempranillo plantings have also gone in at Destiny Ridge, Alder Ridge, Tefft, and Gordon Brothers. Casey McClellan at Seven Hills winery released his first tempranillo in March 2004; I believe that was the first in the state—100 percent varietal, dark and gamy and exotic. I found it immediately fascinating, with a blend of scents mixing roasted meats, vanilla, licorice, clove, and black cherry.

New releases of varietal tempranillo from at least a dozen wineries have since appeared, highlighted by the biodynamic Impulsivo from Cayuse. Whatever its future, tempranillo can be added to the list of European red grapes that demonstrate a remarkable ability to retain some of their Old World varietal character and styling here in New World Washington.

Best Bottles Varietally Labeled Tempranillo

Alexandria Nicole Cellars	Gordon Brothers
Cayuse Impulsivo	Gramercy Cellars

Seven Hills   Trio Vintners

Tertulia Cellars   Zerba Cellars

ZINFANDEL

For years I wondered why Washington produced no zinfandel. It was a phantom grape, reportedly not possible to ripen adequately up in the Far North. Lemberger, though often promoted as Washington's zinfandel, is really not the same at all. Vintners had many reasons for the lack of Washington-grown zin, but all it really takes is a great bottle or two to change their minds. That great bottle has arrived, and been validated in the past dozen vintages, from an obscure Columbia Valley vineyard called The Pines (located, it must be noted, in Oregon).

Though several wineries had made the occasional zin from these grapes, it was Sineann's Peter Rosback who really put the vineyard and indeed zinfandel itself on the Northwest map. Sineann's Pines vineyard zins (both regular and Old Vine) are California-style blockbusters, ultraripe and bursting with flavors of ripe cherry, bourbon, espresso, and chocolate.

On the north side of the Columbia River, things are finally stirring. New zinfandel plantings have begun going in at scattered sites in the Yakima Valley, Horse Heaven Hills, Walla Walla Valley, and Wahluke Slope. Thurston Wolfe does a fine version with the memorable name of Howling Wolfe and also makes a rare varietal primitivo. Recently at Forgeron I was invited to taste a minivertical of six vintages, all drinking well and generously endowed with sweet, ripe red fruit. Trio, a tiny new Walla Walla winery, makes a throat-popping version that at times tops 16 percent alcohol.

Best Bottles Varietally Labeled Zinfandel

Barnard Griffin   Sineann

Forgeron   Thurston Wolfe

Hard Row To Hoe   Three Angels

Maryhill   Trio

Patit Creek

CONCLUSIONS

Quality aside, Washington wines suffer, at home and elsewhere, from a reputation that they are too expensive. This state's marketing mavens and wine writers dutifully trot out statistics proving that on the leading wine media Top 100 lists, Washington places a very high percentage of wines given how little wine is actually made. And wines invariably sell at lower average costs than those from other parts of the world. Makes no difference—the reputation for high prices lingers on.

Why is this? Well, it's easy enough to find examples of tiny start-ups making a couple of hundred cases of so-so wines that are ambitiously priced. They should not be taken as indicative of the overall price-to-quality available in this state. Judge Washington by the quality of its most widely available wines, and a different picture emerges. Yes, Washington needs more of these big wineries, the kind that can produce significant quantities of well-made and inexpensive wines. That takes economies of scale, a genuine commitment to quality, and a major marketing and sales machine to run such operations successfully. For decades Washington's image as a producer of value wines depended entirely on the wineries under the Ste. Michelle Wine Estates umbrella—a good start, but not enough to hit critical mass. That is rapidly changing; these days there are many more value producers making enough wine to have a national presence. Precept has more than a dozen brands priced in the value category, most notably their House wines—a partnership with Charles Smith. They also have value tiers in some of the wineries they have recently acquired, such as Waterbrook and Washington Hills, and Smith's own company is making waves with widely distributed, everyday wines such as his wildly successful Kungfu Girl riesling.

Randall Grahm's Pacific Rim winery expects to reach 300,000 cases in the next half decade, most of it riesling priced from $10 to $12. Hogue (now owned by Constellation) produces around 650,000 cases, and quality is once again on the rise. Ascentia's Columbia and Covey Run brands offer good value, and quite a few smaller wineries have launched brands (Balboa, RiverAerie, Substance, and others) that are priced in the mid-teens.

There is another reason for the "too pricey" reputation, and that ties back to the lack of a signature grape. Though vineyard prices are a small percentage of costs in California or much of Europe, Washington does not have tens of thousands of acres cranking out high-tonnage grapes of the sort that go into the supermarket wines from California, Australia, Spain, and France. So what is grown here is too precious for plonk, and is priced accordingly. Washington has no Central Valley vineyards kicking out 14 tons per acre. The critical mass is not there, and may never be, because the state has barely 35,000 acres of wine grapes.

Most of Washington's 650-plus wineries are tiny start-ups, trying to pay a lot of bills, and they believe they must make at least a small profit, whether or not the competition from overseas can undersell them. So consumers see a row of new and obscure Washington labels in the specialty shops, with price tags that all read $30 and up and quickly get the impression that this is awfully expensive for some winery they've never heard of. The problem is further compounded when a new winery concludes that the way to establish a quality reputation is to spend a lot of money on packaging and put a high price on the bottle. The last couple of years have provided a wake-up call—such tactics are simply not going to work as they once may have.

If you look closely, you will find that in many instances Washington offers better wines, at better prices, than any region in the New World. Let's leave Europe out of it; the Europeans have land that has been family owned for generations, generous tax subsidies from their governments, and other advantages. But comparing apples to apples—Washington to California to Australia to Argentina to Chile to South Africa—I would happily put the best under-$12 Washington rieslings, sauvignon blancs, pinot grigios, sémillons, cabernets, merlots, and syrahs up against any others. Washington will shine.

The Washington Wine Commission's research, based on grocery store wine sales, suggests that total sales of Washington wines priced under $12 account for 87 percent of all Washington wine sales, by total dollars, and as much as 92 percent of all case sales. Those ratios haven't changed significantly over the past six years.

Whether or not these statistics seem compelling, they do show that, relative to its total production, Washington certainly makes its share of affordable wines priced for everyday consumption. They come from a wide variety of grapes, and at least some wines are made in significant quantities and distributed widely. Will Washington ever "compete" with California box wines or the Australian Yellow Tail tsunami or the sea of cheap Languedoc wines? Doubtful. Washington doesn't have to. Quality, not quantity, is the focus here, and that is true at every price point.

4

THE TOP TWENTY VINEYARDS

If you are the type of person who delights in reading through every scrap of information on the back labels of wine bottles, you will no doubt have encountered the word *terroir* often enough to conclude that—at least in the minds of those who make and market wine—*terroir* (and its lesser-known variant, *terrior*) is as common as dirt. In some sense it is dirt, tasted in the flavors that a wine picks up from the soils in which the grapes are grown. But a full explanation of this unique French term encompasses much more than just that, which leads to wine writers going off on quasi-poetic tangents about the "murmuring of the earth" or "the Land-Man Conjunction." However terroir is defined, grape growers and winemakers all seem to agree that it's highly desirable, and therefore they are all pretty sure that they have it.

To simplify, I would suggest that we think of terroir as the expression—in a wine's scents, flavors, and textures—of the combined influences of soil, climate, weather, latitude, elevation, and orientation of a particular place. Taken all together, those site-specific factors create the unique stamp of that place. If you apply that definition in the most generous and generic way, it's pretty clear that terroir does in fact exist every-where. All land has terroir. Your garage has terroir.

But such a broad view renders the term meaningless. What winemakers are really seeking is a grape-growing site whose terroir imparts extraordinary flavors and longevity to the wines it generates. Bob Betz describes it as "a physical reality that leads to growing conditions and ultimately a sensory consequence for the wine." This A-level terroir is uncommon. Only the truly great vineyards, in the most exceptional grape-growing regions, measure up to such high standards. So you will get no argument from me that terroir is the foundation on which all of the world's great wines are built, whether they are Grand Cru Burgundies, first-growth Bordeaux, old-vine Priorats, single-vineyard Barolos, or Grosses Gewachs rieslings.

The search for its own unique terroir(s) is an essential and defining attribute of an emerging wine region. Few would disagree with the assertion that Washington State vintners have already found it in certain select sites. Granted, many are called and few are chosen. All too often I come across a claim such as the following, taken directly from a bottle of Washington wine: "Our belief, a constant for all great wines around the world, is that quality starts in the vineyard. Through attentive viticulture management and passionate winemaking our goal is to create wines that are true to our vineyards [*sic*] terrior [*sic*]."

I've lost count of the number of back labels, press releases, and technical tasting sheets from wineries claiming to have found their "terrior" here in Washington. You may be pretty confident that if they think they have terrior, it's probably tied up in back, barking at the crush crew, rather than lurking in the vineyard.

Apart from the inherent ability of the soil and site to potentially express meaningful terroir, the winemaking must be sensitive and extremely noninterventionist if the subtle scents and flavors—the nuances that reflect terroir—are to remain evident. With rare exceptions, wines that are ripened to "hedonistic" jamminess, marinated in 200 percent new oak barrels, and finished at 15.5 or 16 (or 17) percent alcohol cannot rationally be expected to display tender nuances of site and soil. The sniffs and streaks of mineral, metal, rock, underbrush, herb, leaf, grapeskin, and spice that combine to create layers of flavor in great wines do not survive the sensory overload from fruit ripened to 27 or 28 brix, flavored with roasted barrels, and finished at liquorous, throat-burning levels of alcohol.

One final and critical factor—the vines must have some age. Different grape varieties have different life spans, and there is no doubt that very young vines can generate sweetly appealing fruit. However, most growers will agree that a new vineyard goes through a rather awkward adolescence before slowly settling into maturity after a dozen years or so. Maturity means that the roots are established, the vines bear their fruit more predictably, and the canopy is less aggressively vigorous. In my experience as a wine taster, truly old vines (30-plus years) begin to develop more brambly notes, and the herbaceousness of certain grapes acquires a harmonious softness. Washington has remained phylloxera free and is now blessed with some of the oldest cabernet sauvignon, merlot, and riesling vines in the country. They are most likely to generate the highest-quality wines.

The vineyards profiled in this chapter have demonstrated over a significant period of time that they can ripen fruit that creates distinctive, characterful wines. Most of these vineyards are fought over. Their owners all tell the same story of having to choose from among dozens of winemakers eager for their fruit. More than a few of them hold annual barrel tastings and invite all the winemakers purchasing their fruit to come and compare their wines with others from the same land. That not only serves to benchmark quality but also helps to winnow the field of applicants for future contracts. From my point of view, when several of the state's best winemakers choose to make a vineyard-designate from the same site, it's a clear indication that something special is happening there.

Certainly, stylistic differences exist in any lineup of wines, no matter how similar the source. Yet for these top sites a consistent thread can be found throughout: unique, site-specific flavors that speak volumes about the quality of the vineyard. Most of these vineyards have stood the test of time; they have proven over decades that they are special. Sometimes it is apparent when you walk the rows, and other times it is not. But it always comes through where it counts most—in the bottle.

There is no one formula for designing and tending such vineyards, but certain defining characteristics do seem intrinsic to most of them. Though widely scattered across the state, they are almost always situated on poor soils, at higher elevations with good drainage, and they are farmed sustainably, which means they avoid the use of chemical pesticides, herbicides, and inorganic fertilizers.

In the past decade, experimentation in all aspects of viticulture has continued at a pace never before known in Washington. New vineyards these days are designed with a mix of clones, planted at higher densities, and given precise row orientations. Pruning, trellising, leaf pulling, cluster thinning, and irrigation practices are constantly being fine-tuned. In some vineyards double drip lines are installed, so that single vine rows can be irrigated segmentally, bypassing the more vigorous plants. Infrared aerial photographs can reveal variations in vigor and also contribute to the fine-tuning of a vineyard.

Though by no means the only Washington vineyards deserving of acclaim, those included here are very carefully attended throughout the year by vineyard managers and the individual winemakers who purchase their grapes by the row, not the ton. Although some critics have noted that too many of this state's wineries are in the western Washington population centers, far from the vineyards that supply them, the row-by-row attention that many boutique winemakers give to their purchased grapes can more than compensate. Working closely together, winemaker and vineyard manager decide exactly how each winery's rows will be tended. Overcropping, overripening, overextracting, overoaking, watering back, and using ameliorants (adding tannins and acids) is anathema to terroir. The proof, as always, is in the bottle.

Unlike most great wine regions, Washington is unusual in that many of its best wineries built their reputations with purchased grapes. The brilliant wines of Andrew Will, Leonetti Cellar, and Quilceda Creek inspired dozens of others to try their hand at winemaking, even when they had no vineyard of their own. The Walla Walla AVA, which was federally certified back in 1984, had so few vines that—with the exception of single-vineyard wines from Seven Hills—it was all but meaningless as an appellation until the mid-1990s. But as we enter the second decade of the twenty-first century, many of the leading Walla Walla wineries are focusing on estate-grown fruit.

With its 2007 vintage, Leonetti Cellar wines were, for the first time, entirely sourced from Walla Walla vineyards. This has been a goal for founders Gary and Nancy Figgins since they first planted an acre or so of vines back in the 1970s, but it is really the vision and vineyard expertise of their son Chris that has enabled Leonetti to make the leap to all–Walla Walla fruit. "I think if you look at all the great wine regions and estates," Chris Figgins explains, "they have that vineyard focus. That is one of the ways that you transcend generations. It becomes more about the land, the vineyard, the brand. We are the stewards of the land. Look at first-growth Bordeaux—the winemaker is the winemaker of the day. It's not a cult personality as it is here in the U.S."

Other Walla Walla wineries such as Cayuse, L'Ecole No 41, Pepper Bridge, Seven Hills, and Spring Valley are now growing enough grapes to bring substantial quantities of estate-grown Walla Walla wines to market. And in their vineyard-designated Walla Walla wines, evidence of, not one, but a variety of terroirs can be found.

The genesis of this meaningful exploration of terroir within broader AVAs began in the early 1990s when some forward-thinking winemakers started negotiating purchase contracts at favored vineyards that paid growers by the acre, not by the ton. This gave growers the incentive to take the extra steps, such as green harvesting, required to ripen superior grapes. The most savvy growers began assigning dedicated rows to individual wineries. A stroll today through most vineyards that sell to multiple wineries shows each row neatly labeled with the winery responsible for its care. The more quality-conscious winemakers spend many days throughout the year on the road, checking up on "their" vines and making decisions about pruning, irrigating, green harvesting, and all the many other steps that lead up to harvest.

Unlike California, Washington has not historically been awash in moneyed vigneron wannabes looking to join the elite winemaking country club. Zillah, Mattawa, and Benton City do not sing the same siren song as St. Helena or even Healdsburg. The great majority of Washington start-ups are tiny, shoestring ventures whose owners have found that the quickest way to get started is to rent a little hole-in-the-wall industrial space, buy some used tanks, and purchase enough grapes to make a few hundred cases of wine.

Given this state's geography and west-side population centers, many Washington vintners will continue to rely on purchased grapes indefinitely. In the past decade, wineries such as Betz Family, Boudreaux, Gorman, Gramercy, Januik, Mark Ryan, Rulo, and Stevens have proven that it is entirely possible to make great wine despite owning no vineyards and, in many cases, having to truck their grapes over desert and mountains just to reach the winery. This is not to say that schlepping tons of grapes over hundreds of miles is a joy or a benefit. But many wineries have made it work.

The next phase in this evolution, already well underway, is for the more successful boutiques to begin planting vineyards. As in Walla Walla, the desire to own vineyards, not just tend rented rows, is influencing some of the leading west-side wineries. Andrew Will, Cadence, DeLille Cellars, JM Cellars, Novelty Hill, and Quilceda Creek now own vineyard land in eastern Washington. Robert Karl in Spokane and Syncline in the

Columbia Gorge—opposite corners of eastern Washington—are both invested in vineyards. Wineries large and small are seeing the benefits of growing their own, whether adjacent to the winery or many miles away. Though these wines are not always technically estate-grown, this merging of vineyard owner and winery owner is gathering strength, and that can only enhance the ongoing search for Washington terroir.

Elsewhere in the world, it is accepted wisdom that estate-grown wines are going to be better than wines from purchased grapes. Owning the vineyard makes possible the meticulous care and the accumulation over decades of small bits of vineyard knowledge that ultimately allows the best possible wines to be made. Europeans, in particular, might look suspiciously on the many tiny garagiste wineries that have sprung up in Washington and own no land of their own.

In this revised and expanded chapter, I have doubled the number of listings and divided vineyards into suggested Grand Cru and Premier Cru categories. That division is based on my evaluation of several defining criteria: the age of the vineyard, the owner's appetite for experimentation and collaboration with talented winemakers, the number of vineyard-designated wines (and wineries making them), and the perceived quality of those wines. It goes without saying that all of these vineyards are superior, but I want to give a further impression of the best of the best.

GRAND CRU VINEYARDS

BOUSHEY

Dick Boushey is right out of central casting. He looks the part of a Yakima Valley grape grower. Sturdy, plainspoken, and self-effacing, he conveys with a weathered gaze and measured words an impression of solidity, calm, and fortitude.

His vineyards encompass roughly 80 acres, clustered near his home, a few miles north of Grandview. The first grapes, merlot and cabernet sauvignon, went into the ground in 1980. Boushey admits to "not knowing a whole lot about what I was doing. I had grown them experimentally for three years," he explains, "because there was not a lot of merlot in the state at all. They seemed to ripen well on my site, so I jumped in."

Slowly and methodically he has regularly expanded his plantings, exploring the different soils and elevations (800–1,400 feet) on his land. Syrah, cabernet franc, grenache, and sangiovese have been introduced into the mix of red grapes; grenache blanc, marsanne, roussanne, and picpoul have been added to the existing whites, sauvignon blanc and sémillon. Whether intentionally or not, Boushey finds himself something of a leader among Washington growers with a Rhône grape focus. He seems increasingly confident and receptive to winemaker suggestions and experiments. His regular client base has grown from seventeen to twenty-five in just the past three years, and there is a waiting list. Winemakers who are willing to work with him and whose wines he feels do justice to his grapes make the cut.

Boushey still believes that "the ideal situation is you own both the vineyard and the winery and manage them together to create the wine that you want. But Washington," he quickly points out, "has a different dynamic. How do you make that all work? I make it work by staying in touch with the wines that are made from my grapes and the winemakers."

Many of the leading wineries in the state are in this core customer group: longtime buyers such as Betz Family, Chinook, DeLille, Doyenne, McCrea, Ste. Michelle, and Wineglass and interesting newcomers, notably àMaurice, Brian Carter Cellars, Bunnell Family, Efesté, Fall Line, Forgeron, Fidélitas, JM Cellars, Long Shadows, Ross Andrew, and Sparkman. "We want to grow the best grapes we can," Boushey explains. "I'll do anything people ask, within reason, if it makes good viticultural sense. I'm always game, because I'm trying new things all the time. We've adjusted crop loads, changed canopies, dropped fruit just before harvest, changed watering regimes. Some people have a good viticultural understanding; I want to bounce ideas off them. What I get back is their ideas about flavor profile and the kind of wine they want to make."

The spectacular rise in Washington's syrah acreage began not that long ago, and Boushey was one of the first growers to jump in. He put in the first vines at the request of winemaker Doug McCrea, and has since experimented with new clones as demand for syrah has grown. Not only has he has proven that the grape can do extremely well in his higher-elevation Yakima Valley sites, but the best versions of Boushey vineyard syrah—Betz and McCrea in particular—have a compelling underlayer of game, toasted almond, herb and earth that is unique and distinctive.

To fully appreciate the quality of Boushey fruit, taste McCrea's Boushey vineyard Grande Côte syrah or Betz Family's La Serenne syrah. Bob Betz calls La Serenne his "wild child in the cellar." His tasting notes describe Boushey syrahs as "the most Rhône-like, meaty and smoky and with a hint of wild spice." These grapes are picked up to a month later than the Red Mountain grapes that go into Betz's other syrah. "What I see," continues Betz, "is a clear distinction from California. If the continuum is Australian shiraz at one end and Côte Rôtie at the other end, I think Washington syrah is closer to northern Rhône, while California is closer to Australia. We have a density, a smoke/meat/roasted earth character to syrah that I don't typically get out of California." And Boushey vineyard syrah, as much as any in the state, expresses that distinctive character.

In 2008, Dick Boushey began consulting and managing other vineyard projects, applying his hard-won knowledge to sites on rapidly expanding Red Mountain. Among these new clients are Chris Upchurch (winemaker for DeLille and Doyenne), who is starting a new project of his own; the owners of Efesté winery, who recently bought two unplanted parcels on Red Mountain; and the newly planted Col Solare vineyard. Some of these same clients, Boushey confides, have purchased property next to his own Grandview vineyards, and they will be planting grapes there in partnership with him. All of which bodes extremely well for the rising reputation of Yakima Valley grapes.

It's all working for Boushey right now. Even global climate change is helping him more than most. At a time when some Washington sites are having to fight heat spikes and a tendency for sugar levels to outrun phenolic development, Boushey works to delay harvest. He times his pruning, suckering, and thinning according to the conditions of the vintage. The goal is uniformity, controlling growth, and keeping smaller berries and clusters. Stressing vines, he believes, interrupts the whole ripening pattern. So he aims for a constant moderate. "By the time you see the stress," he says, "it's sometimes too late."

"In the Yakima Valley," Boushey advises, "you want to push harvest into late September and October, when you have the cool nights and the acids stay there. I pick three weeks later than the warm areas, but not at any higher sugar level. There's a big transformation in the flavor profile in that time window, and that's where I want to be. That way you get softer tannins, darker fruit, but still retain some acid for balance."

Historically, many Yakima Valley vineyards struggled to ripen red grapes adequately. Boushey's fruit, particularly his syrah and merlot, shows what properly sited, fully ripened Yakima Valley fruit can achieve. Wines from his grapes show a tangy Bing cherry–tart berry character, sweet and spicy but not jammy, with elegant hints of light herb. Because he brings in his fruit at still-moderate sugar levels (under 26 brix), winemakers often blend their lots of Boushey wine with others from warmer, Red Mountain vineyards.

His most recent vineyard expansion (25 additional acres) was the largest Boushey has undertaken to date, a measure of the confidence he feels as he celebrates his thirtieth vintage. That may be it for a while, though he's thinking about planting a small block of malbec. "I am very cautious about planting right now," he says. "I don't really want to plant much more, but focus on fine-tuning and upgrading to certain new clones that have proven to work better at my sites. Many of my blocks are achieving nice midlife maturity, and I want to maximize their potential over the next ten years."

Still, the experiments continue: changing the row orientation, high-density planting, different trellising, planting new Bordeaux and syrah clones. "I'm responding to what my customers want," he explains. "If they want to grow, I'll grow with them. I'm hands-on, and I like working with smaller wineries. I like to have them feel that they actually own that vineyard."

CAYUSE

There is no single Cayuse vineyard, but because Christophe Baron has created a unique collection of terroir-driven, biodynamically farmed sites, all clustered within a short distance from his winery, I include them all under this general designation. Baron likes to call himself a vigneron, which is French for "winegrower"; but as with terroir, the basic translation does not quite do justice to the full meaning of the word. The term *vigneron* is meant to express the idea that winemaking takes place in the vineyard. And 40-year-old

Christophe Baron, who was born into a family of Champenoise (Baron Albert) whose winemaking history can be traced as far back as the sixteenth century, has imported that age-old concept directly from the Old World to Walla Walla, Washington.

He landed in Walla Walla in 1996, following brief winemaking stints in Australia, New Zealand, and Romania. When he arrived, he knew already that he intended to make syrah. At the time, very little syrah was planted anywhere in Washington, but he set out to explore the fields and orchards surrounding the town, in search of the right place to plant his vines.

The Walla Walla AVA crosses the state line into Oregon, though only recently has the bulk of Walla Walla vineyard been located on the Oregon side. In 1996 Baron was riding with a friend on a quiet road in rural Oregon, a few miles west of Milton-Freewater, when they passed an abandoned orchard. It had recently been uprooted and newly plowed, and he saw what he was looking for. Round rocks, many the size of baseballs, littered the ground. He jumped out of the car and dug into the earth. More rocks. An ancient riverbed cut through this part of the valley. The locals thought he was out of his mind, but he knew he had found the right place for syrah. "It definitely looks like Châteauneuf-du-Pape, this ancient riverbed where I've planted my grapes," he explained in an interview shortly after. "It's a mix of silty loam with a little sand and cobblestone for the first 18 to 20 inches; from there it's pure stone for 200 feet straight down."

Those first 10 acres, painstakingly dug up and hand-planted in 1996, have become the Cailloux vineyard. The winery, established in 1997, was named Cayuse after the Native Americans who lived in the area. Some historians believe that the name Cayuse was actually derived from the French trappers and settlers who called the natives Les Cailloux, literally, "people of the stone." In 1997 and 1998, Baron planted an additional 14 acres in two similar locations nearby. The En Cerise ("cherry") vineyard is 10 acres planted mostly to cabernet sauvignon and syrah, with a bit of merlot and cabernet franc as well. The Coccinelle ("ladybug") vineyard added another four acres of syrah. En Chamberlin was next: 10 acres, planted in 2000 to equal parts tempranillo, cabernet, and syrah. Everything is 100 percent biodynamically farmed, and beginning with the 2004 vintage, En Chamberlin became the first in Washington to be certified by the Demeter organization, an international body that regulates and approves biodynamic farms. Baron's next project, dubbed Armada, is 17 densely planted, stony acres of grenache, syrah, mourvèdre, and tempranillo. Baron calls it his southern Rhône–Spanish experiment.

Three additional vineyards are currently in various stages of development. The first to be planted is the Horsepower vineyard, located on the actual winery property, adjacent to Armada. Two acres, one each of syrah and grenache, some own-rooted and some on rootstock, were planted in 2008. The density is extremely tight—3 feet by 3 feet—4,805 vines per acre.

Almost as dense is a second new vineyard, planted to syrah in the spring of 2009, with 3.5-by-3.5 spacing and 4,000 vines per acre. Still unnamed at the time of publication, this three-acre site is adjacent to the existing En Chamberlin vineyard. As with the other Cayuse vineyards, it is an ancient riverbed, studded heavily with large round cobblestones of granite and basalt. Prior to planting, Baron purchased a pair of draft horses, part of his ongoing commitment to establishing a fully operational biodynamic farm, including not just the vineyards but a completely self-sustained enterprise, generating its own compost and teas from its own farm animals (he's negotiating for goats and sheep at the moment). This newest vineyard is ploughed by horse, using a hand-held plough obtained from a friend in Burgundy.

The third new site, temporarily named Cayuse Canyon, occupies a heart-thumpingly steep site in the Blue Mountain foothills. Planting has not yet begun. Baron has moved away from planting vines on their own roots and now uses a mix of rootstocks, believing that the fertile river-bottom soil of the region does not offer the same protection as the sandy soils found elsewhere in the state. "Since 2000 my vineyards have been grafted onto phylloxera-resistant rootstock," he explains. "If any place in Washington is susceptible to phylloxera, it's Walla Walla. It's just a matter of time."

From the 53 Cayuse acres now in production come four vineyard-designated syrahs, a Bionic Frog syrah, the Impulsivo tempranillo, the God Only Knows grenache, the Widowmaker cabernet sauvignon, two other Bordeaux blends, and a rosé.

With a decade's worth of wines now in release, it is proven that each of the first five vineyards fills a specific niche—Cailloux, the most distinctive of all the single-vineyard syrahs; Coccinelle, the chosen site for the iconic Bionic Frog bottling; En Chamberlin, especially noteworthy for its Widowmaker cabernet sauvignon; En Cerise, for its unusually strong cherry-cassis fruit; and Armada, for its intense and expressive grenache. The philosophy that underlies them is consistent. "Basically the goal is to handcraft wine that reflects the unique expression of each vineyard," Baron explains, "the quality and also the characteristic. In other words, the terroir." A self-proclaimed "freak about terroir," Baron declares, "I'm in love with the earth, with the ground, and I'm trying to express that in my wine. I'm French, after all!"

In pursuit of that goal, Baron is experimenting constantly, at times willing to go to extraordinary lengths and take on extra expense. High-density planting, frequent green harvesting, and the use of native yeasts are part of his methodology. He drops half his crop on the ground long before harvest, stresses the vines further by denying them water, and will send his workers through the vineyards days before harvest to pluck individual green berries from the ripe bunches. Yields are as low as one ton per acre in some instances, though with higher-density plantings, that will rise.

In the winery, Baron is adamantly Old World, using no inoculation, no fining, and no filtration. In many wineries, he believes, purity, integrity, and personality are being lost. "I don't want to be part of globalization," he insists. "That is where biodynamic comes into the equation. It's an ancestral way of farming that creates a perfect environment for the vines."

Cayuse makes just 3,000 cases of wine annually, sold mostly through a (now closed) mailing list. The winery has been making 100 percent estate wines since 2000, the first winery in Walla Walla to commit to exclusively estate-grown fruit. "I don't want to compromise Cayuse's reputation by sourcing elsewhere," says Baron. "To do everything right, you've got to spend a lot of time in the vineyard."

Small wineries in Washington have learned the hard way that the state's frequent winter freezes can best be ensured against by purchasing grapes from vineyards in widely separated locations. But in order to capture his terroir, Baron decided to do what vignerons have done for centuries: to work his land, nearby, and make only the wines whose grapes he has grown. This is especially challenging in Walla Walla, given its recurring history of truly ugly winter freezes. A freeze in 2004 wiped out roughly 80 percent of that year's harvest, but Baron had been burying canes, a labor-intensive process ("it costs me about as much as a new car every year," is how he puts it) that paid off handsomely when he pulled in a full crop. Again in 2009, there was freeze damage, this time limited to his grenache; and again the buried canes saved at least some of the crop.

The Cayuse winery, built in 2005, is spare but functional. Baron calls it La Boîte ("the box"). "I refuse to call this building a winery," he says, with typical Gallic defiance. "To me it is a wine studio, a production studio. We're here to work, to create."

CELILO

Celilo vineyard, home to some of the oldest vinifera vines in the state, will soon celebrate its thirty-fifth harvest. Though long recognized as one of the most distinctive sites in Washington, it was no overnight success. In fact, more than 30 years passed from the time Celilo was first planted until the region it pioneered received its own appellation (Washington's seventh), the Columbia Gorge.

Celilo's 70 acres of vines occupy a southeast-facing slope on Underwood Mountain, an extinct volcano high above the Columbia River. It's well away from the Yakima Valley, Columbia Basin, and Walla Walla vineyards that have largely defined grape growing in Washington and is climatically different from the Horse Heaven Hills vineyards spread above the river farther east. Celilo was so remote when first developed that it even managed to fall outside the massive Columbia Valley AVA.

The late William McAndrew, a Seattle surgeon, purchased the upper part of the property (about 80 acres) in 1971, after doing extensive research on soil, temperature, rainfall, and elevation. "He was a dreamer and a doer," his widow, Margaret, later recalled. His dream, say all who knew him, was to grow world-class wine grapes.

The land was an apple and pear orchard; no wine grapes were grown on the mountain at that time. But there were some experimental vines just a few miles east, at Bingen, where Chuck Henderson had been having some success with gewürztraminer and pinot noir. Dr. McAndrew took notice and began planting his land in 1972. Into the original 20 acres went a scattershot mix of vines obtained from California: chardonnay, riesling, gewürztraminer, chenin blanc, pinot noir, cabernet sauvignon, gamay Beaujolais, Müller-Thurgau, and even a bit of malbec. As was generally true back then, no one had the slightest clue what, if anything, would survive.

In 1974, a second property was purchased, 55 additional acres just below the original site. It was planted in the early 1980s, beginning with cuttings from the original Wente chardonnay. Later, some Dijon 76 chardonnay clones were added, along with a little bit of merlot. Today roughly half of Celilo's vines are original plantings; the rest are later plantings of chardonnay and gewürztraminer, with smaller amounts of pinot gris, viognier, Müller-Thurgau, lemberger, pinot noir, and merlot. Most recently, a test block of grüner veltliner has gone in; the grape is having some early success in the region.

Celilo is unusual in almost every way. It has no winery, relying on others to make wines from its grapes. All of the vineyard is dry-farmed (unirrigated). It is "subalpine," situated on a climatic cusp. Wet, maritime weather blows in from the west, while warm, dry air flows down the gorge from the eastern Washington desert. Celilo's proximity to the Cascade Mountains ensures that rainfall is substantial, an average of 50 inches annually.

The view is a jaw-dropper. Spectacular vistas open in all directions as you look upriver toward the desert, across the river to the verdant Hood River Valley and the looming presence of Mount Hood itself, or west to the flanks of the Cascade Mountains.

Celilo's perch above the Columbia River is more than a photo op; it also helps to mitigate the severe freeze conditions that can affect vines in many Columbia Valley, Yakima Valley, and Walla Walla Valley sites. The elevation (800–1,200 feet) and slope prevent fog and cold air from sitting on the vines. No wind machines or smudge pots have ever been needed or used; no insecticides, either.

The soil, too, is unique: a fine, porous powder that comes loaded with buckshot-sized pebbles. These are about the size and shape of ball bearings and ensure that the vineyard percolates well. This layer of volcanic soil runs as far down as 45 feet, where it hits lava rock, trapping the snowmelt and holding water during the dry summers.

As elsewhere in Washington, the drop in temperature at night during the final weeks of ripening preserves grape acids, while the warm days and southeast-facing slope give the vines the maximum amount of time in the sun, allowing the sugars to ripen fully.

Finally, there is the persistent wind funneling through the gorge. It toughens the skins, helps to control mildew and rot, and concentrates the juices. Not too surprisingly, given its unique location, Celilo experiences more variation in vintage conditions than most sites in Washington.

"Every year is different," says vineyard manager Rick Ensminger. "We can't hardly remember what normal is." He goes on to explain, "Usually spring tells the story. If you get that good start, the rest of the year can be mediocre to good and you're OK. But if you get behind in spring, that can put you on the other side of the fence come harvest. The weather can change so quick."

Apart from the weather, a perennial wild card, it is critters that have made Ensminger's job, shall we say, interesting. "Our biggest enemies are mildew, gophers, and birds," he notes. When the lower vineyard was planted, he remembers, "I went hand to hand with the gophers. They kicked our butt." The gophers are gone, but new challenges come along from time to time. The phone call from his 92-year-old neighbor was one example. "Phone rings and it's the neighbor," Ensminger recalls. "He raises turkeys. I ask him what's up? He says he's got good news and bad news. The good news is, he's got the best crop of turkeys he's ever raised. The bad news, he tells me, is they're all down in my vineyard!" Ensminger rushed out to find dozens of turkeys going one-on-one with his vines, which, conveniently for the birds, had low-hanging bunches just about eyeball-high to a turkey. "I think they liked the merlot," he says ruefully.

Four decades after Dr. McAndrew first scouted the territory, new dreamers and doers are catching on to the potential of Underwood Mountain and the surrounding area. Tidy new vineyards are clustered all around Celilo. Like Celilo, they hope to catch the attention of the dozens of gifted winemakers, from both Washington and Oregon, who believe there is something special in this soil.

Winemaker Peter Rosback of Sineann calls Celilo gewürz "the best marriage of site and varietal in the state." Chardonnays from Woodward Canyon, Harlequin, and Ken Wright Cellars and especially the gewürztraminers of Sineann, Dowsett Family, and Viento consistently prove that these grapes have something extra. Syncline produces that most rare wine, an excellent Washington pinot noir, from the original vines at Celilo. All in all, some thirty wineries in Washington and Oregon are using these grapes, and many, if not most, of them are making vineyard-designates, a sure sign of quality.

CHAMPOUX

It's pronounced "shampoo." And if you ask any serious Washington winemaker where the state's greatest old-vine cabernet is located, Champoux is the first vineyard they will name.

Owner Paul Champoux grew up in the hop industry. So the basic elements of a vineyard—trellises, wires, anchors, vine training, perennial crops, and so on—were quite familiar to him when Ste. Michelle came calling in the late 1970s. They were looking for someone to plant a substantial new vineyard overlooking the Columbia River, 2,300 acres altogether. He took the job, overseeing the initial planting (now part of Columbia Crest) from 1979 to 1983, and stayed long enough to see the first few vintages made.

He admits that he didn't know a whole lot about grapes when he started but had "great mentors," among them Wade Wolfe (Thurston Wolfe), Clay Mackey (Chinook), and Washington viticultural pioneer Walter Clore. He was hooked. And when he concluded his work for Ste. Michelle in 1986, Champoux moved up the road a few miles to manage the vineyard that would one day become his own.

The first wine grapes in what is now the Champoux vineyard were planted in 1972. Seven acres of cabernet sauvignon went into a tiny corner of the 6,600-acre Mercer

Ranch, a vast agricultural enterprise producing corn, carrots, potatoes, and a wide assortment of other fruit and produce. Seven years later, more cabernet was added, along with riesling, chenin blanc, chardonnay, and lemberger. By the mid-1980s, 132 acres were devoted to wine grapes, and a winery was started, named Mercer Ranch Vineyards. The goal, owner Don Mercer grandly announced, was to grow grapes as good as Chateau Lafite.

The winery didn't last long. But under Paul Champoux's management, the vineyard continued to prosper. He began leasing the property shortly after the winery folded in 1989 and continued to expand it, planting nine more acres of cabernet in 1990. Finally, in 1996, he purchased the vineyard with a group of partners that included the owners of Woodward Canyon, Andrew Will, Quilceda Creek, and Powers.

There are now roughly 182 bearing acres: 102 of cabernet sauvignon, 30 of riesling, 5 of chardonnay, 7 of lemberger, 7 of muscat, 8 of cabernet franc, 2 of syrah, 10 of merlot, 5 of petit verdot, and 6 of malbec. Champoux is especially excited about his merlot, planted in 1998 and just now hitting its stride (it can be tasted in Sineann's limited-production Champoux designate.). Nonetheless it is cabernet sauvignon that is the star here, particularly the fruit from the original old vines, dubbed Block One.

Though it is part of the Horse Heaven Hills AVA, the Champoux vineyard does not sit prettily on the bluffs overlooking the Columbia River, as do most of the region's vineyards. In fact it's rather flat and well back from the river. Paul Champoux somewhat candidly admits that if he should ever want to plant additional acreage, "there's other ground around Alderdale that would be a lot better to expand with." But "the Block One soil is a little different," he continues. "It's much older soil there. Not a whole lot of difference nutritionally, but it flakes better than some of the rest. I'm not a soil scientist by any means, but the flavors that vineyard puts off are second to none."

There are many others who would happily argue that all of the land surrounding the vineyard is second to none, though the soils are not identical. Quilceda Creek has purchased the five-acre Palengat vineyard (previously the Matador Ranch), just across the road from Champoux, and is already making a vineyard-designate from the vines. Nearby Phinny Hill vineyard has become a favorite of top winemakers such as Buty's Caleb Foster who seek the best possible Horse Heaven Hills fruit. Robert Karl winery has sited its Gunselman Bench vineyard nearby, and many other wineries pull fruit from the immediate surroundings.

As with so many of Washington's remaining old vines, it was luck and happenstance that prompted the original site selection, nothing like the satellite imagery and hard soil science that motivates such decisions today. As Champoux tells the story, the original seven acres bordered the road, and the huge circle sprinklers that were used to irrigate the ranch crops didn't reach there. "Walt Clore needed to try planting some wine grapes, so here was seven acres that was available."

Champoux gets high praise from his partners and other winemakers who purchase his grapes, especially for his attention to vine nutrition. He says he hasn't used any synthetic fertilizers since 1989, believing that they can be detrimental to microbial activity ("and that's the life of your soil"). To maintain what he calls "live soil," he uses cover crops and compost as feed. Vines are kept balanced by maintaining the optimal pruning-fruit ratio; nutritional balance is achieved by spraying foliar nutrients directly on the leaves. "I'm trying to feed the photosynthesis process and start my sugar building earlier with nutritional balances," Champoux explains. "Magnesium is one of the key nutrients for sugar building at véraison. So I'm trying to get the uptake of magnesium to start earlier." The bottom line for quality, he insists, is having the whole plant be nutritionally healthy. "That's what develops the flavors. That is what has made my vineyard stand out." As if to underscore the point, he adds, "a balanced vine inside and out has helped me to bring these grapes to the next level as my partners and winemakers produce world-class wines."

A wine shop and tasting room (Chateau Champoux) at the vineyard sells a wide variety of wines made from Champoux grapes. Woodward Canyon, Andrew Will, and Quilceda Creek are there of course, but so are vineyard-designates from Buty, Fidélitas, Gamache, Januik, O•S, Three Rivers, Powers, Soos Creek, and Sineann. The old-vine cabernet projects a sturdy muscularity, but more than that, a certain breed that comes of age. Lafite? Maybe not. But Mouton? Quite possibly. Turns out that Don Mercer wasn't boasting after all.

CIEL DU CHEVAL

No roll of the vineyard dice has paid a bigger jackpot in Washington than the decision by partners Jim Holmes and John Williams to plant cabernet sauvignon (of all things!) on Red Mountain (of all places!) back in 1975. Quixotic does not begin to describe their quest. "We needed electricity," Holmes recalled years later, "because there was no power at all. It was like the frontier: no roads, no water, no power, no people—just sagebrush."

What was there was great soil: a surface layer of sandy loam to hold water, then a good mix of calcareous chunks and more sandy loam, then an old riverbed, whose cobbles follow the contour of the mountain slope—quite possibly ancient Columbia River tracks. So they platted roads, brought in power from three miles away, and drilled and drilled and drilled. Running quickly out of funds, they hit a big aquifer at 560 feet. The first 10 acres of vines, planted at what is now Kiona, were a mix of riesling, chardonnay, and cabernet sauvignon, this last chosen simply because it was what the partners liked to drink.

In the early years, grapes were sold to Preston, Quilceda Creek, and Oregon's Amity Vineyards; Kiona wines were introduced in the 1980 vintage. Over time, Kiona built a dedicated winery and expanded the plantings in its 80-acre parcel. Along the way, some friends interested in joining the grape-growing ranks asked Holmes for help planting their newly acquired 80 acres, dubbed Ciel du Cheval (the name is a French take on Horse Heaven, the name of the hills visible to the south). Holmes and Williams purchased it for Kiona in 1991. When the partners split amicably in 1994, the Williams family retained Kiona and its original vineyards, and Holmes took Ciel du Cheval.

Since then, he has turned it into what may well be the most prolific (in terms of variety) and distinctive site in the state. The vineyard now totals 120 acres. Thanks to its location farther east and a bit higher up the hill than either Kiona or Klipsun, Ciel has some of Red Mountain's most shallow soils, and it is somewhat better protected from the fierce winds that hammer the vineyards on the western slopes.

Holmes is a student of the vine and an eager collaborator with many of Washington's most gifted winemakers. Consequently Ciel du Cheval now boasts small blocks of roussanne, viognier, mourvèdre, counoise, grenache, nebbiolo, and Brunello-clone sangiovese, along with more substantial plantings of cabernet sauvignon, cabernet franc, merlot, petit verdot, and syrah.

"There's a prime reason I started planting these in about 1998," Holmes explains. "I have a belief that a little blending makes a better wine. Cab franc of course has always been there, and it is so good for Red Mountain that I put that down. Petit verdot was the next thing. It has a terrible reputation, even in California, but we found a clone that had just become available and planted that. Everybody said don't do that, but now they love it.

"In the same way I began thinking about Rhône varieties. I had mourvèdre; McCrea and Andrew Rich have done it. From my point of view I really liked the outcome. Chasing a little further, I was never really impressed with many of the other Rhône blenders, but I took a wild shot with counoise, never having tasted it. I read the Beaucastel webpage and they used it, they said, for its special qualities. It has a strange color—it doesn't match up with anything. But it's part of the evolution ongoing in the state. If we're going to make top wine, we have to be top blenders. The other element is blending across clones. We have four syrah clones, every one of them different. Again, it's for blending, and my belief is that the winemaker needs the opportunity to express his craft."

Immediately adjacent to the original vineyard are two additional 20-acre plots, joint ventures between Holmes, Quilceda Creek (Galitzine vineyard), and DeLille Cellars (Grand Ciel vineyard). Both wineries were already producing top-tier red wines using Ciel grapes; they wanted more than Holmes could provide, so he offered unplanted acreage instead. More than two dozen other wineries currently purchase fruit from Holmes, who makes no commercial wines of his own (a Ciel estate winery is under consideration). What is most interesting is that no matter who is making the wine, the flavors of the vineyard shine through.

To cite just two recent examples: The 2007 Andrew Will Ciel du Cheval Red is a cabernet franc–merlot blend that captures the sleek minerality of the site and puts the fruit into tight, laserlike focus. The berry flavors, highlighted with crisp acids, strike a pure note and ring true over a lingering finish. A new project, named Grand Rêve, is making a multiwine Collaboration Series from Ciel du Cheval grapes. Vineyard manager Ryan Johnson has contracted five different winemakers to work with select lots of the fruit; the first five releases have included two Bordeaux blends, a pair of syrahs, and a sangiovese.

Despite the different winemaking styles, the vineyard's expression of both power and refinement cuts across all grapes and vintages.

Why is it so good? Holmes points to the extremely high pH of the soils. It ties up nutrients as insoluble minerals, so the vines struggle. It comes back to the calcium carbonate, which controls the pH. The vines never get big canopies, and berry size is little more than half of standard berry size. Napa berries, Holmes says, weigh about 1.3 grams, while Ciel's average about point 88.

The unique site and soil is the starting point, but after 35 years on Red Mountain, Holmes is not about to stop experimenting with every other component of his viticulture. About 15 years ago, he began to get new data, never before available, that allowed him to calculate how much water a vine would need based on the weather reports. His irrigation management evolved rapidly overnight; now there are soil moisture gauges and pinpoint controls on irrigation, varietal by varietal and block by block. One result is softer, rounder tannins than in the past.

Other data have led to a slight reorientation of the vine rows. New plantings no longer go exactly north-south; they're shifted 10 degrees off-axis, so the vines get more sun in the morning, when it's cooler, and less in the afternoon, when it's hot. "It's more of a pioneering venture now than ever," Holmes modestly asserts. "The world's knowledge is expanding. We don't want Ciel to become stagnant; we want it to keep moving forward." In his mind, Red Mountain, despite its rather bleak, desert landscape, will be a tourist destination someday.

Always the realist, he adds, "There's no reason for anyone to visit Red Mountain unless we make great wine there. First, fix your mind on making great wine. If you do that, people will knock down your door to go there. If you don't, what's there? Why would anyone come? It's just a wild spot in the desert. Make great wine, and it transforms into something of worldwide notice. Focus on that. My dream is great wineries that make great wine there on the spot. When I buy wine, I want to know where it came from. A sense of place. To me that's everything."

KLIPSUN

If you visit the Klipsun vineyard on the right sort of day, when a gentle breeze is blowing and the perfume of the grapes in bloom scents the air, it is quite lovely. There's a pergola near the top where you can sit and look out in all directions. Straight west, the hill slopes steeply down toward the snaking line of green trees that hug the meandering Yakima River. Two ridges of mountains are in view: the Rattlesnake Hills to the north and the Horse Heaven Hills to the south. Behind you, to the east, is Red Mountain itself. Looking neither red nor particularly mountainous, it unfolds in large squares of well-manicured vineyards, an occasional stand of trees, and patches of dusty desert.

Patricia (Trish) and David Gelles began planting Klipsun in 1984, following the lead of their friends and neighbors Jim Holmes (Ciel du Cheval) and John Williams (Kiona), who had pioneered the Red Mountain area a decade earlier. Already Holmes and Williams had proven that excellent cabernet and merlot could be grown in this then-desolate place, and winemakers such as Alex Golitzin (Quilceda Creek) and Rick Small (Woodward Canyon) had been eagerly purchasing their grapes.

But in the mid-1980s, Red Mountain was still relatively unexplored and economically risky. Unlike most of the Yakima Valley vineyards that were going in at the time, this was virgin land. The soil had gone untouched since the great floods had recontoured all of eastern Washington 10,000 years earlier. "I think we are lucky nothing was grown here before," Trish Gelles states emphatically. "There were no mistakes to correct. It's always better to farm on virgin land. And sagebrush is a good indication that the soil is good for growing. It's just amazing that no one did it before we did."

Actually, the lack of farming was primarily a consequence of history, points out David Gelles. Red Mountain was not included when the Yakima Valley irrigation districts were established early in the twentieth century. Only in the past few years has the development of the Red Mountain Irrigation District moved forward, driven by the enormous rise in the value of Red Mountain land for viticultural purposes. There are hopes that water rights (rather than relying on wells, as has historically been the case) will be available by 2012.

Though Red Mountain is best known for its Bordeaux reds, the site and soil can ripen almost anything—almost. "We used to have chardonnay," says Trish Gelles, "until we found that Red Mountain is really too hot (chardonnay doesn't like extended high heat). But it's unusual to be able to grow whites and reds both as well as we do."

At first, says David Gelles, they planted their cabernet block as close to the Kiona block as they could, having heard that Andre Tchelistcheff (Alex Golitzin's uncle) had opined that Kiona was growing the best cab in Washington at the time. So to begin, Klipsun was two-thirds white and one-third red; now it is about 85 percent red and 15 percent white. Cabernet and merlot dominate, along with syrah and even a bit of nebbiolo. Sémillon and sauvignon blanc are the remaining whites. But the cab and merlot bring three times the price, and production costs are equivalent, so the remaining white grapes are more or less a gift, left there simply because they make excellent wines and because the Gelleses like to drink white wines from their own vineyard.

The red wines, from a who's who list of Washington's top boutiques, are what built the vineyard's reputation. Klipsun vineyard Bordeaux blends, whoever the winemaker may be, consistently show massively concentrated black fruits, hard tannins, a stiffness to the spine, and a steely minerality. "They're just huge wines," says Trish Gelles, "and long-lived wines, as far as you can tell. There's always a strong cherry and blackberry fruit component. They're just really big."

You'll get different theories as to the importance of Red Mountain soils. Some growers point proudly to the many variations and the mix of glacial rock and wind-blown volcanic dust; others say there is no particular difference from elsewhere. "Our soils were laid down because of a series of huge floods that occurred every 50 to 100 years during the ice age—over fifty in all," David Gelles explains. "I'm beginning to realize that we have the same soils up and down the Yakima Valley, the Walla Walla Valley, and the Willamette Valley. We're all basically dealing with Canadian topsoils."

Red Mountain does get more heat units than any other Washington AVA, with summer temperatures commonly peaking over 100 degrees, the tipping point at which vines shut down. But it makes up for the extreme heat with strong winds, which keep the grapes free of rot and eliminate most pests. And its elevation (grapes are planted between 600 and 1,100 feet, with the newest vineyards climbing even higher) means that once the sun goes down, things cool off considerably. The diurnal temperature swing, especially during harvest, is 40 degrees or more, so the grapes never lose their firm acids, though harvest is earlier here than in most parts of the state.

Klipsun's location, on the lower, most west-facing slopes of the mountain, exposes it to more wind than most of its neighbors, toughening the grape skins, concentrating the juice, and thickening the tannins. Klipsun grapes, especially cabernet and merlot, are in high demand; they have the reputation (the Gelleses neither confirm nor deny it) of being the most expensive in the state. Roughly thirty different wineries purchase Klipsun grapes, and many have their own designated rows. Many happily label the wines "Klipsun Vineyard," for they know that the name brings with it a lot of respect from consumers.

As the vineyard concludes its first quarter century, the Gelleses maintain that they are content with the mix and have no plans for expansion. A couple of acres of malbec were added in 2005; that's it for a while at least. "We may do more clonal stuff as the vineyard ages and we have to replant," Trish Gelles confirms, "but we're still a little way off."

PREMIER CRU VINEYARDS

ALDER RIDGE

Alder Ridge vineyard is owned by Winemakers LLC, now separate from Corus Estates & Vineyards, whose winemaking operations have been acquired by Precept Brands.

The vineyard is one of the state's largest—more than 800 acres—planted in the heart of the Horse Heaven Hills AVA, on a rolling plain set atop a steep bluff above the Columbia river. The first vines went into the ground in 1997, and currently there are twenty-eight varieties in all, including some of Washington's most sought-after Rhônes. Cabernet sauvignon is still the mainstay, but cinsault, counoise, grenache, mourvèdre, and roussanne are also planted.

In 2004 an Alder Ridge brand was introduced, and recently departed winemaker Rob Chowanietz was brought in to oversee the winemaking. He values the extra-long hang time, the moderating effect of the river on both summer heat spikes and winter freezes, and the steady breezes, which toughen the skins and give the cabernet its muscular tannins.

The country in which the vineyard is set is bone-dry desert, averaging roughly four inches of rainfall annually, and the soils are sandy and low vigor. Elevations vary from as low as 300 feet to as high as 1,000. Though basically south-facing, the different slopes and elevations offer a wide range of exposure options. Though considered a warm site, it is generally one of the last vineyards to be picked, due to the dramatic temperature drops at night during the fall. The extra hang time adds structure and density to the Bordeaux grapes, in particular.

Apart from the Corus brands—Alder Ridge, 6 Prong, and Zefina—Alder Ridge fruit is purchased by more than thirty Washington wineries, including some of the state's best boutiques, among them Andrew Rich, Barnard Griffin, Bergevin Lane, Betz Family, Forgeron, Hightower, Januik, L'Ecole No 41, Long Shadows, Owen Roe, Ross Andrew, Rulo, Syncline, and Willis Hall.

COLD CREEK

The first vineyard-designated wine made in Washington State was a Cold Creek cabernet sauvignon. The label reads: "1978 Ste. Michelle Chateau Reserve Cabernet Sauvignon Benton County Washington Cold Creek Vineyards." Along with its historical significance, what is noteworthy about the label is the inclusion of Benton County in the name. Benton County never was, and still isn't, a name associated with fine wine, or with wine in general for that matter. But back then, there was no Columbia Valley AVA or any AVA beyond Washington, which most people identified with the nation's capital. So the marketing mavens at Ste. Michelle decided to throw Benton County at the wall to see if it would stick.

The drive to Cold Creek doesn't look much different now than it did 30 years ago. Heading east from Yakima on Highway 24, you drive for about 35 miles, passing fields of hops, cattle pens, and sheep ranches. The Umptanum Ridge is to your left (north), the Yakima Ridge runs along on your right (south), and the Rattlesnake Hills are the next ridge over from there. There are few if any wine grapes along the drive. Suddenly, a broad expanse of well-tended vines appears on the left, draped across a gently sloping hillside: Cold Creek Vineyards.

Ste. Michelle Wine Estates owns the roughly 900-acre parcel, of which 756 are planted. A five-phase expansion, due to conclude in 2011, will push total planted acreage to about 850. A visitor to Cold Creek may or may not see the creek, which is ephemeral (meaning dry most of the time). Apart from the winter months, it's not likely to be all that cold, either; in fact it is one of the warmest sites in Washington.

Cold Creek, time has proven, is an ideal grape-growing site, with 35+-year-old vines planted in light, silty, well-draining soils. It benefits from some of the warmest and sunniest summer weather in the state, and it sits on a slope that makes it virtually impervious to frost. During the freeze year of 2004, many small (and not so small) Walla Walla wineries, having lost their usual grape sources to the cold, were able to compensate with fruit from Cold Creek, which ripened a full crop.

As in much of Washington, the soils here harbor no significant insect pests—one reason the original block of cabernet, which went into the ground in 1973, is still bearing.

These are some of the oldest cabernet vines in the country. The tough, rugged vines are own-rooted and fan-trained, and the grapes go into a wide variety of Ste. Michelle's best wines, along with up to half a dozen vineyard designates. Cold Creek fruit, especially its riesling, chardonnay, merlot, and cabernet, has been the lynchpin for the Artist Series reserves, the Col Solare reds, the Northstar merlot, the new Ethos series, and some vintages of the Eroica riesling. More recently, a few other carefully selected wineries have been given regular access to Cold Creek fruit, and some have already begun making vineyard designates.

Cold Creek riesling is bright, intensely fruity, and razor sharp; the chardonnays are sensuous, open, and buttery, yet retain the focus and acidity that characterizes the site. Merlots are thick and substantial, and the cabernets are dense, aromatic, tannic, and streaked with mineral and herb.

The vineyard receives on average just five inches of rain a year, but the soil holds moisture well enough that irrigation can be postponed until late June and is tightly controlled after that. The vines grow their canopy without irrigation; when shoot growth slows down, drip irrigation is begun. The idea is to control canopy and berry size by waiting until the shoots really need the water and then giving them just barely enough to survive.

Over the years, Cold Creek has been a training ground for learning the tricks of deficit irrigation. Along with the original (and newer) blocks of cabernet sauvignon and riesling, it is planted to chardonnay, sauvignon blanc, muscat Canelli, grenache, merlot, cabernet franc, and syrah. Most of the newest plantings are Bordeaux varieties dominated by diverse clones of cabernet sauvignon. In addition, a small portion is a mix of Rhône varietals, planted high up on the rocky slope above the original acreage.

Each of these varieties reacts differently to water. The riesling vines, on the advice of Ernst Loosen, who collaborates on the Eroica rieslings, have lately been given more water to grow bigger canopies. This extra shading, Loosen believes, helps to avoid the bitter phenolics that come from overexposure to sunlight, and may also give riesling the lengthy hang time it needs to develop finesse and aromatic structure. Following véraison, irrigation throughout the vineyard is gradually reduced until it is cut off at harvest. Once harvest is complete, the water is turned on until the top two feet of soil are moist. This helps to insulate the roots against winter cold.

Repeated vertical tastings of Cold Creek cabernets have demonstrated that wines from this vineyard can go the distance and evolve, not just survive, in the bottle. The site shows vintage variation more than many Washington vineyards. That, along with ongoing, dramatic changes in vineyard management as well as winemaking techniques, will continue to occur. Given its long (for Washington) history, unique flavor profile, and remote location, Cold Creek may well warrant certification as an AVA sometime in the future.

CONNER LEE

Conner Lee Vineyard is located on Radar Hill south of Othello, Washington—a cool site in a warm region. Planted in the early 1980s and acquired shortly thereafter by Bill Conner and Rhody Lee, it is managed by Tom Thorsen and Jerry Bookwalter (Thorsen-Bookwalter Associates) with on-site management by David Ayalla.

Not technically in the Wahluke Slope AVA—the vineyard is located just a bit to the northeast—Conner Lee shares some of the same sandy-silt soils and general characteristics, though it is considered to be a somewhat cooler site. Spring and fall nights can show day-night temperature variation of as much as 50 degrees. Fall temperatures keep the acids high and the pH low. Vines are ungrafted and the soils provide excellent drainage.

Conner Lee is especially well known for its chardonnay. The grapes mature slowly over a lengthy growing season, without troublesome spikes in sugar accumulation. Arbor Crest winemaker Kristina van Löben Sels, who has been making a Conner Lee chardonnay since the early 1990s, also points out the unusual spiciness of the wine. Both she and Buty's Caleb Foster admire the vineyard's cabernet, cab franc, and merlot, as well, applauding the weight and richness, black currant and cassis fruit, and overall density of the flavors. Other wineries that purchase grapes and on occasion produce vineyard-designates include Barrage Cellars (Nuclear Blonde chardonnay), Gorman (Big Sissy chardonnay), Guardian Cellars (Gun Metal red), JM Cellars, Mark Ryan, and Novelty Hill.

Finally, there is what can only be called the woo-woo factor that sets Conner Lee apart. "The vineyard, unlike any other I have been in," says Van Löben Sels, "has this amazing feel-good energy when you're walking the rows. The way the sunlight filters through the canopy is so uplifting. It has good karma—I notice it every time I am out sampling."

DUBRUL

At the eastern edge of the Rattlesnake Hills AVA, in the heart of the Yakima Valley, is DuBrul, a vineyard so perfectly sited and perfectly managed that it could be the role model for anyone dreaming the dream of growing their own grapes. Hugh Shiels and his wife, Kathy, purchased the 45-acre property in the early 1990s, more than a decade after moving to the Yakima Valley. They had begun their farming adventures at their home a few miles away, growing Concord grapes and some row crops, but their interest in wine soon inspired them to hire consultant Wade Wolfe to help them locate and design a vinifera vineyard. Originally an apple orchard, the land plateaus at about 1,300 feet—a basalt promontory jutting out over much lower pasture land. The south-facing, steeply sloped hillside, strewn with a variety of volcanic rock, basalt, and river rock, much of it covered with a thick layer of calcium carbonate, seemed ideal for growing wine grapes.

Wolfe agreed that the site was promising, and passed the consulting baton to Stan Clarke, who worked with the Shielses as they planted chardonnay, cabernet franc, cabernet sauvignon, merlot, and syrah over a five-year span from 1992 to 1997. Some older riesling vines, dating back to 1983, were left in place and still provide the grapes for rieslings from Owen Roe and Woodward Canyon. The first winery to offer a DuBrul vineyard-designate was Wineglass Cellars. Their 1998 DuBrul vineyard merlot, with its bright fruit and lush, ripe flavors of raspberry, cherry, and vanilla in equal measure, made a strong impression. Many award-winning wines have followed, made by more than a dozen wineries that have won the right to obtain DuBrul fruit, notably Owen Roe, Seven Hills, Tamarack, and Woodward Canyon.

With their science backgrounds (he is an orthopedic surgeon, she a physical therapist) the Shielses have been highly pro-active in doing extensive vineyard research, often in conjunction with the Washington State University Irrigated Agriculture Research and Extension Center in nearby Prosser. Bug studies, quality studies, grow tube studies, aerial infrared photographic studies, geological research, and more have all contributed to their understanding of the land they own and the ways in which they can best manage the vines.

Although it is nowhere near the present-day Columbia River, the ancient course of the Columbia flowed right over Shiels land, as did the ice age floods from Lake Missoula. Volcanic eruptions and wind-blown loess have also contributed to the mix of rock and soil types at DuBrul. Another asset is the excellent air drainage. Says Hugh Shiels: "If you imagine God pouring a giant pitcher of water on top of our site, you can see the water flowing away down to the valley floor. Cold air flows just like water." During the recent freeze of 2004, DuBrul was virtually untouched.

The vineyard is named for Napoleon DuBrul, the great-grandfather of one of the owners. The Shielses' own tiny winery, Côte Bonneville, gets its name from his home, which was built in 1902 and is pictured on the label of their best wine.

ELEPHANT MOUNTAIN

Elephant Mountain is one of the centerpiece sites in the Rattlesnake Hills AVA. It occupies a series of south-facing slopes on Rattlesnake Ridge, ranging in elevation from 1,320 to 1,460 feet—well above the irrigated farmland of the Yakima Valley.

The vineyard property was purchased in 1995 and planted in 1998. It now totals 85 bearing acres, including significant blocks of cabernet sauvignon, syrah, merlot, sangiovese, viognier, cabernet franc, petit verdot, and mourvèdre, along with test plots of marsanne, roussanne, tempranillo, grenache, malbec, barbera, cinsault, counoise, Dolcetto, pinot gris, and carmenère. The soil is sandy silt loam averaging two feet in depth, with a layer of gravel below. It draws water from a deep well rather than from the irrigation canals commonly used at lower-altitude sites in the Yakima Valley.

Owner Joe Hattrup has been an orchardist all his life; this is his first wine grape project. He explains that the rocky south-facing slopes of Elephant Mountain create a beneficial heat sink that helps, along with the elevation, to keep the site warm and dry throughout the growing season. There have been few if any issues with freeze or mildew, although the region has not been severely tested since 1996, which predates the planting.

During its first decade, says Hattrup, Elephant Mountain's average growing season was almost a month longer than most Columbia Valley locations. The moderate daytime highs of the Yakima Valley make for a long growing season, which in turn allows for extended hang time and ideal ripening. "This is not a commodity business," Hattrup insists. "We custom-grow fruit to the customer specifications."

The customers are lining up—always the proof of the pudding as far as new vineyards are concerned. Vineyard manager Denis Gayte, who spent most of the past decade in France as a wine grower, notes that such quality-oriented wineries as J. Bookwalter, McCrea Cellars, O•S, Owen Roe, and Walter Dacon are among them. When asked to describe what he feels are particular vineyard strengths, Gayte replies that "freshness—in French we say 'fraicheur,' which is a wonderful word to describe a wine—balance, power, structure, and in some cases minerality are all characteristics of Elephant Mountain vineyards." Standout varietals include syrah, cabernet sauvignon, tempranillo, and viognier. The reds are often used as blending components rather than featured as single-vineyard bottlings, due to their cool-climate acidity and lightly herbal character.

Two new vineyard projects are also being developed. Sugarloaf is a similar site nearby, about one-third planted, and Hattrup has just purchased another 160 acres in the Zillah district and will begin vineyard development immediately.

LEWIS VINEYARD

Winemakers, like truffle-hunting dogs, have a nose for buried goodies. The surest way to sniff out an excellent new vineyard is to follow the best winemakers. Where are they buying grapes? Who are they collaborating with? Which wines are they doing as vineyard-designates? It was such questions that first brought the Lewis vineyard to my attention, as the source of outstanding, vineyard-designated wines being made by Eric Dunham at Dunham Cellars. Owner Ken Lewis and his wife are octogenarians who entered the wine grape business late in life, but brought with them credentials reaching back into the nineteenth century.

Ken Lewis still has the diary his great-grandmother kept when she came west in a covered wagon as a young girl. Though born in Yakima, he was raised in the Seattle area and spent the first part of his working life as a civil engineer in California, western Washington, and Walla Walla. His parents were apple growers, and part of his work was designing concrete water lines for the Yakima Valley. He and his father bought the first 300 acres of the current property in 1956, and for years Ken Lewis worked in Seattle during the winters and farmed in the summers. The vineyard was not started until 1994, when a few acres of cabernet sauvignon went into the ground, but most of the planting happened between 1996 and 2000.

Currently there are about 120 acres (of 650 total) in wine grapes, a third of it syrah, another third cabernet, and the rest a mix that includes chardonnay, riesling, merlot, and sangiovese. Eric Dunham first purchased Lewis vineyard syrah in 1999 (it came in at a completely ridiculous one-tenth of a ton per acre), and now makes designated Lewis chardonnay, cabernet, and merlot, as well. Half of the vineyard's production goes to Dunham; the rest is sold to such boutiques as àMaurice, Bunchgrass, Januik, Sleight of Hand, Tulpen (owned by vineyard manager Kenny Hart), and Va Piano.

Ken Lewis is a natural-born storyteller and enjoys a good joke, often at his own expense. "Our corporate name is Trailview Farm—look out that window and you can see a road coming down off the Horse Heaven Hills," he explained as we sat in his living room one sunny spring day recently. "My father walked from Ketchum [Idaho] to Prosser, barefoot beside a covered wagon, in 1901. He was six years old." Why on earth would a child undertake such a grueling trek, I wondered. "His father—my grandfather George J. Lewis," he continued, "had missed the covered wagon days and he wanted that adventure, so they did it. He was a wealthy man; his father farmsteaded what is now Sun Valley. We're a family of lost fortunes," he concluded with a wink.

Lost fortunes notwithstanding, the present-day Lewis vineyards (there are several) clearly have what it takes to grow excellent wine grapes. The elevation rises to about 1,200 feet, centered just a few miles north of Prosser, toward the eastern end of the Yakima Valley. Eric Dunham recalls that he had been wanting to make a syrah, and it was not easy to find those grapes back in the late 1990s. He knew a man named John Clark who happened to be a friend of Ken Lewis (yes, they were Lewis and Clark), and Clark connected the dots. When Lewis and Dunham first met, the vineyard was only in its second leaf, and no one really knew what kind of grapes it would produce. "I've heard you make good wine," Lewis told Dunham. "I want somebody to make good wine out of my fruit before I die." He did; other truffle hunters followed, and I am pleased to add Lewis to the honor list of this state's best vineyards.

MILBRANDT

The rapidly expanding empire that comprises Milbrandt vineyards cannot be easily captured in a few paragraphs. Since beginning in 1997, when brothers Butch and Jerry Milbrandt planted their first 60 acres at Sundance, on the Wahluke Slope, they have been on a nonstop growth binge. They grew up in the Ancient Lakes region just a bit farther north, around the town of Quincy, and spent most of their working lives in agriculture and real estate endeavors having nothing to do with wine grapes. But their past business experience has clearly served them well, as has their deep and intimate knowledge of eastern Washington. They purchased Wahluke Slope vineyard in 1998 and began planting: Evergreen, Katherine Leone, and Talcott in 1998; Clifton and Clifton Hill in

1999; Pheasant in 2000; Northridge in 2003; Purple Sage and Clifton Bluff in 2006; Ancient Lakes in 2007; and a still-unnamed new vineyard, also in the Ancient Lakes region, in 2008.

Some of the land is purchased, some leased. "We have paid a lot of money for sagebrush and rocks," says Butch, tongue planted firmly in cheek. "But it put us on the map." "We've worked hard to find some of the best sites in the state," says Jerry, more pragmatically. "Cool high-elevation sites for our whites, for wines with great minerality, acid crispness, and forward fruit. Our reds are planted in the warmer areas, creating wines that are deeply colored, ripe, and generous."

All told, the Milbrandts now control thirteen different sites, all substantial. Nearly 1,600 acres are planted, and they are still growing. They farm ten distinct blocks (roughly 750 acres) of vines on the Wahluke Slope, mostly planted to red grapes, notably syrah. Farther north, in the developing Ancient Lakes region near George, Washington (yes, Martha, there is a George, Washington), another 452 acres are planted at the Evergreen vineyard, with two more sites (totaling 270 acres) set to come into production this year. In this area the focus is on white wine grapes: chardonnay, pinot gris, viognier, gewürztraminer, and riesling. All in all, Milbrandt vineyard names appear on dozens of labels from more than forty different wineries. In a short time, the Milbrandts have become as essential and irreplaceable as any growers in the state.

As if all this were not enough to solidify their position as premium grape growers, the brothers opened their own winery, which doubles as a custom crush facility, in 2005. A new tasting room, in the Prosser Vintner's Village, debuted in 2008.

OTIS

The oldest vines at Otis recently passed the half-century mark, a remarkable age for cabernet and chardonnay in Washington State or anywhere in this country. Because the original vines are planted on their own rootstock and head-trained, they will outlive those that have been grafted onto phylloxera-resistant rootstock. Should the vineyard get whacked by one of eastern Washington's periodic winter freezes, you can train a new trunk up from the roots, rather like a rose bush.

These Otis vines are survivors, pioneers from a distant time when the Washington wine industry was protected by strict trade tariffs and the economics of wine were based on laws that allowed so-called high-ferment wines to be the strongest drinks sold in taverns across the state. Those wines, made from high-yielding, heavily irrigated grapes such as sultana, palomino, alicanté, and salvador, were augmented at fermentation with bags of sugar and turned into high-octane "sherry" and "port." A leading producer of the day was Alhambra. The owner, Otis Harlan, was a savvy businessman who knew that Washington's state-protected wine industry would eventually have to compete on more equal terms. He began keeping an eye on the new wine styles being made in California and decided to plant a few experimental acres of vinifera wines in his Otis vineyard.

The first six acres of Otis cab went into the ground in 1957. Harlan—still hale and hearty as of this writing—recalls that it was initially used to make an inexpensive rosé, a "Burgundy" blend designed to imitate the hearty burgundy of California, and a "port." "We were even thinking of using corks for that wine," he says, a radical departure from the screw-capped wines of the day, "until we found out that not many people had corkscrews!"

The collaboration with Columbia Winery winemaker David Lake began in September 1979. The previous winter had seen a deep freeze; many vineyards were wiped out, and Lake, scrambling for grapes, arranged to purchase a small amount of Otis cabernet and merlot. He was so impressed with the quality of the fruit that he created a special "Millennium" cabernet and predicted that the wine would live long enough to be enjoyed two decades later, when the new century began.

He was too modest. At 25 years of age, the 1979 Millennium was still a remarkable wine, showing brick edges but quite dark, the color of black cherries. Barolo-like, it smelled of tar and leather, rose petals, and cut tobacco; a mature, confident, spectacular wine, nuanced with hints of cherries, raspberries, and tobacco leaf.

Columbia produced a vineyard-designated Otis cabernet sauvignon in every vintage from 1981 through 2006. The wine was always 100 percent Otis and usually pure, un-blended cabernet sauvignon. Those Otis cabernets did not romance you with sweet, succulent fruit or toasty new oak. Often they were rather hard, unyielding wines, occasionally quite tannic, and marked by a distinctive peppery, herbal nose. It has often been noted that the Washington style of making red wine straddles (or defines) an imaginary border between Napa and Bordeaux. Otis cabs clearly fall on the Bordeaux side of that fence; they display the classic herbal aromas of the cabernet varietal, the sort of lightly vegetative scents prevalent in even the best young Bordeaux, along with fairly hard tannins and tightly knit layers of tart red fruit.

These same qualities make them remarkably cellar-worthy. It is not just because the vineyard is so old that it merits inclusion in this chapter. It is because these wines pass the gold standard for greatness: They evolve as well as survive. They develop the nuances of bottle bouquet that Bordeaux lovers rarely find in New World wines.

Today, the entire Otis vineyard comprises roughly 110 acres, with many newer plantings, including 26 acres of pinot gris (Washington's first, planted in 1991, 1996, and 2006); 25 acres of chardonnay (some old vine, others newer Dijon clone); 14 acres of old-vine cabernet and another 16 more recently planted, 17 acres of merlot; 6 of sauvignon blanc; and about 3 acres of syrah. Since 2000, Terry Herrmann has been the vineyard manager, and the fruit is currently under contract to Constellation. Most goes into Hogue Cellars wines, but a little bit is being sold to the new owners of Columbia, who continue to make a small amount of a vineyard-designate for the winery library and mailing list. The future remains cloudy; as this books goes to print, the contract with Constellation is due to expire. Herrmann anticipates that the white grapes will continue to go to Hogue, but the fruit from those ancient cabernet vines may be looking for a new home.

PEPPER BRIDGE

Until very recently, the only vineyards in Walla Walla that added up to any significant acreage were Seven Hills and Pepper Bridge. These days, expansion is everywhere, especially at the higher elevations (across the state line) south of town. Prices for raw land with "vineyard potential" have cooled somewhat, but are still relatively high by eastern Washington standards. Diversity is becoming the hallmark; Walla Walla is already an AVA in need of subdividing. But if a single vineyard can represent the soil, plantings, technological innovation, and commitment to green (sustainable) viticulture that best characterize the region, it is Pepper Bridge.

Norm McKibben and Bob Rupar acquired the Pepper family's original property in 1988; the name Pepper Bridge refers to a low-water crossing on the Walla Walla River. The land was originally a wheat ranch, so the new owners' first inclination was to grow apples. But McKibben had previously been cultivating pinot noir and chardonnay at his (now defunct) 40-acre Whiskey Creek vineyard, some miles north of town, so he and Rupar soon decided to try some wine grapes on the newly acquired land. In 1991, the first five acres each of merlot and cabernet sauvignon went into the ground at Pepper Bridge.

In retrospect, the timing could not have been better. Though there were only a half dozen wineries in Walla Walla, several had already established national reputations. The odd thing was that they couldn't really make Walla Walla wines; only about 40 acres of grapes were planted in the entire valley. So virtually all these Walla Walla winery wines were made from Columbia Valley and Yakima Valley grapes.

The pent-up demand for true Walla Walla fruit was so great that even before the first crop was picked, Pepper Bridge had signed up Woodward Canyon, Leonetti, and L'Ecole No 41 as its customers. It was win-win; the wineries were desperate for local grapes, and the new vineyard quickly benefited from the excellent reputations that the wineries had already built. "That kind of marketing, "says McKibben, "got people to notice Pepper Bridge."

Currently, the 200-acre Pepper Bridge vineyard includes 162 acres of bearing vines, mostly split between cabernet sauvignon and merlot, with 11 acres of syrah and smaller amounts of sangiovese and malbec. A different set of partners owns the Pepper Bridge winery, which maintains control over specific blocks of grapes. Since the eighth or ninth vintage, notes McKibben, the cabernet in particular has become more and more consistent. "The vines," he says with characteristic modesty, "seem to pretty well self-regulate, and it's harder for us to screw them up."

Pepper Bridge sits in one of the valley's colder sites, and the vineyard was hit pretty hard by winter freezes in 1996, 2004, and again in 2008. After the loss of most of the

2004 crop, Pepper Bridge, along with many other low-lying Walla Walla vineyards, began to bury canes for protection. In at least some freeze years that strategy will help to ensure a decent crop the following summer.

Drip irrigation is used, regulated by buried soil sensors that read moisture levels at 12 inches, 18 inches, and four feet. If moisture reaches the four-foot depth, it is more than the vine needs; like many leading vineyards in the state, Pepper Bridge is using less and less water. Theories of stressing the grapes are changing also. "We don't grow our grapes to stress anymore," says McKibben. "Everybody's backed off that now." Too much stress, and pH's "go wild and flavors fall off."

The movement toward sustainable viticulture is gaining momentum in Washington, though the state still lags far behind Oregon and California. There is justifiable doubt about the practicality of being certifiably organic, but many of the underlying principles of organic farming are being incorporated into regular practice. At Pepper Bridge, compost (mostly ground logs along with some winery must and timothy hay), compost tea (applied through the drip lines), and other treatments (molasses, fish compound) are all being used in efforts to rebuild soils sterilized by a century of wheat farming. "We're about as close to organic as we can get without being organic," says McKibben.

More recently, he and Rupar, along with a small group of winery partners, have embarked on a new, still more ambitious project, called SeVein. It comprises 2,000 acres of land on the Oregon side of the valley, rising above their existing Seven Hills vineyard from 1,180 to 1,450 feet. About 1,600 acres are plantable, enough to double the current total acreage of the Walla Walla AVA. The first 350 acres are already in the ground, planted for partners L'Ecole No 41 and Leonetti Cellar and high-profile clients such as Cadaretta, JM Cellars, and retired NFL quarterback Drew Bledsoe.

RED WILLOW

The Red Willow Vineyard got its start in the early 1970s on land purchased by the Stephenson family from the Yakama tribe a half century earlier. Located at the extreme northwestern edge of the Yakima Valley, it is one of the prettiest and most unusual vineyards in Washington State, surrounded to this day on all sides by the Yakama Indian Reservation.

Initially it was farmed to potatoes and alfalfa, with cattle let to graze on the higher slopes unsuitable for row crops. In the early 1970s, Mike Sauer, who had married the granddaughter of the man who pioneered the property, planted a 30-acre Concord vineyard, along with a few experimental rows of chenin blanc and sémillon.

As with so many of Washington's old-vine locations, it was Walt Clore who first got the ball rolling. Clore wanted a weather station installed so that he could compare temperature data with other areas around the state. At the same time, he and Sauer put in a small experimental vineyard. But Sauer already had commercial aspirations, and in 1973 he decided to go ahead and plant three acres of cabernet sauvignon as well. The trials and tribulations of this early planting would test the patience of Job: weeds, rabbits, grasshoppers, drought, and more. But Sauer typically looks on the bright side, recalling those early days with some fondness.

"We were trying to figure out how to pronounce the varieties, let alone grow them," he grins. "The climate was different then. We had several pretty cold winters. The emphasis was on trying to figure out which varieties would survive. Walt put an experimental plot on our land with about twenty different varieties, and it sparked this interest. From about 1983 to 1991 we tried nebbiolo, sangiovese, syrah, cab franc, tempranillo, mataro, malbec, and viognier."

By the early 1990s, a lot of people were jumping into these varieties, but Red Willow was often first. An exceptional partnership between grower Sauer and Columbia winemaker David Lake had formed, one that would last for almost three decades. The first Red Willow vineyard designate, made by Lake, was a 1981 Associated Vintners cabernet sauvignon; those wines are still being made, despite the myriad changes to the Columbia brand and its ever-changing ownership.

"David was always very encouraging," Sauer recalls. "If we would grow it, he would make the wine from it." New vineyards were added regularly, usually on steep hillsides that required weeks of bulldozing. Each new plot, each new grape revealed more and more about this unique site, which sits between 1,100 and 1,300 feet, above the ancient floodplain that created most eastern Washington vineyards. A wide variation of soils—calcareous, sandstone, clay, sand, loam, and silt—were uncovered. And the combination of these poor, ancient, well-drained soils; the east-, south-, and west-facing slopes; and the desert climate (just six inches of precipitation annually) provided perfect laboratory conditions for Lake and Sauer's ongoing trials.

The emphasis shifted somewhat during the 1990s as new sections of the vineyard were developed. The focus then was matching soils to varietals, in hopes of finding the true Red Willow terroir. Then came another round of changes as Columbia Winery, the winery purchasing the vast majority of the grapes, was acquired by Canandaigua/Constellation. "We spent a lot of effort on landscaping at that time," says Sauer, "sprucing the place up." That turned out to be temporary, as well; the Columbia Winery brand now belongs to Ascentia Wine Estates, part of a 2008 sale that saw Constellation divest itself of most of its Washington brands. Where Ascentia will take Columbia is still to be seen, but Sauer thinks it may back away from Constellation's focus on fewer varieties and more marketing. Certainly a return to local control of the vineyard decisions would be welcome.

Though the partnership between Lake and Columbia Winery was both productive and prolific, Red Willow did not enjoy the benefits, as did most of the other vineyards included in this chapter, of receiving input from a more diverse group of winemakers. That too is changing. In recent years, a host of new winery clients have begun purchasing Red Willow grapes—DeLille, Efesté, Fall Line, Mark Ryan, :Note Bene, Owen Roe, Stella Fino, and William Church among them. Columbia purchases now account for less than 40 percent of the total.

Les Vignes de Marcoux, a newer, 60-acre site located about three quarters of a mile west of Red Willow, is carrying on the Sauer tradition of exploring ever more unusual grape varieties, including aglianico, barbera, carmenère, and malbec. Rolling hills and range land rather than steep slopes are found here; newer clones and creative trellising also help to differentiate the site from Red Willow. Clients include Andrew Rich, Betz Family, Owen Roe, and several other wineries whose first wines have not yet been released.

"The past few years have been extremely rewarding," says Sauer. "Old associations with wineries like Columbia and Cavatappi have continued. Relationships with top-end wineries like Betz, Owen Roe, and DeLille have been forged. We are also dealing with smaller and start-up wineries that just have a passion for wine, are willing and enthused to try new and unusual varieties and lots of grapes. Every block and sometimes every row has a specific destination and target wine. It becomes a working relationship, not simply a commodity and a contract."

After more than 35 years, Mike Sauer isn't about to stop experimenting. He's exploring green practices that affect wine quality and worker safety, using compost and biological water treatments to stimulate the soil biology and applying foliar nutrient sprays to promote vine health and minimize mildew and insect problems.

In 2006, another dozen acres went into the ground: three of sangiovese, five of syrah, two of cab franc, a dash of petite sirah, and a touch of Dolcetto. More recently, three acres of cabernet franc and two of sauvignon blanc (a first for Red Willow) were added, bringing the total to 130 acres. "That's it," says Sauer; "all of our suitable ground is developed, and any future planting will be from the removal of existing vineyards. Of course," he adds, "along with this last planting I had to include a few vines of an old Russian variety that Walt Clore had included in that original experimental plot." It comes as no surprise that Sauer is the first in the state to plant rkatsiteli. "It had great growing traits in the vineyard," he enthuses, "I'm sure I will find a small winery to make the wine . . ."

SAGEMOOR

Sagemoor vineyards was founded in 1968, when the original property was purchased out of bankruptcy by a group headed by Seattle attorney Alec Bayless. It was 40 years later that I made my first visit to the site, which includes four vineyards owned by separate partnerships, all under the supervision of Managing Director John Vitalich and General Manager Kent Waliser.

The Sagemoor, Bacchus, and Dionysus vineyards are located a few miles north of Pasco, overlooking the Columbia River and the Hanford Reach. Bacchus and Dionysus are adjoining properties, and from them a visitor can see as far as the Wahluke Slope, where Weinbau, the fourth vineyard in the group, is located. Somewhat confusingly, the name Sagemoor both refers to a specific site and also serves as the umbrella brand for the entire vineyard group.

The oldest vines, thick as trees and battle-scarred by the decades, date from the original plantings, in 1972 and 1973. Still healthy and bearing are about 60 acres of the cabernet, 20 acres of riesling, and another 15 acres of sauvignon blanc. The oldest merlot is at Dionysus, planted in 1980. Currently, a total of 900 acres is in production.

Kent Waliser took over as GM in 2002. On his first day at work, he was told that the vineyard's biggest client had just given notice that it would be phasing out its contracts. Within three years, Waliser learned, roughly three-fifths of his sales would be gone. Such news might have daunted lesser men, but Waliser took it as a challenge. Working with then-vineyard manager Todd Cameron, he began to rethink the whole property. The reason his main client had decided to bail, Waliser concluded, was that grapes at the Sagemoor vineyards were not ripening evenly. The land was not flat, and the soil types and depths varied considerably. A single row of vines might snake down into a gulley and back up a hillside, so some grapes would face south, others north, and still others would be in a hole where the cold air could settle.

Cameron set out to "vigor-map" the vines, carefully noting which blocks or sections grew more quickly than others. Drip irrigation was installed—not in place of, but in addition to, the overhead sprinklers that were already in use. "The whole point was to even up the ripening," Waliser explains. At the same time, he realized that what a large winery might consider a problem, smaller wineries might perceive as an asset. Sagemoor's varied aspects, drainage, and elevation, along with its thriving old vines, were quite appealing to boutique winemakers eager to claim specific rows and blocks as their own.

Waliser and Cameron began dividing up the vineyards into smaller, "niche" blocks and planting new varietals: viognier and roussanne; barbera, carmenère, grenache, mourvèdre, malbec, and petit verdot. They made it their mission to give each winemaker the best possible fruit, tailored exactly to his or her specifications. Derek Way has been the vineyard manager since 2007 and is instituting "best farming" practices designed to ensure sustainability over the long term.

Sagemoor has always been of interest to winemakers who covet the old-vine cabernet. Gary Figgins (Leonetti Cellar), Rick Small (Woodward Canyon), Marty Clubb (L'Ecole No 41), and others are long-term customers. But with the new emphasis on quality and designated vines, the floodgates have opened. As Marty Clubb explains, "Sagemoor used to be overcropped and overwatered. Now they have turned into a powerhouse of acre-managed, specialty lots. To really create quality takes many passes through the vineyard. It costs more for our fruit, but we have more consistent, better-quality fruit as a result."

"I like to think of us as baristas of wine," says Waliser, with a chuckle. "How would you like your grapes today?" Such dedication to customer service has quickly (in wine terms) paid off. Sagemoor is now, Waliser believes, selling to more individual wineries than any vineyard in the state—more than seventy at last count. Best of all, his big client has come back, happier than ever. Among the many Washington wineries relying on

Sagemoor fruit as part of their program are àMaurice, Abeja, Arbor Crest, Barnard Griffin, Barrister, Boudreaux, Corliss, Couvillion, Cullin Hills, DèLille Cellars, Efesté, Fidélitas, Forgeron, Hedges, Isenhower, J. Bookwalter, Januik, L'Ecole No 41, Long Shadows, Reininger, Saviah, Soos Creek, SYZYGY, Tamarack, Three Rivers, Walla Walla Vintners, and Woodward Canyon.

More and more of them are putting the name of the vineyard right on the label. Being selected for vineyard-designated wines is always a sign of quality, and you will now find Sagemoor, Bacchus, Dionysus, and Weinbau designated on numerous bottles from dozens of wineries.

SEVEN HILLS

The original Seven Hills vineyard was started in 1980–81 by the McClellan and Hendricks families. The first four acres were planted to cabernet sauvignon; the next three, in 1982, were merlot. A few white varieties were tried but later pulled and replaced with more cab and merlot. Casey McClellan and Scott Hendricks comanaged the vineyard during most of the first decade, with fruit initially going to Leonetti and Woodward Canyon.

The Seven Hills winery, begun in 1987, was (and is) separately owned. The vineyard had expanded to 20 acres by the late 1980s, but differing ideas about vineyard management—and perhaps different objectives on both sides of the partnership—led to its sale in 1994. A few acres were retained by Scott Hendricks, renamed Windrow, and recently resold to a new partnership. The rest of Seven Hills passed from Hendricks to a group consisting of Norm McKibben and Bob Rupar (Pepper Bridge), Gary Figgins (Leonetti Cellar), and Marty Clubb (L'Ecole No 41). They further expanded the vineyard in 1997 and 1998. The new planting—which currently totals about 175 acres—is Seven Hills East. All but about 20 acres are now in their twelfth leaf.

Seven Hills West, just across the road, includes the original old-block merlot and cabernet vines, as well as another 30 acres or so that have been converted from apples to wine grapes. Grapes from the original vines still go to Leonetti and Seven Hills wineries. Seven Hills West is under different ownership, but since East and West are essentially contiguous, vineyard-designates just lump them all together as Seven Hills. Another, 80-acre parcel, just to the east, is still controlled by the McClellan family. The first 10 acres were planted to Bordeaux grapes in 2003 and named the McClellan Estate vineyard.

The main varietals grown at Seven Hills are cabernet sauvignon, merlot, and syrah. There are significant amounts of sangiovese, cabernet franc, sémillon, and sauvignon blanc and smaller amounts of petit verdot, malbec, and carmenère. The three winery partners use about half of the fruit and sell the rest to more than two dozen other producers, among them Januik, JM Cellars, Otis Kenyon, Reininger, Saviah, Tamarack, Waters, and Walla Walla Vintners.

The old-block merlot and cabernet vines create wines that are relatively soft, very pretty, and beautifully balanced. The black cherry fruit flavors are accented and set against an underlying, earthy minerality. The merlot, in particular, tastes delicious when young, even in barrel, but ages gracefully for a decade or more.

Seven Hills is north-facing, planted on a gentle slope at elevations from 850 to 1,075 feet. It has deep silt-loam soils and excellent air drainage, as it sits just above the old riverbed floor of the valley. Annual rainfall averages about eight inches, and soil moisture is monitored daily by computer, providing data for strictly controlled drip irrigation. Water is mainly drawn from a well drilled more than 1,100 feet down into solid basalt. Several different trellising systems are employed, including vertical shoot positioning and Smart-Dyson split canopy. Sustainable viticulture is the prevailing philosophy, with ongoing efforts such as an internationally approved minimal-chemical program, a further step on the long road to biodynamic status.

The massive SeVein project, which will include as many as 1,600 planted acres when complete, is being pieced together both above and below Seven Hills and will ensure that this vineyard complex remains the center of Walla Walla viticulture for many decades to come.

STILLWATER CREEK

Perhaps the most important potential new AVA in Washington is the Royal Slope, with its band of mostly south-facing vineyards, set in the Frenchman Hills due north of the Wahluke Slope. Stillwater Creek has arguably done more than any other site to establish the name and reputation of the region, as it sells grapes to a number of wineries that in turn make vineyard designates from the grapes. Among them are Arbor Crest, Januik, JM Cellars, and Saviah. Most importantly, Stillwater Creek is the estate vineyard for the Novelty Hill wines, which are also made by Mike Januik.

It occupies one of the steepest sites in the state, with slopes up to 22 percent throughout its 210 planted acres (out of 245 total). Established over three years, from 2000 to 2002, Stillwater Creek includes 53 acres of cabernet sauvignon, 37 of merlot, 30 of syrah, 16 of chardonnay, and smaller amounts of roussanne, sauvignon blanc, sémillon, viognier, cabernet franc, grenache, malbec, mourvèdre, petit verdot, and sangiovese.

Owned by the Alberg family and managed by Jerry Bookwalter and Tom Thorsen, it was the first Columbia Valley vineyard to be certified Salmon Safe (by Stewardship Partners, a Seattle nonprofit promoting fish-friendly practices). Soils are typical for the region: sandy or silty loam with fractured basalt. It's a relatively cool site, yet has found success with a wide variety of grapes.

Although four-fifths of the acreage are in red grapes, it is the white wines from Stillwater fruit (most notably the Novelty Hill bottlings) that have most impressed me. The sauvignon blanc is iconic, a glorious explosion of citrus, tropical, and stone fruits, concentrated and rich; the sémillon belongs with the best in the state. The other whites, including young versions of roussanne and viognier, are also exceptional, laden with mixed floral and fruit aromas, racy and beautifully defined. A varietal grenache—the first from this vineyard—tastes of cranberry, strawberry, and black cherry candy, with a whiff of smoke.

Clonal research has been an important aspect of the vineyard development from the very beginning. Included are numerous Entav selections from France: cabernet sauvignon 2, 4, 6, 8, and 191; merlot 3 and 348; chardonnay 15, 75, 95, and 96; and syrah 174, 300, and Phelps. From such young vines have already come merlots, cabernets, and syrahs with exquisite balance and compact strength.

THE BENCHES/WALLULA

The Wallula vineyard—which has been renamed The Benches by its new owners—occupies a breathtaking bluff rising steeply above the Columbia River just before it bends sharply north and ceases to define the Oregon-Washington border. The Wallula Gap, carved by the river as it cuts into Washington State, is where the massive floodwaters funneled through repeatedly during the last ice age. The vineyard itself is huge, spread along a five-mile stretch of the river, and ranging in altitude from a few hundred to 1,350 feet above sea level. Purchased in 1997 by the Den Hoed family, it is currently planted with 650 acres and has the potential to double that number.

Andy Den Hoed estimates that there are a dozen different soil types on the property, but mostly it is windblown loess, much of it above flood level. With elevations as much as 1,000 feet apart, the vineyard can ripen almost anything well. One hundred forty acres are biodynamically farmed riesling that goes to Pacific Rim (a biodynamic vineyard-designate is produced). Other long-term contracts are held by Ste. Michelle and Oregon's King Estate. Allen Shoup's Long Shadows Vintners was already purchasing Wallula cabernet sauvignon, merlot, and syrah for its wines; Shoup admired the site so much that he formed a separate LLC—Premier Vineyard Estates—and purchased the vineyard itself in March 2008. The Den Hoeds maintain a minority interest and continue to manage the site.

Along with the varieties cited above, small plots of more than a dozen other varietals are being tried. "On the bluffs is the easiest place to see if something works or doesn't work," Andy Den Hoed believes. "All those plateaus are small—from a fifth of an acre to an acre and a half. We can choose the growing style for almost any grape. If carmenère does best on a certain type of slope, whatever it is, we have that. It's not like farming in the Yakima Valley [the Den Hoeds have large holdings there also], where your vineyard is what it is. At Wallula you can pick your shading, your temperature, your growing-degree days, the wind direction!"

The Den Hoeds have initiated trial plantings of albariño, barbera, cinsault, Dolcetto, marsanne, mourvèdre, roussanne, sangiovese, and tempranillo. But under the new ownership, no large-scale experiments will be done—"It's too valuable for experimenting," says Shoup. And too expensive—the price paid is rumored to be the highest ever for Washington vineyard land.

PART 2

WINERY PROFILES

5

THE FIVE-STAR WINERIES

This book's highest accolade—a five-star rating—indicates not only that the wines are exceptional but that the winery, whether large (Ste. Michelle), medium (Barnard Griffin), or small (Cadence), has taken a leadership role in one or more aspects of wine production. Whether in vineyard development and management, exploration of wine styles and varietal grapes, innovative marketing, or offerings of exceptional value, they set the highest standard. In tasting after tasting, visit after visit, vintage after vintage, these producers have helped to improve and define the image of all Washington wines.

As a minimum, these five-star wineries or their winemakers have made at least ten Washington vintages. Most have considerably more. Rob Griffin (Barnard Griffin) is well into his fourth decade as a winemaker in this state; Gary Figgins (Leonetti Cellar) and Alex Golitzin (Quilceda Creek) have each completed three decades and succeeded in transitioning to a new generation. I grant that Abeja, Buty, Fielding Hills, and K are relatively new, but there is a reason that each of them is included here. John Abbott's Washington winemaking experience began at Canoe Ridge in the mid-1990s; Caleb Foster spent eight years at Woodward Canyon prior to founding Buty; Mike Wade is an experienced grower with a great vineyard site and a natural gift for winemaking; and Charles Smith is, well, Charles Smith.

Bottom line: nothing in this book took more of my time and attention than compiling this list of the Top Twenty. Like any list, it can be challenged, argued over, or picked apart. But as I look for the leaders in terms of style, consistency, and value, these are the producers whose wines I believe best display the greatness that is achievable in Washington State.

✱ ABEJA

First vintage: 2001

www.abeja.net

Though Abeja (pronounced ah-BAY-ha; it means bumblebee) has yet to complete its first decade, winemaker and co-owner John Abbott has long-established credentials. After some years at Napa's Pine Ridge and Chalone's Acacia winery he moved to Walla Walla in 1994 to make wine for Canoe Ridge Vineyard, then a new Chalone venture.

Abbott's years at Canoe Ridge produced some of this state's most breathtaking merlots and seductive chardonnays. The experience left him eager to pursue winemaking on a more personal scale, and having conquered merlot, he turned his focus toward perfecting Washington State cabernet sauvignon. Happily, Abbott's quest matched up nicely with Ken Harrison's own plans for a new winery (and B&B) just outside Walla Walla. Ken and Ginger Harrison, John Abbott, and Molly Galt formed their business partnership in 2002, dedicating themselves principally to producing estate-grown cabernet, made to the highest standards, at the property now called Abeja.

Harrison had already begun by planting his 19-acre Heather Hill vineyard, just east of Seven Hills, in 2001. Heather Hill grows mostly cabernet sauvignon, with an acre of merlot and a shy acre of cabernet franc. The small Mill Creek vineyard, which adjoins the winery, was extensively replanted in 2006 and grows four acres of merlot and smaller amounts of chardonnay, viognier, and syrah. Though plans are in the works to develop an 800-acre site north of the winery, near Spring Valley, most of Abeja's grapes are still purchased, and likely to remain so indefinitely.

The chardonnay is primarily Conner Lee (40 percent) and Celilo (40 percent), with some Kestrel View, Smasne, and Gamache. "I want to make sure we're releasing the best possible chardonnay that we can," says Abbott. "I think of this as the reserve." There is only one chardonnay; his point is that what would go into a nonreserve chardonnay is bulked out.

Visitors to the winery, and those fortunate enough to be on its now-closed mailing list, have access to a bright, racy viognier. Made in limited quantities, it's a glorious springtime wine, like drinking flowers. There are also a few hundred cases of syrah from the estate vineyards, sold through the tasting room only. In 2004, Abbott (finally) returned to merlot, making up to 500 cases. Released in November with the (occasional) reserve cabernet, it quickly sells out.

Cabernet sauvignon remains the principal focus and accounts for more than half of Abeja's 3,500-to-4,000-case production. "I think of myself as a second- or third-growth Bordeaux winemaker," Abbott modestly explains, "not first growth." A recent (and typical) cabernet blend included grapes from Heather Hill, Sagemoor (all old vine), Hedges, Kiona, and Wallula. Sweet, toasted nut and butter flavors from barrel aging are perfectly wrapped into clean, vivid, beautifully defined fruit, dappled with a dash of pepper, a whiff of herb, and a brambly, old vine finish, with a hint of black tea.

Reserve cabernets are made infrequently, but are essential for anyone who loves the grape and wants to taste the best that Washington has to offer. Abeja's 2005 reserve was pure varietal and made almost entirely from vines planted in 1972. "We only make a reserve when it's the classic essence of Washington State cabernet," says Abbott, and it's no boast, merely a statement of fact. Classic and classy, with substantial tannins and supple fruit, these are cabernets to lay down for a decade or more.

Though Abeja has been discovered, and the wines are difficult to obtain, visitors to Walla Walla may look for the House Red (formerly the Beekeeper Blend), a modestly priced, cabernet-dominated Bordeaux blend that Abbott makes specifically for local distribution. It's his gift to the community—a wine so good it could easily be the standard-bearer for many wineries.

ANDREW WILL

First vintage: 1989

www.andrewwill.com

A sit-down chat with Andrew Will's winemaker-founder, Chris Camarda, generally begins slowly. Gruff and grizzled, Camarda is a fascinating combination of shy and cynical, and often seems uncomfortable when being interviewed. But sooner or later, some question or other winds him up and sets him off. And given his 20 years of winemaking experience and the years in the restaurant business that preceded them, Camarda's sharp, pointed, opinionated view on all matters vinous usually strikes me as a breath of fresh air.

"It was clear to me that following the California varietal model would not work for Washington," he explained, when asked about his early winemaking. "From the beginning I made single-vineyard wines. It is the pre-eminent idea—aristocratic in winemaking—I admire. Pursuing single vineyards as simply a marketing idea is not very good. But if you are trying to define, give wine a face, a definition, that is the important idea about wine."

Among Andrew Will's early successes were Camarda's single vineyard merlots; he was one of the first in Washington to explore and carefully define the specific flavor characteristics of individual sites. He did this methodically, by eliminating all other winemaking variables. His artistic gifts allowed him to endow each wine with a unique personality, by steadfastly laboring not to put his own stylistic stamp on them.

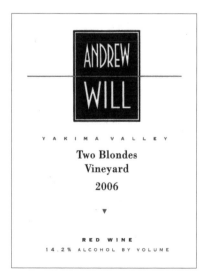

ANDREW WILL

YAKIMA VALLEY

**Two Blondes
Vineyard
2006**

▾

RED WINE
14.2% ALCOHOL BY VOLUME

"I wanted people to see one person making wine the same way, with the same barrels, the same techniques," he recalled, "so what you were left with was the flavor of vineyards. We're interested in the differences between vineyards, not the similarities. Otherwise you might as well make beer."

The vineyards initially chosen—Ciel du Cheval and Klipsun on Red Mountain, Pepper Bridge and Seven Hills in Walla Walla, Champoux in the Horse Heaven Hills and Sheridan in the Rattlesnake Hills—were selected specifically for their ability to express some unique terroir. With the benefit of hindsight, it is clear that Camarda knew what he was doing; he included representatives of the Red Mountain, Walla Walla, Horse Heaven, and Rattlesnake Hills AVAs, though at the time, only Walla Walla was officially designated.

In 2000, he began experimenting with nonvarietal blends. "It wasn't that I didn't like merlot, or cabernet, but I liked the wines that were blended better. More faceted, more lively, more conversational, more liquid," he says. "I didn't even realize it until after I was doing it for a while that for me, as a winemaker, this is the way to make wine. It projects what I think are the best ideas in the wine world."

Since 2003, all Andrew Will wines are nonvarietal blends whose identity is anchored by the vineyard. Ciel du Cheval, Champoux, and his own Two Blondes are the featured sites, this last in the Rattlesnake Hills AVA. He's changed his winemaking also, installing closed-top fermenters, with more precise regulation of heating and cooling. A device he calls the "bubble-ator" gently aerates the wines during fermentation, softening the tannins and creating wines with more texture, less grip, and brighter fruit.

Though 2006 was generally a tighter, tougher vintage than 2005, Andrew Will's wines reversed this pattern. The 2006 releases are expansive, expressive, explosive with berries, cherries, crisp acids, and polished tannins. That said, the 2007s are the best ever made at this winery, and among the best ever made in Washington. The winery's reserve is Sorella, produced from the oldest Champoux vineyard vines. The Annie Camarda syrah, made from Ciel du Cheval grapes, honors his late wife. A lower-priced line of wines called Cuvée Lucia is dedicated to such interesting experiments as Ciel du Cheval sangiovese, Celilo pinot gris, Canoe Ridge sémillon, and from Velvet Canyon, a sémillon–sauvignon blanc blend.

BARNARD GRIFFIN

First vintage: 1983

www.barnardgriffin.com

Though Rob Griffin will soon celebrate his thirty-fifth vintage in Washington and has probably made more award-winning, medal-winning, show-stopping wines than anyone in the state, he is disarmingly modest. "We're too available to be cultish," he says of his Barnard Griffin wines. At 75,000 cases a year ("just exactly where you're not supposed to be—too big to be small, and certainly too small to be big"), he makes a valid point. Unlike most of the wineries listed here, all but a handful of reserve Barnard Griffin wines are widely available and priced accordingly.

Three decades is a milestone that few in this state have reached and even fewer have surpassed. What began, Griffin recalls, as a brief adventure after graduating from UC Davis ("I figured I'd invest a year or two, get my name on the marquee, and come back to California in a blaze of glory," he says) has somehow become a life's work.

He started as winemaker for Preston Wine Cellars, then spent another few years at Hogue; while still there, he and his wife Deborah Barnard started their own enterprise, Barnard Griffin. Throughout his career, Rob Griffin has carved a trail

laden with wonderfully fresh, carefully rendered wines that deliver true-to-varietal, true-to-place flavors. As evidence of his success, Barnard Griffin has steadily grown to become the state's second-largest family-owned winery (just behind Hedges).

Griffin firmly believes that "quality and price are almost unrelated in the wine business." And he sets out to prove the point with each new vintage, determined to make wines that perform far above their modest prices.

The Tulip label wines, which account for all but a few thousand cases of Barnard Griffin's production, include ripe, round, deliciously unpretentious versions of chardonnay, riesling, fumé blanc, sémillon, cabernet sauvignon, merlot, syrah, and a nonvintage cab-merlot. Top bottles are the chardonnay ("the engine that pulls the train, the girl that brought us to the dance," says Griffin); riesling (mostly old-vine grapes, floral and luscious, with the cut and precision of a fine Kabinett); and fumé blanc (often discounted to $6 or $7, where it has no competitors).

Reserve wines feature a diamond label and include lot selections of chardonnay, viognier, muscat, pinot gris, barbera, cabernet sauvignon, grenache, malbec, merlot, petit verdot, syrah, zinfandel, and a fortified syrah. A rosé of sangiovese is one of the finest in Washington. All these reserves are given extra barrel time, up to 100 percent new French oak, and sold primarily through the tasting room and wine club.

The Caraway vineyard, in which Griffin holds a half interest, is an 85-acre site that provides the bulk of his chardonnay. It's also got a few acres each of pinot gris, riesling, sémillon, cabernet sauvignon, and merlot. Relatively cool, it gives grapes a lot of hang time without sugar acceleration. "At one time that was a fault," notes Griffin, ironically adding that "it's now turning into a virtue."

A newer vineyard, near Maryhill in the Columbia Gorge, has been planted to clone 24 cabernet, some zinfandel, and a mix of Rhône varieties. A cooperative project with

Maryhill's owners, it is slated to have its own winery and brand. At the moment, Griffin is making the wines at Barnard Griffin's Richland facility.

Given the astonishing number of wines, vineyards, and winery projects in which Griffin plays a central role, his record for consistently delivering varietal flavors, soundly made wines at every price level, and successful experimentation with such challenging wines as malbec and zinfandel is truly impressive.

The Washington wine industry needs more Rob Griffins. And brand-new wineries, many of whose owners seem to think that a quality statement necessarily begins with a high price tag, might want to consider what sort of a message such hubris sends to consumers. These days, consumers value value, and that is what will continue to make Barnard Griffin one of this state's most successful brands.

BETZ FAMILY

First vintage: 1997

www.betzfamilywinery.com

Bob Betz, the only living Washington State winemaker with an MW (Master of Wine) degree, honed his palate while traveling the globe on behalf of Ste. Michelle and its brands during a career spanning almost three decades with the company. As the company's point man for education and research, he spoke on hundreds of panels and walked the great vineyards of Europe with some of its leading winemakers.

Betz Family winery began as his weekend project, jammed into a tiny, no-frills Woodinville warehouse, total production around 800 to 1,000 cases. But he knew from the start that it would require a full-time commitment to make the wines he could already taste in his imagination. In 2003 he "semi-retired," determined, he told me, "to reclaim parts of my life . . . my garden . . . my wife needs hugging; all those things that time has just eaten away at." His dream winery opened just in time for the 2005 crush; a winery whose every feature has a specific function—to make the best possible wines.

"We face ten critical decisions a day," Betz explains, "and they're not simply on-off. There are always options—which yeast to use? Or the grapes came in at higher alcohol; how much juice do we draw off? Tannin management, punch down, punch over, délestage . . ." he continues, ultimately trailing off into his own thoughts.

Betz Family wines are the brilliant results of such painstaking planning and attention to detail. I once asked Betz how he can make such precise and complex wines while blending from fruit sources so diverse, using as many as five different grapes from four different AVAs. "I blend to a destination," he answered. "If it doesn't hit that destination, I sell it off. If a barrel of finished wine doesn't fit the blend, the only tool I have is selling it off. I don't have a second label."

He sources fruit from the same rows in the same vineyards every year. "Everything that comes into Betz Family fits four criteria," Betz explains. "First, it's got to be a great site; second, a smart grower who understands what it takes to get grapes where you want them; third, a great work ethic and a commitment to farm the land as we design together; and fourth, they must be willing to design a specific area farmed for us and allow us to farm with them."

Betz Family's Père de Famille cabernet sauvignon is a taut, muscular wine, expressing almost pure cabernet sauvignon from Red Mountain fruit, showing exemplary back-of-the-palate grip and concentration, with all the big fruit flavors—plum, cassis, licorice, chocolate, mocha, and more. It is often the most complex and ageworthy wine in the lineup.

The Clos de Betz is the companion wine. With close to 50 percent merlot in the blend, it is usually more open and generous upon release. The vineyard mix ranges from Red Mountain to Horse Heaven Hills to the best of the Yakima Valley, yielding a spicy, toasty, and dense wine packed with berry and cassis fruits.

Le Parrain, the winery's first-ever reserve, began as a single barrel of Red Willow cabernet franc that, Betz explains, "was textural in ways I thought maybe deserved to be bottled separately." It evolved into a six-barrel blend—three of cabernet sauvignon, two of merlot, and the original one of franc. It's a unique effort, offering whiffs of smoke, gun metal, and rock woven through dense red fruits, and may never be repeated.

There were originally just two syrahs—La Côte Rousse, a dark, dense, tannic wine produced from some of the oldest vines on Red Mountain; and La Serenne, sourced from the Boushey (Yakima Valley) vineyard. With an underlayer of game, roasted almond, herb, and earth, La Serenne opens out with decanting, turning silky and supple. What elevates all these Betz wines are their textures, clarity, and sublime complexity. Always carefully structured and beautifully proportioned, they do not overreach, over-extract, or over-fuss with things.

New projects keep surfacing: Bésoleil, a grenache-dominated, southern Rhône red; Chapitre 3, essentially a reserve Côte Rousse; and the newest syrah, La Côte Patriarche. The name honors Mike Sauer (Red Willow vineyard owner) and his longtime collaborator David Lake, the late Columbia winemaker. They were the first to grow and vinify syrah in Washington.

As his wines prove year after year, Betz is a painstaking blender, an MW-level taster, a "complete" winemaker who intimately knows how to work the vineyard, the laboratory, the barrels, and the blending to make superb wines. A cleanliness fanatic, he keeps the barrel room at 50 degrees, does individual monthly SO_2 adjustments, maintains a natural 72 percent humidity, and scribbles a tasting note on every barrel.

Constant improvement is the goal. "There's a chance," he says, "that we haven't yet planted the best vineyard in Washington. That's really exciting! To make wine this good at this stage and still have all these sites to explore. I always go back to what we have here: high light intensity, ample heat during the growing season, dramatic day-night temperature differences during ripening, a general high-stress situation for vines, a long growing season, and a relatively pest-free situation. This is a great area to grow grapes."

BUTY

First vintage: 2000

www.butywinery.com

Caleb and Nina Buty Foster founded their modest Walla Walla winery (it's pronounced "beauty") in 2000, but unlike many of the area's garagistes, they had a wealth of prior winemaking experience. Caleb Foster had spent eight years at Woodward Canyon and worked crush in South Africa and New Zealand, as well as consulted. Beginning with that exceptional background, he has devoted himself to finding ways large and small to tweak his wines and make them even better.

Despite limited resources, and no winery of their own for the first few years, the Fosters made sure to purchase the best possible grapes and to hire consultant Zelma Long to advise them. Working together, they began to explore ways to maximize flavors and textures without using new oak barrels, first in chardonnay and later in their sauvignon blanc–sémillon blend and some of Buty's red wines.

Buty started out at a very competent level, but each year the wines gain something extra in terms of detail and precision; it's clear that the focus on specific vineyards and fermentation techniques is paying off. Buty wines, both white and red, consistently show the sort of nuance and depth that mark the world's best. They keep alcohol levels in check, striving for balance, elegance, and extract. Seamless flavors blend subtle mineral, herbal, and spice components in a style that is clean, a bit lean, polished, complex, and powerful.

A 10-acre estate vineyard is the latest piece of the dream to come into focus. "We spent four or five years looking for the ideal spot in Milton-Freewater—the frost-free zone where the old cherries are," says Caleb Foster. Planted in 2008 and 2009 to syrah, cabernet sauvignon, and what Foster calls "the spice varieties"—mourvèdre, grenache, marsanne, and roussanne—the Rockgarden vineyard is now providing the grapes for Buty's flagship red, Rediviva of the Stones. The vineyard name honors his grandparents

Lincoln and Laura Foster, who for many years served as president and secretary of the American Rock Garden Society.

White wines from Buty are structured for strength, clarity, and concentration. The Conner Lee vineyard chardonnay is always among this state's best. Buty's blend of sémillon and sauvignon blanc (which most recently includes a splash of muscadelle), is focused and fragrant, dense and complex, with exceptional length and viscosity.

The red wines feature tongue-twister names such as Columbia Rediviva and Rediviva of the Stones, or simply list the blend (52% Merlot & 48% Cabernet Franc). Dark, dusty, sappy, and compact, these are muscular and ageworthy. Rediviva of the Stones is roughly half syrah and half cabernet, taking the best flavor components from each. The fruit is blackberry and cassis; and there are scents of leaf, biscuit, and pencil lead.

In 2006 and 2007, Buty released a Champoux vineyard cabernet, their first since 2000. The intention is to make it again each year, as a different source for the Columbia Rediviva has been secured. In addition, Buty's wine club offers a varied and interesting selection of single-vineyard wines under a second label, The Beast. All these wines evoke European breed and elegance, along with a concentration and brightness that speaks specifically of Washington State.

CADENCE

First vintage: 1998

www.cadencewinery.com

Ben Smith is one of several winemakers in this book who learned their craft as members of the Boeing Wine Club. He and his wife, Gaye McNutt, launched their Cadence winery, as many small start-ups do, by contracting grapes from a handful of carefully selected sites. In this instance, it was Red Mountain that they zeroed in on, and by 2004 they were able to

plant their 10-acre Cara Mia vineyard there, under the supervision of Ciel du Cheval's vineyard manager, Ryan Johnson (who now has his own project, Grand Rêve).

Extensive soil studies at thirty-one discrete sites scattered around the small vineyard convinced the owners that they had struck gold. "We have perhaps the most unique and varied soil profiles of any vineyard site on Red Mountain," they enthused. Encouraged, they put in three clones each of cabernet franc, cabernet sauvignon, and merlot and a single clone of petit verdot. Discussions are underway to see if the vineyard can be farmed biodynamically. "The bottom line," says Ben Smith, "is to make better wine."

With the initial (2006 and 2007) releases of the Cara Mia vineyard wines, Smith's confidence has been proven where it counts most—in the bottle. The Cadence Camerata is mostly cabernet sauvignon, sharp and intense, with tightly wound red fruit scents, annotated with leaf and white pepper. The Cadence Bel Canto is split between cabernet franc and merlot and has a juicy center of ripe blackberry and black cherry fruit. Both wines see 50 percent new oak for 18 months.

Cadence also continues to produce red blends from Ciel du Cheval and Tapteil, two of the oldest sites on Red Mountain. What particularly distinguishes Ben Smith's winemaking is the nuanced complexity of the aromas he coaxes out of his young wines. Bouquet is something that great wines develop over time, and young wines, even the best ones, rarely show more than a glimmer of what lies ahead. But sniffing through Cadence releases, I am struck by their detail, even when made from young vines.

The Ciel du Cheval vineyard red blend is elegant and refined, showing scents of dusty coffee, cocoa, and mocha; streaks of chalk, limestone, gravel, and pencil lead; mixed fruits and hints of expressive spice. The Tapteil red, also a Bordeaux blend, is distinguished by a certain dustiness, and an elegant structure whose lightness belies its power. Not the darkest nor the biggest of the Cadence wines, the Tapteil vineyard designates may prove to be among the longest-lived.

Other than a side project for Grand Rêve, Smith and McNutt do not intend to expand into more wines, or more case volume, than they have already comfortably reached—about 2,300 cases total, much of it a pretty, forward, less expensive press wine named Coda. They self-distribute in Washington, but their wines have earned a place on some rarified Manhattan wine lists, alongside Quilceda Creek, Betz Family, and Buty. Good company to keep, and Cadence fits right in.

CAYUSE VINEYARDS

First vintage: 1997

www.cayusevineyards.com

As one of the first, and arguably most influential, of the French-born and trained vignerons to emigrate to Walla Walla, Christophe Baron has dramatically influenced the prevailing ideas about where to plant grapes, which grapes to plant, and how the health of the land is expressed through the flavors of the finished wine.

Cayuse Vineyards has one of the prettiest little tasting rooms on Main Street in downtown Walla Walla, but don't bother going there. Never open, it exists

only for the winery to maintain a Washington bond. Though Cayuse is widely regarded as a Washington winery, the vineyards and winery are in Oregon, in the area west of Milton-Freewater now known as the Rocks.

Baron's family ties are in the Marne Valley, where they own the Champagne house Baron Albert. With a father, two uncles, and several other family members lined up in front of him, young Christophe realized that he would have better luck pursuing his winemaking dreams elsewhere. After studying viticulture and enology in Champagne and Burgundy, he traveled to Oregon and worked briefly at Adelsheim, then interned at Waterbrook in Walla Walla, and spent some time commuting to winemaking assignments in Australia, New Zealand, and Romania. He returned to Walla Walla for good in 1996.

Once he discovered his vineyard sites (profiled in chapter 4), he knew he'd found the right place to make wine his way, free from restraints. Since 2000, all Cayuse wines have been entirely estate-grown, but it wasn't until 2005 that Baron could afford to build his own winery, La Boîte—what he calls "a simple metal box."

From the beginning, Baron's overriding goal has been vineyard development and, specifically, biodynamic farming. He is a passionate man, never more so than when speaking of his biodynamic principles. "When you use forces of death in your vineyard—nasty chemicals—you end up with nasty strains of yeast, and you deal with the risk of stuck fermentation," he explains. "*Biodynamie* is dealing with forces of life, not forces of death. So when I bring the fruit and crush it into my fermenters, I have no worries; it may take some time but it will finish. Three months, so what? You have to wait, and you bottle it when it's finished. That's OK. It's being low-key and not forcing steps. There's life in each bottle, liquid life. You have to respect that."

Cayuse makes about 3,000 cases annually of a dozen or so wines, vineyard-designated and biodynamically raised. Baron's license plate, which reads WWSYRAH, gives a clear indication of his priorities. Small amounts of an excellent rosé and a Cailloux vineyard viognier (now discontinued) are the only nonreds. ("If there is one more white wine I'd like to produce it's riesling," he confesses, "but I'll leave it to the Germans.") The wines are pre-sold to a long-closed mailing list and previewed once a year, on a weekend recently moved from November to early April.

Biodynamic farming; extremely low yields (rarely more than 1.5 tons an acre); wild yeast ("We enhance the life in the vineyards, so our yeasts are healthy; when you use the same strain of yeast, they all taste the same"); daily sampling of every tank during fermentation; experiments with both round and oval concrete fermenters ("They're neutral—you can't hide anything—the juice that we taste coming out of these fermenters is as naked as young wine can be"); no fining or filtering; and very limited use of new oak—all contribute to the uniqueness of the Cayuse wines. They include individual syrahs from Cailloux, En Chamberlin, En Cerise, and Armada, as well as the iconic Bionic Frog, a funky, umami-soaked smorgasbord of charcuterie, bacon fat, soy, seaweed, mulch, chocolate, balsamic—basically, the entire aroma wheel in a bottle.

Camaspelo, Cayuse's Bordeaux blend, is another potpourri of scents and flavors—bay leaf, cut herbs, and a mix of fruits that runs from spicy cranberry to red apple, cherry, plum, and on into semitropical with hints of papaya. The Widowmaker cabernet sauvignon, from En Chamberlin, smacks of cassis and a bit of boysenberry, with an unusual iodine–oyster shell finish. There is a pure tempranillo, Impulsivo, with a pretty, floral nose, more scents of cured meats, some saltiness, and very dark fruit flavors suffused with smoke and tar. The God Only Knows Grenache, which I sense gives Baron more grief and pleasure than any of his other wines, has more sweet, deep, berry flavors, without sacrificing minerality and definition.

In 2007, says Baron, he made his first French vintage in Walla Walla, citing the moderate brix at harvest, matched to excellent physiological ripeness. "You cannot get any better than that," he offers in thickly accented English. "You need alcohol in wine, but it's not the most important thing." Indisputably, the most important thing to this driven vigneron is what he calls "an ancestral way of farming—a complete antithesis to the International style. Purity, integrity, and personality are being lost," he insists, proudly adding, "I don't want to be part of globalization."

CHATEAU STE. MICHELLE

First vintage: 1967

www.ste-michelle.com

Though varietal wines under the Ste. Michelle label were not introduced until 1967, the brand can trace its roots back to Repeal. Capturing such a rich history, along with the growth of the holding company that is now the seventh largest wine company in the country (Ste. Michelle Wine Estates), is beyond the limits of this book. But even a brief survey of the Ste. Michelle brand, and its more limited releases (Ethos, Eroica, the Artist Series reds, the vineyard-designates), provides insight as to why it is unquestionably the most important and influential winery in Washington history.

Tobacco giant UST purchased the Ste. Michelle winery and brand in 1974 and immediately set about expanding its vineyard and winery holdings. In the mid-1980s the parent company launched Stimson Lane under the direction of CEO Allen Shoup, who acquired a diversified, worldwide portfolio of wineries and winemaking alliances. Shoup retired in 2000, and Ted Baseler took over as president and CEO, restructuring the company and tightening its focus on Washington state.

Stimson Lane was renamed Ste. Michelle Wine Estates in 2004. The company now includes in its portfolio six of the seven largest Washington wineries, along with smaller, prestige properties such as Northstar, Spring Valley Vineyards, and wineries in California and Oregon. Chateau Ste. Michelle remains the flagship brand, producing more than two million cases annually—half of it riesling. Its releases cover a broad portfolio ranging from inexpensive varietal wines, to limited single-vineyard chardonnays, merlots, and cabernets, to showcase reserve wines and high-profile collaborative ventures such as Eroica.

Generous with its talent and resources, inclusive in its marketing, and always committed to the larger goal of creating an image of world-class quality for the entire region, Ste. Michelle's managers and winemakers have benchmarked the best wineries in the world, determined to join their ranks. The many different wine labels and tiers are portrayed, more or less accurately, as the products of numerous smaller wineries within the big winery. Ste. Michelle is fond of pointing out that it views its overall size as an asset, giving the company the widest possible range of choices for each individual project.

Nonetheless, there have been some hiccups along the way. During a run of vintages from 2001 through 2003, the red wines suffered a serious decline, becoming tannic, chewy, thin, and leathery. A new winemaker, Bob Bertheau, was hired in 2003, at first to make white wines, but quickly to oversee all production. It is now possible to taste the impact he is having on the entire line of Ste. Michelle wines.

To begin, Bertheau's five different chardonnays are beautifully crafted and distinctive, with better integration of the oak and more softness and complexity in the mouth than their predecessors. The top-of-the-line "Ethos" chardonnay has intriguing streaks of orange peel and citrus zest, along with buttered nuts, toast, and hazelnut flavors, all threaded through the long, silky finish. The Cold Creek chardonnay, which has always delivered extra intensity, drills down into the heart of the palate with refreshing acids and crisply defined fruit.

Ste. Michelle is the biggest producer of riesling in the world, from its widely available Columbia Valley bottling, to vineyard-designates from Indian Wells and Cold Creek, to the Eroica project, a riesling collaboration with Ernst Loosen of the Mosel's Dr. Loosen estate. Eroica recently celebrated its tenth vintage with a stunning retrospective that included not only the regular rieslings but six vintages of the TBA-styled Single Berry Select.

Among its modestly priced varietals, Ste. Michelle consistently delivers soundly made, varietally correct, lively wines. The Indian Wells bottlings, priced just a few dollars higher, are especially good values; the chardonnay and merlot are outstanding. The single-vineyard offerings from Canoe Ridge and Cold Creek—both vineyards have recently been expanded—are distinctive and cellar-worthy; and a perennial favorite is the fresh, spicy sauvignon blanc from the Horse Heaven vineyard.

The Ethos wines are Ste. Michelle's reserve tier, offering chardonnay, cabernet sauvignon, merlot, and syrah. Though well made, round and ripe, and often showing a fair

A DECADE OF EROICA

The prospect of joining a vertical tasting of every vintage of Eroica lured a motley group of writers to the winery's library room on a cloudy weekday afternoon in August 2009. Winemakers Ernst Loosen, Bob Bertheau, and Wendy Stuckey were in attendance, and all ten vintages, from 1999 up through the just-released 2008, were poured together, so we could sniff and swoozle our way through them at our own pace.

I skipped around vintages, first getting a sense of aromas, then dipping into flavors, going back and forth and jotting notes as I did. In the discussion that followed, everyone agreed that all ten wines were drinking well; there is no question that well-made Washington riesling can age for a long, long time. Better yet, the oldest vintages, from 1999, 2000, and 2001, had developed fascinating aromas. My notes on the 1999 read: "Spicy scents of pine needles, apple, some buttery banana, caramel; inviting and rounded out. Delicate in the mouth, with fine details of spice." For 2001: "Light honey, apple, pear, and peach—lovely fruits, spice, good length and elegance."

The 1999 and 2000 Eroicas were 60 percent Cold Creek vineyard grapes; but Bertheau and Loosen have increasingly moved the blend to favor grapes from cooler, higher-elevation sites. The 2007 Eroica, whose youthful, primary fruits and scents are already delicious, was half from the Evergreen vineyard (in the Ancient Lakes region), the rest a mix of Yakima Valley, Horse Heaven Hills, and Columbia Valley sites.

Overall, the cool vintages (1999, 2001, 2007, 2008) were my favorites. The middle years (2002–2006) seemed less complex, a bit fatter, and in some instances, oversulfured. But it could also just be a transitional phase. Eroica seems to require at least eight years to evolve into a mature wine; otherwise, it's best to drink it very young, when the freshness of the fruits and acids is at its peak.

A second vertical presented all six vintages of the Eroica Single Berry Select. This is a late-harvest, botrytis-affected, unctuous dessert wine modeled after the legendary TBAs of Germany. The wines came from vintages 1999, 2000, 2001, 2005, 2006, and 2007. What happened to the middle vintages? I asked. Apparently, there was too much of the 2001 stacking up unsold, so production was halted—a mistake, says Loosen, who argues that the wine shouldn't even be released until it's at least a decade old.

The oldest bottles were in fact showing significant improvement over the younger bottles. They had acquired a lovely, burnished mahogany color, with complex aromas of candied fruits, marmalade, honey, toasted nuts, caramel, sometimes vanilla cream or burnt sugar. The younger vintages were loaded with fruit and sugar, concentrated and long, but primary and not yet knit together. My favorite of the flight was the 2001, the darkest and most thickly unctuous of them all. Second favorite was the 2000, a smooth mix of candied fruits, honey, orange marmalade, butter, acid, and caramel.

amount of buttery oak, they lack the individuality and distinctive terroir of the single-vineyard wines. Chardonnay is Bertheau's strongest suit, and Ethos his finest effort.

Late in 2008, Ste. Michelle owner UST was acquired by an even larger tobacco company, Altria, and there has been a long, uncomfortable pause while the entire Washington wine industry has waited for the other shoe to drop. Rumors abound, though CEO Ted Baseler insists that Ste. Michelle is highly profitable and not likely to be sold off. Altria's chief executive, Michael Szymanczyk, has been quoted as saying, "Our position is that, for now, we are going to keep that business." More troubling, a press release explained that Altria would "hold on to its wine unit . . . because it wouldn't currently fetch enough in a sale." Ouch! That is less than reassuring.

Given its historic importance and dominant role in the development of the Washington wine industry, and the dynamic leadership and winemaking talent now running Ste. Michelle Wine Estates, which is the fastest-growing top-10 wine company in America, it would seem foolish for any ownership organization to rock the boat.

DELILLE CELLARS

First vintage: 1992

www.delillecellars.com

From the beginning DeLille's founders—Charles and Greg Lill, winemaker Chris Upchurch, and Jay Soloff—embodied the ideal mix of marketing magic and winemaking savvy. DeLille developed from a tiny start-up modeled on the best chateaux of Bordeaux (right down to its second label, named D2 for the highway running through the Médoc) to a present-day portfolio of brilliantly conceived, expressive wines. Encapsulated in that arc is the history of Washington's evolution—from an industry dominated by farmer-growers, to one whose quest for quality was largely driven by garagiste wineries such as this, to the present day—when the ideal of using estate-grown fruit is paramount.

DeLille Cellars occupies a picture-postcard setting, from the restored 1890s farmhouse to the meadow dotted with lazily grazing sheep and the occasional peacock. The lovely 10-acre site, high above the Woodinville Valley floor, overlooks Chateau Ste. Michelle and Columbia winery. What it lacked was a vineyard. That was addressed in the spring of 2001, when an 18-acre parcel adjacent to Ciel du Cheval (on Red Mountain) was planted to a mix of three cabernet clones and two syrah clones. Named Grand Ciel, it's tucked into the same sweet spot as Quilceda Creek's Galitzine vineyard, and managed by Ciel's Ryan Johnson.

PRODUCED AND BOTTLED BY DeLILLE CELLARS
WOODINVILLE, WASHINGTON
750ml, YAKIMA VALLEY RED WINE, Alc. 14.9% by vol.

Clonal research is the new viticultural frontier in Washington State. "The one thing all vineyards face," Upchurch explains, "is the potential for uneven ripening, when it doesn't happen in that magic moment that great Bordeaux gets. The idea we had from the start was to get grapes to ripen evenly. Everything was done with the idea that it is possible to get even ripening here in Washington."

They wasted no time making a Grand Ciel cabernet sauvignon, using grapes from the first harvest in 2004. And the wine delivered as promised: 100 percent varietal, pure and concentrated—a complete wine from a single grape and vineyard. The follow-up 2005 and 2006 releases of Grand Ciel confirm that this vineyard captures both varietal character as well as classic Red Mountain highlights of rock and iron. It has the muscle and concentration to develop in bottle over 15 to 20 years. "I think it's the ultimate test of a terroir wine," says Upchurch. "You blend every grape you've got with it, and every grape brings diminishment. I tried every grape I could; if I could improve this wine I'd do it, but . . ."

Chaleur Estate remains the flagship DeLille white and red; with the advantage of sourcing from older vines. The white wine is two-thirds sauvignon blanc and one-third sémillon, from Boushey, Sagemoor, and Klipsun grapes. Upchurch is pulling back on the new oak, a welcome adjustment, and the most recent release is crisper and more steely, with alcohol under 14 percent. Chaleur Estate's red is consistently about two-thirds cabernet sauvignon, one-quarter merlot, and the rest cabernet franc and petit verdot. A subtle and sleek wine, tightly closed upon release, it moves closer with each new vintage to becoming the iconic melding of Washington fruit with Bordeaux classicism.

DeLille's Harrison Hill red wine, also a Bordeaux blend, is sourced from the second-oldest vinifera vines in the state, planted in the early 1960s in what is now the Snipes Mountain AVA. A graceful mix of old-vine bramble, Yakima Valley herbs, and other peppery spices, with dry tannins redolent of Earl Gray tea, this supremely elegant wine wears its flavors like an immaculately tailored suit.

D2 is DeLille's second wine, a declassified wine in the best possible sense—the grapes come from all of the winery's premier vineyard sources, including Ciel du Cheval, Klipsun, Kiona, Harrison Hill, Boushey, Stillwater Creek, Red Willow, and Grand Ciel. Usually half merlot, it is a good barometer for the vintage. From year to year D2 can be ripe or herbal, hot or soft; in superb years such as 2006 and 2007, it is replete with tart red fruits, moist earth, and hints of tar and licorice.

Most recently, a second estate vineyard project, a collaboration with Dick Boushey, has been planted across from the Otis vineyard in the heart of the Yakima Valley. Upchurch also has his own Red Mountain vineyard, on a lower, west-facing flank, again planted under the guidance of Dick Boushey.

DeLille Cellars production is holding steady at 5,000 cases, and the Woodinville chateau is now open for visitors daily. In the autumn of 2009, the owners opened their Carriage House Tasting Gallery just down the road from the chateau, joining a growing nucleus of wineries that already includes J. Bookwalter, Mark Ryan, Ross Andrew, Dusted Valley, Brian Carter, Precept Brands, and several others.

DUNHAM CELLARS

First vintage: 1995

www.dunhamcellars.com

Dunham Cellars is still located at the Walla Walla airport, where it was one of the first wineries to hang a shingle, and just the eighth winery (or ninth, depending on who is telling the story) bonded in Walla Walla. The facility has grown substantially and now includes a separate building for fermentation, a comfy tasting room, and an art gallery and lounge, where wine club events, winemaker dinners, and occasional live music concerts are held.

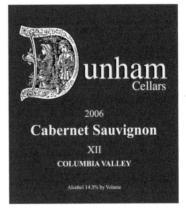

Eric Dunham is the face of the brand, and still the senior winemaker, though day-to-day wine-making duties have been handed off to Dan Wampfler, a former assistant winemaker at Ste. Michelle's Canoe Ridge and Columbia Crest. When Dunham and his parents started the winery, his background consisted primarily of a Hogue internship and a few years as an assistant winemaker at L'Ecole. Dunham Cellars' first vintage, 200 cases of 1995 cabernet, was made while he was still working at L'Ecole; the Dunham winery did not open until 1999.

Dunham wines were exceptional right from the start, and the cabernets, numbered with Roman numerals, were the first from Walla Walla to achieve national notoriety from a brand-new producer since the early days of Leonetti and Woodward Canyon. One hundred percent varietal, with dense, sappy, supple, silky flavors of wild berries and black cherries, the cabs showcased that mix of power and precision that Washington fruit can deliver so well.

In 1999 a Lewis vineyard syrah was introduced, from an exciting new vineyard just north of Prosser in the Yakima Valley. From the start it has been a dazzler, packed with fleshy blackberry fruit and sweet, toasty oak. Big, peppery, and profound, the Lewis syrah proved that Dunham was no one-trick pony. Lewis vineyard chardonnay, riesling, cabernet sauvignon, and merlot have all joined the syrah and are as definitive and essential to the brand as the original cabernet.

Production has reached 15,000 cases. Three-fifths goes into lower-priced labels: Three Legged Red, Four Legged White, and Trutina, a cabernet-merlot table wine. The Columbia Valley cabernet and Columbia Valley syrah account for most of the rest, with the single-vineyard and roman numeral cabs filling out the high end.

Quality has remained consistent through fifteen vintages. Dunham syrahs are exciting wines, purple at the rim, black at the core, spicy, and penetrating, the flavors a fine and textural mix of citrus oil, raspberry, cassis, cinnamon, and toast. Though the Lewis is the topper, recent vineyard-designates from Frenchtown and Double River were strikingly bold, meaty wines, not afraid to show a little funk.

Frenchtown, the 10-acre estate vineyard, was planted in 2000 to cabernet sauvignon, syrah, and cabernet franc. Double River (27 acres adjacent to Basel Cellars) had been leased; 2009 is the last fruit to go to Dunham. The Lewis vineyard remains the source of the winery's best grapes; it is on a long-term lease. Buckley Terrace (two acres next to L'Ecole No 41) is another leased site, planted to cabernet sauvignon and syrah. A new project, Kenny Hill—35 acres near Leonetti's Mill Creek Upland vineyard—was just planted to cabernet sauvignon, merlot, syrah, and malbec and, once established, will be dry-farmed.

Eric Dunham's wide-ranging talents include cooking and painting, as the massive canvases on the walls of the lounge (many also used for his artist-label wines) attest. Dale Chihuly is a friend and mentor. Actor Kyle MacLachlan is another celebrity whom Dunham counts as a close friend; the two men are collaborating on a red wine project called ". . . pursued by bear."

With Lewis vineyard fruit, a second label (Three Legged Red) that soaks up excess barrels and generates excellent cash flow, a multitalented winemaker with celebrity connections, and one of the best music room–winery clubhouses in Walla Walla, Dunham is one of Washington's don't-miss wineries.

FIELDING HILLS

First vintage: 2000

www.fieldinghills.com

Fielding Hills may be the least-visible great winery in Washington. Mike and Karen Wade were well-established apple growers long before they began planting their Riverbend property to wine grapes in 1998. Located a few miles southeast of Mattawa, in the heart of the Wahluke Slope AVA, Riverbend includes 10 acres of cabernet sauvignon, 5 of merlot, 2 of cabernet franc, 5 of syrah, and just a smattering of recently planted carmenère, all surrounded by 135 acres of apples. A bit of malbec may be added in 2010.

FIELDING HILLS

Cabernet Sauvignon

RIVERBEND VINEYARD · WAHLUKE SLOPE

2007

When he realized he was going to try to make wine, Mike Wade signed up for a class or two at UC

Davis; mostly he learned his winemaking by working alongside Charlie Hoppes (Fidélitas) and Gordon Venneri (Walla Walla Vintners). The Fielding Hills label debuted in 2000, and the wines have been entirely estate-grown ever since.

Without exception over the first eight vintages, Fielding Hills wines have been stunningly brilliant. So good, that it makes you wonder how many other exceptional vineyards may be hiding in Washington, selling grapes (or growing cherries) rather than making their own wines. The fact is that Fielding Hills is using just a small percentage of the vineyard's production. The Wades make fewer than 1,000 cases of Fielding Hills wines, though the vineyard produces enough fruit for five times that much.

Initially, they sold grapes to Three Rivers and Hogue. Not until 2006, says Karen Wade, did people want more of their grapes than they had grapes to sell, but now Riverbend fruit is sought after by a number of Wenatchee- and Chelan-area wineries. "I'm not sure we ever thought about vineyard recognition," she admits. Mike Wade is similarly low-key. "We take it at the speed we want," he says. "It takes a lot of pressure off, because we're not putting food on the table with it. We've struggled with where do we go from here and still keep it fun."

I've tasted every vintage of every Fielding Hills release, and I remain extremely impressed by the balance, clarity, definition, and complexity they show across the entire lineup. Mike Wade clearly has a natural talent for crafting elegant, expressive wines. Checking my notes on the thirty that I have scored for *Wine Enthusiast* magazine, I see that all but four rated 90 points or higher. That is flat-out amazing for any winery, let alone one that is brand-new.

The merlots are brilliant, polished, beautifully nuanced wines that can stand alongside the best I've ever tasted from this state. The syrahs, which include a bit of cabernet and merlot in the blend, are supple, silky, and plump, with luscious fruit wrapped in powerful, toasty and buttery new oak. The winery's cabernet sauvignons, cabernet francs, and Riverbend Tribute red (a blend of cabernet, merlot, and syrah) all follow suit; across the board these are supple, juicy, compact, supremely generous.

Fielding Hills proves the primacy of vineyards; the winery is simply a converted orchard shop near the owners' home in East Wenatchee. Plans for a new, improved winery, says Karen Wade, "have not left paper. Too much red tape and no time to fight City Hall!"

JANUIK

First vintage: 1999

www.januikwinery.com

Mike Januik began his wine career as a retailer at a wine shop in Ashland, Oregon, then tried his hand at amateur winemaking, studied at UC Davis, and took his first professional job at (now-defunct) Stewart Vineyards. Januik worked only three vintages there

(1984–86) before moving on to Langguth, Snoqualmie and later Chateau Ste. Michelle. But he made an indelible impression.

Some years ago, I asked owner Martha Stewart (not that Martha Stewart!) about Januik as a young winemaker. "Having Mike for a winemaker," she replied, "was sort of like asking an inexperienced painter to paint the ceiling of your rec room, and then learning that his name is Michelangelo." Januik himself would be embarrassed at such praise, for he is among the most unassuming winemakers I have ever known. But his talent, unmistakable from the very beginning, has finally brought him the ultimate reward: a gorgeous new winery with his name on the front door.

Actually, the name on the front door reads Novelty Hill–Januik, for it is home to both brands. Januik makes all the wines, including 4,000 cases of Januik whites and reds and another 5,100 cases of Novelty Hill. The ultramodern facility, which presents a rather stolid concrete face to the highway, is quite impressive on the inside.

It sports a full quota of the best winemaker toys (a dry fog machine, computer-monitored fermentation tanks, an Italian bottling line), two large barrel rooms, a sleek and open tasting room, a full kitchen, and four private rooms for special dinners and events. In one of them is a grand, 24-foot-long tasting table, fashioned from reclaimed old-growth timber. The landscaped grounds back onto a creek and border the Columbia winery on the north.

His years making wine for Chateau Ste. Michelle gave Januik the opportunity to explore many of Washington's emerging wine regions while accessing grapes from top vineyards such as Cold Creek. Since starting the Januik winery in 1999, he has continued to use fruit from Cold Creek in his cabernets and chardonnays and has added other top-tier vineyard sources, notably Elerding, Champoux, Klipsun, Ciel du Cheval, Seven Hills, and Weinbau.

Januik's white wines are limited to a pair of chardonnays, both graceful and elegant. The Cold Creek designate is tightly structured, with green apple and spiced pear fruit and a lively finish with butterscotch and hazelnut crème. The Elerding vineyard chardonnay shows pineapple, apple, and sweet citrus fruit, tastefully mixed with spicy herb and racy acids.

Red wines are his principal focus. Januik merlots are tight, textured, vertically integrated wines, with more character and snap than most broadly fruity Washington examples. The Klipsun designate is the bottle to buy; its tannins are well managed and mediated, smooth with no roughness or excessively green flavors. The vineyard, Januik admits, has a reputation for producing hard, astringent wines, but, he says, "I handle the fruit differently than most people. I know people that macerate for 30 days; ours are just a week or so."

Januik's Lewis syrahs are saturated, sappy, and precise. He also makes one of Washington's rare varietal petit verdots, from Ciel du Cheval grapes. But his vineyard-designated cabernets are the superstars here. The entry-level Columbia Valley cabernet uses premium grapes from the same sources as his designates: Champoux, Ciel du

Cheval, Seven Hills, and others. Among the single-vineyard wines, it is impossible to choose a favorite, but Januik's first-ever reserve red, a barrel selection blend of Champoux and Weinbau grapes, is the wine he calls "best of the best" and the wine Januik fans have been anticipating for decades.

✱ K VINTNERS

First vintage: 1999

www.kvintners.com

No humble start-up winery in the past decade can match the record that K Vintners founder and impresario Charles Smith has set for growth, financial success, and celebrity status.

A native Californian, Smith spent more than a decade managing Danish rock bands, touring Europe constantly, and wining and dining in style. "It was the classic rock-and-roll life," he recalls— "out late, sleep late." Sometime in 1998—while on a West Coast tour with his band—he left the rock-and-roll life and (briefly) ran a wine shop on Bainbridge Island, near Seattle. That led to an invitation to a dinner party in Walla Walla, where he met Christophe Baron of Cayuse. Baron encouraged Smith to try his hand at making wine there. It seemed like the right sort of place—"a town that thrives on the production of sustenance for people," as Smith describes it.

With $5,000 in his pocket and only a vague notion of how to start a winery, Smith made his first wines the following year, with generous assistance from Baron. Two years later K Vintners opened its doors, near Abeja and Walla Walla Vintners on a historic property east of town that still includes the original 1872 farmhouse. A small vineyard is out in front, but the winery itself is nothing special—just a rather plain shed with a barrel room and tasting table (crushing and fermentation are done elsewhere). Other than a giant "K" in front of the vineyard, the most remarkable thing about K Vintners was—and still is—Charles Smith himself.

His flame-throwing persona—the wild hair, the hyperkinetic enthusiasm, the rock 'n' roll attitude—has certainly played a part in his success. Coupled with his experienced and well-traveled palate, his sixth sense for finding great vineyard sources, and his genius for marketing, it has made him a media favorite. But all that aside, the real key to Smith's success is that his wines not only offer good flavor at a good price but all come with a great story. They give consumers the feeling of being a part of some exciting creative venture, of partaking of Smith's larger-than-life personality, if only through the medium of his wines. Most of all, they bring with them an attitude—clearly based on that rock-and-roll life—that wine should at all times be fun to drink.

K Vintners was just the beginning, as Smith's empire includes a lucrative joint venture with Precept Brands, his own Charles Smith wines, and a still-newer project with Charles Bieler (of Three Thieves). K Vintners' focus is syrah, and there are as many as fifteen different syrahs and syrah blends in a single vintage. To a bottle, K wines are succulent, delicious, and well delineated. The kanji-inspired labels—a stark black slash reads "K" on a plain white background—the silly puns (K syrah indeed), the quirky, boastful names (The Beautiful, The Creator, The Hustler), and the nonmainstream flavors reflect the man himself.

"The idea [of my label design] was to communicate the language of wine to people who don't speak wine," Smith explains. "Back in the old days, they'd have a brand for their livestock; this is like a brand. The letter 'K' is a big-bodied letter, two arms, two legs; it's strong and sturdy. It's anchored to the ground, solid, real; you can't knock a 'K' over. It suggests the wines are strong, balanced, potent."

That they are. The syrahs are joined by a razor-sharp viognier; an exotically perfumed grenache ("The Boy"); a trio of cabernet-syrah blends, mostly from Cayuse vineyard grapes; a tempranillo-cabernet blend; a pinot noir (not yet released); and other, ongoing experiments. Though Cayuse provided much of the fruit and also a winemaking home for K through the 2008 vintage, the growth of both wineries means they've now gone their separate ways. K Vintners is not likely to expand much past the 4,500 cases it now makes; Smith has many other outlets for high-volume wines. At K, he reminds visitors, every wine is made with native yeast, foot-crushed, basket-pressed, and aged in 100 percent French oak.

Smith does not claim to be a technical winemaker. "I don't look at numbers or percentages," he says, "because neither do the people who are buying the wine. I'm making the wines about the feel—like when you are cooking. You really need not to lose sight of the fact that you are making wine for people to drink. It starts in the vineyard, a good site, the right yields, the packaging. It's every single thing. Like a relay race. You can't win the race if any of the runners drops the baton. We never drop the baton."

❋ L'ECOLE NO 41

First vintage: 1983

www.lecole.com

L'Ecole No 41 is the renovated schoolhouse–turned-winery that greets visitors to Walla Walla as they drive east on Highway 12 toward town. Marty and Megan Clubb took over the winery from her parents, who began it as a retirement project in the early 1980s. The third winery to open its doors in Walla Walla, it remains one of the most important, for its history, its vineyards, its forward-thinking owners, and most of all, its wines.

I've entertained many questions about what might be Washington's signature grape, or what my guess is for the next trendy varietal. Sometimes it is more instructive to think about the most notable underperformers. L'Ecole has made its mark with arguably the two most neglected and underappreciated white wine grapes in the country—chenin blanc and sémillon. And that is just the beginning of the long list of successes here.

L'Ecole is now a 37,000-case operation, one of just a few family-owned Washington wineries with a significant national (all fifty states) and international (twenty countries) presence. Two-thirds of the total production is devoted to what Marty Clubb calls the Columbia Valley wines—chenin blanc, sémillon, chardonnay, syrah, merlot, and cabernet sauvignon. "We like being a Walla Walla winery," he says, "but we've lived through the 'bite-us-in-the-behind' winters too. The Columbia Valley lineup protects us economically. It's the value side of our brand, our volume."

The other third comprises Walla Walla Valley varietal wines. The 200-acre Seven Hills vineyard, in which L'Ecole is a partner with Leonetti and Pepper Bridge, provides sémillon, merlot, cabernet sauvignon, and syrah. A new estate vineyard named Ferguson Ridge is higher up the same slopes. Ten acres have already been planted, part of the massive SeVein vineyard project. Non-estate Walla Walla grapes come from Pepper Bridge, Va Piano, Loess, and Yellow Jacket vineyards.

Partnering with his hands-on winemaker, Mike Sharon, who replaced Eric Dunham at L'Ecole in 1996, Clubb makes about 1,600 cases of the Walla Voila chenin blanc. He insists he could sell even more, if the 30-year-old Rattlesnake Hills vineyard could produce more fruit. Walla Voila is a delightful throwback to the early days of Washington winemaking when chenin was a popular off-dry white wine intended as a tasting-room take on Vouvray.

Three different dry sémillons are produced, along with a late-harvest version in some years. The Columbia Valley blends in up to 20 percent sauvignon blanc; it's rich and ripe with pear and melon fruit flavors. The Seven Hills vineyard bottling is barrel-fermented and displays lush, ripe, rich, round, peachy-citrus fruit, while the Fries Vineyard sémillon is often the biggest, creamiest, and oakiest of all. The winery's version of a Bordeaux blanc is called Luminesce, a blend of sémillon and sauvignon blanc that is bursting with fresh pears, orange peel, hints of banana, and toast.

Among the numerous red wines, says Clubb, "merlot is still king at L'Ecole. His Columbia Valley merlot is a Right Bank–styled blend that includes 12 percent cab franc, with a smattering of cabernet sauvignon, petit verdot, and sometimes carmenère. The Seven Hills vineyard merlot is more tannic and sculpted, with cedary, silky black cherry fruit. Along with these wines, the Seven Hills–designated syrah, cabernet franc (wine club only), and Perigee (an old-vine Bordeaux blend) are generally L'Ecole's best wines in most vintages. The two cabernets—one Columbia Valley, the other Walla Walla Valley—are also fine expressions of elegant, old-vine grapes and polished winemaking, both 100 percent varietal.

✳ LEONETTI CELLAR

First vintage: 1978

www.leonetticellar.com

In 1974, Gary and Nancy Figgins planted an acre of cabernet and riesling in their backyard on the outskirts of Walla Walla. Little did they realize that their little vineyard project was a harbinger of a revitalized local wine industry that had lain dormant since Prohibition. After a few more vintages of amateur winemaking, the Figginses bonded Leonetti Cellar in 1977, the first vinifera winery to open in Walla Walla since Repeal. Eleven years later, Gary was able to retire from his day job as a machinist at Continental Can and devote himself completely to wine-making.

Early on, he'd decided to focus on just three or four red wines a year, with the goal of one day using grapes exclusively from Walla Walla vineyards. Though success came quickly and continuously, it wasn't until the late 1990s, as Leonetti Cellar wines profited from a growing national reputation, that a series of land purchases brought substantial vineyard holdings into the fold. It started when Chris Figgins, who had just earned his degree in horticulture from Washington State University, was driving along Mill Creek Road and spotted a for-sale sign on a south-facing hillside. He pulled the sign out of the ground, tossed it in his truck, and raced home, convinced he'd found the perfect vineyard location.

The following year the land, now the Mill Creek Upland vineyard, was planted to cabernet sauvignon, merlot, sangiovese, and petit verdot. Mill Creek Upland grapes have dominated Leonetti's reserve blend in recent vintages and serve as the backbone of the cabernet as well. A second location, at the expanded Seven Hills vineyard, was acquired in partnership with L'Ecole's Marty Clubb and Pepper Bridge's Norm McKibben. The third estate vineyard, the 28-acre Loess vineyard, located directly behind the winery, was added in 2002. It has the same general mix of grapes as Mill Creek, along with a tiny bit of malbec and viognier (the latter wine is made strictly for home consumption). Loess grapes are also sold to Northstar, Pepper Bridge, L'Ecole, Long Shadows (Sequel syrah), and Waters.

The 32-acre C. S. Figgins estate is a fourth project, just a bit east of Mill Creek Upland. First to go into the ground (in 2005) were 11 acres of merlot, the final step to reaching the long-held goal of using Walla Walla Valley fruit exclusively. In 2007, that dream came true. Chris Figgins, who was officially made Leonetti winemaker in 2006, completed his first full Figgins estate harvest in 2008. Along with the Leonetti wines, he is introducing his own brand with a single vineyard Bordeaux blend named FIGGINS that will be released in 2011.

I can't overstate the difficulty of the transition that Leonetti's owners have made in recent years. Though using all-Walla fruit is an admirable goal, it meant trading some older- grapes for younger-vine ones. At the same time, a transition to a second-generation winemaker with ideas of his own has been smoothly completed.

"Chris has long jumped out of my shadow," Gary Figgins confided in a 2007 interview. "That thrills me immensely, and spells big for the future of Leonetti. The wine business is not something you really retire from; even though somebody else is doing the heavy lifting, you're in there with your intellect, vision, and offering up consultation, remembering when the same thing happened and you did this or that." "We're growing up," says Chris Figgins. "There were a lot of guys like my dad; they had to scrape together what grapes they could from bigger growers; they started with no land and little capital."

Based on his first few vintages, I'd say Chris Figgins is improving the ageability of Leonetti wines while retaining the lush fruit and expressive barrel flavors that make them so irresistible. It's taken a few years for the new vineyards to mature. "When we shifted [to estate vines], the wines were good, but they didn't have the compact flavors, the density, that we're seeing now with older vines," says Gary. "We're seeing big flavors kick in with 10-year-old fruit; in fact, we're seeing the intensity of our sangiovese increase so much that with the '06 vintage we are adding an extra year of age."

Leonetti makes about 6,000 cases a year, sold out to a closed mailing list and on allocation to retailers. Released in early spring, the wines include a merlot, a sangiovese, a cabernet sauvignon, and in most years, a reserve. "In terms of the winemaking, we're very much a team," Chris Figgins explains, "with Dad standing back and making sure I don't screw things up. There was never a conscious decision to cut back on oak; I like where we're at now. I want to show off our vineyards. I want to make terroir-driven wines."

The "new" Leonettis are more contemplative, more subtle wines. They are just as innovative as in the past, but moving toward a more contemporary style. There's a floral component to the aromas, tightly-layered fruits, and threads of cedar, cinnamon, and caramel. The tough transition years are comfortably behind, and these new Leonetti Cellar wines respect the winery's rich legacy while confirming that the Figgins family will continue in its leadership role.

First vintage: 1988

www.mccreacellars.com

If I have a question about a grape, a trend, or a winemaking decision that relates to crafting Rhône-style wines in Washington, I turn first to Doug McCrea, Washington State's leading Rhône Ranger, for the answer. McCrea has both pioneered and dramatically elevated the quality of this state's syrahs and other Rhône Valley varietals, while cajoling several high-profile growers into planting heretofore untried grapes such as grenache blanc, marsanne, roussanne, counoise, mourvèdre, and picpoul. He always seems to find himself on the cutting edge of experimentation and works closely with Robert and Jason Haas of California's Tablas Creek, who have been instrumental in making certified, Rhône-sourced clones available for purchase in the United States.

Sometimes older, more established wineries that are no longer the new kid in town or the flavor of the month find it a bit of a struggle to stay visible. McCrea Cellars, with no tasting room and a winemaker who remains less in the public eye than many others, may be making the best and most interesting wines in its history, but can be overlooked by consumers unfamiliar with the winery's essential role in the development of Rhône varietal wines in Washington.

McCrea Cellars' annual production—roughly 4,000 cases—includes a wide array of small-production wines. A Red Mountain grenache is blended with mourvèdre, syrah, counoise, and cinsault. Supple and aromatic, it expresses itself with ripe, sweet strawberry and black cherry fruit, whiffs of pepper and pencil lead, and a full-bodied midpalate.

A Yakima Valley mourvèdre is velvety, loaded with red fruits, and nuanced with smoke and leather. The core reds—four different syrahs—feature different expressions of favored vineyards, AVAs, and barrels. The lineup is superb, but my own personal preferences inevitably lean to Boushey first and Ciel du Cheval a close second; the Cuvée Orleans combines them for dramatic effect.

New in 2008 was a varietal picpoul, Washington's first. Grenache blanc, marsanne, counoise, and cinsault were kept separate following fermentation, but most are destined for blends such as Sirocco blanc. The best of McCrea's white wines, this brings a stony, textural underpinning to a complex mix of citrus, melon, green banana, and papaya. It's a juicy yet subtle wine, with aging potential over the next half decade or so. A companion Sirocco red brings Châteauneuf-du-Pape styling to an intense, smoky, explosively fruity blend of grenache, mourvèdre, syrah, and counoise. The non sequitur red is its Côtes-du-Rhône cousin, from young vines, and sells at a sharply lower price.

A new winery, opened just ahead of the 2005 crush, has allowed Doug McCrea continued opportunity to explore and expand into ever-new varietals. "Keep your eye on tempranillo," he wrote in a recent e-mail. Hmm . . . is that an Iberian Ranger I see off in the distance?

QUILCEDA CREEK

First vintage: 1979

www.quilcedacreek.com

Quilceda Creek has long been an outlier in the Washington wine industry. Founder Alex Golitzin began making wine in his garage, in a sparsely settled part of Snohomish County, well north of Seattle. Occasional visits from his uncle André Tchelistcheff (the late famed enologist and winemaker for Beaulieu Vineyards) provided technical advice. Most young winemakers want to make as many wines as possible, but Golitzin had a single overriding goal: to make a perfect, world-class cabernet sauvignon.

While keeping a day job as a process engineer at Scott Paper, he coupled his mechanical skills to an intuitive sensibility for winemaking. He began modestly, making a barrel a year from 1974 through 1978 using grapes purchased from the Otis vineyard. These were exceptionally good wines, and his reputation was immediately secured with the release of his first commercial vintage, the 1979, which won the Grand Prize at the prestigious Northwest Enological Society judging.

Much like Gary Figgins at Leonetti, Golitzin hung on to his engineering job for many years before retiring to make wine full-time. The Quilceda cabernets of this first decade were all the more astonishing because they were being made in a simple shed with largely scavenged equipment. An important sea change began to occur in the late 1980s and early 1990s, when Quilceda Creek experimented with the idea of making a reserve wine. Paul Golitzin, then barely into his twenties, was the driving force behind the project. Among the many changes he proposed, the use of much more new French oak was the most striking. His father, who had been using four-year-old barrels purchased from Jordan, was dubious at first. "I don't want to over-oak," he told me at that time. "I like it as a flavoring, not as a main course."

The few reserves that were made (in 1988, 1989, 1990, and 1992) convinced Alex that Paul was on to something important. They were so good and represented such a clear leap forward that the father-son winemaking team decided, beginning in 1993, to make them the standard. One cabernet, of reserve quality, was again the focus.

Quilceda Creek cabernet has always had a unique personality, never more so than in the very early years of the Washington wine industry, when there were precious few cabernets of any quality being made here. Black, dense, and tannic, with deep, compact flavors of cassis, anise, and spicy oak, these were wines that seemed to open up somewhat grudgingly over very long periods of time. And they had a Dorian Gray quality about them; they retained their youth and color for unusually long periods of time—decades. At a Quilceda retrospective in 2004, the wines made from 1979 through 1991 (missing only the '82 and '83) displayed Bordeaux-like scents of sandalwood, cedar, licorice, and light herb matched to brilliantly ripe fruit. Several of these wines, though almost 20 years old, were still displaying plenty of berry highlights and purple-blue shades in the glass.

With the success of the experimental reserve wines, the Golitzins had moved away from André Tchelistcheff's influence, though he continued to visit and offer advice. They set themselves a new goal, the attainment of a perfect 100-point score from Robert Parker's *Wine Advocate*. Parker had tasted the 1988 and 1989 reserve wines during a rare visit to Seattle and showered them with praise. As much as anything, that challenged Quilceda's winemakers to do even better.

Vineyard sources changed, but they were always the very best grapes the state could offer: Otis Vineyard in the early years, Kiona through the first half of the 1980s, and then a blend of Kiona, Mercer Ranch, Klipsun, and Ciel du Cheval. In 1997, Mercer Ranch was sold and renamed Champoux. The Golitzins acquired a 21 percent share; it continues to provide some of their oldest cabernet.

Red Mountain vineyards (Ciel du Cheval, Klipsun, and Tapteil) had been the other mainstay, and in 2001, the Golitzins purchased and planted the 17-acre Galitzine vineyard, adjacent to Ciel du Cheval, completely to cabernet sauvignon. They planned to use the grapes in their cabernet, to increase production. But once they had the 2004 and 2005 Galitzine in barrel, they found it didn't match at all. They preferred the expression of the individual sites and decided to keep them separate.

So Galitzine became the first vineyard-designated cabernet sauvignon to be included in the Quilceda ranks (a one-time-only Champoux vineyard cabernet was made in 1997). In 2006, a second vineyard-designate, Palengat, entered the lineup. The grapes come from a newly acquired, five-acre vineyard adjacent to Champoux (Palengat is Jeanette Golitzin's maiden name). Another 30 acres, "right in the heart of Champoux," are currently being planted, moving the winery still further toward using predominantly estate-grown fruit.

Quilceda Creek produces a total of about 6,000 cases of the three cabernets, more than half of it the flagship wine. These are complemented by a very fine Columbia Valley Red Wine, a blend of declassified lots.

The Golitzins did obtain their perfect Parker score—in fact they've done it three times in five vintages. The first releases of the single-vineyard cabernets have been stunningly good, especially when you realize the vines are just now closing out their first decade. The 2006 cabernet, as is often the case, went into a Bordeaux-like state of dumbness for a while, but has the structure, as always, to age for decades.

With new vineyards and wines driving production totals up to 9,000 cases, the availability of these wines may loosen up slightly. Though Washington wines are sometimes criticized for being too expensive, a glance at Quilceda's pricing suggests otherwise. All but the headliner cabernet are under $100 a bottle, and the second wine is $35. I doubt any other wineries in the world with such a stellar track record are offering their wines at such low prices.

Where do you go from here? is a fair question to ask a winery that has achieved so much in such a short time. How much better than perfect can you get? But the Golitzins, a remarkably low-key team (who always credit son-in-law Marv Crum as their co-wine-maker), take it in stride. "The wine can always get better," says Alex. "Worldwide, everybody is getting better at what they're doing." Paul continues: "We've never made our best wine. We can always do better. A 100-point wine today won't be a 100-point wine in five years. The bar is getting raised."

In their own words, the Golitzins are "ruthless" about every aspect of the winemaking. "I'm looking for a stand-alone wine from each fermenter in its own right," Paul explains—"massive fruit, wonderful balance, silky tannin. It's a textural phenomenon that we look for." "Texture is a good word for it," his father agrees. "You've got all these multiple flavors, but on top of that you've got all these different textures."

The concentration and texture of Quilceda cabernets is different from most cult cabernets from Napa; the fruit has a pleasing elegance, the acids are firm but unobtrusive, the tannins are ripe, smooth, and substantial, giving the wines weight and power. The focus, the intensity, the dedication to excellence that has always characterized this winery should serve as a model for many others. Simply put, Quilceda Creek makes brilliant wines in virtually every vintage and has since 1979; an unbroken, unparalleled track record of excellence in Washington State.

SINEANN

First vintage: 1994

www.sineann.com

So what's this Oregon winery doing in the list of Washington's most elite? Good question. But even setting aside Peter Rosback's thrilling Oregon pinot noirs, ignoring his forays into Napa and New Zealand (who else owns a winery with three states and a foreign country among its grape sources?), and focusing simply on the strength of his Washington wines, Sineann belongs here.

Sineann began as the brainchild of Peter Rosback and David O'Reilly (Owen Roe), who created it while they were both working at Oregon's Elk Cove winery. From the start, Rosback was the winemaker, O'Reilly the marketer. When Owen Roe was created, O'Reilly became that brand's winemaker, and the partners went their separate ways.

Rosback began making wine nonprofessionally in 1985, and within three years he'd already sourced the grapes for two wines that are still his most distinctive. He'd stumbled across a bottle of Oregon zinfandel from a long-gone producer, recognized great fruit lurking under bad wine, and managed to track down its source—an almost-forgotten, century-old vineyard near Hood River called The Pines. He began making the wine in 1987, though his first commercial release was not until 1994. Also in '87, he contacted the owners of Mercer Ranch, who had some "old vine" cabernet sauvignon for sale. Those vines, planted in 1972, have been the core of his Block One cabernet sauvignon ever since. Block One is now the core of the Champoux vineyard, the most sought-after cabernet in Washington state. Rosback has been getting those grapes longer than anyone; he was there first.

SINEANN

Cabernet Franc

2008

Champoux Vineyard
Columbia Valley

15.1% Alcohol By Volume

A manic, wiry, long-haired, hockey-playing sushi addict, he has continued hunting relentlessly for fruit from great, often undiscovered sites. He then meticulously sets up the specific rows and viticultural practices he requires, cutting tonnage down to levels as low as one ton per acre in some instances, and begins crafting his intense, brilliant wines.

Sineann's 10,000-case annual production includes as many as thirty wines, but his Washington bottlings are much more limited. The old-vine zinfandel, though grown in Oregon, is technically Columbia Valley fruit. Just across the river, he buys gewürztraminer from Celilo and Oak Ridge, and occasionally pulls in pinot noir from a Columbia Gorge vineyard nearby, though he has not made a designate from it yet.

The Champoux vineyard Block One cabernet sauvignon combines power, texture, and pure pleasure—a seductive mélange of black cherry, cassis, plum, coffee, chocolate, and spice. Tannins are ripe, fine-grained, and have the weight to balance the fruit and oak. In brief, the wine is a triumph of vineyard and winemaker. From younger Champoux vines comes a firm, full-bodied cabernet whimsically named Baby Poux and, in 2007, for the first time, a Baby Poux reserve. A few cases of a dense, intense Champoux cabernet franc are also offered from time to time.

What Sineann does not have, oddly enough, is a dedicated winery. Rosback makes his wines at Medici vineyards, also producing rare, exquisite old-vine pinots for owner Hal Medici. When pressed, Rosback will admit that he probably should have built a winery by now, but then backtracks, saying, "It's all about making great wine. If there was a big quality advantage to a facility, or having my own vineyard, I'd do it. I like a broad variety of wines, and those are the wines I make."

He goes on to list the wines he loves the most. "New Zealand sauvignon blanc; I love it, and I make it. Pinot noir—if you had to go out and buy pinot noir, there aren't that many good ones; you have to kiss a lot of frogs. I make good ones. Old vine zin? I make it. There's no wine like it, not even in California. Block One cab, that's one of the best cab vineyards in the state that is making the best cabernet on the planet in my opinion."

I can't argue with any of the above. Rules are made to be broken, and Peter Rosback breaks most of them at Sineann. He's been making wine his way for 25 years. "I know right now exactly how I want to make wine," he says, and every bottle I've ever tasted proves him right.

WALLA WALLA VINTNERS

First vintage: 1995

www.wallawallavintners.com

For the past few years, Myles Anderson and Gordy Venneri, the founding partners in Walla Walla Vintners, have hosted an annual retrospective tasting of their wines. Walla Walla Vintners debuted with wines from the 1995 vintage, about the same time as Dunham Cellars. (There is some disagreement about who was eighth in the region and who was ninth.) One year the tasting featured cabernet sauvignon; another year it was cabernet franc; and most recently, sangiovese. I have been an admirer of these wines from the very start, as they seem always to display ripe, succulent fruit and luscious barrel flavors, making them instantly appealing. But their aging capabilities were unknown to me, and now that I see how beautifully they develop, my admiration has only increased.

Venneri and Anderson had been amateur winemakers for a decade before turning commercial. "We experimented with oak chips, used oak barrels, beer kegs, food-grade plastic buckets, plastic apple juice containers, Coca-Cola syrup stainless-steel containers, and glass carboys," they recall. "Some tasted bad and some blew up in wine racks." They persisted and, ultimately, they prevailed.

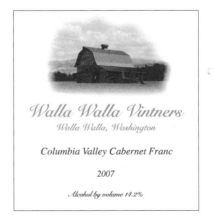

Once they turned pro, success came quickly, and Walla Walla Vintners has steadily grown from an initial production of 675 cases to more than 5,000 cases currently. Their wines are seductive, fruit-forward, soft, and round—

sometimes called "baby Leonettis" by critics. In fact, Venneri and Anderson are good friends with Gary Figgins, and their winery, just across from Leonetti's Mill Creek Upland vineyard, now has its own vineyard, planted in 2008 in a compound that also includes àMaurice and Chan. The 11-acre site is dry-farmed and planted to sangiovese, petit verdot, two clones of merlot, two clones of cabernet sauvignon, and two clones of syrah. The first crop is anticipated in 2010.

Anderson and Venneri purchase fruit from more than a dozen vineyards scattered throughout eastern Washington. They have always had a nose for finding good grapes; their first merlot (1995) used fruit from a new vineyard that no one had heard of— Spring Valley—which quickly went on to great success of its own. More recently, the vineyard mix includes prime spots in Walla Walla, old-vine fruit from Sagemoor and Weinbau, and sangiovese from Kiona and Lewis.

They make sangiovese, merlot, cabernet franc, and cabernet sauvignon and in certain years do a Vineyard Select cabernet or a Sagemoor vineyard-designate, or both. A varietal malbec was made for the first time in 2005, along with a cabernet-sangiovese blend named Bello Rosso; small amounts of petit verdot and syrah are also bottled on occasion, but those grapes are mostly used for blending.

The sangiovese generally includes syrah and malbec in the blend—unusual but delicious, with sweet, sappy raspberry and cherry fruit. Walla Walla Vintners merlots are soft and round, richly aromatic with mocha and chocolate, spiced plum and cherry fruit. They seem to hit peak maturity about eight years after the vintage.

Cabernet franc is a particular strength, sourced from the Weinbau vineyard in the Wahluke Slope, a hot-climate site that is impeccably farmed—manager Miguel Rodriquez was Grower of the Year in 2007. Cab franc in general is often chewy, tannic, and herbal, but rarely luscious, as it is here—a dazzling display of blueberry, boysenberry, raspberry, coffee, tobacco leaf, lead pencil, and more.

Cabernet sauvignon is the winery mainstay, usually a four- or five-grape Bordeaux blend. The Walla Walla Vineyard Select is essentially a reserve, "a precursor to eventually morphing into our own estate wine," says Anderson. Made in 2001, 2003, 2005, and 2006, it is a pure cabernet, intensely flavored and best enjoyed with some extra years of bottle age.

✱ WOODWARD CANYON

First vintage: 1981

www.woodwardcanyon.com

Rick and Darcey Small launched Woodward Canyon, Walla Walla's second modern-era winery, long before the region had shown even an inkling of how important it would become to this state's wine industry. Yet somehow, they knew. They applied for, and received, government recognition of the Walla Walla AVA when there were barely

40 acres of vines in the valley, including their own Woodward Canyon estate, first planted in 1976.

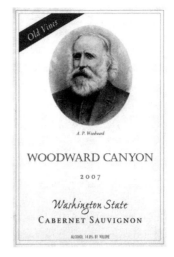

Set on a hilltop a few miles north of the winery in the most arid part of the Walla Walla Valley, it's a dry, windy site on very rocky soil, surrounded by wheat. Huge water tanks at the top of a steep gravel road had to be towed into place and constantly filled in order to get vines established. The topography offers little protection from the occasional arctic blasts. Small is the third generation on the land, which has been both cattle ranch and wheat farm in past decades. "It was never good soil," he admits; "where a lot of the cabernet grows is very shallow and rocky."

Sustainable viticulture has helped to amend soil badly depleted from the years of growing grain. Roughly 41 acres are planted: 7 to merlot, 6 and 6 to cabernet sauvignon and cab franc, 2¹/₂ to chardonnay, and a smattering to sauvignon blanc. The oldest chardonnay vines date back to the beginning; still bearing, they are still an important component of the outstanding Woodward Canyon chardonnay. Most vines are much newer, planted during the 1990s and on into this century, as Small expanded into Bordeaux varietals, Rhône (grenache), and Italian (barbera and Dolcetto). Anyone who has walked the vineyard can't fail to be impressed by the effort it has taken to get grapes to grow.

But the rare estate wines prove that the land has something unique to give back. The Estate red—a reserve crafted from the best lots of cabernet franc, petit verdot, cabernet sauvignon, and merlot—has been produced since 1999 (with the exception of 2004, the freeze year). It's built to age—tight and muscular, with a strong vein of mineral and metal. Still more rare is the Special Selection red, a blend of old-block Champoux cabernet and estate-grown merlot and petit verdot. Made just four times in the winery's history, it is made, says Small, only when repeated tastings prove that certain barrels distinguish themselves from the other Old Vines wines.

The Smalls opened a new tasting room and wine cellar adjacent to the winery in the spring of 2009. It holds an extensive library of Woodward Canyon wines from every vintage, particularly the Old Vines, Artist Series, reserves, and Special Selections. I've been fortunate to taste complete verticals of many of these wines in the past few years, and other than Quilceda Creek, there is no winery in Washington whose red wines can match Woodward Canyon's ability to age gracefully for decades, maturing into fully realized wines of exceptional breed and power.

Production is up to 15,000 cases, half bottled under the less expensive Nelms Road label. "We don't buy bulk wine," Small emphasizes. "Nelms Road wines are all produced by us in-house." They are partially from declassified barrels, partially a selection of younger vines not yet ready for the Artist or Dedication Series wines, and offer outstanding value.

Though Woodward Canyon has long enjoyed a fine reputation for its chardonnays, the winery also makes a thrilling, Sancerre-like sauvignon blanc from estate vines, as well as a dry riesling with old vine fruit from DuBrul. The Rhône and Italian wines—grenache, syrah, barbera, Dolcetto—are brightly fruity and sourced from either the estate, Champoux, or DuBrul vineyards.

Woodward Canyon's Bordeaux varietals and blends receive, deservedly, the most recognition. The Dedication Series cabernets date in an unbroken progression from the first vintage, and many age wonderfully. Since 1995, the wines in this series have been designated "Old Vines." They are made primarily from Sagemoor and Champoux vineyard cabernet vines (Woodward Canyon is a joint partner in the Champoux vineyard) that were planted in the early 1970s.

Woodward's Artist Series cabernets were introduced in 1992. Made in much larger case quantities and priced at slightly more than half the cost of the Dedication Series wines, these are stylish and tight on release, with compact flavors of cassis, black cherry, and berry.

Small is a wiry, boundlessly energetic man whose motor never ceases to rev. He is unusually candid about his winemaking trials, the experiments that went sideways, and the hard lessons he has learned. "When I'm done and out of this, I want to say I never held anything back!" he says quite happily, and no one would ever doubt him. But he does not give himself enough credit for his many triumphs, choosing rather to focus on the contributions of others, the many new projects in the works, his ongoing efforts to establish the estate vineyard, and his tireless evangelizing for all Washington State wines.

6

THE FOUR-STAR WINERIES

The four-star wineries featured here make up only about 7 percent of the state's vintners. Their strengths are proven, and most reach across a broad spectrum of vines and vintages. They often rely upon veteran winemakers, and always draw from exceptional vineyard sources (estate or otherwise). What truly elevates their wines is that they express a specific, individual, stylistic signature that you may attribute to terroir or to the talent of the winemaker, but that rises well above the norm.

As the number of Washington wineries steadily climbs, the quality bar for any particular type of wine is steadily raised. As an example, a decade ago, with maybe a dozen Washington syrahs to choose from, it was no great trick to find the best one, or for that wine to stand out from the rest of the pack. It didn't have to be really good; just better than the rest. Today, with five hundred or more different Washington syrahs in the market each year, the quest to be one of the best has become much more daunting.

In practical terms, you can trust these four-star wineries to make outstanding wines in every vintage. Some reach back a quarter century or more and may not produce the newest, the most trendy, or the rarest wines, but they deliver the quality goods. A few are relative newcomers, included here because they have already demonstrated a substantial commitment to quality, and the ability to reach those lofty goals. They have convinced me that they are tomorrow's superstars.

ALEXANDRIA NICOLE CELLARS

First vintage: 2001

www.alexandrianicolecellars.com

Alexandria Nicole is the winery attached to the Destiny Ridge vineyard. Located in the heart of the Horse Heaven Hills AVA, Destiny Ridge was first planted in 1998 and is just now coming into its prime. There are 266 acres planted to almost two dozen different varietals. Half of the acreage is split between cabernet sauvignon and merlot, and another quarter is devoted to large blocks of syrah, chardonnay, sauvignon blanc, cabernet franc, and riesling. The rest consists of smaller amounts of barbera, carmenère, counoise, grenache, malbec, marsanne, mourvèdre, muscat, petite sirah, petit verdot, pinot gris, roussanne, tempranillo, and viognier.

Destiny Ridge has a fascinating client list, starting with Ste. Michelle but including up-and-coming boutiques such as Darby, Edmonds, and Guardian, along with established players such as Saviah, Tamarack, Thurston Wolfe, Va Piano, and Walter Dacon. But it is vineyard owner Jarrod Boyle who gets first pick and access to the most limited and unusual grapes. Alexandria Nicole Cellars, the winery he founded with his wife, Ali Boyle, in 2001, is where you will find these wines.

He makes a dizzying number of wines—seemingly using every single varietal to make at least a couple of barrels, many bottled as Club Selections. A lifetime resident of the area with a deep knowledge of farming, Boyle first learned vineyard management and winemaking while working at Hogue Cellars. His own wines have improved dramatically in record time, seeming to take a leap forward with each new vintage. Despite the large number of wines being made, quality is remarkably consistent across the entire range.

Alexandria Nicole's white wines are all fresh and juicy, vibrantly fruity, and stainless steel (or neutral barrel)–fermented—no oak bombs here. Boyle's viogniers are exemplary, his Shepherds Mark white—a mix of roussanne, marsanne, and viognier—rich but never tiring. A nicely varietal sauvignon blanc and a luscious off-dry riesling are also offered.

There are something like fifteen different Alexandria Nicole reds, an intriguing mix of varietals and blends, including such unusual (for Washington) wines as tempranillo and petite sirah. One of the best lembergers I've tasted in years—a nod to the past—sells out quickly, as do limited bottlings of malbec and grenache.

Syrah, merlot, and cabernet sauvignon are all strengths, offered in both regular and reserve versions. When Boyle assigns a block number to a wine, it's generally an indication of reserve quality, even if not labeled as such.

The winery has tasting rooms in Prosser and Woodinville and a very active program of wine clubs, which offer members the opportunity to learn firsthand how to work in the vineyard and make their own wines. Prices for the white wines are exceptionally fair. The winery's new Girl Next Door series, with playful pinup labels, adds a fun twist—Roll in the Hay chardonnay, Ooh La La syrah, and Let's Play cabernet are the first three wines in the series. You'll want to collect 'em all.

Assets: a large and excellent vineyard, access to unusual varietals, an entrepreneurial owner-winemaker with a lifetime of farming experience.

AMAVI CELLARS

First vintage: 2001

www.amavicellars.com

Amavi (AH-muh-vee) Cellars is a sister winery (not a second label!) to Pepper Bridge, and the two share talented winemaker Jean-Francois Pellet. The goal here is to offer estate wines (from Seven Hills, Pepper Bridge, Les Collines, and LeFore vineyards) at prices substantially lower than Pepper Bridge. Amavi wines generally use fruit from younger vines and spend less time in new oak.

Amavi does a superb job with sémillon, a grape whose strongest proponents are in Walla Walla (think L'Ecole No 41). In vintage after vintage, the flavors are crystal clear, leesy, and long-lasting, blending pear and pineapple with citrus zest; there is a lively, refreshing acidity, and fermentation in neutral barrels softens the wine. The addition of sauvignon blanc to the blend (in 2008) marked a further improvement. You will have to work very hard to find a $20 chardonnay from anywhere with as much complexity.

Amavi's syrahs are outstanding, especially the Les Collines vineyard bottling (offered exclusively through the wine club). It's meaty, earthy, with nuances of seaweed and rock. In many ways it resembles the Cayuse syrahs, tilting more toward the style of the Rhône than to Australian shiraz. Almost three-quarters of Amavi's 8,500-case production is a smooth, supple cabernet sauvignon, with just a splash of syrah in the blend. Syrah is often blended in with cabernet, and I asked Pellet why he liked the combination. "It changes the aromatics, and helps the mouthfeel too," he replied.

Amavi's new barrel storage and tasting room was opened in the spring of 2010. It is located in the vineyard diagonally across from Pepper Bridge, in an area loaded with destination wineries.

Assets: estate vineyards, an experienced winemaker with European training, a focused lineup of wines, and very competitive pricing.

ANDREW RICH

First vintage: 1995

www.andrewrichwines.com

Andrew Rich makes his wines at the Carlton Winemakers' Studio in Oregon. He's an easygoing, self-proclaimed "vinarchist"—much in the Peter Rosback/David O'Reilly mode. He came to winemaking gradually, following a path that wound through a series of jobs from editing a wine column, to working in retail, then studying winemaking in Beaune, apprenticing at Bonny Doon, and finally moving to Oregon in 1994 to make wine for himself.

"My silly idea at the time," says Rich, "was to live in Oregon but make Washington State syrah." Not so silly after all. Today he makes about 6,500 cases of wine, most of it from Washington, though his Willamette Valley pinot noirs are quite lovely, full-flavored, and nicely perfumed.

Apart from that, Washington wines are the focus. Especially notable are his two roussannes, one a Columbia Valley blend, the other a Ciel du Cheval vineyard-designate. Without being heavy or fat, the Ciel bottling shows more concentration, more acidity and structure, and captures the vineyard's characteristic minerality.

The red wine lineup is quite broad. It includes a pair of meaty syrahs; a spicy, best-selling Coup d'Etat red blended of grenache, mourvèdre, and syrah; and more limited, occasional offerings of varietal counoise, grenache, malbec, petit verdot, and cabernet franc. The Mésalliance red is a masterful blend of merlot, cabernet franc, and syrah—a perfect storm of power, precision, and compact fruit. For a good introduction to the winery style, look for the two value-priced blends, Tabula Rasa white and red.

Assets: a well-traveled palate, excellent blending skills, and a focus on unusual varietals.

ARBOR CREST

First vintage: 1982

www.arborcrest.com

Arbor Crest was founded in 1982 by the Mielke brothers, David and Harold. The family business was orchards and fruit. There were barely three dozen wineries in the state back then, and many of them have disappeared, including Paul Thomas, French Creek, Snoqualmie Falls, Vernier, Haviland Vintners, Rainier Valley Cellars, Neuharth, Salishan, Langguth, and Worden's.

David Mielke began by planting wine grapes at the Wahluke Slope vineyard (sold in 2007 to the Milbrandt brothers). Arbor Crest's early production focused on white wines, highlighted by a fruity, French-oak aged, slightly sweet sauvignon blanc. Success came quickly, and within a few years the winery had grown to become one of Washington's largest. But by the end of the century, with David eager to retire, the brand lost its focus.

Harold's daughter Kristina and her husband, Jim, agreed to move to Spokane and take over the reins. Since then they have steadily improved and revitalized the winery. Kristina Mielke van Löben Sels grew up in the Bay Area, studied fermentation science at

UC Davis, and later worked as enologist and associate winemaker at Ferrari-Carano. Now with eleven Washington vintages behind her, Arbor Crest is again at the top of its game.

The flagship white wine is still sauvignon blanc, with fruit sourced from Bacchus vineyard vines now more than 35 years old. It's stainless steel–fermented, fresh and nicely detailed, with moderate alcohol allowing some of the more subtle varietal flavors—melon, green apple, lime, and grapefruit—to shine. A bargain-priced riesling—also from old vines—is another highlight. The other white, a chardonnay from the Conner Lee vineyard, is generously oaked and roundly fruity.

The expansive red wine lineup includes mostly pure varietals—merlot, cabernet sauvignon, cabernet franc, and syrah—and the occasional vineyard-designate. The top-of-the-line Dionysus red is a Bordeaux blend crafted from some of the oldest vines in Washington. Dark, sappy, and bursting with ripe cassis and black cherry fruit, silky tannins, and juicy acids, it's beautifully knit together. A few limited-edition wines such as malbec and petite sirah are offered through the website and wine club.

Assets: long-term contracts for old-vine grapes, exceptional sauvignon blancs, and an unusual winery tasting room at Cliff House (currently under renovation following a fire).

BARRISTER

First vintage: 2001

www.barristerwinery.com

Barrister is the project of two Spokane attorneys, Greg Lipsker (now retired from the law) and Michael White. They began their professional winemaking venture in 2001 and produce about 3,000 cases of wine annually. Only 120 cases of white wines are made—a Klipsun vineyard sauvignon blanc and (occasionally) a Dionysus vineyard riesling. The red wines, tarry, smoky, dark, and dense, are the stars here.

They include small lots of pure varietals (merlot, cabernet sauvignon, syrah, and cabernet franc), a few vineyard-designates and some well-crafted blends. Despite their imposing color, extract, and tannins, these Barrister wines are not just big and blocky. For example, an old-vine, Bacchus vineyard cabernet sauvignon, blended with a little Artz Red Mountain merlot, is fragrant and compelling, with bright cherry and berry fruit. The merlot pulls it together and seems to provide the thread that tightens the weave of the wine.

The most distinctive expression of Barrister's signature combination of power, weight, massive fruit, and sweet, toasty oak is its cabernet franc. Muscular and spicy, the overwhelming impression is of gorgeous fruit, finished with pretty flavors of toasted nuts. Since its 2001 debut, this is the wine that has won the lion's share of medals for the winery, and deservedly so.

Yet equally good are Barrister's merlots, as muscular and authoritative as any in the state, and priced well below most of their peers. Another gem is the Rough Justice red—a tasty, big-boned, chunky wine done as a different blend every year, priced a little lower than Barrister's varietal wines, and emphatically—say the partners—not a second wine. The goal, they explain, "is to use all four varietals and try to come up with something that meets our style."

Vineyard sources include Seven Hills, Pepper Bridge, Morrison Lane, and Dwelley in the Walla Walla Valley; Klipsun, Artz, Tapteil, and Kiona on Red Mountain; and a couple of prime Sagemoor blocks. Though Spokane is a long way from most of these vineyards, Barrister's owners are hands-on guys: of nineteen separate lots picked in the most recent vintage, sixteen were from designated rows.

Assets: a focus on red wines (notably cabernet franc), a clear sense of the house style, and the ability to seamlessly marry powerful, thick tannins with lush fruit and barrel flavors.

BERESAN

First vintage: 2001

www.beresanwines.com

Beresan (the name refers to a region in Ukraine) is owned by Tom Waliser, a Walla Walla native, apple grower, and vineyard manager. For the past decade or more, Waliser has managed Pepper Bridge and Seven Hills, the two biggest vineyards in the valley, and consulted for several other Columbia Valley growers.

In 1997 he began planting his own Waliser and Yellow Jacket vineyards, 18 acres in all, on stony, dry riverbed—the area west of Milton-Freewater generally called the Rocks. Waliser and Christophe Baron (Cayuse) were the first modern-era vintners to plant wine grapes in the area.

Pointing to the earth and vegetation around his vines, Waliser makes it clear that he has just as many rocks as Cayuse; they're just not visible. Baron, he says, tills his soil intending to bring the rocks up and shake off the dirt; Waliser plants ground cover. "I think there's a classic difference between what Christophe is doing and what I'm doing," he points out. "Both are right, but my philosophy is that Mother Nature wants to bring something up from the ground."

"As you look below the soil, there's a huge amount of microbial activity—a synergy between the vines and what goes on below. There are microrhyzomes that will actually feed the plant sugars they excrete. So I leave the ground cover undisturbed to encourage microbial activity. Plus we're adding compost tea, fish oil, and molasses—carbon-based products that feed the microbes. It's a candy bar for a microbe."

Beresan's production has climbed to about 3,000 cases ("and it will stay there," says Waliser); but new wines—such as The Buzz, a single-vineyard cabernet-syrah, and Viuda Negra, a cab franc–merlot—pop up from time to time. The Beresan standards include a dry, crisp sémillon, and a range of red varietal wines—merlot, cabernet franc, cabernet sauvignon, syrah, and malbec. The Stone River red is a sophisticated blend of cabernet sauvignon, syrah, merlot, and cab franc. Visitors to the tasting room, one of the prettiest in the valley, will often find a surprise or two waiting, such as a Seven Hills vineyard carmenère.

Assets: exceptional vineyards with genuine terroir, an owner with decades of vineyard management experience, a talented winemaker (Thomas Glase) with an elegant touch, and pricing that keeps even the best wines under $30.

BOUDREAUX CELLARS

First vintage: 2002

www.boudreauxcellars.com

Before turning to winemaking, Louisiana native Rob Newsom worked for many years as an expert in rock climbing and alpine gear. As his bio explains, "He has survived a paragliding crash, a flaming helicopter evacuation, and having his tent avalanche-launched off a 4,000-foot alpine wall. He's led 16 expeditions into the Alaska Range, two Himalayan expeditions into the Everest region, fly fished for giant tarpon, barracuda, and bonefish, and summited four of the seven highest peaks in North America."

Being "avalanche-launched" remains my favorite description of Boudreaux Cellars wines, which send your taste buds on a sometimes precarious, always thrilling, "where's the bottom?" flavor glide.

A fishing friendship with Leonetti's Gary Figgins led to Newsom's midlife career change, offering access to rarified barrel and grape sources, along with a tip or two about making wine. There is nothing simple about anything Newsom undertakes, but starting a winery at his hand-built log home, adjacent to a state forest in the Cascade foothills outside Leavenworth, has ramped up the difficulty level in every respect. Off the power grid and hundreds of miles from the vineyard sources he prefers, Newsom has nonetheless built a spectacular, unique facility while learning his craft well.

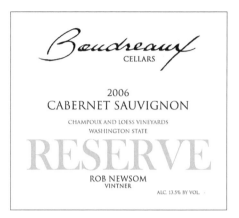

There were some hits and misses among the first few vintages, but I attribute the problems (mostly with white wines) to the lack of a well-insulated barrel and case storage room. That has been addressed, with the construction of an expansive underground cellar, and a new, granite-and-cinderblock winery well suited to combat the extremes of heat and cold in the area. It includes a dedicated tank room, a laboratory, indoor space for labeling and waxing, and a small, cozy tasting bar.

Boudreaux makes 2,000 cases a year of chardonnay, syrah, merlot, and cabernet sauvignon. Acknowledging his superb vineyard sources, Newsom lists as many as ten names on his labels. His 2005 cabernet sauvignon included seven grapes from ten vineyards and six AVAs—quite possibly the first cab/merlot/cab franc/malbec/petit verdot/syrah/sangiovese ever made in Washington. Vineyard-designates from Champoux, Loess (Leonetti estate), Pepper Bridge, Wallula, and Celilo are among the names to search for. The best of the best are the Boudreaux reserve cabernets; gorgeous wines with a rainbow of deeply detailed flavors, from flowers to berries to barrels.

Assets: cult Napa-quality cabernets, outstanding vineyard sources, uniquely beautiful location, live bluegrass music on request.

BRIAN CARTER CELLARS

First vintage: 2002

www.briancartercellars.com

Brian Carter has made wines for a couple of dozen Washington wineries over the past three decades, yet it wasn't until 2006 that he finally opened his own establishment. Headquartered in the thriving Woodinville wine community, Brian Carter Cellars makes about 7,000 cases annually—all blends, not varietals. "That's where the fun is and that's what I want to do," says Carter, adding, "I think blends are an area that Washington State will excel in over the next decade. Only recently has Washington had the number and maturity of good sites for varieties such as petit verdot and sangiovese."

The Auction for Washington Wines named Carter its Vintner of the Year in 2007. He is the only three-time winner of the Northwest Enological Society's Grand Prize. Despite those and many more accolades, Carter remains humble to the point of shyness and has somehow avoided the spotlight more often than he has been in it. He seems more comfortable talking about deficit irrigation, fruit set, and the intricacies of blending than pointing out his own achievements.

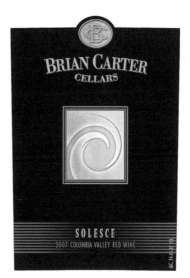

Blending is clearly his forte. He uses Yakima Valley and Wahluke Slope grapes and crafts his wines in a European mode, retaining hints of herb and stone while emphasizing varietal fruit. These are usually wines structured with moderate alcohol levels (averaging around 13.5 percent), sharp acids, and a light touch with new oak.

Carter's most affordable and popular wine is the Abracadabra red. "I overbuy everything," he explains, "so I can have maximum flexibility blending Brian Carter wines. The rest goes into Abracadabra—same grapes, same barrels." A mix of as many as seven grapes and almost as many vineyards, it still adds up to something more than a mish-mash, with ripe fruit, polished tannins, and a lengthy, chocolaty finish.

Oriana is an unusual blend of roussanne, viognier, and riesling; Byzance, a southern Rhône red mixing grenache, syrah, and (sometimes) mourvèdre. L'Etalon and Solesce are Carter's Bordeaux-based reds, and Tuttorosso his super-Tuscan mix of sangiovese, cabernet sauvignon, and syrah. He is one of a very few winemakers with the talent and experience to manage such diversity well.

Assets: depth of winemaking experience, exceptional blending skills, tight vineyard focus.

BUNNELL FAMILY CELLAR

First vintage: 2004

www.bunnellfamilycellar.com

Ron Bunnell is a 1982 UC Davis graduate whose winemaking career began with stints at Beringer, Chateau Souverain, and Kendall-Jackson. He and his family moved to Washington in 1999, when he was hired to oversee red winemaking for Chateau Ste. Michelle. In 2005, Bunnell left to start his own winery at his home on the bluffs above the Yakima River, intending to produce syrah and other Rhône varietals. In 2009, he opened a wine bar and barrel room in the Prosser Vintner's Village.

"When we started our winery," Bunnell recalls, "we wanted to focus. I'm a curmudgeon about cabernet, anyway; I don't like to work with it until it's at least 10 years old. Syrah is much more forgiving in its youth than cabernet. And I love the wines; it's the kind of wine I like to drink."

Bunnell describes his wines as falling into two distinctly different camps. His vins de l'endroit (wines of a place) are vineyard-designated varietals from Milbrandt, Boushey, Stonetree, and other prime sites. Viognier, grenache, and mourvèdre are among the unusual offerings. His vins de l'esprit (wines of the creative spirit) are all blends, including vif, a lively red; à pic, a Washington take on Châteauneuf-du-Pape; and Lia, a grenache-based wine.

Syrahs are designed to spotlight specific vineyards and include brilliant examples from three distinct appellations. The Boushey-McPherson vineyard–Yakima Valley bottling jumps out for its elegance and precision, perfectly showcasing tart, cool-climate fruit flavors. The Horse Heaven Hills bottling, a pleasing mix of citrus, berry, and plum, slides across the palate with the grace of a racehorse, its smooth, ripe tannins leaving a hint of black olive and fresh herb in the finish. And finally, the Clifton Hill vineyard–Wahluke Slope bottling is the most forward and dense of all, with rich scents of mixed berries, spice, fresh herbs, and toast.

A second label, RiverAerie (named for the family farm), roams farther afield, offering value-priced versions of chardonnay, pinot gris, sauvignon blanc, riesling, barbera, malbec, merlot, sangiovese, and more. And a new partnership with the Newhouse family, owners of Upland vineyards on Snipes Mountain, provides access to those older (20+ years) cabernet vines that Bunnell has been lusting after. Look for a new brand, as yet unnamed, to feature them.

Assets: a seemingly inexhaustible winemaker, exciting Rhône-based varietals, and Wine O'Clock, Bunnell's tasting room and café in the Prosser Vintner's Village.

CHARLES SMITH WINES

First vintage: 2005

www.charlessmithwines.com

Charles Smith's expanding empire (K Vintners, Magnificent Wine Company, Charles & Charles) includes a line of wines bearing his own name (and mane—his cascading curls are a brand icon). He calls it his Modernist Project, regionally focused and vineyard-driven. Wines, says Smith, that "taste like the varietal, taste like where they came from, with nothing in the middle [aging, extraction, cooperage] that would delay the message."

The first wine made under this label was the instantly successful Kungfu Girl riesling. With its easy-open screw cap, exotic kanji imagery, and appealing price point, this wine is a wildly popular restaurant pour. Its stablemates include a Boom Boom! syrah, an Eve chardonnay, and a Velvet Devil merlot, all with catchy graphic labels to complement the attention-grabbing names. Production of these value-priced wines has quickly reached 70,000 cases and shows no sign of slowing down.

At the other end of the price spectrum, Smith next rolled out three no-holds-barred 2005 syrahs named Heart, Skull, and Old Bones. Massive efforts, high in alcohol, rich in extract, dense, and concentrated—in other words, cult wines—they were not for the faint of palate (or wallet). Then came the Bomb.

It was not until I became the Northwest editor for *Wine Enthusiast* magazine that I began scoring wines on the 100-point system. My feelings about the pros and cons of that system are well documented in this book, but the fact remains that it is very popular with both consumers and the trade. I have reviewed and scored thousands of wines, but had never found one that I felt deserved the perfect, 100-point score until I tasted Smith's 2006 Royal City syrah, a combination of the previous three. Rich scents of purple fruit, smoked meat, cedar, lead pencil, and moist earth proclaim a wine with genuine gravitas. Tasted on three separate occasions prior to its official release, it repeatedly dazzled me. There was nothing missing, nothing that could be improved, nothing suggesting any shred of incompleteness. From the first sniff to the last sip, the wine delivers extreme pleasure.

What ties these disparate Charles Smith wines together? Not pricing—they sell from $10 to more than $100. It's something intuitive that Smith himself cannot always explain. "I wasn't given a guidebook," he says. "I decided to do it my way, on my own terms, as everyone should. I've never been good at following instructions; I throw myself like Kurt Cobain into the drum kit. You won't see me in a seat at a rock concert—I'm 48 years old and I'll be down in the mosh pit."

Assets: a wide-ranging, fine-tuned palate, a savantlike marketing talent, an iconic image, a sixth sense for finding great vineyard sources, and a flair for doing the unexpected.

CHATEAU ROLLAT

First vintage: 2005

www.rollat.com

Certainly one of the most extraordinary new wineries to have made its debut since the first edition of this book is Chateau Rollat. I have instantly elevated this winery to four-star status—not only because the first three vintages have been outstanding on every level but also because Bowin Lindgren, Rollat's owner-winemaker, has retained Christian Le Sommer as his consultant. Le Sommer's résumé includes work at Chateau d'Yquem and Chateau Latour, where he was general manager and wine master for more than a decade. He recently concluded another lengthy term as the consulting manager for Domaines des Barons de Rothschild.

Lindgren says he spent 35 years "climbing the corporate ladder" with an East Coast pharmaceutical company, then retired with the goal of learning to make wine. He cold-called Le Sommer and badgered him mercilessly until the poor man agreed to make a visit to Walla Walla, a place he'd never heard of, much less seen.

The two men clicked. They agreed on a plan, recalls Le Sommer, to produce "the best possible expression of ripe Walla Walla fruit"—specifically, Bordeaux blends of Seven Hills and Pepper Bridge cabernet sauvignon, cabernet franc, and merlot. Over the first few vintages, some insights into their methodology have begun to trickle out. "We pick much later than anyone else," Le Sommer confides. "We pick on flavor. In Walla Walla, because the temperatures cool down so predictably, you don't cook your grapes by letting them hang an extra couple of weeks."

That's just the start. It is really a combination of sophisticated winemaking techniques—how and when to bleed out juice to enhance concentration; pinpointing exactly how and when sulfites are added; the use of closed fermenters for extended maceration; the use of extensive amounts of dry ice—that results in Chateau Rollat's dazzling results.

Sophie de Rollat (named for Lindgren's grandmother) is the entry-level wine—charming and accessible, "but not simple," says Lindgren. The midlevel wine is simply Rollat, a polished, cabernet-dominated Bordeaux blend, with deep boysenberry, plum, and cherry fruit, firm and full-bodied. This would be the top wine for most wineries. Here that honor goes to the Edouard cabernet sauvignon, a vin de garde—a wine to put away for some years. "I hope it will be a giant among wines," says the winemaker. The 2006 Edouard (honoring Lindgren's grandfather, a well-respected New York sommelier) is indeed a giant. Dense, smoky, and concentrated, with cassis, berry, rock, graphite, and coffee flavors, it is massive and long, still tightly wrapped, with amazing density.

A new label, Ardenvoir, is dedicated to making Rollat's white wines—chardonnay, sauvignon blanc, and sémillon—and offers a generous, fruit-laden rosé as well.

Assets: a gifted, highly credentialed consulting winemaker, with a laserlike focus on Bordeaux grapes.

✱ COL SOLARE

First vintage: 1995

www.colsolare.com

Ste. Michelle Wine Estates and the Antinori family of Tuscany launched their joint-venture Col Solare partnership with the release of the 1995 vintage. Col Solare, which means "shining hill" in Italian, is a blended red wine made predominantly of cabernet sauvignon and merlot, with small amounts of malbec and syrah as well. Oddly, no sangiovese is included in the blend.

Renzo Cotarella, winemaker and enologist for Marchesi Antinori, has been working on the Col Solare project since its inception, and he visits from Italy several times a year. He sees "huge opportunities" in the climate and soils of Washington, explaining (in a translation of his original Italian) that "this permits the possibility to obtain stylistically very particular wines also endowed with a soul." The goal of the Col Solare project, he explains, is "to try to make a wine that represents two different worlds."

Until 2006, all vintages of Col Solare were made at Chateau Ste. Michelle's Canoe Ridge Estate winery in the Horse Heaven Hills AVA. A dedicated Col Solare winery opened on Red Mountain just in time for the 2006 crush. The official ribbon cutting took place the following spring; it was a celebrity-drenched occasion, highlighted by remarks from Piero Antinori.

"It has been a very constructive 12 years," he began. "We have tried in several areas of Washington State to vinify, to experiment. At the end we thought Red Mountain was exactly what we had in mind for our red wine. It is a very special place—a small paradise for making concentrated red wine, with intensity, elegance, and finesse. We think one of Red Mountain's assets is that it is a very small AVA. Small AVAs have more of a chance to become prestigious. Producers can develop strategies together in terms of grapes, marketing, etcetera. Finally, after 12 years, we have picked this to be a home. It has been a dream all these years. Finally it is a reality."

Ste. Michelle CEO Ted Baseler noted: "We needed our own home and vineyard. This is only the beginning. Our plan is to become a one-wine, estate-grown, Red Mountain AVA wine." To further that goal, estate vineyards are being developed, on some of Red Mountain's highest ground. Since 2005, on-site winemaker Marcus Notaro has been using (purchased) Red Mountain grapes in the Col Solare cuvée. The first estate fruit was harvested in 2008.

The winery hosts visitors (by appointment), but is primarily a dazzling production facility with a budget-busting array of gleaming new winemaking gear. The most recent vintages of Col Solare have finally begun showing more of a sense of place. It seems to have found its shining hill at last.

Assets: the expertise and financial support of the Antinori family, a commitment to Red Mountain fruit, and a spectacular new production facility.

COLUMBIA CREST

First vintage: 1984

www.columbia-crest.com

In 1984, when it made its debut, Columbia Crest was a one-wine brand that offered an off-dry blend of riesling, gewürztraminer, and muscat Canelli. But behind that humble offering was a massive vineyard project, the largest ever undertaken in Washington State—an early sign that this would one day become the state's largest winery.

Columbia Crest varietals debuted with the '86 vintage. Chardonnay, sauvignon blanc, sémillon, riesling, gewürztraminer, and chenin blanc were offered, soon joined by merlot and cabernet sauvignon. Brand expansion has continued ever since, and currently the winery makes four separate tiers of wines. The great majority of the total production goes into inexpensive Two Vines and Grand Estates wines.

The newest tier is called H3 (for the Horse Heaven Hills), which occupies a price point just a few dollars higher than the Grand Estates. More important, the H3 wines combine value and reasonably generous production levels with fruit sourced exclusively from the Horse Heaven Hills AVA, which is where the estate vineyard is located. The highest rung on the ladder is given to the Columbia Crest reserve wines, which account for just a tiny percentage of the total production, now more than two million cases a year.

The winery consistently finds its merlots, cabernets, and chardonnays listed in leading wine publications as best buys, among Top 100s, and so on. Its high quality, case volume, and bargain pricing make it the only Washington winery that can compete on a national level with behemoth California brands such as Kendall-Jackson. Credit the 2,500-acre Columbia Crest vineyard, first planted in the early 1980s, which contributes fruit from vines as old as 25 years. Access to so much mature fruit allows winemaker Ray Einberger to pick and choose carefully, so the winery's size becomes more of an asset than a liability.

Einberger, whose background includes time as maître de chai (cellar master) at Mondavi's Opus One, came to Washington in 1993. He first worked at Columbia Crest developing its reserve wine program, before being elevated to the winemaker position in 2003. Einberger is one of those guys who seems to have been blessed with the fun gene. His eyes twinkle, his voice sparkles, even his mustache looks like it's winking at you when he speaks.

He set up the reserve operation as a separate boutique winery within the larger winery, applying French grand cru–style winemaking techniques he had learned at Mouton with the Opus One team. That means handpicked fruit, small open-top fermentation, secondary fermentation in barrel, blending shortly after fermentation, and long aging in new oak. "From grape to finish, it's done by a separate crew; we're going for a small Opus or a small Mouton," he explains with some pride.

Each of Columbia Crest's tiers has a distinct style and marketing niche. Two Vines wines, priced around $8, sell more than a million cases annually, led by the merlot and cabernet sauvignon. The Two Vines style is fruity, immediately drinkable wine; the best of the whites are the riesling and the Vineyard 10 blend. The Grand Estates wines, priced around $11, offer a significant step up in concentration, weight, and the use of new oak. The chardonnay is the best seller, though I believe it is the reds that shine brightest, especially the merlot, cabernet sauvignon, and shiraz.

The H3 lineup, with a suggested line price of $15, is my favorite tier overall, with consistent quality across both white and red wines. The chardonnay and merlot are exceptional; the chardonnay showing cut and precision, the merlot persistent flavors of berry and cocoa. Columbia Crest's reserve wines are priced between $25 and $35, so they compete with many boutique wines from Washington as well as some of the entry-level reds from better Napa Valley estates. There are certainly wines that more than succeed at that level, notably the reserve chardonnay, merlot, cabernet sauvignon, and Walter Clore Private Reserve blend. Special, limited bottlings of zinfandel, cabernet franc, and other rarities are sometimes offered through the wine club mailing list.

Assets: the marketing muscle of the state's biggest wine group; thousands of acres of prime vineyard, and the ability to experiment with small-lot, limited-production wines.

CORLISS ESTATES

First vintage: 2003

www.corlissestates.com

Michael Corliss and Lauri Darneille purchased the rundown, 100-year-old former bakery building that now houses their Walla Walla winery a decade ago, and crushed their first grapes there in 2003. Two previous vintages had been made—and then discarded—

elsewhere. For the next five years, as construction on the winery dragged on and vintages came and went, no Corliss Estates wines were released.

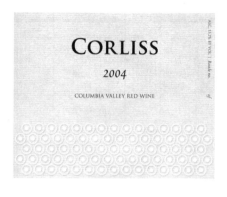

Overcome with curiosity, I arranged to meet Michael Corliss in the fall of 2008. It was the height of crush, and Corliss and then-winemaker Kendall Mix were anchoring a lineup of a dozen or so workers painstakingly sorting grapes. Merlot from Corliss's Red Mountain vineyard was just coming in; the bunches of grapes passed through a gentle destemmer and poured out onto a conveyer belt, where every bit of leaf, stem, and vineyard detritus was picked out by busy hands. By the time the grapes reached the end of the conveyer belt—just before being dropped (not pumped) into fermentation bins—they looked like perfect blueberries, each pristine grape isolated and unbroken.

This is what it takes to make great, not good, wine. Good wines can take many shortcuts and still come out fine. Great wines don't cut any corners. Corliss and Mix took a break to show me around the winery, and along the way explained why it had taken so long to release the first wines.

"I did not at the beginning fully envision that we'd be where we are today," Corliss admits. "It evolved along the way, which is a lot of the reason we've been pretty quiet—taking the journey. When you're on a journey," he continued, "you take a lot of notes and write it up when you finish. After eight years we know very clearly where we're going. We have five great vintages that have been done here at the winery, we've purchased two estate vineyards, and we will acquire another in the next couple of years."

Corliss is a fourth-generation Seattle native whose primary business is as a developer. He was introduced to great wines while still in his early twenties, as part of a group that purchased old wine cellars, including a collection that had belonged to Alfred Hitchcock. Those classic, well-cellared wines shaped his palate, and when he embarked upon his own wine project, it was with the goal of making wines that would age gracefully.

"When you buy and typically drink much older wines, which is what I do, your interest is in how the wine will taste in five, ten, and twenty years," says Corliss. "It is more challenging to set out to build a wine that can last that long. You need to work a lot with the vineyards—where everything starts—how you manage them and crop the fruit, sort the fruit coming in, extract in much longer fermentations, and then manage through a selection process. We're in barrel for 30 to 32 months in about 60 percent new oak."

Corliss and Darneille have the financial resources to micromanage every aspect of the process. Their 42-acre Blue Mountain vineyard was planted in 2001, and grapes have previously gone into some outstanding wines from Nicholas Cole. Their 36-acre Red Mountain vineyard, purchased two years ago from Sandhill, dates back to the late 1980s. The attached winery, completely renovated and renamed RMV Cellars, crushed its first grapes in 2009. A second Red Mountain vineyard was planted in the spring of 2009—55 acres growing all five Bordeaux varietals, plus four Rhônes—grenache, syrah, mourvèdre, and cinsault. Farther west, in the Yakima Valley, the 59-acre Blackrock vineyard was recently acquired and is also being renovated. "It's kind of a diamond in the rough," says Mix.

I can't think of any Washington winery that has set higher expectations for itself, both internally and in the wine community at large. The first releases, from the 2003 and 2004 vintages, included a Bordeaux blend (Corliss Estates red), a cabernet sauvignon, and a syrah. They did not disappoint. Grapes came from Stillwater, old-vine Bacchus and Weinbau, and prime Milbrandt vineyards. All these wines are powerfully fruity, carefully blended, and use their new oak judiciously. In 2006, the proportion of new oak dropped down (as used barrels became available), and in 2007 some estate fruit became part of the program. Corliss Estates and its sister wineries (Tranche and RMV Cellars) are going to be major players in Washington, though Mix has left and the winemaking team is in transition as we go to print.

Assets: vast financial resources, well-chosen estate vineyards in prime locations, and the luxury of taking all the time needed to get it right.

CÔTE BONNEVILLE

First vintage: 2001

www.cotebonneville.com

Among the qualities I value most in wine are those nuances and details that can perhaps best be summed up by the word finesse. Wines with finesse are wines that are balanced, elegant, precise. They may be powerful or they may be fairly light, but they are free of unripe flavors. They may be open or they may be tight and compact, but they offer depth and texture, and the flavors are multidimensional. Wines that are excessively ripe, with high alcohol, high pH, and dominant barrel flavors may be delicious, but they do not have finesse.

Côte Bonneville is the estate winery for DuBrul vineyard, one of the most sought-after sites in the Yakima Valley—precisely because finesse is what DuBrul grapes deliver. Vineyard owners Hugh and

Kathy Shiels moved to the Yakima Valley in 1976 (he is a surgeon, she a physical therapist). They purchased a run-down apple orchard in 1991, hired Wade Wolfe as a consultant, and began planting their 45-acre vineyard in 1992, a mix of cabernet sauvignon, cabernet franc, merlot, syrah, chardonnay, and riesling, all on rocky land that they believe is the ancient bed of the Columbia River. At its highest point, the DuBrul vineyard reaches 1,300 feet.

In 1999—not a vintage that won many accolades from out-of-state critics—DuBrul produced numerous vineyard-designates that won medals for wineries such as Owen Roe, Caterina, Harlequin, Seven Hills, and Tamarack. The Shielses realized they were onto something truly exceptional. And they wanted to make wine for themselves.

"If you believe you're good, if you believe in Washington, and you have the desire to be the best, you have to do it yourself," says Kathy Shiels. "From day one we wanted to make wines we could present on a national level," adds Hugh, "wines that would represent Washington in New York, Miami, Los Angeles."

They started their winery carefully, making 100 cases in 2001; by 2005 they had enough wine to enter the marketplace, and by 2009 production had reached 2,000 cases. One-quarter is the Côte Bonneville red, usually a blend of 60 percent cabernet sauvignon and 40 percent merlot. About 1,000 cases of Carriage House red are produced, a similar blend from different blocks of the estate vineyard. Much smaller amounts of such gems as the Côte Bonneville 2006 DuBrul vineyard cabernet sauvignon are made. A fruit-driven bottle of pure cabernet power, rich, ripe, and sexy, it is essentially the estate reserve. At $200 a bottle, it is also the most expensive red wine ever released by a Washington winery.

Also in 2006, 200 cases of a lush, barrel-fermented chardonnay were added to the lineup, along with other ongoing experiments with syrah and rosé, both offered through the mailing list.

A dozen wineries, carefully chosen, are allowed to purchase DuBrul fruit. Wines to look for include Woodward Canyon's dry riesling and vineyard-designates from Owen Roe, Seven Hills, Tamarack, Stevens, and Sparkman Cellars. But most of all, try to find the estate wines made on-site, and you will be tasting some of Washington's finest terroir.

Assets: the extraordinary estate vineyard, a tight focus on small-production, hands-on winemaking, and the support of several of Washington's best winemakers.

DOYENNE

First vintage: 1997

www.delillecellars.com

Doyenne began simply as the syrah label for DeLille Cellars, and made its debut with the 1997 vintage, when the first syrah grapes from Ciel du Cheval were harvested. DeLille's Chris Upchurch, along with Doug McCrea, were the only vintners offered those grapes. Upchurch, a self-proclaimed "huge Rhône and syrah fan," jumped at the opportunity. In 2004, in an effort to differentiate between the Bordeaux focus of DeLille and the expanding Rhône focus of Doyenne, the latter was officially made a separate winery, and it has actually surpassed its parent in total production, now up to 6,000 cases.

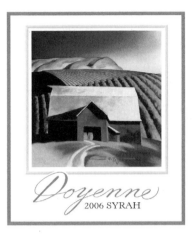

The early vintages of Doyenne syrahs were big wines, tight and chewy, with heavy tannins and an abundance of dark, roasted, espresso flavors. More recently, the winery has moved into a more elegant, more focused style, with beautifully ripened flavors that capture both the floral highlights and pure fruit power of Washington syrah.

"I think Washington is a grand cru winegrowing region for syrah, for cab, and for Bordeaux blends," says Upchurch. "There are two things you have to have—first it's got to be a good place to grow grapes. Second, it's got to be unique in the world; you can't replicate it somewhere else, whether it's the yellow clay in St. Emilion, the 150-year-old Barossa vines, something unique. Washington has the geology, the northern latitude, the natural root stock, volcanic ash soils, the desert heat, and the cool nights."

For Doyenne, he's introduced a varietal roussanne (creamy and thick, with juicy flavors of citrus peel, honey-lemon, and white peach fruits); a Métier white (all Ciel du Cheval viognier, lush and peachy); a Métier red (grenache, syrah, and mourvèdre, spicy and forward); Aix (a syrah-cabernet blend with wild fruits, graphite, and light herbs); and a tangy, mourvèdre-based rosé. The initial ("signature") Doyenne syrah has now been joined by a Grand Ciel vineyard-designate from DeLille's estate vineyard on Red Mountain. In some vintages I prefer the signature, a blend of five clones from four vineyards—Ciel du Cheval, Grand Ciel, Boushey, and Kiona. In others, the Grand Ciel comes out ahead. Either way, both are among the pace setters for the grape in Washington State.

Assets: first pick of fruit from outstanding Red Mountain and Yakima Valley vineyards, a well-traveled winemaker with a particular passion for Rhône wines.

GORDON BROTHERS FAMILY VINEYARDS

First vintage: 1983

www.gordonwines.com

The Gordon brothers planted their first vines in 1980, on a spectacular bluff set 620 feet above the Snake River. Cabernet sauvignon, merlot, syrah, chardonnay, sauvignon blanc, and gewürztraminer are grown, along with experimental rows of tempranillo and malbec. During its first quarter century, the winery had a succession of winemakers; sold grapes to what Jeff Gordon describes as "some really good customers" (L'Ecole, Woodward Canyon, Leonetti, Dunham, and Waterbrook among them); was itself sold (in 2001) and later repurchased (in 2003—complicated story).

During some of these rather painful transitions, the estate wines suffered. But with family ownership restored, a talented new winemaker hired (Tim Henley, who came from Napa's Pine Ridge), and 100 acres of mature vines now being farmed organically, Gordon Brothers seems poised to make its best wines ever.

The unique site—the only vineyard really nearby is Charbonneau—yields wines that are distinctly European in character, with herbal nuances, higher acids, lower alcohol levels, and less obvious use of new oak. Older wines tasted at the winery had developed nicely after 15 years or more—a Gordon Brothers 1990 Merlot showed mature brick and plum colors; scents of fruit pastry, brown sugar, and cherry liqueur; the flavors soft and faded, but pretty and tart. A Gordon Brothers 1988 Cabernet Sauvignon—100 percent varietal and just 12.5 percent alcohol—was another treat, elegant and pleasing with light, tart berry fruit.

Jeff Gordon believes that this is the oldest 100 percent–estate winery in Washington. These days, he proudly admits, no other wineries are taking Gordon Brothers grapes; everything is going into the family's own wines. "The Big Four wines," he says, "are chardonnay, merlot, cabernet sauvignon, and syrah."

Gordon chardonnays come in regular and reserve bottlings; the reserve is the more oaky and buttery, as expected. A light, fresh sauvignon blanc is the other main white wine. Merlot is a best seller, fragrant and refreshingly un-jammy, with tart red berries and plums, perfectly balanced flavors of earth and bark, polished tannins, and hints of cinnamon and cedar. Cabernets and syrahs are just as good, dark and smoky and pungent with roasted coffee scents. Very limited test bottlings of malbec, petite sirah, and tempranillo are in the works; the first tempranillo, released late in 2009, was revelatory—earthy and deep, loaded with coffee grounds, funk, meat, and superrich black fruits.

A second label, called Kamiak, offers a well-made, affordably priced Windust white and Rock Lake red.

Assets: well-established estate vineyards, organic farming, sleeker, more subtly European styling of the less expensive wines, and some interesting, experimental varietals, notably tempranillo.

GORMAN

First vintage: 2002

www.gormanwinery.com

Chris Gorman's rock 'n' roll persona infuses his wines and his tasting room and infects the entire Woodinville warehouse district neighborhood he inhabits ("garage east" he punningly names it). Guitars and rock posters decorate the winery walls, and the wines have a certain swagger to them, with names such as Big Sissy, The Bully, and Evil Twin. Gorman, an engaging rebel who likes to call himself "the anti-winery," comes from a wine sales background and knows the marketing side of the business inside and out.

Gorman and his sometime partner Mark Ryan McNeilly craft similarly bold, occasionally titanic wines, use many of the same vineyards, and manage to ramp up the voltage on their whites and reds without losing a sense of place. These are lavishly endowed wines—big, but never awkward or unbalanced. They are somewhat reminiscent of Leonetti in that winery's formative years, when its wines were so flat-out delicious, you stopped analyzing them and just reached for the bottle to pour yourself another glass.

Gorman's production rarely tops 250 cases of any one wine, with the exception of Zachary's Ladder and The Bully, which reach 400 each—for a total of around 1,500 cases a year. Despite the relative newness of the brand and its small production, Gorman has quickly been noticed; his wines get high scores from all the influential publications and generally sell out well ahead of the new vintage.

The Big Sissy Conner Lee vineyard chardonnay is Gorman's only white, first made in 2006. Fermented in 100 percent–new oak using wild yeast, it piles on the rich toast and butterscotch flavors, with loads of pineapple and candied peach fruit as well; a thoroughly delicious and deeply concentrated wine.

The Evil Twin is an all-Kiona vineyard, syrah–cabernet sauvignon blend, a lovely mix of tart, sappy cassis, smoke, and bright, brambly berry flavors. The Bully cabernet sauvignon is a chewy, cherry-flavored wine; deep and hard and dense.

As with most Gorman reds, The Pixie syrah crosses the 15 percent alcohol line without pausing to breathe, yet remains aromatic, with sweet cherry fruit, spicy tannins, and enough new oak to add butter and butterscotch to the finish. Zachary's Ladder, his lower-priced Bordeaux blend, would be the Meritage wine for many wineries; it's the second wine for Gorman. Compact and dense, it mixes black cherries, iron filings, and rock.

Gorman is no threat with a forklift (he drove one over his own foot a few years ago), but he instinctively knows how to make and market wines that stand out from the crowd. He and McNeilly are well aware that mutual success has made their wines expensive and difficult to find, so they have launched the slyly named Giant Wine Company (which is actually quite small) to market their popular Sinner's Punch and Ghost of 413 value-priced blends.

Assets: a retail and marketing background, a one-man operation ("no employees and, better yet, no board of directors," says Gorman), and the power and passion to make real rock-star wines.

GRAMERCY CELLARS

First vintage: 2005

www.gramercycellars.com

Though sommeliers-turned-winemakers are not uncommon in California, Greg Harrington is the first in Washington to turn from one extremely successful career to another. He passed his master somm exam at 26, working with chefs Joyce Goldstein, Emeril Lagasse, and Wolfgang Puck before deciding to plunge into winemaking. Inspired by the potential he saw in Washington wines, he and his wife, Pam, wasted no time. Shortly after discussing the possibility of making wines "someday," Harrington was in Walla Walla arranging to make wines in a rented facility; he brought in his first grapes in 2005. The couple left their East Coast home in 2006, set up housekeeping in both Seattle and Walla Walla, and launched a winery partnership with Jamie Brown (Waters).

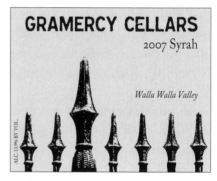

The Waters/Gramercy winery opened in time for the 2007 crush. In 2008, Harrington was named "Best New Washington Winemaker" and Gramercy "Best New Winery" by a Seattle magazine. That year he and Brown also launched their Wines of Substance brand, along with a superdeluxe red wine called 21 Grams. In 2009, in his spare time, Harrington climbed Mount Rainier.

The man is driven, no doubt, but he has as sharply defined and specifically focused a winemaking vision as anyone in Washington. Believing that great wines share common traits—great vineyards, minimalist winemaking, time, and patience—Harrington selects fruit from Les Collines, Pepper Bridge, and Forgotten Hills in Walla Walla, Portteus and Minick in the Yakima Valley, and Phinny Hill in the Horse Heaven Hills. He harvests ripe but not overripe grapes, intervenes minimally in the winemaking, and does not smother the wine in new oak. "Too many wines have excessive alcohol and new oak, are overly fruity, and taste like they could be from anywhere," he writes on Gramercy's website.

Two estate vineyards are being planted to syrah, tempranillo, and Bordeaux varietals. Despite the newness of the winemaker and the winery, Gramercy must already be counted as one of Washington's best—the craftsmanship, quality commitment, and caliber of Harrington's palate mandate it. His syrahs, especially the John Lewis reserve, are intense, peppery, spicy, laserlike wines with sharply defined streaks of herb, wild berry, and earth.

Assets: a world-class palate, great connections to top sommeliers and restaurateurs, and a proven ability to rapidly pull together and effectively manage a first-class winery operation.

HEDGES FAMILY ESTATE

First vintage: 1987

www.hedgescellars.com

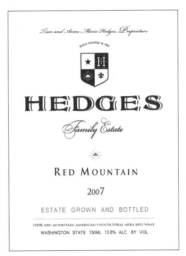

Tom and Anne-Marie Hedges began their family enterprise with a brilliant business plan, marketing Washington wines from a "virtual" winery to buyers in Scandinavia. They parlayed that early success into an audacious vision for establishing vines, a magnificent chateau, and (most unlikely of all) tourism on Red Mountain.

Hedges has always been a smartly run business operation, from its early focus on a single, vivid, fruity blend of cabernet sauvignon and merlot, to its substantial investment in building its vineyards and winery in what might charitably be called the middle of nowhere, to its successful effort to gain legal approval of Red Mountain as an official American viticultural area.

Hedges remains the largest family-owned winery in Washington. Brother Pete Hedges heads up the winemaking team, with assistance from Tom and Anne-Marie's daughter Sarah Hedges Goedhart. Son Christophe is in charge of sales and marketing as well as running the House of Independent Producers (H.I.P.) label.

The workhorse wines for Hedges are the value-priced CMS white and CMS red, which, along with the H.I.P. wines, produce 100,000 cases annually and will soon have their own dedicated winery, sited off the mountain near Pacific Rim. CMS white is roughly two-thirds sauvignon blanc, one-third chardonnay, and a splash of marsanne (the M). CMS red is a roughly equal mix of cabernet sauvignon and merlot, with a bit of syrah (the S).

Some confusion may have arisen from the introduction in recent years of wines labeled Single Vineyard, Two Vineyards, and Three Vineyards and various reserve and block-designated bottlings. Some of these have been discontinued, others have gone through multiple label redesigns, and still others have morphed into the Hedges Family Estate Red Mountain red, which is now the winery's reserve. Almost 12,000 cases of the

2007 Red Mountain red were made, and it marks an important step forward for Hedges, the culmination of a decades-long quest to produce wines with the supple finesse of great Bordeaux. Tart raspberry, boysenberry, and plum fruit wraps into pretty toast, coffee liqueur, and baker's chocolate, all with ripe and fine-grained tannins and plenty of natural acids.

The Hedges estate vineyard was first planted in 1991, to 18 acres each of cabernet sauvignon and merlot and a single acre of cabernet franc. In 1998 and 2000, a two-acre block of Portuguese port varietals was added, along with a bit of petit verdot and malbec. The 40-acre Bel'Villa vineyard is principally devoted to cabernet and merlot, along with three acres of cabernet franc and six of syrah.

In 2003, the Hedges family began applying sustainable agricultural practices to both vineyards, and as of 2008, the Hedges estate vineyard moved into full biodynamic farming. "The real goal is to make the best wine you possibly can," Christophe Hedges explains. "'Biodynamic' says we are going to capture that sense of land in its most unadulterated, raw, cosmologically balanced state."

Assets: prime Red Mountain vineyards, international wine-marketing expertise, biodynamic viticulture, high-performance value brands, and (finally) an identifiable, superpremium reserve.

✱ ISENHOWER CELLARS

First vintage: 1999

www.isenhowercellars.com

Brett and Denise Isenhower grew up in midwestern farm families, studied pharmacy, and came to Walla Walla—and winemaking—after trying their hand at home-brewed beer. Isenhower Cellars was bonded as the valley's twenty-third winery in 1999, and the couple made their first vintage at the original Glen Fiona facility, which has since become Abeja.

They moved the winemaking south of town to Rulo in 2001 and built their own plain, functional winery in 2002, right next door. Production is being cut back to mom-and-pop size—about 2,000 cases—as the winery responds to difficult economic conditions by moving almost entirely to direct sales. Isenhower wines, many with colorful wildflower names and labels, cover a broad spectrum of blends and varietals. I like the attitude they convey— youthful, fresh, convivial, and accessible.

"Wine represents a place better than any other agricultural crop," says Brett Isenhower. "When it's made with respect from vineyard to the bottle, it represents that slice of earth better than anything else."

Isenhower's Snapdragon white is a racy, lightly peppery blend of roussanne and viognier; even better is the vineyard-designate roussanne from Ciel du Cheval, brimming with white peach and pear fruit. The Bachelor's Button is a reserve-style cabernet sauvignon. Supple, brambly, lightly spicy, and svelte, it has the sleekness of a fine racehorse and runs across the palate at a confident gallop. Other regular offerings include Red Paintbrush, a Bordeaux blend; Wild Alfalfa syrah; and varietal bottlings of merlot and cabernet franc. A new series of "recession-busting" wines, featuring dogs on the label, is priced below $20; the Last Straw red has plenty of rustic appeal.

No longer a newcomer to the Walla Walla wine community, Isenhower is moving slowly toward a long-term goal to grow half of its own grapes. The first two acres of an estate vineyard were planted to malbec in 2008. For the near term at least, Isenhower wines will remain blends of grapes from all over Washington State—Yakima Valley, Red Mountain, Horse Heaven Hills, Wahluke Slope—though, strangely, almost no Walla Walla vineyard sources. Grapes are handpicked and hand-sorted, and the Isenhowers avoid modern winemaking additives and enzymes.

It's not just vineyards that are scattered; the actual blends of Isenhower wines change dramatically from year to year. Only the names and label designs are the same. And yet the wines consistently please and have earned the Isenhowers a place in this chapter with the other four-star wineries from Walla Walla.

Assets: creative blends, very pretty labels that stand out in a crowd, hand-built winemaking that puts the emphasis on clean, precise fruit character.

J. BOOKWALTER

First vintage: 1983

www.bookwalterwines.com

Jerry and Jean Bookwalter opened their winery in 1983, making mostly off-dry riesling, chenin blanc, and chardonnay. Jerry works in vineyard management; the winery was a sideline, and it puttered along until problems with other business ventures led to a bankruptcy filing in the early 1990s. When son John Bookwalter returned home a few years later after a successful business career of his own, he did a full-blown SWOT-team analysis (strengths, weaknesses, opportunities, threats)—in PowerPoint no less—and rolled it out to the folks. The prognosis was not so good. The patient was on life support, and John proposed a complete reinvention of the business.

Winemaking consultant Zelma Long was contracted, and thus began a vine-to-wine collaboration that lasted through nine vintages, before being amicably terminated in

2009. Quality improvement, dramatic at first, has since been incremental but steady. The Bookwalters' long history in vineyard management means that exceptionally practiced eyes are on their contracted vines throughout the growing season. Their grapes come from an assortment of well-established vineyards averaging 30 years of age.

The winery is in west Richland and features a tasting room with live music and light food. A second tasting room opened in Woodinville in 2009. John Bookwalter has reorganized the lineup of wines under several different names, many sporting a literary reference (his philanthropic program generates funds for libraries). A subplot is J. Bookwalter's value red, whose white wine companions—Anecdote riesling, Tercet (a roussanne-marsanne-muscat blend), and Couplet (chardonnay-viognier)—are all priced under $20. Foreshadow (formerly Bookwalter's red-label wines) offers both cabernet and merlot. Protagonist is a hot-climate blend made from Red Mountain grapes. Chapter Two is a single, reserve-level wine blended from five barrels (culled from a total of five hundred), always the biggest and the smoothest of all the J. Bookwalter wines.

Not surprisingly, it is the more expensive and limited-production red wines that lift J. Bookwalter to four-star status. These are ripe, rich, heavy, muscular reds loaded with black fruits and often with smoky, earthy tannins. The outstanding vineyard sources include Conner Lee (still managed by Jerry Bookwalter), McKinley Springs, Klipsun, Ciel du Cheval, and Elephant Mountain.

Assets: exceptional vineyard management expertise, a near-decade-long collaboration with Zelma Long, and John Bookwalter's strong business and marketing background.

JM CELLARS

First vintage: 1999

www.jmcellars.com

JM Cellars soon outgrew the basement of John and Peggy Bigelow's Seattle home and, in 2001, moved to its present location, "Bramble Bump," a wooded, Woodinville-area knoll that overlooks Chateau Ste. Michelle's concert grounds. From the beginning, brother-in-law Mike Januik (Januik Winery) has been an inspiration and role model for JM Cellars.

"Peggy introduced me to Mike when he was starting at Stewart," John Bigelow recalls. "For 15 years I watched him go from Stewart to Langguth to Snoqualmie to Ste. Michelle. I was coming up on turning 40, and I wanted to change the focus of my life. I wrote up a business plan and showed it to Mike. He told me which classes to take, which books to read, and which vineyards to buy from, and then left me on my own. Which I was happy for; I wanted to do it myself."

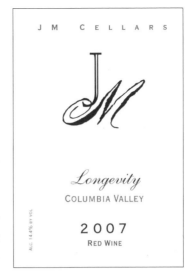

The Bigelows have done it themselves, and done it well; growing their winery steadily, most recently doubling its size from 3,000 cases in 2005 to about 6,000 today. In 2006, John left his day job (channel sales for a high-tech company) for good and hired Tim Drake, whose Woodinville winery experience includes time at Ste. Michelle and Matthews Cellars, as assistant winemaker. That's when things really began taking off.

JM sources fruit from a dozen vineyards, most notably Klipsun, but is moving aggressively toward the goal of becoming an estate winery. Their Margaret's vineyard is part of the massive SeVein project in Walla Walla. It's 40 acres total, with 16 planted so far to cabernet sauvignon, merlot, cabernet franc, petit verdot, malbec, and carmenère. The first harvest was in 2009.

For its white wines, JM produces a Klipsun vineyard sauvignon blanc, a Stillwater Creek viognier, a fine, old-vine chardonnay from Conner Lee fruit, and a rare, late-harvest sémillon. They nicely counterbalance the winery's muscular, nicely proportioned reds. Varietal bottlings of merlot, cabernet sauvignon, and syrah, frequently unblended, use grapes from Klipsun, Kiona, Ciel du Cheval, Boushey, Lewis, Stillwater Creek, and other prime vineyards. Tre Fanciulli (Italian for "three good lads") is the winery's showstopper. It features old-vine Klipsun cabernet blended with merlot and syrah, and it's brimming with delicious black currant, black cherry, boysenberry, and other mixed fruits. A vertical tasting of every vintage (see box) showed me how well these wines can age. Finally, JM's Bramble Bump white and red blends are tasting room favorites that offer great flavor at modest prices.

Assets: access to old-vine fruit, an estate vineyard just beginning to bear, a track record showing consistent improvement, and a classy, classic, signature red.

Tasted in April 2008 at the winery.

JM Cellars 1999 Tre Fanciulli

This is the wine that launched the winery. Klipsun cabernet, Ciel merlot, and Lewis syrah. "I had tasted a cab-syrah blend and I had both in the winery, unblended," Bigelow explained. "I added a little merlot to it to see what that would do. Because it was three grapes and we had three sons who we wanted to name it for, a friend from Italy suggested the name." Still showing a wonderful freshness to aromas of strawberry preserves, leading into black cherry, then adding in black olive, light toast, and even a little peppery note. Plenty of acid and plenty of life ahead.

JM Cellars 2000 Tre Fanciulli

This was made in Walla Walla at Three Rivers. Same vineyards, but more syrah in the blend. Darker and more substantial than the 1999, with plum and cherry and a smoky/peppery vein running through it.

JM Cellars 2001 Tre Fanciulli

This has about a third each of the three grapes—"I was really getting carried away with syrah," says Bigelow. From a cooler year, the wine has a lightly herbal character, with black cherry and cassis. It's seamless and very Bordeaux-like, the most perfectly evolved so far. Some leathery flavors.

JM Cellars 2002 Tre Fanciulli

The fruitiest wine of the tasting, just beginning to soften the rough tannins. The berries come at you in a lovely mix of red, blue, and black, forward and juicy, but this wine does not have the flesh and finish of the 2001.

JM Cellars 2003 Tre Fanciulli

An experiment with 10 percent Russian oak adds a caramelized sweetness to the wine, alongside flavors of black currant, black cherry, smoke, black olive, anise, and black pepper. This is still evolving, integrating, but I like the mass, the density, and the overall character.

JM Cellars 2004 Tre Fanciulli

A stellar effort in a tough vintage. It's got a nice cut to the acids, with more sharp corners and youthful raspberry/strawberry-flavored fruit. Still tight and primary, but well balanced and very clean.

> JM Cellars 2005 Tre Fanciulli
> Very tight, tannic, and somewhat reductive, built to age. There's a mix of rock and barrel underscoring the clean, crisp, tart, mixed berry and cassis fruit. This feels like a mix of 2001 and 2004; one of the best wines of the tasting.
>
> JM Cellars 2006 Tre Fanciulli
> Bright, fresh, and focused, with delicious black currant, black cherry, boysenberry, and other mixed fruits. Give it five years and it's a champ.

LONG SHADOWS

First vintage: 2002

www.longshadows.com

Following a two-decade tenure as CEO of the Ste. Michelle wine group, Allen Shoup decided to forego retirement and instead set about creating Long Shadows. It's a consortium of boutique wineries, each with a focus on a single varietal or blend, produced under the supervision of a world-class, globally recognized winemaker-adviser. French-born Gilles Nicault, who worked at Woodward Canyon from 1996 to 2003, is the on-premise winemaker who oversees the entire portfolio.

"It's a once-in-a-life opportunity," the soft-spoken Nicault admits. "At first I thought, seven brands, people from all over the world; how can I satisfy someone from Germany, from Napa, from Australia, and all over?" The truth is, Nicault is the glue that holds the project together. Though every Long Shadows wine bears the imprint of a celebrity winemaker, without the transparent and meticulous care that he gives the wines day-to-day, the project could not work.

After making the first few vintages in rented facilities, Long Shadows moved into its own $4.2 million winery in 2006, set in the wheat fields a few miles west of Walla Walla. Despite Shoup's description of it as "just a cement box buried in the ground," it's thoroughly modern and strikingly architectural, replete with fine art, and stocked with spare-no-expense winemaking equipment.

Shoup's ultimate goal, as he once explained it, is "to create seven or eight Leonettis—free-standing, 4,000-case wineries that are meeting world standards." So far, each of the wines in the Long Shadows portfolio has its own name, its own label, and its signature style.

Feather is especially popular, a pure cabernet sauvignon made by Napa's Randy Dunn. Concentrated, ripe, and plummy, its red and blue fruits are amplified with ample barrel flavors of toast, chocolate, coffee, and cinnamon, most definitely a Napa-meets-Washington style. Pirouette is a Bordeaux blend (plus syrah, to give it a Washington twist). The winemakers are Napa's Agustin Huneeus and Philippe Melka; it's a substantial, textural, toasty wine, seamless and rich.

Pedestal is Long Shadows' merlot project, made under the supervision of the ubiquitous Michel Rolland in a soft, silky, smoky, voluptuous style. It introduces itself with round cherry fruit and then charges ahead with layers of licorice, citrus, coffee, and rock that enliven the finish. Sequel is a syrah, made by Australia's John Duval, who was head winemaker for Penfolds from 1986 to 2002. There he was responsible for an enormous lineup of shiraz, including the iconic Penfolds Grange. His experience shows in the Oz-like color of Sequel—almost jet black—the spicy berry, plum, cherry, and currant fruit and the silky, polished tannins. Interestingly, Duval uses a splash of cabernet sauvignon in the blend, rather than viognier.

Poet's Leap is Long Shadows' riesling, made under the guidance of Armin Diel of Germany's Schlossgut Diel. Though not technically dry at 1.3 percent residual sugar, it has morphed from a rather round and fruity wine into one that is knife-edged, concentrated, and complex. Loaded with honeysuckle, melon, pear, peach, and hints of sweet grapefruit, it perfectly captures the intensity of Washington grapes and the complexity of German riesling.

In 2004, Long Shadows added Saggi, a super-Tuscan blend that is the project of Ambrogio and Giovanni Folonari. A combination of sangiovese, cabernet sauvignon, and syrah, Saggi has improved since that first vintage, but remains the least-satisfying wine in the lineup, perhaps because so-called super-Tuscan wines themselves lack regional specificity and definition. Chester Kidder is Nicault's personal project, a cabernet, merlot, and syrah blend that showcases his gracious, confident blending skills. Recently, Shoup and a group of investors (most of them partners in Long Shadows) purchased the spectacular Wallula vineyard. That should certainly bring more focus and terroir to any of the company's wines that can base themselves on Wallula's superb fruit.

Assets: world-class winemaking talent, a CEO with big winery abilities and a small winery aesthetic, a varied and fascinating range of wines, and a newly purchased vineyard that is one of the best in Washington.

MARK RYAN

First vintage: 2000

www.markryanwinery.com

Mark Ryan McNeilly is a tall, disheveled, gregarious, and instantly likeable winemaker, and his wines follow suit. They ride big in the saddle, with jammy fruit and plenty of oak and alcohol, and they sport names such as Dead Horse and The Dissident—names with attitude. McNeilly got into the wine business as a salesman for a Seattle distributor, then

Mark Ryan Winery

DEAD HORSE

Ciel du Cheval Vineyard
Red Mountain

RED WINE | PRODUCT OF WASHINGTON STATE | VINTAGE 2007

went to work for Matt Loso at Matthews Estate to learn winemaking. From the beginning, McNeilly has focused on Red Mountain grapes for his signature wines, the Dead Horse and Long Haul reds.

Over time his portfolio has grown, and the unremarkable warehouse district he first made his Woodinville headquarters has become a beehive of start-up grunge wineries. McNeilly, quite to his own surprise, I am sure, is now considered to be the godfather of the garagistes.

The Dead Horse name is a complex pun on Ciel du Cheval, itself a loose translation of Horse Heaven, a reference to the hills that can be seen along the southern horizon when standing in the vineyard. A four-grape, Bordeaux blend, Dead Horse is tannic, liquorous, sweet, and ripe, loaded with flavors of black cherry, plenty of barrel toast, and chocolaty tannins. The Long Haul is McNeilly's right bank–styled, merlot–cabernet franc blend (some petit verdot creeps in at times)—meaty, spicy, herbal, and earthy.

Fleshing out the red wine lineup are a Wild-Eyed syrah, a Crazy Mary mourvèdre, a Water Witch red blend from Klipsun grapes, and a cheaper red called The Dissident, crafted from barrels that didn't make the cut for the Dead Horse and Long Haul. These wines all rock. They take no prisoners, but remain true to the basic strengths of Red Mountain fruit: structure, tannin, grip, and minerality.

"I'm a structure guy—tannin and acid," McNeilly confirms. "I want to make sure everyone knows that Red Mountain is the Côte Rôtie of Washington." Nonetheless, white wines are steadily being added. A pair of viogniers, one from Conner Lee and one from Ciel, made their debut in 2006. In 2007, McNeilly combined them into a single wine, while introducing a fresh and spicy chardonnay that surprised with its complexity and detail. A Dissident white was made in 2007, a sure sign that some rigorous selection is being made for his white wines as well as his reds.

Mark Ryan moved into new quarters in 2009, leaving the funky warehouse district for the more uptown Hollywood section of Woodinville. Ross Andrew and J. Bookwalter are the new neighbors. Now that the godfather and barrels of Dead Horse have arrived, things are sure to get lively.

Assets: a big, generous winemaker who crafts big, generous red wines; an emerging talent for white wines; and a lock on some prime Red Mountain grapes.

NICHOLAS COLE CELLARS

First vintage: 2001

www.nicholascolecellars.com

Mike Neuffer is a quiet man, always a bit reluctant to talk about himself. He made a living in construction in Montana "because I was a third-generation builder; not necessarily what I wanted to do," he confides. "I always thought one day I'd retire and do the wine business. The retirement part never came, but I wanted to leave a legacy for my children. I didn't want them to follow me into a business that was beating me up. So I decided to do something for them and for myself. It just basically was following my passion, my dreams."

He moved to Walla Walla a decade ago, purchased some prime vineyard land near Les Collines, Dwelley, and Leonetti, planted vines, and planned a winery. The wines—all red— were, and still are, dark, chewy, dense, tense, and deeply compact. The first wines from Neuffer's estate grapes were made in 2005, and my notes on all of his 2005 and 2006 wines are quite positive. Although my personal tastes more often run to lower-alcohol, steelier styles, I can certainly appreciate something bigger and more potent if it is a complete and balanced wine without obvious faults.

In 2008, just as the winery was really coming into its own, I received a startling message from Neuffer. "We've decided to change direction," he wrote. "I'm opening a tasting room downtown. We're going to make smaller amounts." Essentially, a partnership with Michael Corliss broke apart. Neuffer kept the inventory and the brand, but sold the vineyards and winery (now home to Tranche) to Corliss. A disappointment certainly, but life goes on, and the new Nicholas Cole tasting room in downtown Walla Walla makes these wines easier to find and to sample.

Whether it's the slow economy or some other factors, Neuffer has dropped his prices significantly, even as his wines are better than ever. The 2005 Estate reserve is the model for what should become the quintessential Nicholas Cole. For the first time, it is cabernet sauvignon–based and could be labeled as such. Dark, chewy, and compact, there are layers of blackberry fruit, lingering flavors that meld smoke, fruit, and acid in perfect proportion. A big wine in a big bottle, for those who like their reds full throttle.

The Camille (Bordeaux blend), Juliet (super-Tuscan style), and Dauphiné (syrah) are all selling for around $35, and I don't have a favorite among them—but if I had to pick one, it would be the 2005 Camille. Dense, liquorous, and smoky, it's the vinous equivalent of a buttery and exotic truffle. The flavors recall the most exotic (and expensive) wines from Spain—concentrated raspberry–black cherry fruit, lots of chocolate, smoke, and spice.

Nicholas Cole also makes a line of GraEagle wines, priced around $25, that use estate-grown fruit not quite ripe enough for the other reds. The Red Wing red is a well-crafted Bordeaux blend. A GraEagle cabernet franc made in 2006 was herbal, peppery, tannic, and dense; I hope it will become a Nicholas Cole regular.

Assets: wines of power and complexity, with a single striking example of each particular style.

First vintage: 1994

www.northstarmerlot.com

Northstar began as a winery devoted solely to merlot, when merlot was king and Washington was angling for the producer crown. The brainstorm of California winemaker Jed Steele and former Ste. Michelle Wine Estates CEO Allen Shoup, it was to be an "icon" project for the company. When Ted Baseler took over as CEO in 2000, he too announced that it was his intention to make Northstar "the best merlot on the planet."

In 2002, just as a dedicated winery was opened across from Walla Walla's Pepper Bridge vineyard, Northstar went through a succession of winemaker changes. Gordy Hill declined to make the move to Walla Walla and now makes wines at Milbrandt. Rusty Figgins made the 2002 wines, then he moved on. David Merfeld has been the man in charge since 2005, and under his watch Northstar has regained its bearings.

Northstar merlots are smooth and satiny upon release, with a lot of expensive-tasting French oak, a testament to the influence of consultant Jed Steele. Both a Columbia Valley merlot and a Walla Walla Valley merlot are made. In most years, my preference is for the former; though production has reached 10,000 cases—four times as much wine as the Walla Walla bottling. It often seems to have more fruit, more depth, and more detail. It's also less expensive.

That said, the 2006 Walla Walla bottling was a gem, perhaps the best Northstar wine to date. Given that Merfeld's 2007, 2008, and 2009 wines are yet to come, his imprint on the winery style is just now being felt. But his commitment, he told me, is to use less new oak. "I want everything in balance," he says.

One thing that has changed completely is the one-time focus on being known strictly for merlot. Northstar now makes cabernet sauvignon, cabernet franc, syrah, petit verdot, and, under its companion Stella Blanca label, sémillon. About 5,000 cases of a Stella Maris red are made; it's a blend of cabernet sauvignon, merlot, syrah, and petit verdot that includes grapes from as many as nine different Columbia Valley vineyards. A fine value at roughly half the price of the Northstar.

Assets: Ste. Michelle's wide-ranging vineyard sources, a first-class winemaking and wine touring facility, and a committed winemaker who has a firm grip on where he is taking the brand.

NOVELTY HILL

First vintage: 2000

www.noveltyhillwines.com

Seattle attorney Tom Alberg, whose venture capital firm specializes in technology start-ups, is the owner of Novelty Hill. The winery's success is centered on two key strengths: its estate vineyard, called Stillwater Creek, and its winemaker, Mike Januik. Stillwater Creek, a steep, south-facing site on the Royal Slope of the Frenchman Hills, was purchased more than two decades ago but not planted until 2000. No expense has been spared, and innovative clonal selection has been chosen, with the goal of creating superior chardonnays, cabernet sauvignons, merlots, and syrahs.

The Novelty Hill/Januik winery opened in Woodinville in 2007. Januik makes all the wines for both. He divides the Novelty Hill releases into Columbia Valley wines, using fruit purchased from Alder Ridge, Chandler's Reach, Klipsun, Weinbau, and other favorite sites; and estate-grown, Stillwater Creek wines. They are brilliant across the entire spectrum. Setting Novelty Hill apart is that rare trifecta—a great vineyard, a great winemaker with almost three decades of Washington winemaking experience, and a price-to-value ratio among the best in the country.

Production levels have reached 15,000 cases total, a number that Januik says is where they will remain. Five white and a half-dozen red wines are being produced from estate fruit alone, and as the vineyard brings more and more fruit online, new varietal wines keep appearing, most recently roussanne and grenache. The vineyard-designated whites—chardonnay, roussanne, sauvignon blanc, sémillon, and viognier—are juicy, mouth-watering wines, bursting with every possible kind of fruit, laced with racy acids, and occasionally showing a distinctive minerality.

The estate reds—cabernet sauvignon, grenache, malbec, merlot, sangiovese, and syrah—are equally thrilling. The syrah's powerful layering of cassis, black cherry, blackberry, toasted nuts, butterscotch, and coffee; the cabernet's nuanced, lightly herbal, thoroughly delicious mix of berries and oak; the firmly authoritative merlot; and the explosively aromatic grenache all portend real greatness for these wines once the vineyard has had a few more years to mature.

Which is not to overlook Novelty Hill's Columbia Valley wines. Januik has been exploring the vineyards of Washington in search of great fruit since the early 1980s—he knows how to find it. The syrah is a particular favorite. On a visit to the winery a year or so ago, I asked Januik how he chose the barrels to use for his vineyard-designates, and he replied simply, "It's a hedonistic thing." All of these wines are hedonistic things, and absolutely not to be missed.

Assets: a veteran winemaker who knows Washington inside and out, a state-of-the-art winery, and an estate vineyard that is headed for greatness.

First vintage: 1997

www.oswinery.com

Formerly known as Owen-Sullivan (a threatened lawsuit, as usual, prompted the name change), O•S is the project of Bill Owen, a wine industry veteran (in wholesale and retail), and Rob Sullivan, a retired banker with, he says, "an entrepreneurial spirit and a wine-loving heart." From an initial run of just four barrels, they've bumped their total production to 5,000 cases, mostly sturdy red Bordeaux blends.

Though I have been critical of these wines in the past, finding them too often volatile and occasionally vinegary, other reviewers have found them "plush and heady." *De gustibus non disputandum,* my mother warned me. In any event, Owen has been working hard to analyze his winemaking process, and now believes that 2008 was "a pivotal vintage for us. I came to the conclusion," he explains, "that yeast of any sort does not function well in a plus-14.5 percent [alcohol] environment, while lactobacillus does. After several years of cautious use of saignée and water exchange, I made 23.6 brix the target no matter what the brix of the must."

Very pleased with the results ("I'm kicking myself long and hard for not having done this sooner"), he intends to stay with that program. Retaining the concentration, muscle, and depth of earlier vintages, yet lowering the alcohol of the finished wines, is a Holy Grail for many Washington winemakers. Whether or not Owen has hit upon the final solution, I give him a lot of credit for looking so hard to find it.

An avid bicyclist (he thinks nothing of riding across the state, mountain passes and all, in the heat of midsummer), Owen has been touring and working with fruit from several excellent Yakima Valley vineyards (Sheridan, Dineen, Meek), as well as better-known sites such as Champoux. A Kabinett-style Champoux vineyard riesling, and S, a Klipsun vineyard sauvignon blanc–sémillon, are his only white wines; the O•S reds are the main stock in trade. From Champoux comes an excellent cabernet franc, with raspberries, strawberries, melon, tobacco, and espresso in the nose and a rough-and-tumble finish. The BSH (hint: the B is for "brick," the H for "house") is a rich blend of cabernet sauvignon, merlot, and cab franc.

R3 is a different blend of the same grapes, "a feminine wine that guys love," says Owen. The Klipsun vineyard red, called M, is primarily merlot, yet the most tannic and tough of them all. The Sheridan vineyard provides grapes for the winery's archetypical

Ulysses red. It's a chocolaty, voluptuous, polished wine, dominated by cabernet franc with a good portion of merlot and cabernet sauvignon. The nearby Dineen vineyard is the source for the O•S syrah; it's superconcentrated—raspberry compote with espresso, smoke, and hints of peppered bacon.

A seemingly tireless experimenter, Owen also makes some interesting one-offs, such as a Meek vineyard petit verdot, a Sheridan vineyard cabernet franc, and a Champoux vineyard cabernet franc. The declassified wine, an inexpensive blend simply named Red, delivers a lot of flavor at a lower price.

Assets: a winemaker with wine wholesale and retail expertise, a focus on Bordeaux blends, access to excellent Yakima Valley fruit, a commitment to making more European-styled wines.

OWEN ROE

First vintage: 1994

www.owenroe.com

James Brown used to be tagged "the hardest-working man in show business." Is David O'Reilly his wine business equal?

O'Reilly, who holds a degree in medieval philosophy from Thomas Aquinas University, was living in Ojai, California, in the mid-1980s, working for Leeward winery, when he first began visiting wineries in Oregon. "I loved the area and I loved pinot noir," he later recalled, "so I decided to move up to the Pacific Northwest and make wine." He first worked at Elk Cove, where he met Peter Rosback, and for a time the two became partners in Sineann and Owen Roe.

They have amicably separated, each with his own brand, both based in Oregon, but making an equal number of Washington wines. O'Reilly's brands include the 30,000-case O'Reilly label, which features an Irish wolfhound, on a lineup of value-priced Oregon wines; the 20,000-case Corvidae wines, a mix of affordable varietals; the 10,000-case Sharecropper's, offering a Washington cabernet and an Oregon pinot; the 7,000-case Abbott's Table, a nine-grape, kitchen sink red blend; and his vineyard-focused, superpremium Owen Roe wines.

These limited-production vineyard-designates are packaged in weighty bottles adorned with rather grim black-and-white photographs of Irish monuments. There are

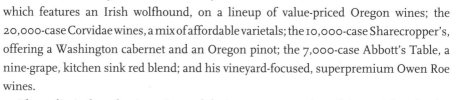

Oregon-sourced pinot gris and a number of pinot noirs, but increasingly, Owen Roe wines are turning to Washington fruit. O'Reilly purchased the Outlook vineyard, in the heart of the Yakima Valley, and is now making his Washington wines in nearby Sunnyside. Of the vineyard's 235 total acres, 90 are bearing, primarily to riesling, merlot, sauvignon blanc, sémillon, and syrah, with a little cabernet sauvignon, cab franc, and test blocks of roussanne and grenache.

Owen Roe's vineyard-designates are selected to be best of type. The DuBrul vineyard, a high-elevation Yakima Valley site, is the source for many of them, including a dense cabernet sauvignon, a powerful riesling with striking minerality, and a beautifully balanced, tiny dancer of a chardonnay. "I made two vows in my life," O'Reilly grins; "one to marry my wife and the other never to make chardonnay. Happily, I'm still married to my wife."

The Lady Rosa syrah is largely sourced from the famed Chapel Block at the Red Willow vineyard. The humbly named but exotically flavored Yakima Valley red wine, says O'Reilly, "exemplifies why I am in the Yakima Valley. It's a right-bank style. Merlot and cab franc are king here."

Owen Roe also makes a Rosa Mystica cabernet franc, stiff and herbal, with unusual cola and root beer flavors; a syrah called Ex Umbris (out from the shadows); Sinister Hand, a red Rhône blend; and one-off gems, such as a Lewis vineyard zinfandel or a Seven Hills (Walla Walla) cabernet. Anything from Owen Roe is going to be memorable and intense, like O'Reilly himself.

The original Owen Roe was a seventeenth-century Irish patriot who fought against Cromwell. "We share his dedication to principle in our work to produce the wines of Owen Roe," O'Reilly explains. "We do not compromise: only the best is good enough."

Assets: a multibrand winery, offering outstanding value wines and exceptional single-vineyard expressions of Yakima Valley fruit.

PACIFIC RIM

First vintage: 2006

www.rieslingrules.com

Pacific Rim brings together several of the critical threads that are weaving the twenty-first-century Washington wine industry. The brand dates back to 1992, when Bonny Doon's Randall Grahm introduced a Pacific Rim riesling. It was dry, most unusual for the time, and it was crafted from a mix of grapes from Washington, California, and Germany.

Grahm's interest in Washington riesling hit its tipping point more than a decade later when he decided to radically downsize his Bonny Doon winery and hired Nicholas Quillé to oversee the restructuring. Quillé, who holds degrees in winemaking from both the University of Dijon and the University of Reims, along with an MB from the

University of Washington (can you say overachiever?), quickly downsized himself out of a job. Once Bonny Doon had been reduced to a tenth its former size, he began thinking about what to do next.

"I went to Randall and said I thought I could do something with Pacific Rim," Quillé recalls. "It was a 15 minute, Warren Buffett–type conversation. I asked him, 'Wouldn't it be nice to have a producer in North America that focuses solely on riesling—someone who would really hang their hat on that grape, and take it to a deeper level?'"

Grahm agreed to keep the Pacific Rim brand, relocate the winemaking to Washington State, and focus almost exclusively on making a full lineup of rieslings. Local partners, the Den Hoed family played an important role, developing a biodynamic vineyard (at Wallula) and funding a $5.7 million production facility that opened in West Richland just in time for the 2007 crush. Production is already up to 140,000 cases, and the goal, says Quillé, is to reach 300,000—95 percent of it riesling—within a few years.

Pacific Rim's portfolio now includes a chenin blanc, a gewürztraminer, a raspberry dessert wine, and a pair of blends called Autumnus—fourteen different wines in all. Though Grahm is the celebrity winemaker bankrolling the brand, the real stars of the show are growers Bill and Andy den Hoed, and Quillé himself, who is both general manager and winemaker.

Most impressive are Pacific Rim's four single-vineyard rieslings, each a showcase for a different winemaking style. One, from Willamette Valley grapes, is done in the style of a German Kabinett. Another, from the Yakima Valley, is what Quillé describes as Alsatian. A third is biodynamically farmed—handpicked, hand-sorted, and handmade, with no additions of yeast or nutrients or acid. The fourth, also from Wallula, is a bit sweeter and riper, more like the classic Washington Johannisberg rieslings.

Other offerings include rieslings labeled Dry, Sweet, and Organic—helpful to consumers—and a White Flowers Brut sparkling riesling. "The thread that we followed on our wines," explains Quillé, "is first Washington . . . then riesling . . . and third the green aspect of what we are doing. That's a theme we've been ramping up. WineWise was begun in the spring of '08; we wanted to do something for wineries, pushing a little harder than what the vineyard folks have done. Our primary goal is to raise awareness and create a frame so people can assess their performance."

Assets: a focus on riesling; value pricing; a commitment to green, organic, and biodynamic viticultural practices; a French-educated winemaker with a strong business background.

First vintage: 1998

www.pepperbridge.com

Norm McKibben acquired the Pepper family's former farm in 1988. The name Pepper Bridge refers to a low-water crossing on the Walla Walla River; at one time it was the only place to ford the river for miles in either direction. McKibben and his partners planted their first 10 acres of vinifera vines in 1991 and expanded the vineyard to around 200 acres over the next several years. The plantings include a variety of wine grapes, predominantly cabernet sauvignon, merlot, and syrah.

Pepper Bridge grapes were in demand from the very beginning; back then there were only about 40 acres of wine grapes growing in the entire Walla Walla Valley. Rick Small (Woodward Canyon), Gary Figgins (Leonetti Cellar), and Marty Clubb (L'Ecole No 41) were the first customers. "That kind of marketing," says McKibben, "got people to notice Pepper Bridge."

The estate winery was founded in 1998, and the spacious, gravity-flow crush facility opened in 2000. A barrel room and tasting room were added in 2003, nestled into a hillside in the middle of the vineyard. The winery uses a combination of fruit from two estate vineyards, both sustainably farmed—Pepper Bridge and Seven Hills.

McKibben hired Swiss-born winemaker Jean-Francois Pellet in 1999, and Pellet has since become a partner in Pepper Bridge and other McKibben projects, notably Artifex, a custom crush facility. Believing that a winemaker who doesn't express his terroir is not doing his job, Pellet has done a masterful job of coddling the wines along as the vineyards matured. McKibben agrees that terroir is very important in the making of world-class wines: "You're going to get a little more variation from vintage to vintage," he points out, "because you're not trying to mask it."

Pellet predicted that he would need five vintages to learn the vineyard, and sure enough, the 2003 vintage marked a clear turning point for both the merlot and the cabernet. Flavors ever since have been less herbal, more classic expressions of strawberry preserves, blackberries, and cassis. A bottle of the 2003 Pepper Bridge merlot, tasted recently at six years of age, was developing very pretty, secondary fruit flavors and aromas and was nowhere near its life's end.

"After 10 years I'm talking terroir," Pellet confirms, with a little shy pride. "We all want that sense of place. It's a vague word, but it means a lot to me." Terroir shows up in little ways, rarely obvious, but the sort of subtle harmonics that turn a one-note wine into a symphony. Working with just two vineyards—Pepper Bridge and Seven Hills—

Pellet can reach for details that are easily lost when too many grape sources, grapes that are too ripe, maceration that goes on too long, too much new oak, and the like affect the winemaking.

Pepper Bridge wines have complexity and balance—they don't stop. Many wines start fruity and die, or crack up and show odd flavors, but these keep going; they are seamless and nicely integrate the elements of herb, fruit, and barrel toast. They are released young, but are built to live.

Along with the regular bottlings, Pellet also makes a pair of vineyard reserve reds (Pepper Bridge and Seven Hills) that carry the same flavors up a notch or two in intensity. The Seven Hills is a favorite, with pretty aromas including a sweet hay note, an elegant lightness to the body, and a mix of sweet grain, berry, and light herb.

Thanks in part to an aggressive program of organic management, an effort to rebuild soil after decades of wheat farming, Pepper Bridge wines are on a steep curve of dramatic improvement. "Not only are the vineyards getting better," Pellet enthuses, "but I'm getting better. One thing I really enjoy is that you can have all the money in the world but you are not going to speed up Mother Nature; you just have to be patient."

Assets: one of Walla Walla's oldest vineyards, a skilled, European-trained winemaker, a tightly focused brand, and an absolute dedication to sustainability.

REININGER

First vintage: 1997

www.reiningerwinery.com

Chuck Reininger, like Rob Newsom of Boudreaux, was a professional mountaineer who worked as a climbing guide in Argentina, Alaska, and Washington. He learned winemaking at Waterbrook before opening his modest winery, playfully dubbed Shackteau Reininger, in 1997. It was just the tenth winery in the Walla Walla Valley and among the first to be located at the airport, now home to a thriving, incubator-style community of garagistes. A few years ago, Reininger moved his winery six miles west of town, renovating two old potato sheds into an impressive 15,000-square-foot winery and tasting room. Nearby is the Ash Hollow vineyard, in which he is a minor investor and from which he receives cabernet, merlot, and syrah.

Reininger makes about 3,500 cases annually, all wines from the Walla Walla AVA. Another 6,500 cases are made of a very fine sister label called Helix by Reininger. First produced in 2002, Helix is designed for larger-production Columbia Valley wines—a way to expand, Reininger explains, without cannibalizing the founding brand.

Chuck Reininger seemed to lock onto his style early on, and has kept it consistent, thanks to excellent grape sources and a confident touch with his barrels. Reininger wines surmount vineyard and vintage variation; they are supremely smooth and supple, creamy and delicious. Now well into his second decade of winemaking, he is experimenting with a number of unusual varietal wines as well as sophisticated Bordeaux blends. "One of the things I really enjoy is I want people to experience the varietal," he explains. "So they see what Washington really can do with these grapes. We've come out with a malbec and a carmenère; I've also got a blend together that's cab, merlot, franc, malbec, petit verdot, and carmenère."

Reininger cabernets are open and forward, showing juicy cherry and strawberry flavors, dotted with herb and spice, finished with luscious milk-chocolate flavors. The merlots are even better: smooth and seamless, juiced up with spicy berry and plum, then softened with barrel flavors of butterscotch, milk chocolate, and coffee. These wines seem to glide along on a carpet of silk, tossing out bursts of spice and herb along the way.

The Ash Hollow vineyard syrahs are more herbal and at times scorchingly acidic, distinctive and concentrated, with dense flavors of cranberry and pomegranate.

There is a late-release, sangiovese-based blend called Cima that Reininger calls his "Super Wallan." The Helix wines go from strength to strength, improving with each new vintage. The Helix sangiovese, syrah, Stone Tree vineyard SoRho red, and Stillwater Creek vineyard merlot are simply outstanding.

Assets: great barrel management; two well-defined, separate but equal brands; and a consistent, accessible and consumer-pleasing style.

ROBERT KARL CELLARS

First vintage: 1999

www.robertkarl.com

Robert Karl Cellars, founded in 1999 by physician Joseph Gunselman and his wife, Rebecca, has gone from strength to strength with never a stumble. Vintage after vintage has been beautifully crafted, sleek, compact, and polished. Both Bordeaux blends and varietal wines consistently score well in my tastings.

Joe Gunselman has proven himself to be a meticulous winemaker with a talent for blending that is particularly evident in his reserve and cabernet wines. I can't help but find a studied, precise, clinical, physician's approach in these

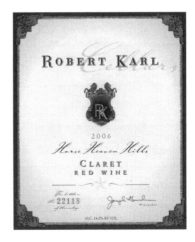

wines, but I mean that as a sincere compliment. They are clean and polished: Gunselman is to reds what Rulo's Kurt Schlicker is to whites. These red wines, when first released, are locked up tight; they must be decanted.

Beginning with the 2003 vintage, the Gunselmans have sourced grapes exclusively from vineyards in the Horse Heaven Hills AVA. They purchased their own eight acres on Phinny Hill, near a block of vines planted for them a decade ago. Their love for the area began back then, while on a hunt for grape sources. Says Joe Gunselman: "To me it has a magic to it; it just hit us the first time we traveled there. We didn't know there were a lot of vineyards already there; we just knew it was the place."

Robert Karl wines offer exceptional quality for the price and are styled for long-term cellaring as much or more than for immediate enjoyment. A little sauvignon blanc is the only white wine made, for this is truly a red wine specialist. Few wineries still make a Claret, but Robert Karl's five-grape version is iconic, and a great introduction to the brand. Along with the winery's cabernet sauvignon, it best represents the Robert Karl signature style. A home run from the very first vintage, the cabernet now blends grapes from Gunselman Bench, Phinny Hill, and McKinley Springs. Dense, deep, and angular, it's loaded with bright berry flavors mixing raspberry, strawberry, and boysenberry. Much smaller amounts of a Gunselman Bench vineyard-designated cabernet are now being made; it's a bit more forward and open, but with the same tight structure.

In 2006, for the first time, Robert Karl also made a varietal cabernet franc. A limited amount of syrah, with fruit from the McKinley Springs vineyard, is produced, showing tangy flavors of boysenberry, raspberry, and tart cranberry, hints of meat and smoke and bacon, and crisp acids that seem to etch the flavors into sharp relief. The Inspiration reserve is Robert Karl's most expensive and limited wine, a complex, sappy Bordeaux blend. Any of these wines may be cellared for a good ten years; I would be very surprised if they did not in fact have lifetimes measured in decades.

Assets: a focus on red wines from great Horse Heaven Hills vineyards; a winemaking style that is precise, compact, complex, and structured for cellaring.

RULO

First vintage: 2001

www.rulowinery.com

Kurt and Vicki Schlicker choose to self-distribute their Rulo wines to keep their prices as low as possible. They do not seek out, nor do they need, high praise from influential critics; they sell every bottle and have a growing legion of admirers. You may not be familiar with their wines. But if you love clean, bracing flavors, flavors that seem to crystallize the essential components of wine—fruit and acid—and capture the sparkling clarity of the grapes, Rulo is for you.

Built in 2001, the functional winery is adjacent to the owners' home a few miles south of downtown Walla Walla. Chardonnay, sauvignon blanc, viognier, cabernet, and syrah are the focal points. It cannot be overstated: Rulo wines offer extraordinary clarity and focus. They profile immaculate fruit with bracing acid and tread lightly on the new oak. Kurt Schlicker—a practicing anesthesiologist—takes full advantage of his degrees in microbiology, pediatrics, and anesthesiology and runs a tight ship. His wines have nothing clinical about them; they are never boring or stripped, but you get the feeling they have been well cared for.

Combine is one of several sauvignon blancs made, all vivid and bracing, like a dash through a cold mountain spring. Another is pure Evergreen vineyard fruit, spicy, minty, and sharp, almost Sancerre-like. The Ceres white blends in chardonnay; it's barrel-fermented, herbal and intense. Chardonnay is another Rulo focus; some are barrel-fermented, some are done in stainless, revealing brilliant, bright, apple fruit, and mouth-cleansing acids. The Walla Walla viognier displays flavors of lime and citrus and rock that seem to fade forever.

Rulo's red wines include a fresh and forward blend called Syrca, roughly three-quarters syrah and one-quarter cabernet. There are several syrahs, most notably the Silo reserve, a riot of subtle, extended flavors—berry, currant, rock, and earth. Cabernet sauvignon is offered as a pure varietal, dense and ripe with black fruits, black olive, earth, and rock.

Case production has topped out at 3,000. Two small vineyards (one leased, one owned) are being developed, in the Rocks near Cayuse. Syrah, viognier, and chardonnay are in the ground. "We're the only knuckleheads who have planted chardonnay down there," Schlicker chuckles, adding, "I think it's gonna be a killer—that's what we're betting on." I would bet he's absolutely right.

Assets: immaculate winemaking, beautifully crafted wines of intense clarity that sell at prices well below fair market value.

SAVIAH CELLARS

First vintage: 2000

www.saviahcellars.com

Richard Funk studied microbiology at Montana State, intending to brew beer for a living. A move to Walla Walla in 1991 sparked an interest in wine, and his work over the course of a decade as an environmental health specialist with the county brought him in close contact with the wineries. He helped them to untangle water quality and wastewater management regulations, while he scouted out the best vineyard locations and grape sources. Since he founded Saviah Cellars, winemaking has become his full-time occupation.

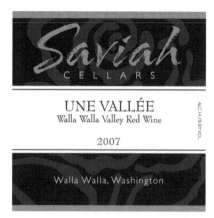

Starting with just 300 cases the first year, production has reached 4,200, all small-lot varietals and blends. But as with many successful, family-owned wineries, there is also a cash cow on board; at Saviah it's a generous merlot-based blend called The Jack. Funk makes 5,000 cases of The Jack and it usually sells out quickly. Priced around $15, it doesn't cut corners on the fruit, and it also sports one of the cleverest labels in the state, a sepia-toned jack of clubs. It is due to be joined soon by a syrah-based version named The Jack of Diamonds.

Saviah's signature style for both white and red wines begins with lovely aromatics and brings in juicy and fine-tuned fruit flavors, restrained use of oak, and balanced wines across the board. The chardonnays, sourced from Stillwater Creek grapes, are whole-cluster pressed and barrel-fermented. "Succulent" is the word that keeps cropping up as they roll across the palate; they're juicy and loaded with a mix of apple, pear, and light tropical fruit, especially pineapple. A barrel-aged, white Bordeaux blend named Star Meadows is a recent addition to Saviah's white wines.

Red wines are the mainstay here, and new varietals have been steadily added. They now include a floral, spicy cabernet sauvignon, a sweetly herbal cabernet franc, and a pair of sharply etched syrahs—one from Red Mountain, the other from Stillwater Creek. The Big Sky Cuvée is Funk's Columbia Valley Bordeaux blend, but his best wine is most often Une Vallée, its companion Walla Walla Valley red. Pepper Bridge, Seven Hills, and McClellan vineyard grapes go into this round and approachable blend of cabernet sauvignon, merlot, and cabernet franc. These are the oldest blocks of fruit that Saviah uses, and along with its sweet and tangy flavors of cherry and berry, Une Vallée has the structure to age for up to a decade.

Funk also consults for Watermill winery and has embarked upon several joint vineyard projects with that winery's owners. The first Watermill estate grapes were harvested in 2007, 12 acres planted in the Rocks to cabernet franc, malbec, mourvèdre, syrah, and tempranillo. A 10-acre syrah vineyard is being developed nearby.

Assets: owner-winemaker with a deep and detailed knowledge of the Walla Walla Valley, access to excellent grapes, an ability to craft wines with generous aromas and succulent fruit flavors.

SEVEN HILLS

First vintage: 1988

www.sevenhillswinery.com

Though it is one of Walla Walla's founding wineries, Seven Hills remains somewhat underappreciated by the critics. Perhaps it is the less ripe, lower-alcohol, more European styling of the wines, or the quietly modest personality of the winemaker, Casey McClellan. For those who prefer grace over power, there are many hidden treasures to be found here.

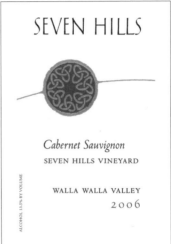

McClellan's family was instrumental in planting the Seven Hills vineyard almost 30 years ago. It was the first—and for many years the most important—source of grapes in Walla Walla. No longer owners of that property, McClellan and his wife, Vicky, nonetheless source Seven Hills grapes for some of their best wines. A McClellan estate vineyard was planted in 2003, also located on the Oregon side of the valley, and now totals 20 acres, all Bordeaux red grapes.

The Seven Hills winery, originally in Oregon, moved to downtown Walla Walla a decade ago, where it shares a beautifully renovated, historic brick building with the Whitehouse Crawford restaurant. A wide range of wines is offered, but McClellan is a veteran who handles them all well, makes them in a consistent style, and never seems to slip up. Seven Hills certainly has its share of admirers, as production has reached about 14,000 cases. To his surprise, most of the growth, says McClellan, is fueled by his riesling.

That wine, Germanic in style with streaks of sweet honey and tea, coupled with the snap of natural acids and a mix of pretty fruits, is half from Evergreen vineyard, half from 30-year-old Yakima Valley vines. An Oregon pinot gris and a Wahluke Slope viognier, both fresh and crisply defined, are also made annually.

Seven Hills Columbia Valley reds include a fragrant, soft merlot and a somewhat austere cabernet sauvignon. Several more substantial cabs are made: vineyard-designated, pure varietals from Ciel du Cheval, Klipsun, and Seven Hills; and a Red Mountain reserve, a tight, steely, complex and challenging wine, with concealed muscle and depth.

Among the more unusual wines, done in limited case quantities, are a varietal tempranillo, a malbec, a petit verdot, and a rare Walla Walla carmenère. Pentad is the winery's most complex wine, a cabernet-dominated Bordeaux blend that includes a generous portion of carmenère. Subtle and soft, aromatic, and laced with herb and savory spices, it is a delicate, evocative, and challenging wine that rewards your attention.

Assets: a long track record making wine in the Walla Walla Valley; excellent vineyard sources (the same rows from the same old-block vines are harvested every year); and graceful, unpretentious winemaking.

SHERIDAN VINEYARD

First vintage: 2000

www.sheridanvineyard.com

Scott Greer, a former pension planner who confesses he simply set out to buy himself a gentleman's farm in the Yakima Valley, now stands in the front ranks of an ongoing regional renaissance, centered in the valley's Rattlesnake Hills. Greer purchased 76 acres of orchard and Concord grape land in 1996. Chris Camarda (Andrew Will), who was advising him, snagged 36 adjacent acres to establish his own Two Blondes vineyard. With DuBrul and Dineen also nearby, they are in the heart of an exciting grape-growing region.

The first four acres of Sheridan cabernet sauvignon went in the ground the following spring. "I made every single mistake you can possibly make in that first four acres," Greer cheerfully confesses. "I'm leaving it in the ground as my ode to how naïve I was." Sheridan's site sits on a hilltop at 1,200 feet, with very shallow, rocky soil and a caliche underlay. Over the years he's added merlot, cabernet franc, malbec, petit verdot, syrah, and a few rows of sauvignon blanc and sémillon—64 acres in all, most of it split between the two cabernets.

Camarda mentored him with both vineyard management and winemaking, and the sociable Greer says he relentlessly questioned every winemaker who would acknowledge his presence. "I searched out the wines I had a lot of respect for, tried to learn the philosophy behind the winemaking as much as possible," he recalls. "I learned that you can never make the wine better than the quality of the fruit coming in the front door, no matter how good you are. But you can certainly go backwards."

Greer is a quick study. He now manages the nearby Dineen and Meek vineyards, and sells his own fruit to Stevens and O•S Winery. His winemaking he describes as very low-tech: open-top fermenters, manual punch-downs, and so on. All 4,000 cases produced annually are estate-grown, the lion's share going into his inexpensive second wines under the Kamiakin label. The Sheridan label is reserved for a chewy and dense, unfined and unfiltered cabernet franc; a leafy, textural cabernet sauvignon; a merlot-cabernet–cab franc blend named Mystique; a two-cabernet blend named L'Orage; and exceptional syrahs that smell and taste like ripe, almost raisined grapes, hung meat, boysenberry syrup, smoke, tar, and coffee, all infused with wild herbs.

There are also reserve bottlings of the syrah and cabernet, given more time in barrel and bottle, and overall a big step forward in terms of power, depth, and detail.

Assets: high-quality estate fruit, in a location that encourages longer hang times and delivers complex, herbal flavors at moderate alcohol levels.

SOOS CREEK

First vintage: 1989

www.sooscreekwine.com

Soos Creek's Dave Larsen was the first of an impressive number of Boeing Wine Club alumni to make it to the big leagues. He crushed his debut commercial vintage in 1989. Fifteen vintages later, he finally retired from his day job as a Boeing financial planner to take on winemaking full-time.

A new winery building at his home in south King County was completed in 2009, allowing Soos Creek production to reach 1,500 cases annually, all red wines. "I have no grandiose plans of getting too big," Larsen modestly insists. "I like being small; I like doing everything myself."

The winery is named after a little creek located nearby, and its wines are easily spotted on retail shelves by their distinctive label graphic of a horse outlined in thick, black ink. Thanks to his early start and Boeing purchasing power, Larsen immediately lined up impeccable vineyard sources, Ciel du Cheval, Champoux, and Charbonneau among them. He remembers seeking out their fruit because, he says, "Woodward Canyon, Leonetti, and Quilceda Creek were already doing great things with it." At the time, he wondered why more people weren't after the same stuff he was.

Now they are, and newcomers must wait in line for those grapes. Soos Creek does well by them. For his first eight vintages, Larsen made only cabernet. At a vertical tasting early in 2008, he poured every cabernet he'd made from 1989 through 2002 (missing only 1993, "which suffered an untimely death a few years after bottling," he explained). My personal favorites were the 2001 Artist Series #1, 1999 Columbia Valley reserve, and 1997 Columbia Valley. But the oldest wines were still drinking nicely, especially the 1992 Ciel du Cheval cabernet, blended with 8 percent Champoux merlot. It was the first time the alcohol reached 14 percent, and at 15 years of age the wine remained firm, tannic, and chewy, with tart red fruits in fine condition and a fat, meaty finish.

For over a decade, Soos Creek produced four or five different wines annually, including two standout, single-vineyard cabernet sauvignons from Champoux and Ciel du Cheval. In 2007, for the first time, Dave Larsen also made a syrah and a merlot. Soos Creek's Champoux vineyard red weaves together black fruits, spices, and licorice; the Ciel du Cheval offers sleek and juicy red fruit flavors of cranberry, raspberry, pie cherry, and even a bit of pomegranate, backed with substantial acids.

The Sundance red is made with what Larsen dismisses as "leftovers," but these are not your mama's leftovers. At $20, it's much like the Quilceda Creek red, that winery's entry-level blend, benefiting from the same care as the label's most prestigious wine. At Soos Creek, the top-of-the-line wine is the Artist Series red, a blend of grapes from Champoux, Ciel du Cheval, Weinbau, and Dineen—select vineyards that represent four of the best AVAs in Washington. It's almost exactly half-and-half cabernet sauvignon and cabernet franc and tastes like beautifully ripe blackberries, boysenberries, and cassis, adding layers of chocolate and baking spices as it winds through the finish.

Assets: outstanding vineyard sources, ageworthy red wines with density and concentration.

* SPRING VALLEY VINEYARDS

First vintage: 1999

www.springvalleyvineyard.com

For over 100 years the Corkrum family has farmed wheat at its Spring Valley ranch, 12 miles northeast of Walla Walla in the rolling hills of the Palouse. In 1993 Shari Corkrum Derby and her husband, Dean Derby, a former football star, planted two acres of merlot, a successful experiment that quickly grew to include 45 acres of merlot, cabernet sauvignon, cabernet franc, petit verdot, malbec, and syrah.

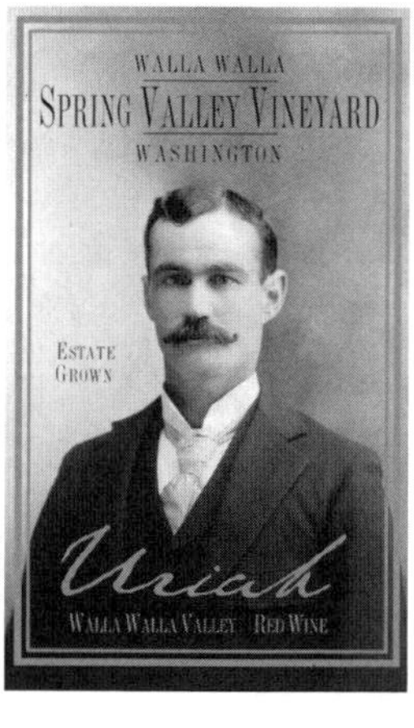

From the first vintage, their Spring Valley grapes were in demand, going to Cadence, Walla Walla Vintners, Reininger, and Tamarack, among others. Encouraged by the results, the Derbys launched their own winery. Their first wine, 1,000 cases of a merlot-dominated blend named Uriah, honored Shari Corkrum Derby's grandfather and pictured him in a vintage photograph on the label. It remains the flagship blend.

Spring Valley's lineup has grown to include Frederick, a cabernet sauvignon–dominated blend; Derby, a pure cabernet; Nina Lee syrah; and Muleskinner merlot, all dedicated to various Corkrum ancestors, with labels featuring old photographs and brief biographies. A Katherine Corkrum cabernet franc was introduced in 2007.

Tragedy struck late in 2004, when son Devin Derby died following a car accident. It sent the winery into disarray, created discord among family members, and ultimately led to the sale of the brand, though not the vineyard, to Ste. Michelle Wine Estates. The new owners have retained Serge Laville, a Frenchman who joined the winery as Devin Derby's assistant in 2002, as winemaker. Winery equipment was updated, and another 70 acres of land leased from the family and planted mainly to cabernet franc, cabernet sauvignon, and merlot, with smaller amounts of petit verdot and malbec. With the first expanded crop in 2009, production of Spring Valley wines can be expected to more than double, from 5,000 to as many as 12,000 cases.

Spring Valley wines share and display terroir-driven flavors quite distinct from those of any other Walla Walla Valley subregion. Intense, almost syrupy berry flavors are augmented by streaks of sweet herb, grass, leaf, and bark—grace notes, if you will, that characterize this unique site. The fruit is ripened to rather high alcohol levels and buoyed with powerful acids. Though some wines, especially the syrah, can approach 16 percent alcohol—too much for my taste—these big, brawny, chewy, complex, and generous reds are among the most distinctive and powerful in Washington. Others are taking notice, and new vineyard projects from Precept and Abeja are in the works nearby.

Assets: a unique vineyard location, full-throttle reds, and the financial and marketing power of Washington's biggest winery group.

STEPHENSON CELLARS

First vintage: 2000

www.stephensoncellars.com

Dave Stephenson took short courses at UC Davis in the late 1980s, concentrating on brewing science. He moved to Bellingham, where he planned to open a brewery; worked odd jobs, and started reading about Walla Walla. After visiting a few times in the late 1990s, he pulled up stakes and moved to town, doing custom crush work at Waterbrook for Christophe Baron, Charlie Hoppes, and Mike Januik, who were all starting wineries. "It was an amazing place to work as an apprentice," Stephenson recalls.

He's gone on to do a great deal of consulting, for such Walla Walla wineries as Otis Kenyon, Russell Creek, Sapolil, and Zerba. Stephenson is a

quiet, unassuming man, and to hear him tell the story, he has mostly been dragged kicking and screaming into this work. Nonetheless, he made time to begin his own winery project in 2000.

He launched Stephenson Cellars with as little fanfare as possible, renting a tiny shack out at the airport, small and tucked away off the main avenues. He made just six barrels (140 cases) of syrah, with fruit purchased from Dave Minick in the Yakima Valley and Forgotten Hills in Walla Walla. In 2002 he added another three barrels from the same two vineyards, along with 90 cases of Forgotten Hills merlot. By 2003 he was up to 500 cases, mostly syrah and cabernet sauvignon. In 2004 one barrel of a reserve syrah was made, and currently he's expanded to 1,200 cases a year, yet remains determined to keep it small. "I get a little queasy making large amounts of wine," says Stephenson, "because I lose track of barrels. I want to know every individual barrel; I can feel the trade-offs if I go beyond that."

Syrahs are what Stephenson does best, sourcing grapes from a handful of carefully selected sites, occasionally making a vineyard-designate or a reserve. "I don't want to make 'bell curve' wines," he writes on his website, "the ones where you blend varieties together for predictable flavor profiles that have been proven to please most wine drinkers. I like to accentuate what's edgy about particular lots. So I'd be the first to admit that my wines aren't for everyone."

A 2006 Forgotten Hills viognier was his first foray into white wine, "put through malolactic and treated like Burgundy." Also quite good that year was his merlot, a ripe, textural, sexy wine with a finish that refuses to quit. A downtown Walla Walla tasting room opened in 2009, and a nonvintage red table wine was added to the lineup. Nonetheless, Stephenson Cellars remains one of the least-known, though most interesting, boutiques in town.

Assets: a consultant's wide range of winemaking knowledge and experience, and a special knack for syrah.

STEVENS

First vintage: 2001

www.stevenswinery.com

A protégé of Matt Loso (ex–Matthews Cellars), Tim Stevens worked both there and at Sheridan before setting off on his own. His initial production was 100 cases of Champoux vineyard cabernet franc, a rather quirky start indicative of the unusual style of Stevens wines.

Tim and his wife, Paige, do just about everything at the winery, which moved to bigger quarters (still in Woodinville) in the summer of

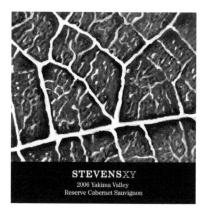

STEVENS XY
2006 Yakima Valley
Reserve Cabernet Sauvignon

2008. They make about 2,500 cases of red wine, 300 of white, and a very small amount of rosé, sold at the tasting room only. The labels, starkly beautiful black-and-white depictions of the owner's original works of art, are as attention grabbing as the wines themselves. Stevens wines sell out quickly, mostly to mailing list and tasting room customers; they are rarely seen in wine shops or on restaurant wine lists.

Trim, elegant, sharply defined, and long lasting, Stevens cabernets are personal favorites. He draws grapes primarily from select Yakima Valley vineyards—Sheridan, Dineen, and Meek, all managed by Scott Greer; and DuBrul, which provides the core of his exceptional XY reserve.

The 424 red (cabernet sauvignon, cabernet franc, and a little merlot) displays earthy details in both nose and mouth and tastes of mushroom, wet leaf, and moist earth, along with coffee and blueberry components. The Black Tongue syrah is an immense, brooding wine with a spectacular mix of black fruits, cassis, earth, soy, and forest floor. Stevens's Sheridan vineyard merlot, dark, subtle, and beautifully proportioned, glides across the palate like Apollo Ono dancing with the stars. A few cases of malbec may come and go quickly, and a less expensive red blend called Oui is now offered, perhaps as solace to those who look longingly at the "sold out" signs on the other Stevens wines.

Representing the white wines are a full-bodied sauvignon blanc and a bone-dry viognier. Immaculate and light, the viognier clocks in under 13 percent alcohol, yet delivers ripe fruit flavors. Though Stevens remains a bit of a local secret, all of these wines belong on anyone's list of Washington's best.

Assets: a tight focus on a handful of truly great Yakima Valley vineyards, and a particular gift for making Yakima Valley cabernet sauvignons.

SYNCLINE WINE CELLARS

First vintage: 1999

www.synclinewine.com

Syncline, a 5,000-case winery founded in 1999 by James and Poppie Mantone, has been a leader on so many fronts I lose count. They are one of a handful of wineries on the West Coast using the Vino-Seal glass closures. They have recently joined the ranks of grower-producers working with biodynamic techniques. Syncline wines have been instrumental in bringing acclaim from outside the region to the Columbia Gorge AVA, which spans the Washington-Oregon border on the eastern edge of the Cascades.

James Mantone is bookish and intense, with wide-set, open, inquisitive eyes—not shy, but not demonstrative either. While backpacking through Oregon in the summer of 1995, he found work at a custom crush facility making small batches of wine for a wide range of clients. "It was like working at ten or twelve different wineries, all at the same time," he recalls.

He tasted some early Rhône Ranger efforts from McCrea Cellars and Glen Fiona, wines so good that he started driving north to visit eastern Washington wine country and meet the growers. "I started to see some great potential in the land," he recalls. "Everybody was still chasing merlot, which they picked in the first weeks of September, and they didn't get a frost till November! So I asked myself, 'Well, what's wrong with the rest of the growing season?' And I started looking into some late-ripening varietals."

A marriage and a move north brought James and Poppie Mantone to the Columbia Gorge to raise a family and build a winery. From the start, the Mantones have produced well-structured, detailed, and highly aromatic wines. Better still, they are priced affordably and crafted for both near-term enjoyment and cellaring. Their business approach is based on the European model—small, family-owned—"what one or two people could do," says James. "You make the best wines you can," he modestly explains, "upgrade equipment when you can, pay as you go."

The Mantones' focus on southern French varietals keeps expanding as they work with blends of cinsault, mourvèdre, counoise, and grenache, along with syrah and viognier. Branching out still further afield, recent Syncline releases include one of Washington's first grüner veltliners. Mantone is cultivating a small estate vineyard (Steep Creek Ranch) biodynamically and replacing barrels with concrete tanks, noting that in his view "oak flavors muddy the wines."

The vibrant, juicy Subduction red, Syncline's least-expensive wine, accounts for a third of the winery's 5,000-case production. Cuvée Elena is its more expensive sibling, a smorgasbord of concentrated plum, prune, and cherry fruit. Syncline's Celilo vineyard pinot noir, produced from vines planted in 1972, proves that Washington is not entirely befuddled by that snarly grape. Other delights include a tangy rosé, a sparkling chardonnay, and two-barrel offerings of cinsault, grenache, and mourvèdre. In brief, nothing from this groundbreaking, family enterprise ever disappoints.

Assets: Rhône grape focus, European production methods, unique vineyard sources, commitment to organic (and some biodynamic) viticulture.

TAMARACK CELLARS

First vintage: 1998

www.tamarackcellars.com

Tamarack Cellars' Firehouse red has become the iconic Walla Walla mutt wine, much as owner Ron Coleman's legendary Iceberg Diner is the town's most-loved burger joint. It's too bad Coleman doesn't serve his wine with his burgers; it would be a match made in heaven.

The Firehouse accounts for about two-thirds of Tamarack's 18,000-case annual production. "I always wanted to make affordable wine" Coleman explains. "It's almost impossible to do that without volume. Not cheap wine, but affordable wine." Coleman is one of Walla Walla's most liked and most affable winemakers, but he's not shy with opinions. Having worked in wine sales (at restaurants, retail shops, and several wineries) before opening his tasting room doors at the airport, he has a more worldly, less dreamy view of the business than many of the newcomers.

"People are buying their wines as cheaply as they can these days," he told me in a recent interview. "Restaurant wine sales are way off. People are still buying good wine, but taking it home. Firehouse sales are enormously strong; cabernet franc also. Merlot is holding its own, but syrah is a tough sell."

Along with Firehouse (named for his first crush facility, an old fire station), Coleman makes ample amounts of chardonnay, cabernet sauvignon, cabernet franc, merlot, sangiovese, and syrah and is especially fond of vineyard-designates. He already does designates from DuBrul, Sagemoor, Ciel du Cheval, and Seven Hills, with Wallula, Tapteil, and maybe Weinbau due to follow. "I want people to be able to taste seven great vineyards in one spot," he says. The idea is to have a reserve winery within the winery, all vineyard-designated and focused on red blends with Bordeaux grapes.

Though I once criticized Tamarack for being a bit formulaic, I am happy to retract those words. Recent vintages are extremely consistent, very well made, interesting to taste through, and they particularly shine with chardonnay, cabernet sauvignon, cabernet franc, and the growing lineup of single-vineyard wines. Visitors to the modest tasting room will also find an astonishing collection of large-format bottles offered for sale.

Assets: a winemaker-owner with retail experience, an expansive range of single-vineyard wines, and a couple of outstanding value wines.

WATERS

First vintage: 2003

www.waterswinery.com

Waters founding winemaker Jamie Brown, formerly a partner in James Leigh Cellars, is well connected in Walla Walla, and launched his new project with grapes purchased from a handful of select sites, notably the Leonetti estate vineyard. It was a James Leigh Cellars syrah that introduced Brown to sommelier Greg Harrington, who liked the wine so much he decided to move to Walla Walla and start making wines of his own.

Harrington and Brown, along with managing partner Jason Huntley, built the Waters winery

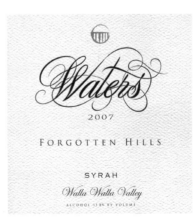

2007

FORGOTTEN HILLS

SYRAH

Walla Walla Valley

ALCOHOL 13.8% BY VOLUME

next door to Va Piano, just in time for the 2007 crush. Along with their own wines, they collaborate on a project called Wines of Substance, offering well-made varietal wines priced in the midteens and a superpremium Bordeaux blend named 21 Grams.

All three single-vineyard syrahs are exceptional at Waters. The Loess (Leonetti), Forgotten Hills (estate-owned), and Pepper Bridge vineyards furnish the fruit. Brown tickles out detailed nuances that render each wine distinctive, showing a different facet of Walla Walla terroir. Good as they are, his less expensive Columbia Valley syrah does not suffer by comparison. Though not labeled as such, it is also vineyard-specific, sourcing grapes from the Minick vineyard in the Yakima Valley.

Interlude is Waters' blend of Bordeaux varietals, sourced since 2005 from Walla Walla vineyards. Brown also makes a pure cabernet sauvignon, a barrel-fermented viognier, and a dry rosé.

Several estate vineyards are in various stages of development. Forgotten Hills, a 7.5-acre syrah, cabernet sauvignon, viognier, carmenère, and counoise vineyard planted in 1996 by artist Jeffrey Hill, was acquired in 2007. Mars Hill is a 27-acre parcel with 10 acres planted, also in 2007; at 1,300 feet it is directly above the Seven Hills vineyard and grows cabernet sauvignon, merlot, malbec, and tempranillo. Old Stones is nearby, but at a lower elevation, in the rocky soils of the old riverbed, and is planted to cabernet sauvignon, syrah (both Phelps and Tablas Creek clones), viognier, grenache, mourvèdre, and petit verdot.

Jamie Brown's considerable talents as a winemaker were on display at a retrospective tasting of several dozen James Leigh Cellars and Waters wines in the spring of 2009. With the range of new, estate vineyard sources at his disposal, quality at Waters, already quite high, can only continue to rise.

Assets: excellent new production facility, access to outstanding Walla Walla fruit from both estate and contracted vineyards, a proven gift for superb syrah.

7

THE THREE-STAR WINERIES

Many of the three-star wineries listed here were included in the "Rookies" section of the previous edition of this book; others with a bit more experience were given numerical ratings that qualified them for inclusion in the chapters covering the top 15 percent of all the wineries in the state. Newer additions to this list include some old hands on an upward quality curve and a few exceptional newcomers not previously reviewed that have jumped ahead of the Rising Stars in chapter 8 simply by virtue of overall quality and the undeniable excitement being generated by their first vintages.

As always, I place a high value on a consistent track record, so the shorter the track record, the more promising the winery must be to merit a three-star rating. What you can expect from these sixty wineries, representing less than 10 percent of the state's total, is that their best wines stand out from the pack. Not every wine in every vintage will be a star, but at least some will offer either unusual value, evoke a distinct sense of place, or reveal a particular specialty. Quite frankly, a few wineries are included simply because they have excellent potential that may not (yet) have been fully realized. The more successful that Washington wines become, the more challenging it is to rise above the competition. These are the wineries—old and new—to watch most closely. For each I have also called out a best bottle (or bottles)—either a particular varietal or specific vineyard bottling.

ÀMAURICE CELLARS

First vintage: 2004

www.amaurice.com

Family-owned àMaurice Cellars (the name is a tribute to the owner's late father, Maurice Schafer) occupies a choice spot on the eastern edge of Walla Walla, in the foothills of the Blue Mountains. Walla Walla Vintners is just across the road, Leonetti's Mill Creek Upland vineyard a stone's throw away. The Shafers have good instincts as far as not only where to be but whom to be with—they signed up Rich Funk (Saviah) to consult on the first vintage or two, hired Kenny Hart to manage the vineyard, and sent winemaker-to-be Anna Shafer down to Argentina to work a couple of vintages with Paul Hobbes.

The 13-acre, sustainably-farmed estate vineyard, planted in 2006 and first harvested in 2008, grows a mix of cabernet sauvignon, cabernet franc, petit verdot, merlot, syrah, viognier, and malbec. Those grapes are augmented with purchased fruit from a well-chosen list of Columbia Valley growers.

The vivacious daughter, Anna Shafer, has quickly energized the brand, generating a great deal of favorable press, especially for the winery's viognier and malbec. More important, she has taken over the winemaking reins full-time, and it was with great interest that I tasted the first of her estate-grown wines. She has quickly shown herself to be an astute student of the vine, making canny vineyard choices for purchased fruit and crafting wines that convey a sense of individual style.

Malbec seems destined to be this new winery's signature bottling, and Shafer's enthusiasm for the grape is based on her real-world experience in Argentina. "I think malbec grows better in Washington than in Argentina," she says and then explains why. "The amount of UV in Argentina can't be duplicated, but here we are own-rooted, on deep soils, while they have clay and hardpan. Argentina has harvest rain and hail, and malbec will rot really easily. They have green mold and black mold; we don't have any."

Excellent vineyard management, a great location, a talented winemaker, and what appear to be deep pockets are among the many advantages that this young winery holds.

Best wine: malbec.

ALDER RIDGE/ZEFINA

First vintage: 2001

www.preceptwinebrands.com

Corus Estates and Vineyards developed these brands, along with the 812-acre Alder Ridge estate vineyard, which sells fruit to dozens of Washington wineries. Corus was recently acquired by Precept Brands, but the vineyard remains under private ownership.

From 2004 to 2009, the winemaker was Rob Chowanietz, hired to do the inaugural crush at the Alder Ridge winery as well as to oversee an ambitious ramping up of estate production. The five-year goal was to reach 20,000 cases of Alder Ridge cabernet, and another 5,000 of everything else. That may change, but the quality of the estate fruit is certain most apparent in these cabernets, which are the top-tier wines. Though the vines are barely a decade old, the vineyard's location—high above the Columbia River in the heart of the Horse Heaven Hills AVA—is proving to be one of the best in the state.

The Zefina wines occupy a lower price tier and include a Serience white (viognier and roussanne) and a Serience red (Rhône blend), along with unusual varietal bottlings such as tempranillo, sangiovese, and zinfandel, which might still be considered experimental.

Best wine: Alder Ridge cabernet sauvignon.

ANIMALE

First vintage: 2001

www.animalewine.com

Animale is what the French call a garagiste operation. Winemaker Matt Gubitosa, a geologist by trade, has converted the basement of his Seattle home into a snazzy winery, laboratory, and barrel room. Which makes him more of a basementiste, I suppose.

Animale operates at the fringes of what could be considered commercial. Its entire annual production barely tops 200 cases. Small brings with it many challenges; no matter how careful a winemaker may be (Gubitosa maintains an immaculate cellar), producing wine in tiny batches makes it easier for bacteriological and oxidative problems to appear.

Gubitosa is committed to a winemaking approach that includes no new oak, no fining or filtering, and focuses on cool-climate flavors. His varietal wines are expressive in both nose and mouth, often deceptively light, but occasionally turning up the voltage, as did a recent, rare Washington petite sirah and a companion petit verdot. His "estate-grown" pinot noir, which debuted as a single half bottle and more recently quadrupled production to a two-bottle total, somehow captures the unique zeitgeist of this unusual winery.

Best wine: grenache.

APEX AND APEX II

First vintages: 1988 and 2001

www.preceptwinebrands.com

Apex was originally the superpremium label for a group of wineries that also included W. B. Bridgman and Washington Hills. In 2004 the Washington Hills brand was sold to Precept, and in 2008 Apex and Apex II also became part of the Precept portfolio.

Precept CEO Andrew Browne envisions Apex as a "white tablecloth prestige brand" selling for $15 to $30. Apex II, which was introduced as a value brand by the previous owners, will continue, says Browne, as a mainstream "opportunity" brand, priced under $15. With the change in ownership, it's a given that the lines will be expanded. Both Apex and Apex II had been inconsistent over the years, but showed particular strengths in the Apex dry riesling and cabernet and the Apex II sauvignon blanc. The first releases made under the new ownership, with a different winemaker and different grape sources, will begin with the 2009 vintage wines. They should give an indication of where the brands are going. Precept has a full plate, with many recent acquisitions as well as in-house brands, all being tried out, digested, and tweaked. But based on the history of the Apex and Apex II lines, and Precept's marketing and sales expertise, they warrant inclusion (albeit with a virtual asterisk) in this chapter.

ASH HOLLOW

First vintage: 2002

www.ashhollow.com

High school buddies John Turner and Steve Clifton (of California's Brewer-Clifton winery) were the lead principals in what was initially just a Walla Walla vineyard project. The vineyard occupies some of the farthest-west flatland in the AVA—hot and dry in the summer but prone to winter freezes.

Planted between 1998 and 2005, it produces cabernet sauvignon, malbec, merlot, and syrah. A second vineyard named Lakeshore grows 12 acres of cabernet sauvignon, malbec, and petit verdot near Leonetti's Loess vineyard just east of town. New investors have come into the mix to fund the vineyard expansion and pay the costs of starting up a winery (wines are being made at Bergevin Lane). Both Turner and Clifton have moved on, and there has been a winemaker change as well, with Tony Lombardo—a recent graduate of the community college's winemaking program—hired as of the 2009 vintage.

With all that going on, it is difficult to predict what Ash Hollow's future will be. The winery has made very little white wine to date, focusing mostly on estate-grown red varietals and several blends. The premier white wine is the Somanna, half sauvignon blanc and half pinot gris. The Terassa reserve is the high-end Bordeaux blend, generously oaked; the Nine Mile red offers the best value. The newest releases include a Four Horsemen red and a Den Hoed vineyard gewürztraminer.

Best wine: estate cabernet sauvignon.

BALBOA

First vintage: 2003

www.balboawinery.com

Balboa operates out of its own tasting room at the Beresan winery, adjacent to Pepper Bridge, and recently opened a second outlet in downtown Walla Walla. Thomas Glase makes wines for both Beresan and Balboa. His Balboa wines are (mostly) value-priced, always fresh, and infallibly interesting. The original, colorful labels, drawn by Amy Glase with childlike charm, have been replaced, as have the screw-cap closures. Apparently, the new labels and composite corks use recycled materials and carry less of a carbon footprint.

Balboa's single-vineyard varietals are sourced from the Mirage vineyard, and they are among the very best under-$20 reds made in Washington. Glase's winemaking skills are topflight, and, given his connection to vineyard manager Tom Waliser, he has no trouble obtaining excellent fruit. My favorites among the regular Balboa releases are the fruit-driven versions of merlot, syrah, sangiovese, and cabernet sauvignon. There is also a reserve red (syrah-merlot); and a cabernet-syrah named Sayulita, after a favorite surf spot on the Mexican coast. This wine will always be a single-vineyard blend, though the vineyard may change from year to year. The 2006 Sayulita, from the LeFore vineyard, is a gorgeous bottle, smooth and tightly woven with veins of earth, pepper, black olive, black coffee, black fruits, and licorice.

Two other Balboa offshoots are the Mith white and Mith red Bordeaux blends—a joint project of Glase and L'Ecole No 41 winemaker Mike Sharon. The white wine, a sémillon–sauvignon blanc sourced from Klipsun vineyard fruit, is especially good. It is encouraging to see other new Washington wineries starting as Balboa did, by offering polished, professional winemaking, pure varietal wines, moderate alcohol levels, and affordable prices.

"We want to make affordable wines representative of the varietals and where they were grown," says Glase. "My job is to make wine so you can drink it, not put it in your cellar and wait ten years. I don't have any wine in my cellar; why should anyone else?"

Best wine: Sayulita.

BERGEVIN LANE

First vintage: 2001

www.bergevinlane.com

Annette Bergevin and Amber Lane left San Francisco Bay Area careers in telecommunications to return to Bergevin's hometown of Walla Walla. French-born-and-educated winemaker Virginie Bourgue joined them early in 2003 and helped to design the new winery from scratch, expanding the all-red lineup by adding viognier and sémillon. Danish-born Steffan Jorgensen became winemaker in 2006 and continues to infuse Bergevin Lane wines with a European sense of style.

Production has leveled off at around 11,000 cases, much of it devoted to the very popular Calico white and Calico red blends. Grapes are purchased from a variety of vineyards in Walla Walla, the Horse Heaven Hills, and the Wahluke Slope.

Bergevin's viognier has been a success from the beginning, and Jorgensen seems to have improved it even further, blending in 8 percent roussanne and barrel-fermenting it. The winery's Columbia Valley syrah is crafted in a European mold, herbaceous and aromatic, with rich scents that mix the purple fruits with intimations of herb, chocolate, and cracker. Several limited-release syrahs are also made: most recently they include a barrel select, a Princess, and a bottling called Oui Deux.

Intuition, Bergevin Lane's reserve Bordeaux red, offers complex, spice-box flavors that blossom into a lovely, supple wine nuanced with mineral, leaf, and leather.

Best wine: Intuition reserve.

BONAIR

First vintage: 1985

www.bonairwinery.com

Gail and Shirley Puryear (his title, winemaker; her title, wine goddess) purchased and planted their first few acres in the Rattlesnake Hills in 1979–80. They began making wines under their Bonair label in 1985 (winery number 29 in the state), with Mike Januik consulting. Ongoing purchases have brought the total vineyard acreage up to 35, including most notably a 40-year-old site at 1,200 feet that the Puryears believe is the oldest vineyard in the Rattlesnake Hills.

The Bonair winery is a popular tourist destination, and much of the 8,000-case annual production is sold on-site. Tour buses are welcome, the vineyards are right at hand, there is a banquet facility, and the winery occupies a lovely plateau in the heart of the Rattlesnake Hills AVA. Gail Puryear was the principal author of the AVA petition and still lobbies hard for its acceptance. Slowly but surely he has made a believer out of me by proving that it's elevation and soil based, as AVAs should be.

Bill Mechem is the assistant winemaker and also oversees his own small side project called Whisper Ridge. Among the broad range of wines being made, the white wines are the standouts, especially the vineyard-designates. The old-vine, Morrison vineyard cabernet sauvignon is also interesting, as is the port-style blend of estate-grown Touriga Nacional, Tinta Çao, and Tinta Madera.

Best wine: dry gewürztraminer.

CAMARADERIE CELLARS

First vintage: 1992

www.camaraderiecellars.com

Camaraderie began, as have so many Washington boutiques, as a weekend hobby. One hundred pounds of grapes were purchased in the fall of 1981, five gallons of cabernet sauvignon were produced, and that first wine won a gold medal at the Puyallup fair in 1983. The hook was set.

"The best things in life are meant to be shared," says winemaker Don Corson. For him and his wife, Vicki, and business partner Gene Unger (who keeps all things mechanical humming along), that means wine and food and friendship. Hence the winery name. An intense, dynamic man with a natural gift for teaching and an inspirational zest for wine, Corson has navigated the hurdles of commercial winemaking and steadily grown the enterprise, which now produces around 3,200 cases of reds and another 600 of white.

Camaraderie lays claim to being the farthest-northwest winery in the continental United States. That tells you something about the winemaker. Moving grapes 300 miles over desert, mountain passes, and the Puget Sound in the midst of crush doesn't faze him. "We're working with seven different vineyards in five AVAs," Corson explains matter-of-factly. "I really like being able to blend the best from the individual vineyards."

Camaraderie's forte is clearly its cabernet-based reds. Top vineyards such as Artz, Meek, Milbrandt, and Chandler Reach provide the raw materials, which Corson fusses over relentlessly. He wants his wines to be ranked among Washington's best, but he keeps his prices affordable and is adamantly non-elitist.

Camaraderie's best red, named Grâce (pronounced "grahhss"), is full, seamless, and rich, a five-grape Bordeaux blend modeled after Chateau St. Jean's Cinq Cépages. The merlots are substantial and loaded with smoke and cedar, and Camaraderie also makes a fine malbec and one of the better cabernet francs in the state.

Best wine: Grâce.

CANOE RIDGE VINEYARD

First vintage: 1992

www.canoeridgevineyard.com

Canoe Ridge Vineyard (not to be confused with Canoe Ridge Estate, which is owned by Ste. Michelle Wine Estates) was founded in 1990 as a joint venture between California's Chalone Wine Group and a number of shareholders from Washington State. Marking the first time Chalone had expanded beyond California, the founding set the stage for a dedicated $2.5 million winery to accompany the vineyard, which had been planted the previous year.

The timing was good because the AVA now known as the Horse Heaven Hills was just beginning its expansive growth and development. Explorers Lewis and Clark had first spotted a five-mile-long, canoe-shaped geological formation running east-west about 900 feet above the Columbia River; hence the name. The 143-acre vineyard is planted primarily to merlot and cabernet sauvignon, with chardonnay, cabernet franc, and syrah filling in the rest. The moderating influence of the river helps minimize the risk of winter damage, and the steady winds prevent rot or mildew problems.

John Abbott (now at Abeja) made the first vintages of Canoe Ridge. A meticulous and talented craftsman, he helped to establish the brand as a producer of some of the best merlots and chardonnays in Washington. With Abbott's departure in 2002 and an ownership change in 2005 (the winery now belongs to industry giant Diageo), Canoe Ridge seemed to lose focus for a time. In the middle of crush in 2005, Diageo brought in a talented Frenchman, Christophe Paubert, to make the wines. Paubert's résumé included winemaking stints at Chateau d'Yquem, Chateau Gruaud-Larose, and New Zealand's Montana winery.

He immediately announced himself as "a terroir winemaker." Which meant, he explained to me in an early interview, "you will never express terroir if you overripen, overoak, and keep your wine two years in barrels. First you need to want to express it; then you need to know how. I don't do lots of funny things; I taste the juice lees, and if they're good, I increase the turbidity of the wine. If the lees are not good, I remove them. I focus on showing the fruit."

With Pauillac as his model, Paubert introduced substantial changes in both vineyard and barrel management. In March of 2009, to celebrate the twentieth anniversary of the planting of the estate vineyard, he orchestrated a massive tasting of Canoe Ridge merlots (see box). Then, abruptly, he resigned to become winemaker and general manager of Stags' Leap winery in Napa (not Stag's Leap, which is part of the Ste. Michelle portfolio). "It is too bad," Paubert told me shortly before his departure in July 2009; "I have spent three years finishing other people's wines while starting my own. And now, just as my first wines are being released, I am leaving."

I expect very fine wines from Canoe Ridge in the 2006, 2007, and 2008 vintages, which were all made under Paubert. Ned Morris is his replacement, and he too brings solid production and vineyard management expertise to the job, so Canoe Ridge remains on track. Production has reached about 30,000 cases, two-fifths of it merlot, one-fifth cabernet sauvignon, and significant amounts of chardonnay, dry riesling, and gewürztraminer.

Best wines: Block 13 reserve merlot and Block 1 reserve cabernet sauvignon

---

CANOE RIDGE VINEYARD TASTING

In March 2009, I sat down with Christophe Paubert and tasted through Canoe Ridge Vineyard merlots from 1993 (the first year they were made) to 2006, Paubert's first vintage as winemaker. (Note: he left the winery just ahead of the 2009 crush.) Many were poured from magnum. We discussed the importance and value of making wines that cellar well, and Paubert shared his thoughts as we sat and sipped.

"It's a cultural thing that has changed a little in this age," he began. "In Bordeaux the young wines were so tannic you couldn't enjoy them without aging. It was also recognized that only great vintages and great terroir could age well; so it stood for the quality of the château. Now the evolution of the winemaking makes wines more approachable early on, and a change in consumption habits also. I think the best can age as well as before, but they are easier to enjoy when young. So the life span begins earlier and can go as long as before. One of the pleasures of wine is to see it evolving through the years. If you have a cellar and several bottles of a certain wine, you have the pleasure of drinking it, and another pleasure, which is to see it evolving. The other dimension of that is that there are some vintages that are very different one from the other; it is a way to measure that. Some food also matches better with an aged wine; when it matches well, that is magic."

Here are my notes on the tasting. Wines with stars were favorites.

1993 Merlot
Columbia Valley; 13.5%
Mature scents and flavors, drinking very well, nice round mouthfeel, still has cooked plum and cherry fruit and good balance.

1994 Merlot
Columbia Valley; 13.5%
Tighter and fresher than the '93, with more tannin, better muscle and structure; very cabernet-like. Firm, slightly bitter tannins, but sturdy and well made.

1995 Merlot (magnum)
Columbia Valley; 13.5%
First hints of barrel smoke and toast. Some brett also; comes out in the finish. This is drying out, perhaps because of the brett. Smells better than it tastes.

1996 Merlot (magnum)***
Columbia Valley; 13.5%
The color on these first few wines is very consistent; still alive but plenty of russet/sunset at the edges. This is nicely mature, firm; polished tannins. Flavors show black cherry, charcoal, smoke, earth, licorice . . . best so far by far.

1997 Merlot (magnum)
Columbia Valley; 13.5%
Black cherry candy with a hint of cola. Seems like a lighter vintage overall, but this has held up well, with interesting spice and mint highlights.

1998 Merlot (magnum)
Columbia Valley; 13.5%
Darker in color, showing less age, tasting very good. The length is impressive, with some granular tannins, sweet cherry, and plum. It has a little fracture between the middle and the finish, and runs quickly into the tannins, suggesting that it may not age as smoothly from here on.

1999 Merlot (magnum)***
Columbia Valley; 13.5%
Substantial, almost black in the center, comes to a powerful focus, with complex and still–densely buried notes of licorice, smoke, tar, and hints of tobacco. Power and the structure on display; chewy, muscular, dense, and compact.

1999 Lot 10 Reserve Merlot (magnum)
Columbia Valley; 13.5%
Lot 10 means tenth tank entered into the winery; it's the same block (13) as the other reserves. Lacks the balance of the regular; it's more tannic, with some volatility in the finish.

2000 Merlot
Columbia Valley; 13.5%
Very expressive of the vintage—open, rather loose, a bit chewy, with secondary strawberry fruit flavors. Drinking at its peak. Color is dark and tannins are substantial, but the overall weight and balance are not up to the best.

2000 Lot 13 Reserve Merlot (magnum)
Columbia Valley; 13.5%
Has a strong eucalyptus note; it's juicy in the mouth, with higher acidity than the regular bottling. Shows some green, herbal, slightly stemmy edge to the tannins—more Bordeaux-like, but drinking well.

2001 Merlot (magnum)*
Columbia Valley; 13.5%
A rich, evocative nose, hints of floral, bark, cinnamon, some barrel flavors; a little sweetness to the tannins. Drinking well, with more complexity than the 2000, more length; it's a well-modulated and graceful bottle probably at its peak.

2001 Lot 10 Reserve Merlot (magnum)
Columbia Valley; 13.5%
More depth and darkness right in the aromas; definitely picking up the new oak, with streaks of butter and caramel showing under the red fruits. Acids seem a bit adjusted, not entirely integrated.

2002 Merlot
Columbia Valley; 14.5%
This bottle had an experimental plastic cork—"They don't age," says Christophe Paubert. This smells cabbagey, old, dull; it was about when overall quality took a dive down. (These plastic corks were used only for some of the production in 2002 and 2003.)

2002 Block 13 Reserve Merlot (magnum)
Columbia Valley; 14.2%
A little dumbed down . . . the wine is holding something back. It's got more than it's giving me right now. Some mint comes out, some spice, and a little heat.

2003 Merlot
Columbia Valley; 14%
Tannins are ripe but not flabby; they have a snap to them that subs for acid. There is also a toffee character that comes through, along with cherry fruit. A perfectly drinkable but somewhat flat-lined wine.

2003 Block 13 Reserve Merlot*
Columbia Valley; 13.9%
All French oak is used for the reserve; the fruit is the same as the regular bottling, but here the oak adds butter, caramel, hazelnuts, and pretty toast.

2004 Merlot*
Columbia Valley; 14.5%
Very pretty nose, smooth and supple; this shows a lot of grace. Polished, showing really well, with graphite, minerality, earth, some hints of herb, and pretty, precise fruity plum-cherry-strawberry flavors.

2004 Block 13 Reserve Merlot**
Columbia Valley; 14%
This block consistently shows a mint-eucalyptus-oily character; it's lively, juicy, and fresh. Very tight and young, with raspberry-cherry fruit, vivid acidity, some menthol. A bright, acidic, tangy, spicy wine with lots of life ahead.

2005 Merlot*
Horse Heaven Hills; 14.5%
Dark and substantial, good concentration, fine balance, grip, and a chewy, tannic core. Black cherry, some boysenberry, juicy and textural. Should age very well.

2005 Block 13 Reserve Merlot***
Horse Heaven Hills; 14.5%
This is big, juicy, loaded with fruits, lots of depth and ripeness. Berries and cherries and smoke and toast; this is textural, grainy, chewy, and rich.

2006 Merlot
Columbia Valley; 14.2%
Tasted pre-release; it has precision, detail, and focus not previously seen. Complex and peppery, made for aging; it needs more time in the bottle.

2006 Block 13 Reserve Merlot***
Columbia Valley; 14.7%
Tasted pre-release. Very tightly wound with black cherry, licorice, iodine, earth, wood; very tight but substantial. Great potential.

CHANDLER REACH

First vintage: 2000

www.chandlerreach.com

The 42-acre Chandler Reach vineyard, which overlooks (but does not occupy) Red Mountain, not only provides fruit for owner Len Parris's wines but also sells to a growing number of smaller producers outside of the Yakima Valley. The site, says Parris, is always windy, and warmer earlier than Red Mountain, though eventually Red Mountain catches up.

Parris is a genial man in his late fifties, a builder-developer for most of his life, who also founded a premium, drive-through coffee business called Jitters. His winery is modeled after a Tuscan villa (Washington has more than a few of these, oddly enough), and the estate vineyard grows a bit of barbera and sangiovese, but the strengths are the Bordeaux grapes: cabernet sauvignon, cabernet franc, and merlot.

Current production is 6,800 cases. "We handpick, always have," says Parris, "and pride ourselves on providing fruit as clean as we can. We pick into cherry packs (that are worn on the body and open up on the bottom) to try to be as easy on fruit as possible. Which doesn't make a lot of sense, because in a couple of hours we're gonna crush them into oblivion . . . but we get a lot of comments that 'yours is the cleanest fruit we're given,'" he adds, with evident satisfaction.

The estate wines are steadily improving as the vines age and Parris gets more vintages under his belt. "Winemaking is like golf," he says. "You know the shots but the courses are different every year. Is it raining? Is it windy? By the time you've perfected it, you have to play a different course."

Look for the estate select red wines and the Parris Estate reserves, which now include cabernet sauvignon, cabernet franc, and sangiovese. The winery's lower-priced red blend, 36 Red (named after the winery truck), offers especially good value and sells out quickly.

Best wine: Parris Estate reserve cabernet sauvignon.

CHATTER CREEK

First vintage: 2000

www.chattercreek.com

Ask Chatter Creek winemaker Gordy Rawson how many hats he wears, and he quickly replies, "All of them." Not that a lot of small, start-up wineries aren't essentially solo operations. But at 1,500-plus cases, Rawson's Chatter Creek winery is not all that small; nor, given his quarter century of winemaking experience, is it a typical start-up.

Rawson belongs to the mad scientist school of winemaking, which is to say he is unafraid to try anything and seems to revel in the challenge of something new. An early experiment with apple wine won best of show at Woodinville Wine Festival; he made his first zinfandel and riesling in 1984 and followed with gamay, Müller-Thurgau, merlot, and sparkling wine in 1985. Book learning and relentless experimentation guided him, along with plenty of generous advice from wine sellers and winemakers, including Columbia's David Lake, for whom Rawson served as cellarmaster from 1985 until mid-1998.

He launched his own winery by making sparkling wines in the late 1990s, until a trademark infringement lawsuit closed the door on that venture. "How anyone could have gotten a cheap Russian vodka confused with a $20 bubbly I have no idea," Rawson says, with more than a hint of exasperation. Needing a new name and a new label for his wines, he hit on Chatter Creek, a favorite fishing spot from his childhood. "I was looking for something that wouldn't get me sued," he explains.

Chatter Creek production includes an interesting mix of white and red wines: pinot gris, viognier, grenache, single-vineyard syrahs, cabernet sauvignon, cabernet franc, and nebbiolo. The syrahs and cabernets are standouts. Grapes are mainly sourced from Yakima Valley, Horse Heaven Hills, and Wahluke Slope vineyards. In 2005, a small winery and tasting room were opened in the burgeoning Woodinville warehouse district, and from time to time winemaker dinners are cooked and hosted at the winery.

Best wines: the single-vineyard syrahs.

CHINOOK

First vintage: 1983

www.chinookwines.com

Kay Simon and Clay Mackey are the wife-and-husband winemaker-vintner team behind Chinook (the name references a warm wind that blows through the area, not the famous salmon). This much-loved winery was among those that pioneered the suddenly fashionable Prosser area almost three decades ago. Before that, Simon spent some years making wine for Ste. Michelle, one of the first women in the country to work for such a large winery; Mackey was the Chateau's vineyard manager at the time.

The Chinook style is tight, controlled, and precise. "Compatibility with food is an ever-present winemaking goal," says Simon. "All of our wines are fermented to dryness and then aged in barrel and bottle until we feel that they are ready to enjoy with a meal." Made in a converted red barn on the outskirts of Prosser (the tasting room is in the old farmhouse), Chinook wines are technically exact and infallibly consistent. They are the classic expression of Yakima Valley fruit.

Chinook's chardonnays, 100 percent barrel-fermented, are scented with mint, lime, orange peel and full-flavored without being fat. The sémillons are tart and sharp, with varietal fruit flavors of fig, lime, and grapefruit. Sauvignon blanc completes the white wine lineup—also barrel-fermented, lightly toasty, and rich.

Turning to the Chinook reds, you will find the merlot at its best in a very ripe vintage such as 2005. A small cabernet franc vineyard is planted at the winery; along with purchased grapes, its fruit is made into both a dry rosé and firm and tart varietal wine. In some years a cabernet sauvignon is offered also, and a pair of budget-priced, Yakima Valley white and red blends. The dry and racy Chinook cabernet franc rosé, released and quickly sold out each summer, remains a favorite among Seattle sommeliers.

Best wine: cabernet franc (especially the rosé).

COEUR D'ALENE CELLARS

First vintage: 2002

www.cdacellars.com

This Idaho winery produces wines almost exclusively from Washington grapes, with particular success making viognier and syrah. It's family owned by Kimber Gates and her parents, Charlie and Sarah Gates. Production is roughly 3,400 cases annually. Vineyard sources are impressive: Alder Ridge, McKinley Springs, Elephant Mountain, Elerding, Boushey, and Stillwater Creek among them.

Though we all know that wines are made in the vineyard, extra credit must go to winemaker Warren Schutz, a UC Davis graduate with Napa Valley winemaking experience at Far Niente and Chappellet. Although schlepping grapes to Coeur d'Alene from vineyards more than 200 miles distant is no cakewalk, it is no different than what dozens of west-side Washington wineries do each year.

What does set Coeur d'Alene Cellars apart is simply the quality in the bottle, apparent from the very beginning and consistent across an expansive lineup of Rhône varietal bottlings. The syrahs include a Washington bottling from a mix of sites, vineyard-designates from Stillwater Creek, Alder Ridge, and Boushey; another simply labeled Envy (from McKinley Springs fruit); a reserve syrah named Opulence; and a fortified, oak-aged, port-style dessert wine. Coeur d'Alene has also added a varietal mourvèdre called MO.

In fact, everything I have tasted from this winery, including the non-Rhône varietals, the inexpensive blends, and the chardonnays, has been very well made. They are hampered a bit by their location. (They don't qualify for membership in the Washington Wine Commission and must label all their wines, even those from prestigious single vineyards, with the generic Washington AVA, since the grapes cross a state line.) But in terms of quality they have earned a place alongside some of Washington's most consistently excellent producers.

Best wine: Boushey syrah.

COLUMBIA

First vintage: 1967

www.columbiawinery.com

Where to begin? The ups and downs of Columbia throughout its first half century of existence (the fiftieth anniversary is due to be celebrated in 2012) could fill this book. Were a movie to be made, it should not be named merely *Sideways*—I'm thinking instead that the old Yardbirds song "Over Under Sideways Down" would be more appropriate.

To briefly recap: Columbia began as Associated Vintners, the weekend pastime of a group of University of Washington professors. In 1967 they bonded the winery and produced their first commercial wines, a riesling, a gewürztraminer, a pinot noir, and a cabernet sauvignon. Over the years the business has weathered the sale of its vineyards, a change of names (from A/V to Columbia), several changes of owners and of venue, and an absolutely bewildering array of label designs.

The guiding light throughout a quarter century of Columbia's history (1979–2004) was winemaker David Lake (recently deceased), an MW with distinctly European tastes. In the spirit of the amateur wine lovers who pioneered the A/V brand, Lake experimented tirelessly. Most famously, his long-standing collaboration with grower Mike Sauer of Red Willow vineyard pioneered syrah in Washington State, which they planted in 1985 and first vinified in 1988. They were also the first to make a Washington pinot gris and have been among the first for a dozen other varietals, including viognier, cabernet franc, barbera, malbec, mourvèdre, sangiovese, nebbiolo, and tempranillo.

But breaking new ground is rarely easy, and Columbia has faced more than its share of hurdles, not all self-imposed. Confusion with Ste. Michelle's Columbia Crest, the state's largest winery, still haunts the brand (the two have no connection). A profusion of wines, labels, and special limited bottlings has made it difficult for consumers and critics to get a solid fix on Columbia's strengths. Lake himself acknowledged that the style of wines he produced ("not too high in alcohol, not overtly oaky, truly drinkable wines that work nicely at the dinner table with food") were "not necessarily the wines that win the top awards. And the pressure is very much to try to get the big awards, the high-percentage-point scores."

That pressure was exacerbated during the time (2001–8) that the winery passed into the hands of industry behemoth Constellation Brands. Divested in 2008 (along with some of Constellation's California holdings), Columbia now belongs to California-based Ascentia Wine Estates. Included in the deal was sister winery Covey Run, whose winemaker, Kerry Norton, was quickly promoted to fill the vacancy created by David Lake's retirement. No sooner had that matter been resolved than Columbia appeared to have lost the lease on its Woodinville headquarters, forcing it to move its production facilities to the Yakima Valley.

But wait! A new lease was negotiated, a tasting room remodel completed in 2009; and Ascentia's CEO, Jim DeBonis, has promised better days ahead. "When I look at all of these brands," he told me shortly after the purchase was announced, "I think they've been under the shadow of a 200-pound gorilla. Every single one of them is of critical importance to us and to our ability to succeed on an ongoing basis. They are going to get exactly what they deserve, which is the limelight."

Historically, Columbia's white wines have been elegant, crisp, and shellfish friendly, especially the sauvignon blancs, sémillons, and pinot gris. There is a fine off-dry gewürztraminer and an equally lovely Cellarmaster's riesling, and the Wyckoff vineyard chardonnay can be a dead ringer for a village Burgundy from a warm vintage.

The single-vineyard cabernets (from Red Willow and Otis) stand stylistically with classified-growth Bordeaux and show a similar capacity to improve with age. The most recent releases indicate that a transition to rounder, fruitier, more forward (but less iconic) wines was already underway by 2005. Given the bumpy road the brand has traveled of late, I am content to list it at three stars. But with the new, solid, seemingly sensitive ownership, an experienced winemaker in command, and a few more vintages to reorient Columbia stylistically, it will, I sincerely hope, return to the very top ranks.

Best wines: Wyckoff vineyard chardonnay; Red Willow vineyard cabernet sauvignon.

COUGAR CREST

First vintage: 2001

www.cougarcrestwinery.com

In 1996, Deborah and David Hansen exchanged San Francisco Bay Area careers in pharmacy and veterinary medicine for life on a Walla Walla farm, where they had been developing 125 acres of orchard. Cuttings from Windrow (part of the early Seven Hills vineyard) and Cailloux vineyards went into the ground at Cougar Hills in 1998, and the Golden's Legacy vineyard was added in 2000. A third vineyard (Stellar) was sold in 2006 to Otis Kenyon.

The first Cougar Crest winery was a modest affair, set among the many start-ups at the Walla Walla airport. Production has steadily grown to 10,000 cases, buoyed by excellent scores from out-of-state critics, but the Hansens have kept things focused. An expansive new facility opened in 2008 west of Walla Walla near Reininger and Long Shadows; and a new label, Walla Walla River Winery, was added, based at the old airport location. That winery is taking the Hansens in some interesting new directions, with a varietal tempranillo and a varietal malbec among the first releases.

The principal Cougar Crest wines are estate-grown, beginning with a stony, floral viognier and a delicious grenache rosé with up to 25 percent viognier blended in. Syrah, merlot, cabernet sauvignon, cabernet franc, and a red blend called Dedication Two are also offered, along with the occasional reserve, produced only when Debbie Hansen feels that the vintage has produced some lots that are "identifiably unique."

Best wine: the reserves are standouts.

COUVILLION

First vintage: 2004

www.couvillionwinery.com

A small vineyard and winery, set in the rolling hills of the Palouse, just a few miles north of Walla Walla, Couvillion is the project of winemaker Jill Noble and her wheat farmer husband, Craig. Jill is a registered nurse, who went to sign up for Spanish lessons at the nearby community college and instead enrolled in the viticulture and enology school. Following an internship at Abeja ("a pivotal moment as far as really falling for the winemaking part of this"), she and Craig observed the success of neighboring Spring Valley Vineyard and decided to diversify their own wheat farm into wine grapes.

In 2003, three acres went in—cabernet and mourvèdre—at an elevation of 1,500 feet. Problems followed immediately: birds wiped it out, winter freezes decimated it, water has to be trucked up (there is no well). Six years into the project, no estate wines have been released. But the Nobles are undaunted. "We have up to 160 acres that could be turned into vineyard," Jill confides.

From purchased fruit, mostly Lewis and Sagemoor vineyard grapes, Couvillion has released dry riesling, sauvignon blanc, merlot, cabernet sauvignon, and a Bordeaux blend named Equilibré. The wines are quite competent ("It's more than a crush, it's an obsession" Jill writes), and I do hope that the vineyard will ultimately reward their efforts as well.

Best wine: cabernet sauvignon from Sagemoor vineyard.

COVEY RUN

First vintage: 1982

www.coveyrun.com

In 1999, Covey Run (founded as Quail Run) brought in winemaker Kerry Norton from Oregon's Eola Hills Wine Cellars. Though it might seem to be a big switch in terms of both climate and wines, Norton was one of Oregon's most eclectic winemakers. During his eight-year run at Eola Hills, he produced flavorful, herbaceous sauvignon blancs, roundly fruity chardonnays, and spicy cabernets, along with good budget versions of pinot gris and pinot noir.

He continued in the same quiet, steady mode at Covey Run, a 300,000-case winery now part of Ascentia Wine Estates. From 2001 through 2008, Covey was owned by Constellation Brands, and Norton was given the freedom to chase down his own vineyard sources. Better fruit meant better wines, and through the mid-2000s, the brand seemed to improve with each successive vintage.

There are three tiers. The Quail Series wines, priced between $7 and $9, showcase bright, expressive fruit flavors. The bottles feature the quail label, a graphic reference to the original winery name. Among the white wines, the pinot grigio, dry riesling, and chenin blanc are standouts; but everything from the muscat to the gewürztraminer to the chardonnay (partly barrel-fermented in real barrels, not tank staves or chips) is worth trying.

In the summer of 2005, Covey Run introduced the Winemaker's Collection, line-priced at $13 and aimed primarily at the restaurant trade. Covey Run's Reserve Series, priced just a dollar or so higher, debuted around the same time. Included are a chardonnay, a merlot, a cabernet sauvignon, a syrah, and (occasionally) a sémillon ice wine.

When Kerry Norton took over as winemaker at Columbia in 2007, he was replaced at Covey Run by Kate Michaud. Her first releases are just coming out. During the transition, it seemed that the wines lost a bit of their luster; the Quail Series, though affordably priced, no longer overdelivered. The reserves, now sporting a new label design, are a cut above their cheaper stablemates, but in their price range they need to step up a bit to reach Covey Run's previous standards.

Best wine: reserve chardonnay.

C.R. SANDIDGE

First vintage: 2000

www.crsandidgewines.com

Ray Sandidge began his winemaking career on Long Island, at Pindar Vineyards. He later spent time at Georg Breuer in Germany, then worked a series of jobs in the Yakima Valley before moving to Lake Chelan Winery, the largest producer in the new Lake Chelan AVA, to become director of winemaking.

Among his many current projects is C.R. Sandidge, a 2,500-case, family-owned enterprise that makes a number of wines styled for the tasting room trade, such as Glam Gams rosé and Whistle Punk red. More important, Sandidge taps his excellent vineyard contacts to source grapes from an unusual roster of Yakima Valley sites, including Boushey, Klingele, Minick, and Kestrel, along with Stone Tree in the Wahluke Slope.

As president of the Lake Chelan Wine Growers Association, he has begun sourcing fruit from local vineyards. It will be especially interesting to follow the work of this experienced craftsman as he explores this unfamiliar terroir.

Best wine: The supersweet dessert wines labeled KISS.

DES VOIGNE CELLARS

First vintage: 2004

www.desvoignecellars.com

Darren DesVoigne comes out of the dot-com world; his brother Derek owns Cuillin Hills. Initially, the main focus at Des Voigne was intended to be sangiovese, but across the lineup of red wines it is difficult to pick a favorite; they are all substantial, dense, and flavorful.

The packaging features beautifully drawn, full-color renditions of jazz musicians, and some of the wines are named for music festivals—Montreux syrah and San Remo sangiovese, for example. Something about the plushness of both wines and wine labels inspires flights of descriptive fancy. Enthused about the Emcee merlot, I wrote, "This is a sweetly plummy, cherry pie–flavored merlot that does for a meal what a pillow does for a bed. Lie down and enjoy the lush cherry fruit, the sandalwood scents, and the spice." The Duke (mostly zinfandel but lately with petite sirah, syrah, cab franc, and even lemberger in the mix) is a crowd favorite, the Solea red showcases Kiona's Red Mountain fruit, and the San Remo sangio may come from Walla Walla one year, Red Mountain the next.

In 2008, a barrel-fermented viognier-roussanne named Menina Flor was added to the lineup; nice to have a white wine in the mix. Prices are in the mid- to upper twenties, and for the quality—not to mention the fun—these wines are among my favorites.

Best wine: the Emcee merlot.

DOMAINE STE. MICHELLE

www.domainestemichelle.com

Consumers may rightfully be suspicious of inexpensive bubbly from big, corporate wineries. Visions of Cook's come to mind. But Ste. Michelle's bubbly brand offers consistent value across a full lineup of styles.

The basic offerings include a Brut, a Blanc de Blancs, an Extra Dry (same as the Brut, but sweeter), a Blanc de Noirs, a Frizzante, and a pricier vintage sparkler called Luxe. They are all made by the méthode champenoise, but the Luxe uses only free-run chardonnay juice and is given up to five years of aging.

The Blanc de Noirs is consistently the best of the lineup; some of the others can be excessively foamy and a bit chalky through the finish. But the Blanc de Noirs is a pretty, pale copper, lightly pinot scented, and a good quaffer; go there.

Best wine: the Blanc de Noirs.

DONEDÉI/GIBBONS LANE WINERY

First vintage: 1999

www.donedei.com

Donedéi is the brand name for the wines of Gibbons Lane Winery, founded in 1997 in Tenino, just south of Olympia in western Washington. According to winemaker and co-owner Carolyn Lakewold, the name translates as "gift of God." Beginning in 1999, a few hundred cases have been produced each year, roughly one-third of them merlot, the other two-thirds cabernet. Production now hovers between 750 and 1,000 cases annually, "depending on the whims of nature," says the winemaker.

Lakewold left behind a career as a college English professor (and NCAA fast-pitch coach) to apprentice with Doug McCrea and Bob Andrake, before building her own winery (with husband Fred Goldberg) and releasing a 1999 merlot. Cabernet sauvignon was added a year later, and those two wines remain the sum total of the winery's modest production.

Grapes come from Red Mountain's Artz and Ciel du Cheval vineyards and from Elephant Mountain in the Yakima Valley. Both wines include merlot, cabernet sauvignon, and cabernet franc in different proportions and use French and American oak barrels. Dense, chewy, and powerful, they are dark, smoky, tannic wines, usually given an extra year or two in bottle before being released. Lakewold has recently been invited into the lineup of very talented winemakers who are participating in the Grand Rêve winery project on Red Mountain.

Best wine: the cabernet sauvignon.

DUSTED VALLEY

First vintage: 2003

www.dustedvalley.com

Dusted Valley is owned by the Johnson and Braunel families. The two couples met at the University of Wisconsin, where they individually studied food science and tourism and hospitality. The consulting winemaker for the first couple of vintages was Steve Lessard; more recently Gordy Hill has assisted with blending trials, fruit sources, and overall style, while making the budget-priced Boomtown label wines at the Wahluke Wine Company.

Young, energetic, and good-humored, Corey Braunel and Chad Johnson work closely together on all winery and vineyard decisions ("no particular division of responsibilities"), while their wives handle the finances. In order to keep expenses down, wines are being made at Bergevin Lane. In the spring of 2008, they planted the 20-acre Stoney Vine vineyard in the area known as the Rocks, to a mix of syrah, petite sirah, mourvèdre, grenache, tempranillo, Touriga nacional, and viognier. The first wines should be from the 2010 vintage. Several other vineyards are leased, which brings the total under cultivation to nearly 100 acres.

Boosted by the success of their Boomtown wines (up to 20,000 cases), they have been able to keep the growth of the primary Dusted Valley label more moderate. Now at around 4,000 cases, and sporting a much-needed new label design, Dusted Valley offers a well-rounded lineup that includes old-vine chardonnay and viognier from Kestrel vineyard fruit; their own Stained Tooth syrah (clever marketing and Wisconsin oak barrels differentiate it from the Walla Walla syrah); a serviceable cabernet; and more limited wine club offerings such as a reserve syrah and a nicely nuanced malbec. A westside tasting room opened in Woodinville in the summer of 2009.

Their motto neatly sums up their philosophy: "As we say in the Dusted Valley, crack that [screw] cap! The first two glasses are for your health, the second two for ours!" In just a few short years, Dusted Valley has developed its own slightly zany marketing style, coupled with good winemaking, a focus on vineyard development, and a solid business plan. This is a winery already close to earning that fourth star.

Best wine: reserve syrah.

FALL LINE

First vintage: 2003

www.falllinewinery.com

Fall Line winery is located in south Seattle and is owned and operated by Tim Sorenson, who teaches university-level economics, and his wife, Nancy Rivenburgh, also a university professor (in communications). Just to prove how all-encompassing the wine fever is when it strikes, Sorenson, who holds a Ph.D. from Harvard, began his professional wine experience as part-time retail help in a downtown Seattle wine shop, then donated time as an unpaid cellar rat at Cadence winery (now a neighbor) before building Fall Line in 2003.

He's locked in some excellent fruit sources, Boushey, Artz, and Red Willow among them, and has even convinced Dick Boushey to plant a little tempranillo for a Fall Line blend, first harvested in 2009. The name is a geological term that also relates to alpine skiing, and references the most natural line of descent between two points on a slope.

Case production hovers between 1,200 and 2,100 annually; it slid a bit in 2007 ("a bridge year" says Sorenson) as the winery began shifting from an AVA-centric to a vineyard-centric focus. Beginning in 2008, there will be three vineyard-designated Bordeaux blends—from Artz, Boushey, and newly added Red Willow—and a fourth wine that is pure cabernet from the oldest (1980) Boushey vines. "I'm a focus person," Sorenson explains; "the focus on three vineyards all in the Yakima Valley has simplified my life tremendously." In 2011, a Boushey tempranillo will be added, the only non-Bordeaux varietal.

In the early vintages, Fall Line wines were competent but somewhat indistinguishable from many other new winery releases. But the refined focus, the excellent vineyard sources, and Tim Sorenson's increasing confidence as he adds more vintages to his résumé all bode well for the future.

Best wine: the Boushey-sourced wines.

FIDÉLITAS

First vintage: 2000

www.fidelitaswines.com

Winemaker Charlie Hoppes came to Washington via a stint at Ste. Michelle and was in charge of day-to-day winemaking operations at the winery's Canoe Ridge facility during its formative years. In 1999, Hoppes left the Chateau to become the winemaker for Three Rivers winery in Walla Walla, staying there for three vintages before setting off on his own. For the past decade he has developed his Fidélitas winery while serving as winemaker for Goose Ridge and Gamache and finding time to consult for a growing number of Washington start-ups.

Fidélitas, Hoppes explains, means "faithful, loyal, and true." "Faithful to Bordeaux grape varieties, loyal to classic winemaking techniques, and true to Washington State's Columbia Valley terroir." It's more than a slogan; it captures a way of doing business and a road map to the intended style of Hoppes's wines. "My goal is to try to get the very best fruit that I can and put some blends together. I like to think that there's always a better vineyard out there, and I like to try some new ones every year."

In 2007, Hoppes reached another goal, opening his own winery on Red Mountain. It's not a fancy facility, but it has proven to be a popular stopover for visitors to the area, with an expansive tasting bar pouring many of the winery's dozen or more selections. Total production has reached 7,500 cases, mostly reds, including single-vineyard offerings from Champoux and Boushey. There are only two whites—a sémillon and a Bordeaux blanc blend called Optu White.

The most expensive wines come in extremely heavy glass bottles. Not meaning to single him out, but I would like to see more eco-friendly packaging introduced here, as well as at other wineries in Washington whose bottles look and feel like medieval weaponry.

His fruit sources, as you would expect from a veteran winemaker, are from well-established vineyards such as Boushey, Champoux, Gamache, and Klipsun. He offers quite a few pure varietal bottlings—merlot, malbec, and cabernet sauvignon, which is increasingly his focus. A small estate vineyard—three acres of three different cabernet sauvignon clones—was planted adjacent to the winery in 2009.

Smooth, rich, and unabashedly oaky, Fidélitas wines are consistent and flavorful, with a clear stylistic vision, a pure fruit core, and a lush mouthfeel. The m100 red wine honors the winemaker's grandmother Mary: "Standing strong at 4 foot 8 inches, this passionate, stubborn, loving, opinionated, caring, tough, God-fearing, Lawrence Welk–lovin' gal passed away at 100 in December 2005."

Best wines: the Champoux vineyard designates.

FORGERON CELLARS

First vintage: 2001

www.forgeroncellars.com

Forgeron winemaker Marie-Eve Gilla, who is married to Gilles Nicault of Long Shadows, has been making wines in America since the early 1990s. Her first years in Washington State were spent at Covey Run, Hogue, and Gordon Brothers. At Gordon Brothers she became enamored of the concept of making wines that straddle the border between American and French styles, sturdy wines with a lot of character.

In 2001, she helped to found Forgeron Cellars, headquartered in a turn-of-the-century blacksmithing shop in Walla Walla (*forgeron* is French for "blacksmith"). "Washington sunshine," she explains, "is a lot more consistent than in France. We like the French wines because they are elegant and balanced and meant to age. So we're trying to create an elegant wine that showcases the American fruit but is subtle enough and balanced enough to age."

With typical French dedication to cooler vineyard sites, Gilla has sought out those vineyards that can deliver the fruit she wants to make her wines her way. "I'm really picky," she admits; "I want things just so. It's about the grapes, the site, the relationship with the grower."

The winery's ongoing strengths are its chardonnays and zinfandels. Though she believes that there's a lot of chardonnay in the world, but not that much good chardonnay, Gilla recognized early on that hers was a style that people like and want, so she has made it a focus at Forgeron. Her chardonnays are given a rather lush treatment with generous new oak.

A retrospective tasting of the winery's first six zinfandel vintages proved their ageworthiness and showcased their balance. All six wines were drinking well, reflecting changes in vineyard sources and vintage variation. For winemakers with Old World training, vintage variation is not something to be pounded out of the wines. Rather, it is something to be nurtured and cherished.

Forgeron's merlots and cabernets have really come into their own in recent vintages, with single-vineyard bottlings from Pepper Bridge, Champoux, and Boushey among the highlights. Total production is up to roughly 5,000 cases.

Best wines: chardonnay and zinfandel, for their style and uniqueness.

FORT WALLA WALLA CELLARS

First vintage: 2001

www.fortwallawallacellars.com

Jim Moyer and Cliff Kontos are the partners behind Fort Walla Walla Cellars. They arrived independently in Walla Walla in the late 1960s, and eventually both began doing a little home winemaking. Moyer lives next door to Gary Figgins, another one-time home winemaker, who offered some helpful advice. Eventually, he and Kontos, who had become golfing buddies, decided to "do it for real" and started Fort Walla Walla Cellars.

They make about 1,900 cases of syrah, merlot, and cabernet sauvignon annually, all from Walla Walla fruit, much of it grown at Pepper Bridge and Les Collines. "Part of our style is we underpress all of our grapes," says Moyer. "It gives us wines that are lower in tannins than typical wines; a style we like because it shows more fruit, and it's approachable at a younger age."

A few wine club– or tasting room–only only wines are offered; all their wines run to a round, supple, chocolaty style, open and forward and quite appealing.

Best wine: the red blend called Treaty.

GAMACHE VINTNERS

First vintage: 2002

www.gamachevintners.com

The Gamache vineyards, located north of Pasco near Bacchus and Conner Lee, were first planted by Bob and Roger Gamache in 1982. A total of 185 acres is in the ground, a diverse mix of cabernet sauvignon, merlot, malbec, syrah, cabernet franc, pinot gris, chardonnay, riesling, sauvignon blanc, viognier, and roussanne. The oldest block is riesling planted in 1983; there are also sauvignon blanc from 1985 and cabernet sauvignon from 1985, 1990, and 1994.

Since its inception, Gamache vineyards has been primarily a contract grower for various Ste. Michelle Wine Estates brands, notably Northstar merlot, Eroica riesling, and Columbia Crest reserve cabernets. A number of smaller producers also purchase Gamache grapes, including àMaurice, Abeja, Bergevin Lane, Boudreaux, Fidélitas, Tamarack, and William Church.

The Gamache brothers started their own label with the 2002 vintage, hiring Charlie Hoppes (Fidélitas) as their winemaker. "We were swallowed up for years by the big company, and we wanted to see what we could do on our own," Bob Gamache explained. The wines were immediately impressive, especially because the syrah, cabernet sauvignon, cabernet franc, and merlot are 100 percent varietal and all estate-grown. Production has climbed to around 3,000 cases, including a tasty selection of white wines and a moderately priced Boulder Red.

Cousins of Paul Champoux, the brothers make a few hundred cases of a reserve Gamache–Champoux vineyard select cabernet sauvignon that is a 50-50 blend of old-vine fruit from the two vineyards. Cassis and blackberry flavors, along with substantial streaks of earth and tannin, black olive, and coffee define this wine. In 2009, a new tasting room in the Prosser Vintner's Village was opened, with an on-site barrel room. A dedicated production facility is still in the works.

Best wines: riesling and syrah.

HARLEQUIN WINE CELLARS

First vintage: 1999

www.harlequinwine.com

Named in homage to Picasso, Harlequin Wine Cellars is the handiwork of Robert Goodfriend and Elizabeth Cook. Goodfriend brings a chef's sensibility to his winemaking. He was a self-confessed "science geek" in college and then went into restaurateuring in Santa Fe. His next stop was California's Central Coast, where he worked for a time at Wild Horse, in charge of the crush pad. It was the first time, he remembers, that he had ever tasted pinot noir grapes. It was an epiphany. "I put them in my mouth," he told me some years later, "and it made sense. I realized this is what the fruit tastes like. It all worked for me, from a culinary standpoint."

Goodfriend sources grapes from all over the Northwest: pinot noir from Oregon's Hoodview vineyard, chardonnay from the Celilo vineyard in the Columbia Gorge, and viognier from the Wahluke Slope. The syrahs are sourced from Wahluke Slope and Yakima Valley vineyards. From time to time a Jester's Red or basic Claret have been offered. Sadly, this winery seems to be falling behind in new releases, and may have gone out of business by the time you read this.

HIGHTOWER CELLARS

First vintage: 1997

www.hightowercellars.com

Like many young couples with a winemaking dream, Kelly and Tim Hightower started small, working day jobs while making a few hundred cases of their "handpicked, hand-sorted, handmade" wine in a funky warehouse in Woodinville. They next found 15 acres of undeveloped (and relatively cheap) vineyard land on Red Mountain, back when water rights were as rare as trees, and moved from Woodinville to Benton City in the fall of 2002.

The Hightowers retrofitted an old barn on the property as a small winery, and began planting their 10-acre estate vineyard in the spring of 2004. It grows cabernet sauvignon and merlot, with small amounts of cabernet franc, petit verdot, and malbec. In 2007, they harvested their first grapes. The vineyard name—Out of Line—refers to the vines' 11-degree offset from standard north-south orientation. Using GPS to rotate vine rows in this way creates more evenly balanced ripening on both sunrise and sunset sides of the vine.

A modest, cozy tasting room opened in the spring of 2008. Along with the estate fruit, grapes for their high-toned, glossy red wines continue to be sourced from a variety of vineyards, including Alder Ridge in the Horse Heaven Hills, Pepper Bridge in Walla Walla, and Artz and Shaw up on Red Mountain. Along with merlot, cabernet, and the occasional vineyard-designate, Hightower offers a series of lower-priced Murray wines featuring the winery dog on the label.

"We started off with the idea of just making one wine," says Tim. "I don't want to make twenty wines. But it's beneficial to have three or four with the distributor." A spring 2007 vertical tasting showcased Hightower merlots from 2000 through 2004 and Hightower cabernets from 1997 (the first) through 2004. Nothing was over the hill, and all were soundly made. Yet nothing stood out from the rest of the pack as unique or exceptional.

I don't wish to damn Hightower with faint praise. I include this winery happily in this state's top third, I applaud its industry and commitment, and I hope it will continue to look for its own unique expression of that valuable Red Mountain terroir.

Best wine: Red Mountain Red.

HOGUE CELLARS

First vintage: 1982

www.hoguecellars.com

Why was Hogue Cellars—one of this state's founding wineries—left out of the first edition of this book? That question has come up more than a few times, and it's a good one. I have long admired and valued the contribution that the Hogue family made to the development of the Washington wine industry. I remember vividly the introduction of the Hogues' first wines, at a Seattle tasting in the mid-1980s, and how thoroughly delicious and fresh and exciting they were.

But in 2001, when the winery passed out of family ownership and into corporate hands—first Vincor, and now Constellation—it all changed. Good winemakers came and went, but overall quality tanked, even as production grew. Dozens of wines were produced, in a confusing profusion of price point–driven tiers. Many of the wines released from the 2002 through 2004 vintages were terribly disappointing, my notes stocked with words such as volatile, thin, chalky, vegetal, bitter, burnt.

Happily, things are definitely looking up for Hogue. The state's third-largest winery (up to 650,000 cases annually) passed from Vincor to Constellation in 2006 and was Constellation's only Washington winery not sold to Ascentia in 2008. The Hogue family still owns the vineyards. Co Dinn became director of winemaking in 2007 after a decade there as white-winemaker.

About one-quarter of the total production is riesling, with chardonnay and pinot gris the other important whites. Cabernet sauvignon and merlot are the major red wines. White wines have generally been significantly better than the reds—tart, bright, and fruity. The reds can be tannic and somewhat dilute, but the most recent offerings of the low-cost wines have been Best Buy caliber. Rough tannins were an issue, but Dinn insists that the winery is working to amend the problem, while admitting that for a while they were overextracting and tannin levels were too high.

Three-quarters of Hogue's wines are packaged under the $10 red label—tank-fermented and released within a year of harvest. The $16 Genesis line is a selection of fruit from the best vineyards; the pricier Hogue reserves get extended aging in new French oak; and the Terroir series is reserved for what Dinn calls research and development—very limited production vineyard-designates, mostly sold through the tasting room.

Best wines: the red-label white wines.

JLC/JAMES LEIGH CELLARS

First vintage: 2001

(website in development)

Spofford Station, the superb estate vineyard, is the ace in the hole at JLC. The first four vintages were made by co-founder Jamie Brown (now at Waters), who focused on that vineyard's fruit to craft a series of outstanding varietal merlots, cabernets, and syrahs, along with red blends named Palette.

My notes on these wines are loaded with superlatives, for their power, their varietal typicity, the explosive aromas that often blended fruit with funk—good funk. The 2004 Spofford Station syrah—one of the rare Walla Walla wines from that freeze year—was a gorgeous mix of Rhône-like herbs, spices, earthy funk, and tight, tart fruit, I wrote, blended seamlessly and expanding into a luscious rainbow of fruit and earth and herb.

That said, the first of the post-2004 releases seemed to suffer a bit. The remaining partner, Lynne Chamberlain, appears to be stretched a bit thin, trying to grow the grapes, cultivate the grapes, harvest the grapes, crush the grapes, make the wine, sell the wine, and work another job in real estate. She is also wrestling with the issue of what to call her winery—JLC? James Leigh Cellars? Spofford Station? Right now, it's a little bit of all three. The only certainty is that Spofford Station grows great fruit. Stay tuned.

KESTREL VINTNERS

First vintage: 1995

www.kestrelwines.com

Begun by a Florida couple as Kestrel View Estates back in the mid-1990s, Kestrel has as its main asset the estate vineyard the two purchased, originally planted by Mike Hinzerling more than 35 years ago. From those vines come old-vine estate chardonnays, cabernets, and merlots; newer plantings provide fruit for the estate viognier, malbec, and syrah. The winery was opened in 1999, in the Prosser Wine and Food Park—a strip mall just off the highway east of town. Despite its unprepossessing looks, Kestrel makes it a pleasant stop, with many wines available and a sizable gift shop.

Production has climbed to 35,000 cases—90 percent red wines. There are occasional bright spots among the myriad offerings, especially the viognier and (usually) the co-fermented syrah. Most of the red wines are all over the map in terms of style and quality, with no surefire success from one vintage to the next. With such excellent fruit, the perpetual hope is that things will settle into a more predictable groove, but sometimes there is leathery funk (a brett issue?), sometimes wines that are simply thin and characterless, sometimes the opposite—pruney, raisined, prematurely aged wines.

The most popular wines are the least expensive—the Lady in Red nonvintage blend and its cheesecake-label shelf mate, Pure Platinum White.

Best wine: Winemaker's Select Co-ferment estate syrah.

KIONA

First vintage: 1980

www.kionawinery.com

This Red Mountain pioneer and longtime grower of exceptional grapes—fruit that is eagerly sought after and fought over by many of this state's best winemakers—is one of the most difficult wineries in Washington to rate. The problem is that Kiona the vineyard and Kiona the winery are light years apart in consistency. Though the vineyards—more than 130 acres of prime Red Mountain real estate—are impeccably run and excellent in all vintages, the Kiona wines have not been as reliable.

Scott and Vicky Williams are the owners, but Scott's parents, who pioneered Red Mountain in the mid-1970s, maintain some ownership in the original estate vineyard. That first vineyard was planted in 1975, Scott Williams confirms. He was in high school at the time, and as he recalled in a recent interview: "We had no idea what would do well. The criteria was, would the vines survive our climate and make commercially acceptable wine?" That original planting has grown to 65 acres and still includes some of the original riesling and chenin blanc. Here and at two other Red Mountain sites (The Ranch at the End of the Road and The Heart of the Hill), Williams grows syrah, lemberger, petit verdot, mourvèdre, sangiovese, zinfandel, malbec, carmenère, chardonnay, and gewürztraminer. He sells grapes to as many as forty different wineries, and also makes about 35,000 cases of Kiona wines annually, a mix of up to twenty different white, red, and sweet dessert wines.

A complete overhaul of Kiona's barrel room and tasting room was completed in 2007, adding barrel storage, office space, a meeting room, and a catering kitchen. It's a lovely facility whose covered deck offers panoramic views of the original vineyard, the Horse Heaven Hills, and Red Mountain itself.

Barrel storage in the old facility, Williams acknowledges, was "an issue." The new barrel room is underground, is well insulated, and holds the temperature between 55 and 68 degrees year-round without air conditioning. That seems likely to have a positive impact on the reds. Kiona the winery has always done a bang-up job with its late-harvest and ice wines; they are world-class. Among the dry whites, the reserve dry riesling is a standout. Were only the vineyards and dessert wines considered, this would be a five-star enterprise. There is no reason it should not reach that level with its red wines, given the exceptional material it has to work with.

Best wines: late-harvest and ice wines.

LATAH CREEK

First vintage: 1982

www.latahcreek.com

Mike Conway earned his winemaking stripes under California's John Parducci in the late '70s and then moved to Washington to make wine at Worden and at Hogue before starting Latah Creek in 1982. His wines have always been value-oriented, everyday, everyman offerings, and the white wines in particular show a confident veteran hand at work. Since 2005, Mike and Ellena's daughter Natalie has been the assistant winemaker.

Production has leveled off at about 17,000 cases annually, much of it riesling and the winery's unusual Huckleberry d'Latah, a riesling and huckleberry blend. There is also a Maywine, which mixes white wine with woodruff (an herb) and strawberry concentrate. Though the wines are unpretentious and often on the sweet side, they are meticulously made and offered at user-friendly prices. Latah Creek's rieslings, muscats, and other off-dry, tasting room favorites (such as a Prosecco-styled, light sparkling wine called Moscato d'Latah) give customers consistent and soundly made wines vintage after vintage.

Most of the winery's sales are through the tasting room, mailing list, and a few outlets in the Spokane area, where the winery is located. Red wines being made currently include sangiovese, merlot, a cabernet-syrah blend, a reserve petit verdot, and a very nice cabernet-syrah-zinfandel blend called Vinosity.

Best wine: off-dry riesling.

MORRISON LANE

First vintage: 2002

www.morrisonlane.com

Dean and Verdie Morrison planted their first four acres of syrah just outside Walla Walla in 1994. The original vineyard has grown to 28 acres, and the dazzling array of varietals produced makes it one of the most eclectic in the state. More than half the acreage is devoted to syrah; also included in the rest of the mix are viognier, cinsault, carmenère, counoise, Dolcetto, sangiovese, nebbiolo, and barbera. An additional five acres— noncontiguous—is being leased. That plot is one of the highest in Walla Walla at 1,800 feet.

Morrison Lane grapes were a hot commodity from the very first harvest. Among the wineries that lined up to purchase them were Seven Hills, Cayuse, K Vintners, Walla Walla Vintners, and SYZYGY. Currently, Morrison Lane vineyard-designates are being made by K Vintners and Willis Hall.

The winemaker for the Morrison Lane winery is son Sean Morrison, who is also the cellarmaster at Abeja. Estate grapes are used almost exclusively; a couple of Columbia Valley wines were made in 2004, when the estate vineyard was frozen out. The various wines show clear varietal identities, and such unusual offerings as the Morrison Lane Dolcetto, cinsault, and counoise varietal bottlings are especially interesting, as is the 33⅓ red, a co-fermented blend (a third each) of syrah, counoise, and viognier. Production is about 1,200 cases annually (except for 2004), largely sold out of the tasting room.

The multitalented Morrisons are a musical family as well: Dean on stand-up bass, Verdie on piano, Sean on guitar (married to vocalist Kate Bray). Their Main Street tasting room is often the setting for some excellent jazz jams.

Best wine: 33⅓ red.

:NOTE BENE CELLARS

First vintage: 2001

www.notabenecellars.com

:Nota Bene Cellars stands as a testament to the steep learning curve faced by many of the tiny underfunded start-ups in the wine business. Tim Narby and his wife, Carol Bryant, had the misfortune to start their shoestring winery in September 2001. For a time, his aerospace industry job seemed about to vanish, even as the winery bills piled up.

They had not yet released their second vintage before they found themselves doing a complete label redesign, prompted by the comments of a would-be distributor in the Midwest who didn't like the old triangular style. They also outran their own business plan. "I was only supposed to be at 500 cases by 2003, the third year," Narby sheepishly admitted, "and I was at 1,100. I shouldn't have done that."

The early misfires did not prove fatal, and Narby and Bryant, who spent almost two decades doing home winemaking before turning pro, are now on solid ground, stylistically and financially. "I tend to harvest late," Narby explains. "I like jammy, plummy, big New World flavors. I don't have any problem with what made Napa famous."

Calling upon his Boeing Wine Club experience and connections (he was Boeing's grape procurement officer), he's been able to line up grape contracts with several of the best vineyards in the state, including Stillwater Creek, Stone Tree, Conner Lee, and Ciel du Cheval. The wines—all red—include a pair of Bordeaux blends named Miscela and Abbinare. Similar in style, they use grapes from different vineyards. There is also a fine syrah; several vineyard designates (Ciel du Cheval, Conner Lee, and Verhey); and a grenache-syrah blend called Una Notte. Very consistent in quality, these wines make it difficult to pick a favorite, but the Una Notte stands out for the bright fruit and lush barrel flavors.

Best wine: Una Notte red.

OTIS KENYON

First vintage: 2005

www.otiskenyonwine.com

A sense of wry humor underscores this Walla Walla winery's labels. Its burnt edges pay ironic homage to owner Steve Kenyon's grandfather, a dentist who was accused back in the 1920s of burning down his competitor's office. He soon mysteriously disappeared and was presumed dead; a half century later, Steve Kenyon explains, he tracked down his grandfather and found him alive and well. Reunited with his family, he lived to be 101.

The back label copy is a nonstop parade of awful puns: "The Otis Kenyon name inflamed emotions in the Walla Walla Valley in the 1920s. Today this exceptional wine region ignites the passion of another generation of Otis Kenyons." There is even a blended wine called Matchless—it took me awhile for that one to sink in. Puns aside, the wines are seriously good, made under the supervision of consulting winemaker Dave Stephenson, with fruit drawn from some of Walla Walla's best sites.

The modest production facility is just down the road from Cayuse, and the property—yet to be planted—includes acreage adjacent to Christophe Baron's En Chamberlin vineyard. A second site, the Stellar vineyard, was purchased from the owners of Cougar Crest in 2006. Estate wines have been produced since 2007, the goal being to have those grapes constitute about half of the 2,000-case annual production.

Included in the portfolio are varietal bottlings of cabernet sauvignon, carmenère, malbec, merlot, and syrah; there are also very limited offerings of reserve wines, such as a Seven Hills vineyard merlot. The syrah is surefire, with grapes from Patina, Va Piano, and Windy Ridge, but the merlots—both regular and reserve—offer the most density, richness, and seductively smoky barrel flavors.

Best wine: merlot (both regular and reserve).

PAGE CELLARS

First vintage: 2000

www.pagecellars.com

A decade ago, Jim Page, a corporate pilot by trade, was flying winemakers Eric Dunham and Matt Loso back to Seattle from a Florida sales meeting. Before they landed, he'd been inspired to start a winery, and Page Cellars became one of the first microboutiques to settle into the industrial warehouse district of Woodinville. Matt Loso took on the role of consulting winemaker, but the early releases of red blends from Red Mountain fruit seemed a bit overdriven, high-toned, and alcoholic. Loso later confided that it took a few vintages before he was allowed to pull things back and get away from the big huge red syndrome.

From 2005 forward, there has been steady improvement. A rare Klipsun vineyard sauvignon blanc turns the usually snarly, gooseberry-flavored grape into a honeyed pussycat, ripe and tropical, with a toffee candy finish. The Shaw vineyard red blend brings mass and muscle, polished tannins, and plenty of chocolaty oak. Not shy, but delicious. Several syrahs are produced, notably the Lick My Lips bottling from Wahluke Slope grapes. Case production has topped out at 2,500. Libra de Carta is the declassified second-label red.

Best wine: sauvignon blanc.

PRECEPT BRANDS

First vintage: 2003

www.preceptwinebrands.com

There's a dearth of cheap and good Washington wine in the marketplace, and Andrew Browne is a man with a mission—find it, make it, and sell it. The ebullient, curly-haired CEO of Precept Brands believes that, despite a global downturn in wine sales, his company is still in really good shape. "We've got a nice solid base of business, and it's growing incrementally within a realistic pattern," he explains. "We're not just sitting on our laurels; we continue to challenge the status quo as an industry."

Although the Precept portfolio includes brands from overseas, it is solidly anchored in Washington State. Browne and his partners have acquired or joint-ventured with marquee wineries such as Waterbrook and Willow Crest, turbo-charged Charles Smith's wildly successful Magnificent Wine Company (House, Steak, and Fish wines), revamped once-faltering Apex and Washington Hills, and introduced a smorgasbord of supermarket-friendly labels, including Rainier Ridge and Barrelstone, Sockeye and Pavin & Riley, Shimmer, Avery Lane, and Pine & Post. Most recently, Precept acquired Corus Estates, with its Alder Ridge, 6 Prong, and Zefina brands and winery.

In a few short years, Precept has become the third-largest wine company in the state, with a bullet. A Grandview bottling plant was opened in July 2005, and a massive production facility and tasting room debuted just outside Walla Walla in 2009. Though Precept has always relied on purchased grapes, the company is evolving rapidly toward an emphasis on owned vineyards. The first is Canyon Ranch (previously Snipes Canyon Ranch), a 500-acre Yakima Valley property slated to double in size from its current 150 planted acres. Existing varietals are chardonnay, pinot gris, merlot, syrah, and malbec; coming soon are riesling, gewürztraminer, and more pinot gris. A smaller vineyard is being planted near Spring Valley in northeastern Walla Walla County.

The reasoning behind so many different brands? Precept has set out to develop a diverse lineup of Washington wines designed to overdeliver on quality, particularly at the cheap end of the spectrum. "We try to maintain what I call extreme value in Washington State," Browne explains. "In the past, if you wanted a $5 wine, you couldn't find it in Washington. That's been one of our challenges—to continuously overdeliver."

Some of the early Precept efforts were less than stellar, but these days, quality improvements are tangible across the board. The strategy is simple enough: find people that do the viticulture or the winemaking, or both, well. Let them do it, and give them all the technical support they need. Then let Precept do what it does best.

"We're good at making packages, working with distributors, going out there and getting the public to try the wines," says Browne. "It's really hard for anyone to do the whole process alone; farming, making, selling, branding, and doing the PR for the wine. We're finding people who do a remarkable job with some portion, but bash their heads against the wall talking to distributors."

At the value end of the spectrum, look for Pine & Post, Waterbrook, Washington Hills, Washington Hills Summit Reserves, Avery Lane, and the House, Steak, and Fish wines. Pendulum, Sol-Duc, and Browne Family are premium projects priced higher. See separate entries for Alder Ridge, Apex, Waterbrook, and Willow Crest.

Best wine: Browne Family cabernet sauvignon.

ROSS ANDREW

First vintage: 2000

www.rossandrewwinery.com

Ross Andrew Mickel is a friend and contemporary of restaurateur Mark Canlis and Betz Family winery's Carmen Betz. It was through Carmen's dad, Bob Betz, that he first found wine work, as crush help at DeLille Cellars in 1998. The following year he worked briefly in Australia, then came back to join Betz as cellarmaster, where he stayed for almost 10 years. Their original warehouse space is now the home for Ross Andrew winery.

Mickel picked up a great deal of practical information from his years at Betz Family, along with a certain real-world perspective on the requirements of the job. "We're glorified janitors," he states matter-of-factly. "We walk around with sprayers of alcohol; if we have to break down a piece of equipment, we spray it with alcohol to keep it clean. We'll spend an hour or two setting up, another two cleaning up. The sanitation time is a lot more than the actual task. There are too many things that can screw a wine up; you've got to pay attention to SO2 levels, VA levels, top regularly; there's a lot of little things that need to be done."

Mickel does all of those little things, and his wines reflect that attention to detail. Production is up to 2,600 cases, including a couple of white wines (one from Oregon grapes, the other from the Columbia Gorge) and a flight of reds. Highlights are a gamy, three-clone Boushey vineyard syrah and a focused, elegant cabernet sauvignon built on Klipsun and Ciel du Cheval fruit. Mickel is one of the five winemakers participating in the Grand Rêve project (profiled elsewhere). He and his business partners, Ned and Sheila Nelson, also design winemaking equipment through their American Basket Press company.

Best wine: Boushey vineyard syrah.

RUSSELL CREEK

First vintage: 1998

www.russellcreek-winery.com

Cabernet, merlot, syrah, and sangiovese are the specialties at this low-key Walla Walla winery. Larry Krivoshein is a self-taught winemaker who turned out full-bodied reds for a decade before getting his winery bonded. His wines are solid and fleshy and still feel a bit homemade—not in a bad way, but reflecting a rougher, more casual, less contemporary style that harks back to an earlier time in Walla Walla.

Tributary is Russell Creek's Bordeaux blend (with a splash of syrah for good measure); the Winemaker's Select bottlings have garnered some good scores and reviews from the national press, and show more oak, more tannin, and more chocolaty flavors than the regular bottlings.

Best wine: Winemaker's Select cabernet sauvignon.

RYAN PATRICK

First vintage: 1999

www.ryanpatrickvineyards.com

Ryan Patrick owners Terry and Vivian Flanagan farm three different vineyards—58 acres altogether—all located east of Wenatchee. Bishops is 20 acres, set on a basalt bench above the Columbia River and planted to merlot, cabernet sauvignon, cabernet franc, and chardonnay. Homestead, another 20 acres, has been in the family for over half a century and grows chardonnay exclusively. The newest vineyard is Vivian's, which also overlooks the river, and grows cabernet sauvignon, cabernet franc, barbera, and nebbiolo.

Terry Flanagan retired from a career overseas in 1996 and returned to his childhood home determined to start a winery. It was named for sons Ryan and Patrick Flanagan. Patrick was tragically killed in a car accident in the summer of 2004; Ryan manages the Indian Wells vineyard for Ste. Michelle Wine Estates and oversees all vineyard operations for Ryan Patrick.

Winemaker Craig Mitrakul worked at Ponzi in Oregon and Three Rivers in Walla Walla before joining Ryan Patrick in 2004. Since then, Mitrakul has kept a steady hand on the tiller and added some innovations of his own, most importantly his reserve cabernet sauvignons, which are pure varietal with a fine balance of fruit, earth, acid, and supple tannins.

The winery produces about 5,000 cases annually—a mix of chardonnay, sauvignon blanc, barbera, cabernet sauvignon, and syrah. The everyday Rock Island Red (named for the town, not the railroad line) offers excellent value in a Bordeaux blend with lively spicy, cherry-flavored fruit front and center. Recently, a "naked" (i.e., no oak) chardonnay has joined the estate chardonnay bottling; both are nicely styled, the estate version mixing its melon-apple fruit with barrel notes of vanilla cream and toasted cracker.

The winery production facility is in Quincy, but a new tasting room opened in the faux-Bavarian wine town of Leavenworth in the summer of 2009.

Best wines: estate chardonnay and reserve cabernet sauvignon.

SAGELANDS

First vintage: 1984

www.sagelandsvineyard.com

You can't miss Sagelands, which rises above I-82 just as you enter the Yakima Valley south of Yakima. It was first planted and opened (to great fanfare) by businessman David Staton, but struggled with too many wines, high overhead, and a lack of focus. Pink Riesling was its best-selling wine for a time; need I say more?

The property changed hands throughout the 1990s and was eventually purchased by Chalone and renamed Sagelands. Currently owned by Diageo, Sagelands is best known for its moderately priced Four Corners merlot and cabernet sauvignon but, other than that, has yet to find either a focus or a style to call its own. The Four Corners concept—blending grapes from the Wahluke Slope, Horse Heaven Hills, Rattlesnake Hills, and Walla Walla Valley—works as a marketing concept but so far has been meaningless as far as the wines are concerned. Many wineries blend grapes from around the state; it is mostly a protective measure to ensure a grape supply if a freeze knocks out a particular region.

The other Sagelands wines—riesling, chardonnay, some generic blends—are unremarkable. But with deep-pockets Diageo behind the brand, there is always a chance for real improvement.

Best wine: Four Corners merlot.

SAINT LAURENT

First vintage: 2001

www.saintlaurent.net

As you motor down the fir-covered eastern slopes of the Cascades past the town of Wenatchee and follow the river as it winds south and east, the landscape, though drier and more desertlike, is spectacular. At Saint Laurent, in the hills above the town of Malaga, apple and cherry growers Mike and Laura Mrachek have jumped into the wine business. They've renovated a pretty little farmhouse—originally built from a Sears & Roebuck kit—added a pond and waterfall, and furnished the tasting room with lovely antiques and offer a pleasing lineup of wines from their Wahluke Slope vineyard, part of a 500+-acre agricultural enterprise named Lucky Bohemian Farms. A small estate vineyard near the tasting room grows riesling and an unusual varietal called St. Laurent.

The first 60 acres on the Wahluke Slope were planted in 1999. The total has since expanded to more than 260 acres of chardonnay, riesling, cabernet sauvignon, merlot, and syrah. Craig Mitrakul, who also makes wines for Ryan Patrick, oversees production at the winery. Along with the named varietals, he produces a red blend named la Bohème and a cheaper duo dubbed Lucky White and Lucky Red.

Best wine: la Bohème.

SLEIGHT OF HAND

First vintage: 2005

www.sofhcellars.com

Trey Busch, a nattily dressed Nordstrom alum, first made his mark as a winemaker at Basel Cellars, where his intense syrahs and excellent Merriment red were standouts. One of Walla Walla's most congenial individuals, he soon got the urge to start his own winery and found backers Jerry and Sandy Soloman while attending the Sun Valley wine auction. Busch quickly secured some juice and made his first blends, opening his downtown tasting room in June 2007 with The Magician (gewürztraminer), The Spellbinder (a nonvintage red), and The Archimage—an old-vine, right-bank, Bordeaux blend.

The winery name, labels, and tasting room décor, inspired by a Pearl Jam song, reference the world of magic. Wines are being made at Saviah, and production has jumped up to 3,000 cases, most of it The Magician and The Spellbinder. With changing grape sources and just small case quantities of Busch's best wines, it's a little early in the going to pin a definitive label on Sleight of Hand. But the white wines have been especially good, notably The Enchantress, a supremely rich chardonnay from an old Yakima Valley planting.

The reds, as might be expected, are consistently well made. The Spellbinder is the table wine anchor; there are also about 300 cases each of Levitation syrah, The Illusionist Red, and Archimage, a merlot–cab franc blend. In the spring, a few cases of a Magician's Assistant rosé are released and quickly snatched up by tasting room visitors. And on Spring Release weekend, a real magician entertains in the winery's downtown tasting room.

Best wine: The Illusionist Red

SMASNE CELLARS

First vintage: 2003

www.smasnecellars.com

Robert Smasne grew up on a farm in the central Yakima Valley; his great-grandfather homesteaded there, and his father first planted wine grapes in the 1970s. "I grew up right next to Otis vineyard," Smasne says cheerfully. "Dick Boushey is my dad's neighbor.

I was becoming a winemaker before I knew it; we'd sneak into vineyards just to taste the grapes."

With such a fast start, it's not surprising that Smasne, still in his mid-thirties, has already racked up an amazing career. He's assisted in the winemaking at Covey Run, Pepper Bridge, Amavi, Cayuse, and Alexandria Nicole. He is a partner with Alan Busacca in Alma Terra; makes wines for fourteen different labels and wineries, including Skylite Cellars, Gård Vintners, and Upland Estates; consults at Chandler Reach and Timber Rock (in Idaho); and along the way has started his own Smasne Cellars.

As talented as he is, it seems clear that Smasne has overloaded his plate. Consequently, there are some brilliant wines, some duds, and quite a few that fall in between, even in his own portfolio. The Smasne reds show a lot of new oak, at least when first released, though that can be misleading—sometimes, as red wines gain additional bottle age, the oak integrates. Smasne's whites can be outstanding, but again vary widely.

Among a lineup that currently includes varietal riesling, gewürztraminer, chardonnay, cabernet, carmenère, petit verdot, syrah, and various blended wines, the vineyard-designates (Smasne estate, Phinny Hill, and Lawrence) are the standouts. A second label, Farm Boy, offers simple, budget-priced wines, and an even newer project, Rosella, will donate all proceeds to charity. Whew!

Best wine: estate dry riesling.

SNOQUALMIE

First vintage: 1984

www.snoqualmie.com

The full and complete history of Snoqualmie could fill this book, so we'll skip right to the present and simply say that it has become one of the most important wineries in the state, offering an expansive lineup of value-priced wines. Winemaker Joy Andersen has been the unsung heroine of the rise in quality.

To this observer it has often seemed that Snoqualmie got the last, worst fruit from the long list of parent company Ste. Michelle Wine Estates' vineyards. Too many red wines tasted unripe, vegetal, and charmless. It is perhaps no accident that the sole successes during the first half of the 1990s were the winery's muscat and gewürztraminer, grapes that no one else was eager to claim. But, perhaps influenced by the opening of a dedicated tasting room in Prosser, the quality tide began to turn about the time the century did, and Snoqualmie wines have been remarkably good in most vintages since.

There are numerous tiers of line-priced wines. The Columbia Valley bottlings have graphic, colorful labels promoting the small-town farm community appeal of the region. The Snoqualmie Naked line, first introduced in 2003, has been expanded to include organically grown and vinified riesling, gewürztraminer, chardonnay, rosé, merlot, and cabernet sauvignon, all with minimal added sulfites. So far, only the naked gewürztraminer and riesling have been recommendable, but with fruit coming from the largest certified organic vineyard in the state, look for quality to improve across the board. The reserve wines are a mixed bag, with syrah being the most likely to shine.

Snoqualmie's first 100 percent organic wine, a 2008 riesling with no added sulfites whatsoever, debuted in 2009. To Andersen's credit, she points out that the wine is perishable and should be consumed within six months of its release.

Scattered throughout the Columbia Valley offerings are many fine values, especially among the whites: the sauvignon blanc, as light and clean as a spring breeze; the chardonnay, with a splash of viognier in the blend; and the Winemaker's Select riesling, off-dry and reminiscent of fresh-pressed apple cider.

Best wine: rieslings, naked or fully clothed.

SPARKMAN CELLARS

First vintage: 2004

www.sparkmancellars.com

For years, Christian Sparkman was best known as the personable manager of the Waterfront Restaurant in Seattle. Through an ongoing series of winemaker dinners, he fine-tuned his palate and made the contacts necessary to obtain choice grapes for his dream project—his own winery. "I'm now in a position to call guys up who know what the hell they're doing," Sparkman explains in his beguiling southern drawl. "They have been great to me."

The idea came to him and his wife, Kelly, just after their first daughter, Stella, was born in 2004. "We thought that it would be nice if I didn't have to work at night by the time she went to school," Sparkman recalls. After five years of working essentially two full-time jobs, raising two young children, and using borrowed equipment while stretching loans from their families and a second mortgage on their home, the Sparkmans have reached the point where the winery is completely self-sustaining.

The wines justify the sacrifices. Mark McNeilly (of Mark Ryan winery) consulted on the first few vintages, but Sparkman has gained enough confidence to fly solo these days, albeit with consulting help from enologist Erica Orr. As production levels off at 2,500 cases, the lineup includes a barrel-aged Lumière chardonnay from Stillwater Creek grapes; the Red Mountain–sourced Ruby Leigh and Stella Mae reds; a Boushey vineyard syrah called Darkness; a companion syrah named Ruckus; an Outlaw merlot; an old-vine, Klipsun vineyard Kingpin cabernet sauvignon; and a Wilderness red, what Sparkman calls "our D2, for us to kind of tinker." All the reds are high-alcohol, dense, seductive, and thoroughly delicious wines, from a first-class array of vineyards, including Klipsun, Kiona, Ciel du Cheval, Boushey, and DuBrul. Sparkman is already close to being a four-star winery; just a little more time and it will be there.

Best wines: Kingpin cabernet, Darkness syrah.

SYZYGY

First vintage: 2002

www.syzygywines.com

In astronomy, a syzygy is the perfect alignment among three celestial bodies, such as the sun, moon, and Earth during a total solar eclipse. That perfect alignment has not yet come to this SYZYGY, which makes about 2,000 cases total of syrah, cabernet sauvignon, a wine simply named Red, and the superpremium Saros, a malbec-tempranillo-cabernet blend. "My original intention," says owner and winemaker Zach Brettler, "was to drink more wine for less money. But it's proved to be the exact opposite."

Started just before the number of Walla Walla wineries quintupled, SYZYGY has excellent vineyard contracts in the valley. Syrahs are thick and sappy, with no rough edges. The cabernets are classically styled, 100 percent varietal, from excellent vineyards such as Conner Lee, Sagemoor, and Klipsun. The red blend changes vineyard sources completely from year to year, but is usually quite good, loaded with berry flavors, sharp acid, and spice. Saros (another obscure astronomical term) is conceived as a three-varietal blend, "a place to put new varietals," Brettler explains. A recent partnership split means that SYZYGY is being realigned, with Brettler now solely in charge.

Best wine: syrah.

TAGARIS

First vintage: 1987

www.tagariswines.com

Michael Taggares founded his winery in 1987 (Tagaris is the proper Greek spelling of the family name), but though launched more than two decades ago, Tagaris only recently has emerged as a winery to watch in this state. That's thanks largely to the current winemaker, Frank Roth, who was hired just before the 2006 harvest. The son of Coke Roth, a Tri-Cities businessman and vineyard owner, Roth apprenticed in Canada at Sumac Ridge and Hawthorne Mountain vineyards, then spent 10 years as cellarmaster for Barnard Griffin.

A new Tagaris winery was opened nearby in 2005, with a sizeable restaurant attached. Under Roth's guidance, the Tagaris brand has been repositioned as a producer of small lots of unusual wines such as counoise, mourvèdre, sangiovese, tempranillo, malbec, and petit verdot, all from estate vineyards. There is also a well-made, dry chenin blanc. Along with the successes are some wines with noticeable faults, possibly because the winery prefers to use neutral barrels exclusively—none less than six years old.

A second label, Eliseo Silva, is value priced, with easy-drinking varietal offerings of cabernet sauvignon, merlot, syrah, chardonnay, and sauvignon blanc. Eliseo Silva is the ranch manager and oversees 1,000 acres of apple orchards and three vineyards. The 200-acre Areté vineyard dates to 1983; the 100-acre Alice vineyard grows many of the newer varieties; and the 144-acre Michael vineyard (source of many of the Snoqualmie Naked wines) produces organically certified cabernet sauvignon, carmenère, cabernet franc, merlot, muscat Canneli, cinsault, barbera, and sangiovese.

A new label—pumpkin orange with a kanji-style red T painted on it—accompanied the rollout of all the new Tagaris varietals.

Best wine: the Eliseo Silva lineup is most consistent.

THREE RIVERS

First vintage: 1999

www.threeriverswinery.com

You can't miss this imposing winery, which sits just off the main highway leading into Walla Walla from the west. It was founded as a three-way partnership among retired telecom executives Steve Ahler, Bud Stocking, and Duane Wollmuth. They built a destination winery complete with conference rooms, a spacious deck, a 14,000-square-foot cellar and barrel room, a large gift shop and tasting room, and a three-hole golf course.

Charlie Hoppes made the inaugural vintages and then passed the winemaking baton over to Holly Turner, whose deft sensitivity, particularly in her white and red Bordeaux blends, set a stylistic standard for the brand through much of its first decade. But sales failed to keep up with the 15,000-case production, and early in 2008 the winery was acquired by California's William Foley. The last of the original partners left in 2009.

Turner, whether by choice or necessity, has been making a large number of wines, and therein lies a potential problem. The website lists fourteen varietals, a white and red Meritage, and up to half a dozen vineyard-designates and mailing list–only wines. Many of the vineyard sources are first-rate—Sagemoor, Champoux, Boushey, Milbrandt—but how can one winemaker trot around to so many different locations and keep track of her grapes? Might it not be easier to establish a national identity by showing only your very best wines?

In the year or two preceding the Foley acquisition, Three Rivers releases were disappointing. The River's Red, once a fine everyday value, turned generic. None of the varietals stood out from the competition. But with the newly released 2007 reds and 2008 whites, a return to previous form seems to be taking shape.

Best wine: the merlot.

THURSTON WOLFE

First vintage: 1987

www.thurstonwolfe.com

Thurston Wolfe has carved out a unique path, even in a state laden with pioneers. Wade Wolfe, a lean, square-jawed man in his early sixties, holds a Ph.D. in plant genetics from UC Davis. Soft-spoken and unassuming, Wolfe arrived in Washington in 1978, hired by Chateau Ste. Michelle to be its technical viticulturalist. Back in the day, he encouraged growers to follow basic viticultural practices: cut back on irrigation, rein in crop loads, and the rest. He made it his personal mission to investigate alternative red grape varieties for eastern Washington (at the time, cabernet sauvignon and pinot noir were the two most commonly planted).

The Thurston part of Thurston Wolfe is his mother's maiden name. It was chosen because, as his practical-minded wife and business partner, Becky Yeaman, explains, "Yeaman Wolfe or Wolfe Yeaman just didn't sound right." When he left Ste. Michelle to start his own winery, the focus was dessert wines: a black muscat, a late-harvest sauvignon blanc named Sweet Rebecca, a pair of ports. Table wines began to enter the mix in the mid-1990s, when the winery moved from downtown Yakima to Prosser (a new tasting room opened in the Vintner's Village in 2006).

Grenache and lemberger, some of the state's first zinfandels, and most recently, varietal bottlings of sangiovese, syrah, petite sirah, primitivo, and tempranillo have joined the lineup, sometimes briefly. Thurston Wolfe offers few white wines, but a pinot gris–viognier blend called PGV (viognier–pinot gris–muscat blanc) is a lip-smacking success.

Wade Wolfe's somewhat quixotic pursuit of esoteric table and dessert wines presented a bit of a financial challenge to the winery in its formative years. But nonmainstream varietals (so-called "sport varieties") are quite trendy now. Thurston Wolfe wines are never flashy; they reflect the quiet confidence of the winemaker, his deep knowledge of grapes and vineyards, and his focus on the clean, intense expression of pure varietal fruit. The Howling Wolfe zinfandel and the Zephyr Ridge petite sirah are at the top of the list, but the superstar is the JTW Reserve Premium Dessert Wine, a portlike blend of Touriga, souzao, petite sirah, zinfandel, and cabernet sauvignon.

Best wine: JTW Reserve Premium Dessert Wine.

VA PIANO VINEYARDS

First vintage: 2003

www.vapianovineyards.com

Va Piano Vineyards is located south of Walla Walla in prestigious company: Pepper Bridge, Northstar, Beresan, and Saviah are neighbors; Rulo, Isenhower, Basel, and a host of newer wineries are nearby. Owner Justin Wylie is the fourth-generation son of a Walla Walla family whose century-old business is stone monuments, and he brings a very sharp business mind to all of his enterprises.

"Making good wine is just half the battle," says Wylie. "I'd rather have my marketing degree than go to school for viticulture and enology. It's crucial in today's world. Why is your wine purchased and how is it positioned when there's a lot of good wine out there? I really enjoy that side of it."

To help fund his new winery, he organized the building to include rentable, bonded incubator space, then auditioned for the best possible tenants. He came up with Trust, Tertulia, Otis Kenyon, Gramercy, and Chateau Rollat. "I figured I was only as good as the people around me," he explains. "I wanted people I could learn from." He's also a partner in the Octave vineyard project above Seven Hills.

Va Piano's 13-acre estate vineyard was planted to cabernet sauvignon, syrah, merlot, cab franc, and petit verdot in 2000. Just as it was beginning to bear fruit, Wylie lost his whole crop to the freeze in 2004. He says he came out of it unscathed, even calling it a "blessing in disguise" as his vines had a full year to rest and he'd already contracted for other grapes as insurance.

About two-thirds of the estate grapes are sold to other wineries, while in its own releases, Va Piano uses a mix of vineyard sources that has evolved over the first six or eight vintages without entirely settling down. The estate wines, a Columbia Valley cabernet and a companion syrah, are muscular, tannic, and textural, made in mailing list–only quantities.

Bruno's Blend is an agreeable nonvintage red that raises funds for a former Gonzaga University professor engaged in charitable work. Wylie's most recent offering, again with a clever business spin, is the Aloysius cabernet sauvignon, which benefits Gonzaga's Alumni Scholarship Fund, while appealing to 50,000 alums as potential customers.

Best wine: syrah.

✳ VIN DU LAC

First vintage: 2002

www.vindulac.com

Vin du Lac was one of the first wineries to open its doors in Washington's newly christened Lake Chelan AVA. Larry Lehmbecker and Michaela Markusson are the proprietors; he makes the wines, she handles the business. The cozy winery overlooks the lake and includes an inviting tasting room and a cheerful bistro serving small plates of seasonal foods.

Lehmbecker made both wine and beer as a hobbyist for many years before pursuing winemaking professionally, spurred on by regular visits to Provence. There are three main tiers of wine being made: the Fresh White series wines are all stainless steel–fermented, sport colorful party labels, and appeal to tasting room visitors who may prefer a little sweetness in their whites. The Barrel Select wines—mostly reds but with a soft and buttery chardonnay—are workmanlike efforts from purchased grapes. Best is the cabernet franc.

At the top tier are the LEHM Estate wines, sourced from the vineyard adjoining the winery. Dry riesling, sauvignon blanc, and pinot gris—all very good—show improvement from year to year as the vines age. Fresh and lively, they are already helping to define a particular style for the region—with more finesse than power, but plenty of flavor enjoyment. In the summer a small amount of an off-dry LEHM rosé (a blend of cabernet franc and sangiovese) is also available.

Best wine: LEHM dry riesling.

WALTER DACON

First vintage: 2003

www.walterdaconwines.com

Winemaker Lloyd Anderson introduces his Walter Dacon winery with a trio of syrahs named Belle, Beaux, and Magnifique. Heavily influenced by Rhône varietal pioneer Doug McCrea, Anderson ages one syrah in French oak and the second in American and offers the third as a reserve selection from his favorite French barrels.

Though designed and priced differently, Anderson's winemaking style keeps all three syrahs in lockstep. My tasting notes over the first few vintages describe (and score) them very consistently. All display scents and flavors of smoke, coffee, charcoal, and tar, with dark, dark fruits. In other words, barrel flavors are a major component here. The grapes are sourced from Elephant Mountain, The Ranch at the End of the Road, and Destiny Ridge—Yakima Valley, Red Mountain, and the Horse Heaven Hills respectively.

Skillfully made and quite flavorful, these are wines that will please many palates. A fruity, forward, luscious, over-the-top viognier debuted in 2006, along with a Red Mountain sangiovese and a fourth, Boushey-vineyard syrah called Appanage. The Boushey fruit is so distinctive and distinguished that it sets this wine well apart from the other three.

Best wine: Boushey vineyards Appanage syrah.

WATERBROOK

First vintage: 1984

www.waterbrook.com

Until its sale to Precept Brands late in 2006, this 42,000-case winery was one of the largest family-owned operations in the Northwest. It was Walla Walla's fourth winery when it was founded in 1984 by Eric and Janet Rindal, and it quickly established itself as the value brand in the region.

Good as Waterbrook was, it inevitably lost momentum during the years of transition. But Precept CEO Andrew Browne has promised to make it his "home-run brand"—and has the ambitious goal of creating what he calls "the Ste. Michelle of Walla Walla."

With that in mind, a massive new winery—the Walla Walla Wine Works—has been constructed west of town, near Reininger, Three Rivers, and Cougar Crest. With room for 10,000 barrels, more than sixty tanks ranging from 1,000 to 30,000 gallons, and a 300,000-case annual capacity, it is the production center for the expanding Waterbrook line, as well as several other Precept ventures. John Freeman will continue as winemaker. Included on the property are a large tasting room and visitors center, where a wide variety of Precept brands can be sampled.

As before, Waterbrook will keep a focus on value-priced varietals, mostly whites, including well-crafted chardonnay, sauvignon blanc, riesling, and pinot gris. A step up in price and quality are the two Waterbrook Mélange wines—blanc and noir—kitchen sink blends of many grapes that show plenty of good fruit flavor. The Waterbrook reserve wines have been repackaged in longer, slimmer bottles and now include chardonnay, cabernet sauvignon, merlot, and syrah. None disappoint; for the $22 price they are generous, varietal, and plush; the new-oak flavors suggest far more expensive wines. Finally, there is a tight, concentrated Waterbrook Meritage, a selection of fruit from the best sources (including Stone Tree and Loess).

Waterbrook's Blackrock vineyard was sold separately to Michael Corliss, but will continue to provide purchased fruit, along with Precept-owned Canyon Ranch and Willow Crest. A new, 80-acre vineyard is being planted in the vicinity of Spring Valley, so that Waterbrook will once again have estate fruit from the Walla Walla AVA.

Best wine: reserve merlot.

WHITMAN CELLARS

First vintage: 1998

www.whitmancellars.com

In any critical selection in which a cut-off point must be reached, someone is going to be on the bubble. The last man cut from a baseball team just before the season starts. The job candidate who makes it all the way from a field of hundreds to number . . . two. Whitman Cellars was for me one such "bubble" winery in this book's first edition, but as Steve Lessard, who took over the winemaking in 2002, has settled comfortably in, bringing exceptional vineyard contacts with him, Whitman has begun to release wines that show polish and personality.

Lessard is an easygoing native of California, educated in food science at CalPoly in San Luis Obispo. During his college years he worked odd jobs at more than half a dozen wineries—"little places that shared equipment," he explains, "and I came with it. I'd work harvest for three different wineries and all different grapes." From college he did stints at Hacienda, Stag's Leap Wine Cellars, and Delicato, then on to Hedges for six years, and finally to Whitman Cellars.

There are just two white wines: a barrel-fermented, sweetly toasty viognier and a delicious riesling, introduced in 2008. The popular Narcissa red is modeled after Hedges Three Vineyards—a blend of cabernet, merlot, cabernet franc, and syrah. Toasty, smoky scents underscore sleek berry fruit; though done in a somewhat lean style, it's nicely balanced. Two other proprietary blends—Killer Cab and Del Rio Red—have recently been added, joining well-oaked, varietal bottlings of merlot, cabernet, and syrah, mostly sourced from excellent Walla Walla vineyards. Production rests at 5,000 cases annually.

Best wine: cabernet sauvignon.

WILLIS HALL

First vintage: 2003

www.willishall.com

Winemaker John Bell is an alum of the Boeing Wine Club and made many vintages as an amateur winemaker before launching his own venture in 2003. The names Willis and Hall were chosen to honor his father and grandmother. Production began at a modest 1,200 cases and is now around 3,000.

The main focus is on four or five wines each year: one or two syrahs, a cabernet-based blend, a merlot-based blend, and a viognier. But there are many small-production wines that range more widely.

Most of Bell's nicely polished wines hover in the 13 percent alcohol range, a welcome respite from the palate thrashers that so many boutiques produce. He sources his grapes from several vineyards that are a bit off the beaten track—Snipes Canyon Ranch, Chandler Reach, and Destiny Ridge among them—and he loves to explore nonstandard grapes such as Dolcetto, tempranillo, malbec, nebbiolo, and sangiovese.

It would be astonishing if every wine in such a young and broad portfolio hit a home run, and they do not. But when Bell rings one up, it's a pleasure. The best Willis Hall bottles share many similar strengths: soft, ready to drink, and unusually pretty, with supple flavors that speak of pie cherries, strawberries, and plums, and a pleasing, toasty finish. He is convinced that Washington State is the ideal growing region for many of the world's not-so-well-known varieties, such as tempranillo. "I'm a stew and casserole type of guy," says Bell. "I spend a lot of time at the blending table, figuring this out."

Best wine: syrah.

First vintage: 1995

www.willowcrestwinery.com

Willow Crest scores well on the strength of its excellent vineyard practices and its pioneering efforts with pinot gris. Grower David Minick planted his first wine grapes in 1982, at an elevation of 1,300 feet in the sweet spot (north of Prosser) of the Yakima Valley.

Though he ran both vineyard and winery for many years, he recently entered into a joint venture with Precept Brands that looks to be win-win. "I was wearing too many hats," Minick admits, "growing, making wine, doing bookkeeping, running a tasting room. Instead of hiring my own sales and marketing team, it makes a lot of sense to be involved with Precept."

The Minick vineyard includes 215 planted acres. Pinot gris, riesling, and syrah are particularly noteworthy, and Precept plans to expand Willow Crest production (currently about 8,000 cases) to more than 30,000 cases, all from estate-grown grapes. The bulk of that production will be riesling and pinot gris, with smaller amounts of syrah, cabernet franc, and some tasting room reds. Anything that Minick grows has the raw ingredients to become very fine wine, and Willow Crest wines usually deliver far more flavor than their modest prices would suggest.

Best bottles: pinot gris, cabernet franc, and syrah

8

THE RISING STARS

The number of bonded Washington wineries has motored past 650, accompanied by the now-customary fanfare trumpeting the industry's steady growth—the state ranking number two in the country, winery numbers quadrupling in just a decade, and so forth. Though I too applaud the growth and do not wish to turn curmudgeonly, the fact is that the vast majority of these new wineries are so small as to be insignificant.

Some are virtual; others barely rise above the hobbyist level. All but a handful make very limited amounts of wine. Provided that the wine is decent, the prices not over the moon, and especially if they have a conveniently located tasting room, they can sell almost all of it to visitors, mailing list subscribers, and a few regional retailers and restaurants. The owners of these start-ups often work day jobs or are retired; they don't need a business that actually makes money.

When the state passed the six-hundred-winery mark, a local paper interviewed one of the newcomers. The owner was refreshingly candid. She admitted that her winery had yet to see its first crush. Their plans were to make maybe 200 cases of wine annually. Growth? No way—that would turn the winery into a "job" and it would no longer be any fun. On such fragile scaffolding is much of Washington's growth being built.

I would guess that, moving forward, the total number of functioning wineries in this state is likely to plateau, perhaps even shrink slightly, as the effects of the global economic downturn continue to resonate throughout the industry. Certainly there will be some consolidation and slowing down, even among the big players. To cite just one example, the Crimson Wine Group, whose portfolio includes Archery Summit in Oregon and

Pine Ridge and Domaine Alfred in California, recently halted plans for its Double Canyon winery in the Horse Heaven Hills. The plug was pulled despite a well-sited vineyard now in its fifth leaf and two vintages of wine already in barrel. The vineyard will be continued as a stand-alone project for the indefinite future.

Cheap land (about a tenth the cost of vineyard land in Napa) and a well-deserved reputation for quality should help to ensure that major wine industry players with at least a toehold in this state—Constellation, Diageo, Foley, Ascentia, Pacific Partners, and others—are likely to stay. Ste. Michelle Wine Estates, now the seventh-largest wine company in the country, is the essential cornerstone, an irreplaceable entity whose future under its new ownership remains, as this book goes to press, a bit uncertain.

In terms of image, the little boutiques—almost all producing fewer than 2,500 cases annually—play an important role. The perception of Washington State as a quality region chock-full of charming, artisanal boutique wineries churning out fascinating wines helps to drive the engine of growth for all wineries, large and small.

At the moment, a few well-funded new enterprises such as Corliss Estates and Drew Bledsoe's Doubleback winery are able to garner the immediate attention of collectors and the press. But the great majority of Washington's newcomers are obscure, underfunded bootstrap operations. Some arise from the owner's midlife change of course; other new entrepreneurs are simply moonlighting while hanging onto their "real" jobs. Graduates of the state's two- and four-year enology and viticulture training programs may augment their first full-time winery jobs by making a few barrels of their own, placing them under a separate bond in the host winery, and setting up their new business with little more than a mailing list and a website.

Turnkey incubators such as Artifex, co-ops such as the Winemakers' Loft, and custom crush operations such as the Wahluke Wine Company also provide relatively low-cost entry to the wine business. But the big challenges remain. How can a small, unknown winery—especially one that must rely on purchased grapes—carve out a distinct identity for itself?

The disappointing reception given to so many Washington syrahs in recent vintages points to some of the problems they face. Though I remain convinced that syrahs from Washington are often excellent, even exceptional, their impact on the broader marketplace has been more of a whimper than a bang. To the consumer—not to mention the national wine press—it seems that almost every new winery has at least one syrah, sometimes several; and many of them are sourcing their grapes from the same handful of growers, charging the same relatively steep prices, and coming out with the same flavors. Is it any surprise that the press yawns and consumers stroll over to the Côtes-du-Rhône?

When a young winery offers something interesting and well made, such as the malbecs and sangioveses and tempranillos that are popping up, pricing often becomes an obstacle. Argentina (or Italy or Spain) pretty much own the market for these wines in the minds of consumers. And why not? Their $10 bottles can be as good as Washington's

$25 bottles. They have cheap land, cheap labor, old vines, and many more acres/hectares under cultivation. Consumers don't care what your business costs are! They are concerned only with how many dollars are coming out of their wallet when they buy a bottle of wine.

It's not that there isn't a viable future for these Washington wines at some point in time, but until there are many more acres of vines in the ground here, prices are not likely to become truly competitive. It is up to the little guys to make wines that are so unique and compelling that price ceases to be the overriding consideration. When you taste a wine such as Buty's Phinny Hill vineyard malbec, with its extraordinary finesse and meticulous attention to detail, how can you not be thrilled at the potential for this grape here in Washington?

So how do you find such wines? The rising stars profiled here are a good place to look. In many respects, and especially for consumers seeking cutting-edge, artisanal wines not yet discovered by out-of-state critics, this is the most important chapter in this book. Here are the new, unheralded wineries most likely to cut through the 650-and-growing clutter and make a name for themselves. Also included are a few older wineries on a quality upswing.

The ability to do quality work over the course of many vintages is one of the hallmarks of a first-class winery and winemaker. Anyone can get lucky once or twice. Time will sort out who among these newbies got lucky, and who is for real. Nonetheless, these rising stars are off to a good start.

Full disclosure: though almost all of these eighty entries are newcomers, the seemingly inexhaustible torrent of newly bonded hopefuls has not stopped, and not all who may be worthy of consideration are included here. Publishers set both page limits and deadlines, and authors must occasionally sleep.

ADAMANT CELLARS

First vintage: 2006

www.adamantcellars.com

Devin Stinger spent 22 years in high-tech in the Portland (Oregon) area, but like so many recent transplants to eastern Washington, he says he always wanted to get into the wine business. He and his wife, Debra, jumped into the winery pool out at the Walla Walla airport, taking the first of the cute new winery incubators built by the Port in 2006.

Adamant—the word refers to an especially hard substance, such as a diamond—did its first crush that year, sourcing grapes from Spofford Station and Les Collines. More recently, a small vineyard has been planted to tempranillo and albariño south of town. The most unusual wine is a sparkling tempranillo rosé. Tasted pre-dosage, it was quite intriguing, a worthy stand-in for pinot noir.

Among the more traditional efforts, I especially like the Winemaker's Select, a fifty-fifty blend of cabernet and merlot. So far, with just 1,200 cases produced annually, the Adamant Cellars wines are selling out quickly, so the mailing list is the best option for finding them.

AIRFIELD ESTATES

First vintage: 2005

www.airfieldwines.com

One of the most exciting trends in Washington wine is the resurgence of grower-winemakers. Airfield Estates, whose distinctive tasting room tower is a Prosser Vintner's Village landmark, is the project of the Miller family, Yakima Valley wine grape growers for over 40 years. With an 850-acre estate vineyard to source from, Airfield (named for a World War II airbase that was located nearby) is in an enviable position.

Marcus Miller is the winemaker and general manager and has quickly assembled an impressive résumé, including stints at Canoe Ridge and Tsillan in Washington and Montana Brancott in New Zealand. So here is proven viticultural expertise, a catchy winery name and story, and a young and enthusiastic winemaker—all the potential in the world. The labels are clever and appealing, and everything is bottled under screw cap—very forward thinking. Right now, the best wines from among the profusion of German, Bordeaux, Rhône, and Italian varietals on display are the whites—particularly the riesling, the regular (not unoaked) chardonnay, the Thunderbolt sauvignon blanc–sémillon, and the Lightning chardonnay-viognier-roussanne.

The reds are less successful—inky and high in alcohol (most over 15 percent), they often show abrasive tannins and taste chalky through the finish. Syrah—particularly the reserve bottling—is the best of the varietals; the everyday blends, notably Bombshell red, offer the best flavor bang for the least bucks. And the Foot-Stomped syrah rosé is worth grabbing for the label alone.

ALMATERRA

First vintage: 2006

www.almaterrawines.com

The AlmaTerra motto is ". . . inspired by terroir"—which would not generally inspire much enthusiasm, given that so many are called, and so few are chosen. But the founders have the street cred to back up the boast. Alan Busacca holds a Ph.D. in earth science and soil science, taught for many years at Washington State University, and has been instrumental in writing the applications for several Washington AVAs. "I am a savant of landscapes," he writes. "I have a nose for deciphering the nuances, history, and intricacies of a seemingly simple or ordinary hillslope, especially if it is in service of finding great vineyard sites."

With exactly that goal in mind, Busacca has teamed with winemaker Robert Smasne to make single-varietal, single-vineyard wines expressive of particularly important (in their view) sites in Washington. The first wines include syrahs from Ciel du Cheval, Minick, and Coyote Canyon, as well as a three-vineyard blend called Coéo.

In some sense AlmaTerra's white wine project is the more intriguing, as it will offer single-vineyard viogniers from Upland, Coyote Canyon, and Chukar Ridge vineyards. The first release includes the AlmaTerra 2007 Coéo Three Vineyard Viognier: a very promising beginning, juicy and citrus-laden, with lime and grapefruit, a refreshing hint of tonic water, and a splash of sweet sun tea, all in proportion. The two Coéo wines are designed as complements to the single-vineyard offerings, to show what a winemaker can do with blending.

"The fruit is all brought in at a brix level that is mature for each specific vineyard," Smasne explains; "otherwise all wines are given the same yeast, fermentation style, cooperage, aging, and racked, filtered, and bottled on the same days. Each lot is topped with its own wine, so it's 100 percent single-vineyard."

The credentials of the founders, focus of the project, and professionalism of the first few releases suggests that AlmaTerra will ultimately achieve its dual goals of crafting wines that not only express their place of origin but educate consumers about Washington terroir as well.

BAER

First vintage: 2000

www.baerwinery.com

Winery founder Lance Baer died unexpectedly in the spring of 2007, just as his young winery was on a major upswing with good reviews and a dedicated following. The winery remains in family hands, with sister Lisa Baer now at the helm. She has moved it into the cluster of boutiques on the north side of Woodinville, near such luminaries as Gorman and Guardian Cellars.

Since 2004, Stillwater Creek has been the exclusive vineyard source for all Baer wines. "Lance locked in good vines early on," Lisa explains. Production is up to about 2,400 cases, three-quarters of it the flagship Ursa, a merlot-dominated right-bank Bordeaux blend. The 2005 and 2006—the last two vintages made by Lance Baer—were both delicious, plump, sweetly fruity, and immediately accessible.

The cabernet-dominated Arctos red blend was not made in 2005 and 2006, but is back in production as of 2007. A new wine, a reserve cabernet franc named Maia, will also be released shortly. A lovely chardonnay named Shard has also returned after an absence of several vintages. Lisa Baer says she intends to continue down the path set by her brother, giving the wines two years in barrel and one in bottle prior to release. With the highest of hopes and fingers crossed for the future of this promising winery, I wish her all success.

BARRAGE CELLARS

First vintage: 2006

www.barragecellars.com

Several things stood out as I tasted the first releases from this Woodinville winery. First impressions are just that, but Barrage is off to a good start. The packaging is attractive, and the enthusiasm of the owners, Kevin and Susana Correll, is contagious, as when they write that they "hope to barrage the palate with the intense and unforgettable flavors of Barrage Cellars wines."

More important, Kevin has done his due diligence as a winery volunteer, taken the UC Davis short courses, opened his winery in the Woodinville 'hood, where help and neighborly advice is close at hand, and lined up exceptional vineyard sources—Boushey, Conner Lee, Destiny Ridge, Elerding, and Marcoux.

Among the first releases, the 2006 Elerding Vineyard Double Barrel Cabernet Sauvignon was a standout, offering cassis and black cherry fruit, wrapped in rich coffee/mocha flavors. The 2006 Boushey Secret Weapon Cabernet Franc showed a good grasp of varietal flavors, with polished, powerful tannins; the 2007 white wines were also well made.

BASEL CELLARS

First vintage: 2001

www.baselcellars.com

No visitor to Walla Walla's Basel Cellars is likely to forget the experience, given its headquarters—a rustic, 13,000-square-foot mansion set in rolling hills south of town (note: the facility may be rented for weddings and other grand events). "Casual grandeur" is the stated aesthetic, modeled somewhat after Yosemite's Awahnee Lodge and Mt. Hood's Timberline Lodge. Basel makes 6,500 cases of wine annually, primarily red. The lineup begins with a basic claret and includes vineyard-designated cabernets and syrahs and a Bordeaux blend called Merriment. In the fall of 2009, Basel introduced an independent label called The Earth Series, emphasizing affordable price points and earth-friendly winemaking.

From 2001 through 2005, winemaker Trey Busch (now at Sleight of Hand) turned out some dramatic successes, notably with grapes sourced from Lewis, Seven Hills, and Spofford Station. With the change in winemakers—Justin Basel is now in charge—have come changes in vineyard sources and a move to mixing American oak barrels in with the

French. Vineyard-designated wines from Chelle Den Millie and Mirage have been supplemented with estate-grown, Pheasant Run bottlings. The most recent releases, especially the Pheasant Run merlot and the estate Merriment, seemed to pull back on the exposure to new oak and showcase riper fruit—a clear improvement. The white wines have not yet come up that far, but it's early in the going for this young winemaker.

BUNCHGRASS

First vintage: 1997

www.bunchgrasswinery.com

William VonMetzger, the long-haired Coloradan who has been making wine at Walla Walla Vintners since 2005, is now involved with a new project—the revival of the Bunchgrass winery. Bunchgrass was just this side of a hobby winery, making about 300 cases a year, notably the popular Founder's Blend. As of the 2005 vintage, Bunchgrass was semiofficially wrapped; the owners were getting up in years and wanted some fun time.

In 2006, VonMetzger began making a few barrels of his own under the Walla Walla Vintners bond. Through a happy set of circumstances, those wines became the first to carry the new Bunchgrass label. Several partners are helping him revive the brand, including the original owners and Gordy Venneri of Walla Walla Vintners. Production remains quite small, between 400 and 600 cases.

The new Bunchgrass wines are stylish and modern. The first syrah, from Lewis vineyard fruit, revealed a smoky, meaty, brambly fruit character, with a leafy note under very pretty raspberry fruit. The red blend called Triolet was mostly cabernet, elegant and approachable but not too light. In the works is a Morrison Lane vineyard syrah and a revived Founder's Blend made with cabernet franc and merlot.

CADARETTA

First vintage: 2006

www.cadaretta.com

The Middleton family, which owns Cadaretta, trace its Northwest roots back to the late 1800s, when Middleton forebears launched a forestry products company on the Olympic Peninsula. The name Cadaretta honors a ship that once carried lumber for that company. The Middletons ventured into the vineyard business in the mid-1980s, growing table grapes in Bakersfield, California. They later expanded into wine grapes in Paso Robles, where they opened the Clayhouse winery in 2003.

But their hearts remain in Washington State. "We wanted to bring it back closer to home," says Rick Middleton, "full circle. I like Walla Walla because it feels like a real place; it was a town long before there was wine, and I think that's what makes it real."

Jumping in big, the Middletons purchased 357 acres in the SeVein vineyard and began planting their Southwind estate in the summer of 2008. There are twenty-two clones in the mix—three each of sauvignon blanc, cabernet sauvignon, merlot, and syrah; two of petit verdot; and smaller amounts of sémillon, viognier, counoise, grenache, and cab franc.

Cadaretta wines are made at Artifex, a winery incubator in which the Middletons are also partners. The sauvignon blanc–sémillon, modeled on the Australian SBS style, is already distinguished, with lush, bright, fresh fruit flavors of pineapple and grapefruit. The first Cadaretta chardonnay, from 25-year-old Champoux vines, brought firm, crisp, lean flavors of apple and pear. The red wines—cabernet sauvignon, merlot, syrah, and a superpremium Springboard Red—are sourced from a wide range of vineyards. The cabernet, based on Abeja's Heather Hill fruit, is especially good.

CASCADE CLIFFS

First vintage: 1990

www.cascadecliffs.com

One of the pioneers of the Columbia Gorge AVA, Cascade Cliffs offers a most unusual lineup of wines, with an emphasis on estate-grown, northern Italian varietals. The vineyard was begun almost 25 years ago, but the winemaking was amateurish until a change of ownership in 1997 put ex-banker Bob Lorkowski in charge as managing partner and winemaker.

Lorkowski notes that his grandfather was a moonshiner, and wine was drunk frequently at home. "I was fascinated by fermentation," he adds. Experience gained at Paul Thomas, Cavatappi, and Chinook also contributed to his knowledge, but his focus on Piedmont varietals is strictly his own.

The high-acid barberas, Dolcettos, and nebbiolos are the winery's main calling cards; of the three, the barbera is the must-have wine. There is also an interesting mix of estate-grown, non-Italian reds, including cabernet sauvignon, merlot, petite sirah, and syrah. Most unusual of all Cascade Cliffs wines is the Symphony, a cross between muscat of Alexandria and grenache gris that is somewhat reminiscent of viognier.

Given its unique lineup and stunning location in the Columbia River Gorge Scenic Area, this is a winery that should be on anyone's must-visit list.

CAVU CELLARS

First vintage: 2006

www.cavucellars.com

Just opened in the spring of 2009, CAVU Cellars is making a splash with barbera, of all things, which is being done both as a rosé and a full-flavored dry red wine. Also among the winery's first releases are a stylish sauvignon blanc, a single-vineyard malbec, and a single-vineyard cabernet sauvignon.

Winemaker Joel Waite has a retail background, including some years as a private chef and caterer in the Washington, D.C., area. After moving back to eastern Washington, he took the two-year course in Walla Walla, worked for a time at Maryhill winery, and seems already to have charted an interesting and distinctive course for this new, small, family-owned operation. Case production is right around 1,100.

CHELAN ESTATE

First vintage: 2002

www.chelanestatewinery.com

In the spring of 2000, Chelan Estate became one of the first wineries to start planting in the newly minted Chelan AVA. As it wraps up its first full decade, Chelan Estate is still finding its way—not too surprising when you have a new winery in an untested wine region. Winemaker-owner Bob Broderick started with an interesting mix of chardonnay, viognier, cabernet franc, merlot, and pinot noir—Dijon clone, own-rooted, planted meter-by-meter, and hand-pruned.

It soon became apparent, says Broderick, that one clone wasn't going to do it on its own; it was missing the aromas and the big center palate he was seeking. So grafted clones from Oregon were added to the vineyard. Though some of the original vines have already been ripped out, a commitment to estate-based wines remains.

The schedule for new releases seems to be backing up; the winery was still showing the very first releases from the estate vines as this book was going to press. So it is not possible to fully evaluate the potential of either the site or the winery.

So far, the most interesting aspect of both the AVA and the winery is the commitment to pinot noir. Pinot has been largely absent from the otherwise loaded Washington viticultural smorgasbord, but as more marginal regions are developed—marginal in a good way—it is entirely possible that a Washington style of pinot will begin to emerge. If and when it does, it would not surprise me to find Chelan Estate among its champions.

COVINGTON

First vintage: 2003

www.covingtoncellars.com

David and Cindy Lawson are the owners of this Woodinville boutique, which sources fruit from Yakima, Walla Walla, Horse Heaven Hills, and Red Mountain vineyards. David started hobby winemaking after a successful navy career, took some classes at UC

Davis, and has blended into the Woodinville matrix, with small-batch offerings of sémillon, viognier, sangiovese, syrah, blended reds, and rarities such as cabernet franc and malbec.

Assistant winemaker Morgan Lee interned at Columbia Crest and helps out in both barrel room and tasting room. The white wines—a varietal sémillon and viognier—are full of fruit and nicely balanced. The reds are solid; the most interesting being the Alder Ridge malbec and the cabernet franc sourced from Kiona and Seven Hills. Covington has also enjoyed recent success with its Kiona vineyard–sourced sangiovese, which brought in some nice awards.

The top wine is the Artisan Series Cabernet Sauvignon, a reserve Bordeaux blend. Again, excellent vineyard sources (in 2006, Klipsun and Kiona) suggest that Lawson has the right contacts to get the best possible material for his wines. Though little-known outside the region, Covington has already attracted a lot of interest and loyalty from its local customer base and is definitely a winery to watch in the future.

CUILLIN HILLS

First vintage: 2004

www.cuillinhills.com

The actual Cuillin Hills (pronounced "coolin'") are on the enchanting Scottish island of Skye. The winery is in Woodinville, one of a pair owned by brothers Derek and Darren DesVoigne. They opened together in a small warehouse space in what is known as the 'Hood. Derek is in charge of Cuillin Hills, whose debut was launched with a lovely, chocolaty 2004 sangiovese.

Derek DesVoigne first worked as assistant winemaker at Chelan's Vin du Lac, then joined his brother to start their separate-but-connected wineries. A pair of Cuillin Hills syrahs from the 2005 vintage showed skillful winemaking also, and the winery has progressed smoothly without a stumble in each new vintage. Wines from both Rhône and Bordeaux varietals remain the focus as Cuillin Hills barrels its fifth vintage.

The claret is true to its name (no syrah slipped into the blend), rather soft and open, a drink-now wine. The first (to my knowledge) vineyard reserve—a 2006 Weinbau vineyard cabernet franc—was also a solid effort, loaded with tangy boysenberry and plum-flavored fruit; the oak (25 percent new) lightly handled, adding whiffs of toast and coffee.

Fewer than 1,000 cases are made in total, meaning these wines are hard to find outside a few local retailers and the tasting room and mailing lists. Derek DesVoigne is already showing a confident touch with oak and sourcing interesting grapes. I expect the best is yet to come.

DAMA

First vintage: 2003

www.damawines.com

Dawn Kammer and Mary Tuuri Derby are the partners in this venture (hence the name, a shortened "Dawn and Mary"). DaMa is headquartered in a cozy tasting room in downtown Walla Walla. It was launched in the spring of 2007, more than two years after Mary Derby's winemaker husband, Devin (Spring Valley Vineyards), was killed in a tragic auto accident.

Both women have restaurant wine backgrounds and use their combined expertise to craft blended wines from purchased juice. Since they are essentially acting as négociants, it is difficult to pin down a specific style for DaMa, but the winery's goals—to create affordable wines that appeal specifically to women—are admirable. Dawn Kammer's background includes 20 years in the fashion and cosmetics industries, and along with its colorful, fashionista labels, DaMa sometimes ties its wine tastings to trunk shows and other women-friendly events.

Kammer and Derby crushed fruit for the first time in 2008, making 10 barrels of wine from the Goose Ridge vineyard. They intend to craft a red blend to be called DaMa Natrix. The punny name fits right in with their wine club, dubbed DaMa Nation, and the winery's nonprofit contributions to women's causes, which they call the DaMa-Know effect. Don't let these groaners affect your thinking about the wines, which are stylish and just plain fun.

DARBY WINERY

First vintage: 2005

www.darbywinery.com

Darby English has only recently joined the growing ranks of garagistes setting up shop in the Woodinville warehouse district. He spent some years in the restaurant business, worked briefly for an Arizona distributor, and took some winemaking courses at a community college near his West Seattle home. But he appears to be one of those gifted naturals whose achievements far outstrip their slender résumés.

Natalie English describes her husband's winemaking venture in this way: "It started in the basement of our home . . . spread to the garage . . . then he had a tent in the front yard. That's when I knew it was out of control."

There is a skillful hand at work both in blending and structuring his limited lineup of wines, and a thoughtful design aesthetic in the wine labels also, which are on rich paper stock and resemble old postcards, with antique handwriting and what appears to be a botanical drawing of a cluster of rose leaves. That attention to rich detail comes through in the wines, starting with Darby's viognier-roussanne blend, named Le Deuce.

Loaded with ripe and delicious melon, sweet pineapple, and stone fruits, Le Deuce brings a gorgeous creamy texture and a mouth-tickling sensation of richness that never turns thin, bitter, or hot. In 2009 the blend will include marsanne from Boushey. Darby's red wines—a Bordeaux blend called Purple Haze, a cab-syrah-franc–petit verdot blend curiously named CHAOS, and syrahs named the Dark Side and Aunt Lee—also reveal a fine touch with blending and barrel management.

The focus on very small lots of wines crafted from Bordeaux and Rhône varietals is expected to continue as Darby ramps up to roughly 2,100 cases. I can't wait to see more from this exceptionally talented start-up.

DEN HOED

First vintage: 2005

www.denhoedwines.com

The Den Hoed family emigrated from Holland just after World War II, moved cross-country to the Yakima Valley a few years later, and built an empire. Andreas and Marie Den Hoed planted their first wine grapes in the Yakima Valley in 1956; today the family farms thousands of acres. In the mid-1990s, sons Bill and Andy partnered with Andreas to purchase and develop their most ambitious project, the Wallula vineyard, and now they have completed the circle with the first releases of their Den Hoed Wine Estates wines.

Rob Newsom (Boudreaux Cellars) and Gilles Nicault (Long Shadows) were chosen to make the two wines, one to honor each parent. The first to be released was the 2005 Marie's View Red, a blend of cabernet sauvignon, merlot, syrah, cabernet franc, and sangiovese—all fruit from the Wallula Vineyard. Tasted just after bottling, it strongly resembled Newsom's Boudreaux wines—a ripe, rich, sexy bottle.

The 2006 Andreas Cabernet Sauvignon is a masterful effort, smooth, silky, chocolaty, and rich with ripe cherry fruit. A big, supple bottle, it unwraps itself gracefully to reveal streaks of graphite, licorice, smoke, and coffee. Even before its official release, this gorgeous, pure Cabernet was drinking so well that it could pass for a bottle from one of Napa's cult boutiques.

DOMAINE POUILLON

First vintage: 2005

www.domainepouillon.com

Alexis and Juliet Pouillon—"Les Vignerons," reads their card—have unusual credentials for such newcomers: joint U.S.-French citizenship, a connection to organic pioneer Restaurant Nova in Washington, D.C. (founded by Alexis's mother), a background in soil science, and experience working at Chateau Beaucastel in France.

Beaucastel is the source of many of the vines planted in their five-acre, biodynamically farmed vineyard. It is not surprising then that Domaine Pouillon, located just above Syncline in the Columbia Gorge, specializes in Rhône varietals. The Pouillons moved to the gorge in 2005, and Alexis soon found work as a winemaker at Wy'east and Marchesi vineyards, as his own project was getting started.

Domaine Pouillon's first releases were labeled Domaine Pierre Noire until a trademark issue forced a change. Grapes are sourced from vineyards in both the gorge and the Horse Heaven Hills, handpicked in small lots, and crafted in lots as small as a single barrel. Just 1,500 cases total are produced annually, and wines from the estate vineyard have not yet appeared. But what is in the market already is very fine.

Deux is a chardonnay-viognier blend; Blanc de Moulin mixes roussanne and viognier. Both are sleek, textural and immaculately clean. The red wines include a Barrel Select cabernet sauvignon, a nonvintage Rhône blend called Black Dot, and a 50-50 syrah-cabernet named Cuvée en Amont, based on a country wine from Les Baux de Provence that the Pouillons shared on their first date.

All of these wines reflect skillful artisanal craftsmanship and most sell at modest prices.

DOUBLEBACK

First vintage: 2007

www.doubleback.com

Launched on a windblown mountaintop in the summer of 2008, Drew Bledsoe's Doubleback winery is at first glance the sort of celebrity-based project common in California, though still a novelty here in Washington. Happily, all signs point to this being much more than the usual lackluster effort with a famous name on the label.

Bledsoe was the number-one pick overall in the 1993 NFL draft. Now retired after a record-setting, 14-year pro career, the Walla Walla native is taking a hands-on, quality-driven approach to his winery project. It starts, he says, with the dirt. Determined to produce estate-grown wines using sustainable and site-specific viticultural practices, he enlisted Leonetti Cellar's Chris Figgins as his consulting winemaker. Together they are developing his two vineyards and making the first wines.

"Once I began to entertain the idea of retirement," Bledsoe explains, "it became apparent that I was going to need to create a new avenue in which to channel my energy and interests. I was fascinated by the growth of the wine industry in my hometown of Walla Walla. I was intrigued by the whole production process. I always will be confused by people who collect wine for the sake of owning it and showing off bottles. Wine is not something that should be set on the table and fawned over. It is something to be shared and enjoyed."

The first vintage of Doubleback, released in the spring of 2010, is a 2007 cabernet sauvignon made with fruit purchased from several Walla Walla vineyards. All of these early vintages are being made by Figgins at the Artifex facility, while he oversees the establishment of the vineyards. The 40-acre McQueen vineyard was planted in the spring of 2008, part of the expansive SeVein project. A second vineyard, the Flying B, is located in Oregon's Columbia Valley. Its 89 acres were planted in 2006, to a mix of Bordeaux grapes and syrah. Both sites are expected to contribute fruit to future Doubleback wines.

Given the exceptional resources at work to craft these wines and vineyards, it seems likely that the first release, a serious, dusty, dense, dark, and complex effort in the Leonetti mold, is no flash in the pan.

DOWSETT FAMILY

First vintage: 2007

www.dowsettwines.com

Chris Dowsett's winemaking credentials began as a child; his family started Oregon's Laurel Ridge winery in 1984. He studied horticulture at Oregon State and then worked in Australia, planning to make sparkling wines. Back in the States he did lab work at Mondavi, Schramsberg, and Stonestreet before settling in at Walla Walla's Canoe Ridge, where he and John Abbott developed a fondness (and talent) for making gewürztraminer.

A collaborative winery project called Latitude 46 was next, then Dowsett spent some years as the in-house winemaker at Artifex, an upscale custom crush facility in Walla Walla, and most recently claimed a position as assistant winemaker at Buty. Dowsett Family is his tiny—300-case—personal project, and it continues his love affair with gewürztraminer.

The grapes for the Dowsett Family gewürztraminer are sourced from the Celilo vineyard, from vines planted in 1984. Previous vintages of this wine, made for Latitude 46, were arguably the best version of the grape made in the Northwest—and this continues to hold true. The wine is consistently fragrant and floral, matching the lush perfume to exotic passion fruit, grapefruit, and citrus flavors.

Dowsett Family also makes a pretty, Châteauneuf-style red wine called Devotion, a blend of syrah, mourvèdre, and grenache. A varietal mourvèdre is being contemplated.

DUMAS STATION

First vintage: 2003

www.dumasstation.com

This little winery, on the highway between Waitsburg and Dayton, north of Walla Walla, is the project of Jay DeWitt and Doug Harvey, the owners of Minnick Hills vineyard. All the estate wines come from that fruit, or from Jack DeWitt's Breezy Slope vineyard at the base of the Blue Mountains.

The winery itself is a converted apple-packing shed, which harks back to the time a century ago when apple orchards rather than wheat fields were the region's main industry. Dumas Station was the local railroad stop, and the winery logo commemorates it with an old steam engine chugging along.

Small amounts of cabernet sauvignon, merlot, and syrah are produced, all displaying the excellent fruit with no-frills winemaking. Among recent releases I was especially fond of the syrah. Both estate vineyards are at relatively high altitudes, and Minnick Hills was one of the few in the valley to produce fruit in the freeze year of 2004. These very limited–production, moderately priced wines are certainly worth seeking out for a taste of Walla Walla fruit from one of the few major vineyards north of town.

EDMONDS WINERY

First vintage: 2003

www.edmondswinery.com

Owner and winemaker Doug Petersen began studying the miracle of fermentation as a home brewer. One day in 1999, he tells me, he stopped in for beer-making supplies and noticed a sign reading "Get your grapes." Next thing he knew, he was up to his neck in 500 pounds of cabernet. "I had never done it," he cheerfully admits; "I didn't have a clue."

Years spent working as a banquet chef at the Seattle Convention and Trade Center helped to tune his winemaking palate, and steady improvement as an amateur led to his first commercial vintage in 2003. Two years later, Peterson and his wife, Lael, moved their Edmonds winery to the Woodinville warehouse district, into the same tiny space that was the first home of DeLille Cellars.

Production has grown from 130 cases of a single cabernet in 2003 to about 1,300 cases of as many as eight different wines, all red. Grapes are purchased by the pound, not the acre. "We look for the guy that has the vineyard and he's a farmer," Petersen explains. "We want the guy to be in the vineyard, actually doing the work!"

In its first four or five vintages, Edmonds has crafted some interesting wines, especially the Slide Ridge Bordeaux blend and the Solstice, an even mix of syrah, cinsault, and mourvèdre. The emerging style centers on wines of moderate alcohol (under 14 percent) that display bright, fresh fruit flavors nuanced but not clobbered with new oak. If there is a criticism, it is one common among young wineries—excess volatility, which makes some wines taste sharp and unbalanced.

EFESTÉ

First vintage: 2005

www.efeste.com

The rather awkward name of this promising young winery is a rehash of the initials (F, S, T) of the partners, Daniel Ferrelli, Patrick Smith, and Kevin Taylor. The winery's chief asset is winemaker Brennon Leighton, a heavily tattooed ex–grunge rocker whose "wine epiphany" was a 1985 Cheval Blanc tasted while working as a busboy in California. Some years later he enrolled at UC Davis and, following graduation, worked several vintages at Chateau Ste. Michelle, specifically in its Eroica program.

The first Efesté wines—1,800 cases, all reds from the 2005 vintage—were made under the supervision of consulting winemaker Chris Upchurch (DeLille, Doyenne). Upchurch helped the new winery establish vineyard contracts with an honor roll of growers, including Klipsun, Ciel du Cheval, Kiona, and Boushey.

Red Mountain will continue to be an important focus, as the partners have purchased and planted 42 acres of Rhône and Bordeaux grapes that will begin bearing in 2011. They also own a 25-acre Yakima Valley vineyard being developed and managed by Dick Boushey. In addition, Leighton has used his own contacts to line up fruit from Evergreen, Weinbau, Sagemoor, Bacchus, and Red Willow, much of it from original old block plantings.

The winery is located in a modest warehouse space in Woodinville, where production has quickly climbed to 6,000 cases. Leighton is truly passionate about terroir. "I don't want to put my handprint on a wine," he insists. "I don't fine, I don't filter, and I use 100 percent native yeast. I'm trying to be really gentle, like it's an artifact. The purity of the vineyard—what can a certain varietal do from a certain vineyard? That's what excites me."

That excitement is conveyed across the entire lineup. These are elegant, highly aromatic, and complex wines, but neither fruity nor massively oaked. The Feral sauvignon blanc and Eroica-style riesling both come from the Evergreen vineyard and are acidic, racy wines. The reds include a pair of syrahs, one Red Mountain, the other Boushey; Final-Final, a polished blend of cabernet and syrah; and Big Papa, a complex, dusty, old-vine cabernet. With such graceful and ageworthy wines, Efesté feels like a long-term winner.

ENSEMBLE CELLARS

First vintage: 2003–2004

www.ensemblecellars.com

Before upending his life and moving to Walla Walla to study winemaking and open a winery, Craig Nelsen was a water guy. He owned or managed water-related businesses in El Paso, Boston, and here in the Northwest. Following the sale of his last company, he set out to taste, and learn about, as much wine as possible. This, by the way, is an excellent strategy.

In 1999 he opened a wineshop—Water to Wine—in Gig Harbor, while moonlighting as a violinist in the Tacoma Symphony. Many bottles later he was visiting Walla Walla on a wine-tasting mission when he learned about the new college for viticultural studies. Goodbye Gig Harbor, hello Walla Walla. Two years later he graduated with a degree in enology and viticulture, and quickly moved on to become assistant winemaker at Nicholas Cole.

Ensemble Cellars, which references his musical as well as vinous activities, is headquartered out at the Walla Walla airport. Nelsen makes about 400 cases of a single wine each year. It's a Bordeaux blend, but here's the twist—each Ensemble wine is also a blend of three successive vintages. Named simply Release Number One, Release Number Two, and so forth, they include grapes from a mix of AVAs and vineyards, notably DuBrul.

It would take most of this chapter to explain the blending process. Nelsen spends a month or so each spring working on the wines in their various stages. For example, in 2009 he was doing separate blending trials for the finished version of Release Number Five, the initial two-vintage components of Release Number Six, and the first vintage for Release Number Seven, while bottling the next wine to be released (Number Four).

His goal, he explains, is to avoid off-years—"kind of a Champagne cuvée, nonvintage approach with high-end Bordeaux blends as the goal." The finished wines are indeed consistent, ready to drink upon release, and soundly made. My personal quibble? This approach blends away all terroir, vineyard character, and vintage variation. The wines seem just a bit flat, as if put through a real workout. So far, I admire the thinking more than the drinking.

FLYING TROUT

First vintage: 2004

www.flyingtroutwines.com

Winemaker Ashley Trout—that is her real name—moved to Walla Walla to attend Whitman College, where she double-majored in anthropology, and film and rhetoric. She had barely landed when fate stepped in, disguised as a job offer from Chuck Reininger, who was looking for part-time help at his winery. "I thought this was the coolest thing ever," she later recalled. "Chuck made the job sound so awful that he scared everyone else away. There were four guys plus me, and I was so enamored with this idea of doing something completely different from how I was raised that I said yes. So there I was—a cellar rat at 18—doing punch-downs, inoculations, all that jazz."

The story continues. "After graduation, I knew I wanted to do wine as a profession, but I felt I should do something totally unrelated first. I went to Japan and taught English.

In Japan I had a big rock-climbing accident and I broke everything. By the time I finally got out of the wheelchair, crush was over. I didn't want to wait another nine months for crush, so I went to Argentina. I knocked on doors, saying I speak fluent Spanish and English and I've worked for four years in a winery and you don't even have to pay me."

While there, she learned lab work, her career hampered only temporarily by a moderate-sized explosion. Flying Trout winery opened its tiny tasting room (recently moved south of town) in the spring of 2007. Trout makes wine both in Walla Walla and Argentina—what she calls "a fascinating experiment with bihemispherical terroir"— roughly 1,000 cases annually. Not too surprisingly, it is her malbecs that garner the most attention, though she also makes a fair amount of syrah, along with sangiovese, cabernet-carmenère, Argentine torrontés, and other experiments. The mailing list offers the best access to these wines.

FURION CELLARS

First vintage: 2005

www.furioncellars.com

Any wine named Wicces Basium (the witches' kiss) is bound to excite the imagination. The flagship offering from this tiny boutique in Everett (just north of Seattle), it's a pretty, beautifully integrated blend of syrah, mourvèdre, and grenache from Walla Walla's RiverRock vineyards.

Furion's Micole Miller also makes a Columbia Valley syrah and small amounts of chardonnay—total production no more than a few hundred cases. His style is more elegant than over the top; the syrah brings a floral nose and smooth, soft flavors of candied cherries and molasses.

GÅRD VINTNERS

First vintage: 2006

www.gardvintners.com

The Lawrence vineyard was planted in 2003, inspired by—and happily located near—the wildly successful Stillwater vineyard. The grapes are new, but the Lawrence family has been growing apples and cherries on the Royal Slope of the Frenchman Hills for more than four decades. South-facing and high in altitude (up to almost 1,700 feet), this is in one the most northern growing regions in the state, yet still can muster the heat units to ripen an astonishing variety of grapes, including riesling, roussanne, pinot gris, cabernet sauvignon, grenache, and syrah. Where else but in Washington do you see such a mix?

Gård Vintners, launched in 2006, is the Lawrence family winery—the word means "farm" or "estate" and reflects their Norwegian roots. Among the first releases were a dry riesling, a syrah, a cabernet sauvignon, and a syrah-cabernet blend called Don Isidro in honor of the vineyard manager.

Winemaker Robert Smasne uses estate-grown fruit exclusively. Total production has grown from 500 to 1,250 cases in the first three vintages. This combination of a vineyard site with outstanding potential, owners with substantial agricultural expertise, and an up-and-coming consulting winemaker would seem to be a surefire recipe for success. The first releases, not surprisingly, were relatively light, given the youth of the material. Best among them was the syrah.

GIANT WINE COMPANY

First vintage: 2005

www.GiantWine.com

The Giant Wine Company (which is actually quite small) is the project of Chris Gorman and Mark McNeilly. Though each has a winery of his own, and they produce such memorable wines as The Evil Twin and Dead Horse, they do not offer any wines under $20. Giant's mission is to fill that gap.

The first releases from Giant were labeled The Ghost of 413 and included a white and a red. Outstanding values at the time, they were followed up a year later with a pair of Sinner's Punch wines, again both a white and a red, and also very well made for their $14 price point.

The Ghost name was introduced with a variety of explanations. "Since this is purchased wine," says McNeilly, "we didn't know how associated we wanted to be with it." Naming them Ghost wines was in part an effort to be invisible. The 413, adds Gorman, is a veiled reference to the bond number of his original winery, which was to be called Sleeping Giant. Then again, he says with a knowing grin, April 13 is the birth date of Ricky Schroder, Thomas Jefferson, Ian Fleming, and Baron Rothschild. You pick.

By any name these wines fill a gaping hole in the market: the need for solidly made Washington wines priced in the $12–$14 sweet spot. It generally requires the economies of scale of a big winery to offer such wines, which is why so very few boutiques even try. Kudos to Gorman and McNeilly for taking a giant step forward.

THE GLACIAL LAKE MISSOULA WINE COMPANY

First vintage: 2002

www.lakemissoulawine.com

With a Blaine, Washington, headquarters, this may qualify as the most northern winery in the state—the owners actually live in Vancouver, B.C. The name (now shortened to GLM on the label) references the great floods that carved out much of eastern Washington many thousands of years ago.

GLM's flagship wine remains a Bordeaux blend named Deluge, done in a style that favors maximum extraction and generous use of new French oak. "We reject wine pseudoscience (biodynamics, organics) and fads (ultra-ripeness, high pH, must dilution, terroirism)," write owners Tom Davis and Tracey DeGraff on their website. Fair enough; reject away. In place of such things, they offer some of the most unusual statistics I've ever seen on a wine label, such as this entry on the 2003 GLM Deluge: "Total phenolics: .787 AU (UV absorbance @ 280 NM)."

The first release of Deluge was two-thirds cabernet sauvignon and one-third cabernet franc; subsequently that ratio has been upped to three-quarters–one-quarter. The grapes for the first five vintages were from Kestrel View's estate vineyard. Beginning with the 2007 vintage, malbec from the Verhey vineyard is in the blend.

Two additional wines are now made: a saignée rosé blend from the grapes for the 2008 Deluge, and a tasting room malbec-based red blend. Total annual production is up to 350 cases.

GOEDHART FAMILY

First vintage: 2006

www.goedhartfamily.com

This tiny Red Mountain operation makes just a single syrah each year, from Bel'Villa vineyard grapes. They have an inside connection to the fruit—Sarah Goedhart is the daughter of Tom and Anne-Marie Hedges. Hedges is where Brent Goedhart makes these wines, but the barrel room and a small tasting room are located just up the hill in the family home.

The first releases—from 2006 and 2007—are styled very much in the Hedges manner, which is to say they are European and relatively light, emphasizing clean fruit flavors with noninterventionist winemaking. "Unfiltered, unfined, and unscored," say the Goedharts. Brent started his career on the bottling line at Santa Barbara winery, later spent time working for Lou Preston at Dry Creek, and did some interning at Snoqualmie before starting this project. "It's fun to wear all the hats instead of just doing one job all day long," he says.

Case quantities are quite small, and the wines are sold almost exclusively through the mailing list and at the tasting room.

GRAND RÊVE VINTNERS

First vintage: 2005

www.grandrevewine.com

Grand Rêve (great dream) seems to have all the pieces in place to be one of this state's most exciting properties in the years ahead. The founding partners are Paul McBride, a retired high-tech entrepreneur, and Ryan Johnson, the personable vineyard manager for several of Red Mountain's most prestigious sites, most notably Ciel du Cheval.

Their project is both visionary and long-term. In order to get wines into production as quickly as possible and to pursue their goal of showcasing the best of Red Mountain terroir, the partners have devised a Collaboration Series program. Six winemakers have been offered special lots of Ciel du Cheval grapes and challenged to create the best wine they can. "Sort of a Long Shadows of Red Mountain," McBride explains, "except here it's the grower choosing the winemakers, and the fruit all comes from a single vineyard and AVA."

The first releases (about 200 cases of each were made) included Bordeaux blends from Ben Smith (Cadence) and Carolyn Lakewold (Donedéi), syrahs from Ross Mickel (Ross Andrew) and Mark McNeilly (Mark Ryan), and a one-time-only sangiovese. Chris Gorman became the fifth winemaker starting with the 2008 vintage; Syncline's James Mantone is the sixth, crafting a Rhône-style red wine to be bottled as Collaboration VI and released in 2011. Each of the first Collaboration Series wines I've tasted has succeeded in the difficult task of capturing the attributes of the vineyard and the strengths of the winemaker, without being too imitative of the winemaker's existing brand.

The far more challenging task facing Grand Rêve Vintners is the establishment of the estate vineyard. Situated on the highest slopes of Red Mountain, above Col Solare, it is 20 acres of rock, rock, and more rock. Nine distinct soil types have been identified on the property and matched to specific clonal selections. Some of the land is above the ancient flood zone. It's taken four years to plant the first 11 acres; 40 percent is syrah, 20 percent cabernet sauvignon, and the rest a mix of merlot, cab franc, grenache, mourvèdre, petit verdot, and viognier.

"Ryan's always been inspired by Priorat and Côte-Rôtie," says McBride. "That meant we had to pound 13,000 T-posts by hand in the rock." "The entire vineyard," Johnson is quick to explain, "is designed to be farmed in microblocks where varieties, clones, trellising, and irrigation are meticulously matched to soil and topographical character."

The Collaboration Series wines have been produced in every vintage since 2005, and they are a great introduction to Grand Rêve. But the full realization of the founders' great dream will have to wait awhile longer, until the vineyard is bearing and the estate wines are made. That is an exciting prospect.

GUARDIAN CELLARS

First vintage: 2003

guardiancellars.com

Jerry Riener, an undercover narcotics officer by trade, learned winemaking by volunteering his time and talent, first at Matthews Estate, later with Lance Baer, and for the past six years with Mark McNeilly at Mark Ryan. Riener is an equipment guy with a love of motors, tools, farm gear.

"I started in this business with the simple goal," he modestly explains on his website, "to drive a forklift." A man of apparently boundless energy, he seems to exist on no sleep, and has for years. "I work at the winery five or six hours every morning before going to work," he tells me matter-of-factly. During crush, when wineries are going at full speed day and night, he takes vacation time from police work to do his winemaking. "The focus at Guardian Cellars," says Riener, "is to continually strive to produce the finest single varietals and blends from Washington vineyards. Plus, making kick-ass wines is a nice change from my day job of arresting people."

Guardian Cellars got started with just two barrels of cabernet sauvignon made at McNeilly's winery in 2003. Additional wines were added the following year. In November 2007, Guardian Cellars made its official debut, releasing the '03 cabernet, the '04 Gun Metal, and an '04 Red Mountain syrah. Total annual production has climbed from less than 200 to roughly 1,500 cases as of the 2008 crush and now includes a clean, lightly grassy sauvignon blanc (Angel) from Klipsun vineyard grapes.

Riener's sense of gallows humor is apparent on many of his labels, variously named Gun Metal, Chalkline (a second label "for wines that died before making it into the final cut"), and The Wanted. The Mark McNeilly influence is visible throughout, and to good effect.

HARD ROW TO HOE VINEYARDS

First vintage: 2004

www.hardrow.com

Formerly Balsamroot winery, the new name Hard Row To Hoe, according to winery owners Don and Judy Phelps, celebrates the "entrepreneurial spirit" of a local man who operated a rowboat taxi service ferrying copper miners to a Lake Chelan brothel (at Point Lovely, no less!) back in the 1930s.

There is no question that the Hoe wines are spirited, some pushing 16 percent alcohol, all showing real guts and character. One major asset so far has been the vineyard from which most of the grapes have been purchased—Riverbend, which belongs to the owners of the Fielding Hills winery.

Hard Row To Hoe's estate vineyard, managed by Don, is being planted and maintained organically using sustainable growing practices. In 2005 the first two acres of cabernet franc went into the ground, followed in 2006 by two acres of gewürztraminer and riesling, and in 2007 with additional blocks of sémillon, sauvignon blanc, malbec, and chenin blanc.

The early releases, all from purchased grapes, included a dense and syrupy zinfandel, a classy cab franc, and one of the better barberas I've tasted from this state. Most wines are sold from the tasting room and mailing list. A second label—Shameless Hussy—offers especially fine value.

HESTIA CELLARS

First vintage: 2004

www.hestiacellars.com

Though the first releases from this new producer were limited to quite small quantities—65 cases of sémillon, 100 of a Meritage red, 150 of a merlot—the wines were very well made. The Charbonneau vineyard sémillon was done in a lean, clean style, accenting cool-climate flavors of lime and tart melon, with an underlying hint of stone. The Meritage and the merlot, both from Horse Heaven Hills vineyards, also showed a skillful winemaker at work.

Shannon Jones is the winemaker and owner. His family roots go back to southern Italy and Greece, hence the winery name and logo (Hestia was the Greek goddess of the hearth). Grapes are primarily sourced from the Andrews vineyard in the Horse Heaven Hills, with supplementary fruit from Boushey, Dineen, and Stone Tree. A tasting room was recently opened in one of the Woodinville business parks.

A pair of Dineen vineyard-designates released in the spring of 2009 marked a real step forward in quality. The syrah was sharp and precise, with cool-climate hints of lemon zest and citrus. The cabernet sauvignon, 100 percent varietal, also showed pure fruit, balance, and concentration.

HORAN ESTATES

First vintage: 2003

www.horanestateswinery.com

Tragedy has touched the lives of the founders of Horan Estates, and the wines are named in remembrance of those who are gone. The original Horan settlers arrived in the Columbia Valley in the 1800s. Winemaker Doug McDougall is the great-grandson of Michael Horan, who established the original farm and homestead.

The eight-acre estate vineyard is on the south side of the Frenchman Hills, north of Royal City. Though the site is mostly planted to syrah, there are also small amounts of cabernet sauvignon, merlot, cabernet franc, mourvèdre, cinsault, and viognier. The winery is in Wenatchee Heights.

Horan's HVH Red honors the winemaker's late grandmother. It's a substantial effort, dense with concentrated berry, cherry, and cassis fruit. The CWM Syrah is named for Corey Wayne McDougall, the winemaker's son, killed some years ago in a snowmobile accident. Ripe, high in alcohol, and toasty, with sappy red fruit flavors, it also brings some earthy tannins into play. The estate-grown fruit and the focus on a handful of red wines, especially syrah, are this winery's core strengths.

LAHT NEPPUR WINERY

First vintage: 2007

www.lahtneppur.com

Court Ruppenthal's cozy roadside brewery sits just at the edge of Waitsburg, in the northeastern corner of Walla Walla County. He makes an ever-changing array of craft beers and, within his first few years, was named best brewery in the state at the prestigious Ellensburg Brewfest. Not content to rule brew-dom, he has launched a winery venture, first with a fortified syrah cleverly named O-Courto, and next with a Walla Walla cabernet sauvignon. Don't expect to find these wines anywhere but in the neighborhood any time soon, but it is yet another reason to make the tiny town of Waitsburg—home, too, of jimgermanbar and the Whoopemup Hollow Café—a must-see on any visit to Walla Walla wine country.

LONE CANARY

First vintage: 2002

www.lonecanary.com

Winery founder Mike Scott had Wild Canary wines and labels ready to go when threats of a trademark infringement lawsuit sent him back to the drawing board. The brand's Tweety-bird logo and the name Lone Canary were the result. A Washington winemaker since 1980, Scott began his career at the now-defunct Worden winery, briefly joined Mike Conway at Latah Creek, and launched Caterina in 1993, where he remained as winemaker until starting up Lone Canary in 2002.

Though the emphasis at Lone Canary has increasingly shifted to red wines made from Italian varietals, the results have been spotty. Too often the wines come across as overripe and pruney, and the DuBrul vineyard reserve, which should on the face of it be the best of them, is often the most dried out and disappointing.

Sauvignon blanc was always and still remains the star. It's all-stainless-fermented, made in a sharp, spiky, pungently grassy style. The fruit flavors combine pear and pineapple, gooseberry and lime—think New Zealand without the canned-pea flavors. Sauvignon blanc accounts for as much as half of the winery's 4,500-case annual production.

LOST RIVER

First vintage: 2002

www.lostriverwinery.com

Right from the start, I was impressed with the barrel-fermented sémillon from Lost River. When I tasted the 2003 for the first time, the brilliant bouquet of honey and flowers, matched to rich, ripe pear, apple, and blood orange fruit flavors, suggested that here was a new winery able to craft that magic combination of elegance, texture, and length.

Though no one-hit wonder, Lost River has not yet found a way to repeat that initial magic. The sémillon has been joined by a lively, stainless steel–fermented, whole cluster–pressed pinot gris and a clean and refreshing sauvignon blanc–sémillon blend called Rainshadow White.

The red wines include well-made versions of merlot, cabernet sauvignon, and syrah and a Bordeaux blend called Cedarosa. Modestly priced and medium-bodied, they are a bit too generous with the new oak, but the winemaking is solid and the flavors true. So far they do not differentiate themselves from so many other similar wines from other small, start-up producers.

The most recent releases suggest that this is a winery still in the experimental stages of carving out its identity. A syrah-viognier carries the amusing name Côte-Wall; another new wine is a limited-production nebbiolo. And the potentially iconic sémillon, which was not made in 2007, makes a return in the 2008 vintage. Winemaker John Morgan calls it his true reserve, only made when he is "really tickled by a particular lot." As John Hurt once sang, "I'm satisfied and tickled too."

LULLABY

First vintage: 2007

lullabywinery.com

Virginie Bourgue arrived in Walla Walla six years ago with one of the more impressive wine résumés the town has ever seen. She was raised on a farm in Bonnieux (in Luberon, north of Provence), was educated first at a viticulture and enology school in Avignon, went on to earn a master's degree in enology in Champagne, next worked a year at Louis Roederer and another at Nicolas Feuillatte, and finally moved to the United States to do an internship at Ste. Michelle. Which led to an offer to become the winemaker for Bergevin Lane—all by the time she was 30 years old.

Bourgue's sensitive, delicate touch with wine grapes was evident from the beginning. She once explained to me that, although the grapes are usually the same, she immediately found that American wines are more powerful than French wines. "It seems the American wine drinker needs that," she theorized. "Here, if the nose is good—fruity, like candy—people will say, 'Yeah!' They are almost buying by smelling. If it stinks, they say, 'I may not be brave enough to put that in my mouth.' In France, it is the opposite. If it stinks, they say, 'Wow—it must be good!'"

Her success at Bergevin Lane quickly led to further opportunities, and from 2006 until the spring of 2010, she was the winemaker for Cadaretta. While there, she started Lullaby, her "evening and weekend project." The initial releases showcased Bourgue at her finest. The first Lullaby rosé was a blend of grenache, syrah, and a dollop of viognier, barrel-fermented in neutral oak, dry and fruity, with sneaky complexity. The Lullaby viognier, also barrel-fermented, shows a wide variety of fruits—apricot, peach, papaya—and places them in a refined, silky setting. A cabernet-merlot blend will be the next wine released.

WANT MORE?

Here are some under-the-radar, soon-to-be-rising stars, and a couple of old hands undergoing a renaissance.

The sheer number of new Washington wineries making their debut in the past few years has run smack into my own personal limitations of time and space (still, as always, the final frontiers). On this list are the wineries that are all generating some kind of buzz and are definitely worth checking out. I've included a word or two about them and listed a website if one exists.

Caterina (new owners are rapidly reviving this brand), www.caterinawinery.com
Cedergreen Cellars (old-vine chenin blanc is noteworthy), www.cedergreencellars. com
College Cellars (WWCC enology program winery), www.collegecellars.com
Corvidae (new Owen Roe line of moderately priced varietals), www.corvidaewine. com
Daven Lore (WSU's Dr. Dirt is one of the owners), www.davenlore.com
Five Star Cellars (big reds, big scores), www.fivestarcellars.com
Five Zero Nine (Seattle wine lovers group, California winemaker), www.509wines. com
Garrison Creek Cellars (gorgeous facility adjacent to Les Collines), www. garrisoncreekcellars.com
Gifford-Hirlinger (estate fruit brings rapid improvement), www.giffordhirlinger. com
Gilbert Cellars (estate-grown fruit, especially riesling and syrah), www. gilbertcellars.com
Goose Ridge (vast vineyard holding; Charlie Hoppes makes the wines), www. gooseridge.com
Hence Cellars (estate malbec), www.hencecellars.com
Hyatt Vineyards (latest releases are vastly improved), www.hyattvineyards.com
Kerloo Cellars (Walla Walla syrahs—very impressive debut releases), www. kerloocellars.com
Lantz Cellars (People's Choice at Sexy Syrah event), www.lantzcellars.com
Paragon (Tom Glase is consulting winemaker), www.paragonwinery.com

Patit Creek (new owners, steadily improving), www.patitcreekcellars.com

Patterson Cellars (good blend called BDX), http://washingtonwinecompany.com

Pomum Cellars (tempranillo specialist), www.pomumcellars.com

Pondera (a variety of Bordeaux blends), www.ponderawinery.com

Portrait Cellars (estate winery of Red Mountain's Shaw vineyard), www.portraitcellars.com

Robison Ranch Cellars (getting a lot of buzz in Walla Walla), www.robisonranchcellars.com

Sapolil Cellars (popular Walla Walla tasting room with live music), www.sapolilcellars.com

Seia (syrah specialist), www.seiawines.com

Shady Grove (interesting new varietals), www.shadygrovewinery.com

Southard (first releases very impressive), www.southardwinery.com

SuLei Cellars (outstanding debut, especially roussanne), www.suleicellars.com

'37 Cellars (Rob Newsom of Boudreaux consults), www.37cellars.com

Townshend Cellar (Spokane winery, value-oriented), www.townshendcellar.com

Tru (new Walla Walla sparkling wine specialist), www.trucellars.com

MAISON BLEUE

First vintage: 2005

www.maisonbleue.com

Winemaker Jon Martinez summed up 2008 this way: "I changed professions, moved, got married, and started a new business. Did I leave something out? It was a very busy year."

It was the year his tiny winery opened its doors in the Prosser Vintner's Village, the culmination of many years of planning, scrimping, and plain hard work. Originally from Kansas City, Missouri, Martinez commuted cross-country while studying winemaking, then gave up a successful dental practice to set up shop in Washington.

Maison Bleue began by specializing in wines from southern French and Mediterranean grapes, most notably roussanne. The first white wine releases were a bit on the ripe side, but distinctive. They included a viognier and a roussanne that were mirror image blends in 85-15 proportions, both finished off-dry; and an even sweeter roussanne named La Vie Douce that was the best of show. Future versions of the viognier-roussanne blends will be barrel-fermented to complete dryness.

His overriding goal, says Martinez, is to produce pure varietal, single-vineyard wines exclusively from Yakima Valley grapes. He is already well on his way to meeting that challenge, with two estate vineyards already in production. The Dutchman vineyard, a cooperative venture with the Den Hoed family, includes the largest planting of albariño (6.5 acres) in Washington, along with smaller amounts of roussanne and marsanne. In

2008, Martinez purchased a 21-acre Yakima Valley site, renamed it French Creek, and set about renovating its 30-year-old, 9-acre block of Wente clone chardonnay. He will fill the rest of the acreage with new plantings of grenache, mourvèdre, and syrah.

Though he never intended to make chardonnay, he jumped in with characteristic energy and focus, turning out a nicely sculpted, bright, and citrusy wine with refreshing acids and moderate levels of alcohol. Also in production are at least four different red wines, most important among them a syrah and a syrah-grenache blend from the Boushey vineyard. Maison Bleue is just getting started, but I am already very impressed with the creativity and energy that Jon Martinez is bringing to this project.

MANNINA CELLARS

First vintage: 2004

www.manninacellars.com

Mannina Cellars has maintained a tight focus over its first few vintages, specializing in sangiovese and filling in with merlot, cabernet sauvignon, and a value-priced red blend called Cali. Hobby winemaking turned professional for owner Don Redman, an environmental engineer by training—there must be something in the Walla Walla air. But by keeping production small, taking a measured approach, and pulling in fruit from Seven Hills, Pepper Bridge, Les Collines, and other top vineyards, Redman is off to a good start.

The Cali Red, a Bordeaux blend (which sometimes tosses in syrah or sangiovese also), is a fruit-driven, very pretty wine and the best buy as well. The sangioveses—four vintages so far—are blended differently each year, but may include small amounts of merlot, cabernet, and/or syrah. Lightly toasty and offering strawberry-raspberry fruit, they are steadily improving and succeed in their goal of emulating the lightness and elegance of Chianti. The first few merlots were the most substantial wines to date from Mannina, with ripe fruit at center court and new oak nicely holding down the perimeter.

In the spring of 2009, the 30-acre estate vineyard went into the ground, a mix of vines including merlot, cabernet sauvignon, sangiovese, cab franc, syrah, barbera, and nebbiolo. The 2006 Birch Creek vineyard cabernet sauvignon, made from fruit sourced nearby, is a preview of good things to come.

MARYHILL

First vintage: 1999

www.maryhillwinery.com

Maryhill makes a dizzying assortment of wines, and for most of its first decade, quality has been up and down. The winery location—a spectacular setting near the Maryhill

Museum overlooking the Columbia Gorge—is a tremendous asset. Production has grown from 4,500 to 80,000 cases annually. Name a varietal, they make it, usually in two versions.

Even the simple blends, such as the Winemaker's White and Winemaker's Red, can be good one year, funky the next. The regular tier's most consistent wines are the aromatic whites, such as gewürztraminer and sauvignon blanc. The reds include a wide range of unusual varietals—cabernet franc, malbec, sangiovese, barbera, grenache, zinfandel, and so on.

The Proprietor's Reserve wines, which can cost up to $40, should be Maryhill's best, and occasionally a particular wine in a single vintage has met that standard. But how to explain the all-too-frequent disappointments? Some are pruney, some earthy, some funky, some bitter, some clobbered with oak. The unmistakable scents and flavors of tack room leather afflict more than a few of them. The winery even calls out, in its tasting notes, the "exotic, bold, leathery aromas" in its barbera. A little too leathery for my taste, I'm afraid.

Given its superb location, visitor extras such as a summer concert series, and the owners' roll-out-the-welcome-mat attitude, it would be curmudgeonly to exclude Maryhill from this book. But the fact that the winery can't seem to hold on to a winemaker—Garry Penner did the 2008 crush, and he was replaced by Richard Batchelor in 2009—is clearly a problem. It would be really nice to see Maryhill's portfolio settle into some consistent quality; it's time.

McCORMICK FAMILY VINEYARDS

First vintage: 2006

www.winesofthegorge.com

The owners are part of the well-known McCormick spice family. Their family-owned vineyards are located on both the Oregon and Washington sides of the Columbia Gorge, while the winery tasting room occupies a stunning perch high on the Washington bluffs, 1,000 feet above the river. The vineyards are farmed organically, and seventeen different varieties have been planted. In addition, McCormick sources grapes from other local growers.

Memaloose is the oddly named label, which commemorates a Lewis and Clark campsite directly below the winery. In 2006 the winery made its first wine, a Memaloose Corps Red, mostly cabernet franc, with a little sangiovese and cabernet sauvignon blended in. In 2007 a white blend was added, along with a syrah-grenache named Mistral Ranch, a blend of Italian varietals called York's Reward, and a version of Corps Red renamed Idiot's Grace. Tart, acidic flavors characterize these young wines from young vines, but they are well crafted by winemaker Brian McCormick, with good balance and texture.

McKINLEY SPRINGS

First vintage: 2003

www.mckinleysprings.com

With 1,600 acres of vineyard in the Horse Heaven Hills, the Andrews family would seem well endowed with grapes. The Andrewses began as grape growers with just 16 acres of cabernet sauvignon three decades ago, and now grow nineteen different varietals, including rarities such as nebbiolo, cinsault, barbera, and mourvèdre. Their Horse Heaven Ranch and McKinley Springs vineyards sell to some of the state's premier wineries—Andrew Rich, J. Bookwalter, Robert Karl, Northstar, and Syncline among them.

The McKinley Springs estate winery is a fairly recent addition. Though they set out to specialize in red wines—notably cabernet sauvignon and syrah—the best wines to date have come from white grapes such as chenin blanc, roussanne, and viognier. Fragrant and fresh, all three of these lovely wines deliver pleasing aromas that mix fruit and flower, leading into elegant and textural flavors that are far more nuanced than the reds.

Among the reds, the malbec is the standout. All the rest must overtake the heavy-handed barrel scents and flavors, which seem to overwhelm the fruit. The malbec succeeds with a mix of cherry, plum, mocha, coffee, and spice.

MEEK FAMILY ESTATE

First vintage: 2004

(no website)

Meek Family Estate, just across from Red Mountain above Benton City, includes 54 acres of vineyard. Planting to Bordeaux and Rhône varietals was begun in 2001 and is ongoing, at first under the supervision of Fred Artz and more recently with the help of consultant Scott Greer of Sheridan winery.

Though owner Michael Meek relocated from Seattle to Minneapolis in the early 1990s, he has pursued his lifelong dream of vineyard ownership from afar. The vineyard's excellent location immediately resulted in high-quality fruit, already in demand from such wineries as Andrew Will, Sparkman, Stevens, and Sheridan.

Since 2005, a small percentage of the crop has gone into the estate's own limited-production wines. There are two different labels. The WJ Meek label honors the owner's late grandfather, a home winemaker himself, and so far includes a Bordeaux blend and a syrah. Fruit is sourced from the estate and the nearby Minnick vineyard. The first vintages of these wines offered exceptional value.

The Meek Family label is devoted exclusively to wines made from estate grapes. First made in 2005 and 2006 by Scott Greer, they included a varietal petit verdot, a syrah, and a Bordeaux blend named Inherit (as in "the meek shall inherit the earth"). I found all three of these wines to be extraordinarily ripe, their colors saturated to blackness, their scents bordering on pruney. That said, they offered substantial flavors, all in the dark spectrum, and established a style (reminiscent of Greer's own Sheridan reserves) that will certainly appeal to many consumers.

In 2008, Meek Family produced its first white wine, a sauvignon blanc made by Tim Stevens, who recently succeeded Greer as consulting winemaker. Stevens has shown an outstanding touch with his own wines, and there is every reason to believe that under his direction the Meek Family wines will continue to impress.

MERCER ESTATES

First vintage: 2005

www.mercerwine.com

Mike Hogue and Bud Mercer, both Washington vineyard pioneers, became partners in this new venture in part to bring the next generation—Mike's daughter Barb and Bud's son Rob—back into the winemaking business. A 70,000-case production facility and barrel room were built on the eastern outskirts of Prosser, and opened to the public in 2008.

The first wines were also released that year. Most of the production of Mercer Estates is divided among four white varietals—a succulent, juicy riesling, a crisply refreshing pinot gris, a sauvignon blanc, and a chardonnay, all first made in 2007. Two red wines complete the lineup, both from Horse Heaven Hills grapes and made in much more limited quantities.

Winemaker David Forsyth, who spent 23 years at Hogue Cellars, is in charge. Especially promising is the prospect that future Mercer Estates red wines will eventually be based upon fruit from a new vineyard, planted in 2006. Named Dead Canyon, it occupies a previously unplanted, 120-acre site adjacent to Champoux—which was, of course, originally part of Mercer Ranch. Dead Canyon grows cabernet sauvignon, merlot, and syrah. Given its superb location and all the talent behind it, this could well become one of the best sites in the Horse Heaven Hills.

MERRY CELLARS

First vintage: 2004

www.merrycellars.com

It is not uncommon for new wineries to offer a lot of different wines; it is the rare young winemaker who can rein in the natural urge to experiment widely with as many different grapes as possible. Nonetheless, what usually happens is that a few strengths emerge, and (one hopes) some tightening of the lineup results.

Merry Cellars is still in the early phases of that process. Winemaker Patrick Merry set up shop in downtown Pullman (home of Washington State University) and immediately made a viognier, a blended white called Soirée, a chardonnay, and merlot, cabernet sauvignon, syrah, and Crimson reds (honoring the college's Cougar colors).

In 2005, the winery made its first carmenère and sangiovese, added a varietal sémillon and sauvignon blanc, and introduced its first vineyard-designates. More wines have followed, making it impossible to get a clear sense of direction. One red wine has stood out from the pack—the carmenère, with fruit sourced from Seven Hills vineyard. It is structured like a modest Bordeaux, with the peppery and herbal character of the grape, along with accent notes of dried sage. Among the white wines the sémillon and sauvignon blanc have been the most interesting so far.

MICHAEL FLORENTINO CELLARS

First vintage: 2005

www.michaelflorentinocellars.com

The Winemaker's Loft, a winery incubator in the Prosser Vintner's Village, was the brainchild of Michael Haddox, who used it as a vehicle to start up his own project, Michael Florentino Cellars. Haddox began his winemaking career after completing his military service, first taking a job on the Columbia Crest bottling line and learning the trade by working his way up from there. He founded the Loft in 2006, briefly made it his headquarters, and attracted a number of other start-ups, most notably Maison Bleue.

In the spring of 2009, the Loft ran into financial difficulties, the business changed hands, and Haddox, whose winery had already outgrown the space, attempted to relocate it in Kennewick's Southridge Village development. Sadly, those plans fell through; Haddox sold the brand and has moved out of state. Though it is impossible to predict the ultimate outcome, any wines remaining in the market that carry the Michael Florentino Cellars label will be well worth buying. The last note I had from Haddox read: "I hope to have a new wine back into your hands in the near future. Stay tuned."

MILBRANDT VINEYARDS

First vintage: 2005

www.milbrandtvineyards.com

Brothers Butch and Jerry Milbrandt own a growing empire of acclaimed vineyards clustered in the Wahluke Slope–Ancient Lakes heart of Washington State. Though the first vines went into the ground just a dozen years ago, the roll call of Milbrandt properties—some purchased, others leased—now includes Sundance, Katherine Leone, Talcott, Clifton, Pheasant, North Ridge, Purple Sage, Wahluke, Ancient Lakes, Evergreen, and others. There are thirteen separate sites and 1,600 acres in the ground, but still more remarkable is how familiar most of these vineyard names have become. They appear on dozens of labels from more than forty different wineries.

The Wahluke Wine Company is the Milbrandts' custom crush facility. It opened in a spare metal shed barely in time for the 2005 crush, the first vintage for their own brand as well. The plan, Butch recalls, was to overbuild the facility to a capacity of 250,000 gallons, intending to slowly grow to fill that size. It was immediately too small. They expanded to one million gallons in 2006. Still too small. A million and a half gallons were made the following year, much of it for Charles Smith and Precept Brands. In terms of total production, Wahluke is now the fourth-largest winery in Washington State.

Gordon Hill has been the winemaker since 2006. Under the Milbrandt label, he makes three separate tiers of wine. The Traditions wines include purchased fruit and sell for $13–$15. The Estates wines cost about $10 more and are sourced from specific vineyard blocks. Included are well-made versions of syrah, merlot, malbec, petite sirah, and a fragrant red blend called Three Estates. The newest wine is a superpremium red blend called Sentinel. Each Sentinel release will focus on a specific Milbrandt site. Many of these wines are sold only at the tasting room, in the Prosser Vintner's Village, or through the winery's mailing list.

The most affordable and widely available Milbrandt wines are among this state's finest values. Look for white wines from the Evergreen vineyard and red wines from any of the Wahluke Slope sites.

NEFARIOUS CELLARS

First vintage: 2004

www.nefariouscellars.com

Heather and Dean Neff split the winemaking duties at their Nefarious winery right down the middle, Heather (whose card reads "Head Chick") doing the whites, Dean doing the reds. Their first estate vineyard—named Rocky Mother—was planted in 1998 in Pateros, a few miles north of the Lake Chelan AVA. Eight test varieties went into an acre of ground, and the thinking was that pinot noir would be the principal success in the area. With that in mind, the Neffs moved to the Willamette Valley to study enology and spent three years making pinot noir.

Upon returning to Chelan, they changed course. Rocky Mother was replanted all to syrah, while an adjoining parcel, named Stone's Throw, got 2.5 acres of riesling. Their Defiance vineyard, seven acres on the south shore of Lake Chelan, went into the ground between 2005 and 2007, with more syrah, viognier, and a bit of malbec.

Remarkably, all the Nefarious wines released to date have been exceptional. The Stone's Throw vineyard riesling seduces immediately with scents of honeycomb, beeswax, and a mix of citrus blossoms; it's rich without being tiring, bone dry, yet carrying a lovely sensation of sweet blossom. The Defiance viognier, from very young vines, is also elegant and stylish, and the first Defiance syrah was nuanced and aromatic.

The other red wines are just as impressive. Sourced from several different Columbia Valley vineyards, including Riverbend on the Wahluke Slope, are a cabernet sauvignon, a cabernet franc, a malbec, and a syrah, all supple and muscular, polished and precise. From their Rocky Mother vineyard comes the Neffs' best syrah, its flavors so beautifully wrapped that it would be easy to overlook the complexity—the density—that they present.

Based on their early work, I'd have to say that Nefarious is one of the most exciting new wineries to appear in the last few years.

NxNW

First vintage: 2005

www.nxnwwine.com

Oregon's King Estate winery is backing this new project, based in Walla Walla, and pronounced "North by Northwest." The labels are very technical yet classy, listing vineyards, blocks, soils, harvest dates, blend, process, and cooperage. The first two vintages (2005 and 2006) were made at King Estate, but beginning with the 2007 crush, the wines are being made at the Artifex custom crush facility in Walla Walla.

The main vineyard sources are Seven Hills and Pepper Bridge in the Walla Walla AVA, Wallula in the Horse Heaven Hills AVA, and Elephant Mountain in the Yakima Valley. The stated intent of the project is to specialize in cabernet and syrah from inland vineyards—a nice complement to the King Estate wines.

In addition to the nationally available Columbia Valley cabs, a limited-production, sequentially numbered Walla Walla Valley cabernet and a pair of syrahs are sold only at the winery. Given the vast resources that King Estate brings to the enterprise, it would not be surprising if NxNW continued to expand its presence in Washington State.

O WINE COMPANY

First vintage: 2006

www.owines.com

Stacy Lill is the wife of one of the founding partners in DeLille Cellars. Along with Kathy Johanson, she has established O Wines to fund scholarships for underprivileged young girls. O was introduced with a single chardonnay, affordably priced, and recently joined by a companion O Red, a blend of syrah, merlot, cab franc, and sangiovese.

Good works aside, the O chardonnay is a delicious bottle, full-flavored, fleshy, and dolloped with buttery oak. I have not tasted the red, but am confident in its quality. There are a number of similar ventures in this state, but the wines are often secondary to the causes. Along with Va Piano's Bruno's Blend, O is the best of all.

OLSEN ESTATES

First vintage: 2006

www.olsenestates.com

A longtime Yakima Valley grape grower, the Olsen family unveiled its first vintage in 2006. The Olsens' focus is on Rhône- and Bordeaux-style blends crafted by winemaker Kyle Johnson, who came over from Ste. Michelle's Canoe Ridge Estate. Grapes are sourced from the Olsens' 70-acre vineyard, first planted in 1980 and now growing nineteen different grape varieties.

It's a welcome trend throughout the state that growers with decades of vineyard expertise are opening wineries, and the best wines seem to come when professional winemaking talent is hired as well. The first releases of Olsen Estates wines were promising, especially the rieslings, chardonnays, and syrahs. More recently, the 2007 reds—syrah, petit verdot, and a special Heritage syrah—were superb. This winery appears to be a superstar in the making.

Note that Olsen Hills is the less expensive lineup; the Olsen Estates wines are the pricier reserves.

. . . PURSUED BY BEAR

First vintage: 2005

www.pursuedbybearwine.com

This buzz-worthy Columbia Valley cabernet sauvignon is a collaboration between artist-winemaker Eric Dunham (Dunham Cellars) and actor Kyle MacLachlan (*Desperate Housewives, Twin Peaks*). MacLachlan, a Yakima native, met Dunham at a wine tasting some years ago. A friendship evolved, a wine project was hatched, and the result is this sophisticated cabernet sauvignon.

MacLachlan credits director David Lynch with introducing him to fine wine. His interest in Washington reds piqued during visits home to Yakima; he spoke to his good friend Ann Colgin (of Napa's Colgin Cellars) about the possibility of doing a wine of his own. She was encouraging and contributed hard-to-get, custom-made Taransaud barrels to the project. Production is up to about 365 cases, sold through the website and in restaurants, and a second wine, a puncheon-aged syrah named Baby Bear, is also in the works.

Very much in the Dunham mold, … pursued by bear cabernet is supple and smooth, with delicate floral aromas over pure, powerful black fruits. The name refers to an obscure stage direction from Shakespeare ("Exit stage right, pursued by bear").

RAMSEYER VINEYARDS

First vintage: 2005

www.ramseyervineyards.com

John and Heather Ramseyer are among the new wave of vineyard owners exploring the potential of the Rattlesnake Hills AVA in Washington's Yakima Valley. Their five-acre site, near the Dineen, Sheridan, and Two Blondes vineyards, is planted mainly to cabernet and merlot, with small plots of the other three Bordeaux reds. The first estate-grown grapes are from the 2009 vintage.

Since 2005, a single cabernet sauvignon has been produced annually from Dineen vineyard grapes. Scott Greer (Sheridan) is the consulting winemaker. Named simply Vintage One, Vintage Two, and so forth, it is 100 percent cabernet sauvignon. A dense and richly fruity red with soft berry-mulberry flavors and soft tannins that wrap around the palate and linger seductively, it is available only through the winery mailing list. Nonetheless, a fine debut.

RASA VINEYARDS

First vintage: 2007

www.rasavineyards.com

Brothers Markrand (Pinto) and Yashodhan (Billo) Naravane are the founder-owners of this new Walla Walla venture dedicated specifically to syrah. They are high-tech veterans who "ditched it all to go completely native in the wild, cutthroat world of winemaking." Wild and cutthroat it may be, but the first releases from Rasa have the right stuff to make it big.

Billo, the first to move to the valley, brought with him one of the most unusual career-change stories I've ever heard. Born in India, he and his family moved to the United States when he was still in grade school. Billo went on to considerable academic success with advanced degrees in applied mathematics and computer science. But after 15 years, he explains, the fun had gone out of computer work.

"I decided that I didn't want to live a life without passion," he admits. It was time to make the change to a career in wine. He was accepted into the (very difficult) master's program at UC Davis, where he took every course in both enology and viticulture, graduating in August 2008. Meanwhile he and his brother scouted for land, settling on Walla Walla, when they found it was one-tenth the cost of California "and every bit as good."

The Naravanes, it is quickly apparent, do not shy away from daunting tasks. In less than two years they purchased a 28-acre site in the Rocks and began readying the land for grapevines. Billo is teaching viticulture at the college, and the first Rasa wines (from purchased grapes) are already in bottle and barrel.

The 2007 QED syrah (QED stands for *quod erat demonstrandum,* "what was to be demonstrated") is supple, almost voluptuous, dark, sappy, packed with compressed black fruits, streaked with iodine and coffee. It shows excellent length and opens with scents hinting of game, earth, sweet mocha, lead pencil, and cedar. A reserve called Principia (tasted pre-release from barrel) is even bigger.

Initial production is 750 cases; the plan is to introduce a number of single-vineyard syrahs and cabernets into the lineup, for up to 3,000 cases total. An estate vineyard is in development—28 acres in the Rocks. It will be planted to syrah, viognier, roussanne, grenache, mourvèdre, tempranillo, malbec, and possibly cabernet and cab franc.

RED SKY

First vintage: 1999

www.redskywinery.com

Red Sky's Jim and Carol Parsons owned a wine and cheese shop before opening their Woodinville winery. The Parsons like to give their wines an extra year or two of bottle age before release, so the current vintages may appear to be backed up. That is intentional. "Our wines are not made for early release," says Jim Parsons. "The goal is to make wines that increase in intricacy over time."

Production began with just 50 cases in 1999 and is up to about 1,000 cases a year. As of the 2006 vintage, Carol Parsons took over the winemaker reins from John Ogburn. Erica Orr is consulting on the technical and lab work.

Red wines—especially the Serendipity reserve—are their strength; also good are the merlot, the syrah, and the cabernet franc. A pleasant sémillon is also made.

REYNVAAN FAMILY VINEYARDS

First vintage: 2007

www.reynvaanfamilyvineyards.com

Mike and Gale Reynvaan are splitting their time between a home on Vashon Island and a new home, vineyards, and winery in Walla Walla. Two sites have been planted. The first 16 acres, named In the Rocks, was planted between 2005 and 2008, to a mix of Rhône grapes a little cabernet sauvignon. The first crop (of syrah) was picked in 2007.

Another 10 acres, named Foothills in the Sun, adjoins the winery. Planted in the spring of 2008, it includes syrah, viognier, and cabernet also. The Reynvaans introduced their first wines at a private barrel tasting in the fall of 2008, a full year ahead of their official release. The three wines included a Rhône white varietal blend, a syrah co-fermented with viognier, and a syrah co-fermented with marsanne. Christophe Baron (Cayuse) is consulting for son Matt Reynvaan on all viticultural and winemaking decisions. Given the commitment to quality vineyards, the top-flight consultant, and the preview tasting of the first few wines, I am confident that this young winery, off to a very good start, is one to watch closely.

RÔTIE CELLARS

First vintage: 2007

www.rotiecellars.com

It's refreshing to see a new producer with a clear focus and a real talent for getting the job done. Rôtie Cellars released its first three wines in the spring of 2009 to immediate applause from those fortunate enough to taste them. This Rhône specialist, based in Walla Walla, is set on making just 800 to 1,000 cases annually, working with traditional Rhône grapes and blends, limiting the use of new oak to capture true fruit flavors, making wines with moderate alcohol levels, and never fining or filtering.

Rôtie's 2007 Southern Blend Red Wine, from Horse Heaven Hills grapes, was classy stuff: silky, smooth, layered, and beautifully integrated throughout. The blend— 55 percent grenache, 35 percent syrah, and 10 percent mourvèdre—created a full, fleshy wine whose finishing tannins were polished and ripe, with no rough edges.

Also impressive was the 2007 Northern Blend Red Wine, a Columbia Valley syrah co-fermented with 3 percent viognier. Streaked throughout with a mix of tart berry, wild herb, green olive, and coffee bean, it was a fine-tuned effort with the sort of seamless complexity that few wineries—much less new wineries—ever achieve. Completing the first release was the 2008 Southern White, a 50-50 viognier-roussanne blend loaded with floral and mint aromas, soft and penetrating in the mouth, with phenolic bite showing only in the lengthy finish.

SAN JUAN VINEYARDS

First vintage: 1999

www.sanjuanvineyards.com

Though many successful wineries have been established on the islands of Puget Sound, they face two difficult hurdles. The first is simply logistical—how to get eastern Washington grapes to the wineries, when hundreds of miles, mountain passes, and (often) ferry travel are involved. The second is the challenge of establishing estate vineyards, often with lesser-known grapes and without the extensive farming experience that most growers can rely on.

San Juan Vineyards has successfully met both challenges. A wide variety of wines from Yakima Valley, Columbia Gorge, and Columbia Valley grapes are offered, always competent, occasionally excellent. Memorable bottles have included a barrel-fermented pinot gris, a Celilo vineyard chardonnay, and several syrahs.

From the estate vineyard on San Juan Island have come a series of light, delicate, elegant white wines fashioned from siegerrebe and Madeleine angevine grapes. At their finest these recall some of the wines of eastern France (Savoie), Switzerland, and the Trentino–Alto Adige region of Italy.

STELLA FINO

First vintage: 2005

www.stellafino.com

Based in Milton-Freewater, the Oregon side of the Walla Walla AVA, Stella Fino owners Matt and Marlene Steiner intend to focus on Italian varietals. The winery is named for Matt's great-grandmother, the inspiration for the brand.

The Steiners left financial careers in Manhattan to find a simpler life. The first few Stella Fino vintages focused on sangiovese, barbera, and a simple, quaffable barbera-sangiovese blend called The Boot. The lone white wine is a pinot gris. Grapes will eventually be sourced from a planned 35-acre estate vineyard on the north fork of the Walla Walla River. The newness of the winery, inexperience of the winemaker, and decision to make Italian varietals all suggest that a learning curve is definitely in this winery's immediate future, but it should be fun to watch.

STEMILT CREEK

First vintage: 2002

www.stemiltcreekwinery.com

Jan and Kyle Mathison belong to a Wenatchee farming family whose roots go back more than a century. The small winery, with annual production around 1,300 cases, is a small part of their fruit-growing business but uses estate-grown grapes exclusively, from their south-facing vineyard above Stemilt Creek. The Mathisons have planted seven acres of merlot, seven of cabernet sauvignon, an acre and a half of cabernet franc, and two acres of syrah.

Jan is making the wines with help from other locals in the business. The Stemilt Hill Red is a tasting room bargain, while the merlot and the cabernet sauvignon have a smooth, chocolaty appeal reminiscent of such wineries as Fidélitas and Reininger. My favorite so far is the Cabernet Franc, which brings the same smooth, round fruit-forward flavors as the other wines, but adds in more details with citrus, olive, and green tea flavors streaking through. The finish gets downright sexy, with a strong wash of chocolate and caramel.

STEPPE CELLARS

First vintage: 2005

www.steppecellars.com

This modest operation located in the Rattlesnake Hills AVA is notable for its winemaker, German-born Anke Freimuth-Wildman, who worked for the Hogue winery previously. Not too surprisingly, she is particularly adept with riesling and gewürztraminer, both of which are made in off-dry, tasting room styles that showcase pretty Yakima Valley grapes. The dry white wines are less interesting; the reds (cabernet, merlot and syrah) pleasant and fruity.

WINES OF SUBSTANCE

First vintage: 2006

www.winesofsubstance.com

This clever project is a collaboration among Jason Huntley and Jamie Brown (Waters) and Greg Harrington (Gramercy Cellars). Drawing on the periodic table of elements for graphic inspiration, they launched the brand with a head-turning website and an ever-growing lineup of wines that offer not only substance but inspiration.

"Substance enables us to play at the top of our game," says Harrington. "I don't have to force anything to fit [the Gramercy Cellars portfolio]." Consumers are the beneficiaries, as Substance offers handcrafted, quality-driven wines at less than half the price of the main brands. The focus throughout is on single-varietal wines, many from unusual varietals.

The labels show blocky white letters on a black background (a sort of reverse K Vintners), using abbreviations such as Cs (for cabernet) and Me (for merlot). The wines are very well made, in a style that might be dubbed sommeliatarian—that is to say, restrained, elegant, food-friendly. Among the many interesting releases are a pinot gris, a counoise, a malbec, and a cabernet franc. Great stuff all around.

Wines of Substance is in some sense the poster kid for the youth movement among Walla Walla winemakers. Standards are much higher, competition more cutthroat, and costs are far beyond what anyone imagined 20 years ago. It's pleasing to note that, in response to the relentless, price-driven competition from well-capitalized corporate brand makers, there are few if any gimmick labels coming out of the region.

Instead there is a welcome trend toward clever, artistic label designs, interesting varietals (often 100 percent, single-vineyard expressions of terroir), moderate levels of alcohol, restrained use of new oak, and a genuine effort to offer value pricing across an entire portfolio.

SWEET VALLEY WINES

First vintage: 2005

www.sweetvalleywines.com

In April 2007—the same week that the Walla Walla sweet onion became the official Washington State vegetable after winning a knock-down, eye-for-an-eye battle with the russet potato lobby—Sweet Valley Wines was officially named Washington's five-hundredth winery. Though such milestones are questionable at best, the tiny winery, whose first vintage consisted of a few hundred cases of a single red wine, found its named splashed across press releases and trumpeted in the wine media.

With encouragement and some guidance from Chris and Gary Figgins (Leonetti Cellar), managing partners David and Karen McDaniels—one of four couples who share ownership—have handed over the winemaking chores to their son Josh. He has already expanded the lineup to include viognier and syrah, merlot and cabernet, tempranillo and a springtime rosé.

A dedicated winery is planned, and case production, now at 2,000, is anticipated to triple. The first few vintages have been hit-and-miss, but the successes—especially the viognier and the Double Barrel Red—are promising.

TERTULIA CELLARS

First vintage: 2005

www.tertuliacellars.com

Tertulia is one of a cluster of new wineries just north of the Oregon border in Walla Walla. It is the project of Jim O'Connell and Greg Lark, both from out of state and both involved in hospitality businesses. The first three vintages were made at Va Piano. A nearby 14-acre parcel was purchased and planted in 2007, and the winery finished in time for the 2008 crush.

Just under nine acres of grapes are in the ground, including two each of tempranillo, syrah, merlot, and viognier and a smidgen of roussanne and cabernet sauvignon. A second vineyard—13 acres located just south of Seven Hills—is being developed with a mix of grenache, syrah, mourvèdre, counoise, cinsault, and carignan.

The first winemaker was Ryan Raber, a recent graduate of the two-year wine studies program in Walla Walla. Despite making more than a dozen wines from so many different vineyards all at once, he hit the mark with more than a few of them. The first wines from Raber's replacement, Quentin Mylet, have yet to be released.

Tertulia's viognier, syrah, carmenère, malbec, and tempranillo have all been varietally true and nicely nuanced. A cabernet sourced from three excellent Horse Heaven Hill vineyards also shows depth and detail. The Sobra Red—a less expensive blend (the name is Brazilian slang for "leftovers")—is so far the best value in the lineup.

TILDIO

First vintage: 2002

www.tildio.com

Milum and Kate Perry built this cozy winery adjacent to their eight-acre vineyard about a mile east of Lake Chelan. Tildio is Spanish for "killdeer," a shore bird that migrates through the area each spring. "Killdeer winery," says Kate, doesn't sound nearly as appealing as Tildio.

With a UC Davis degree in enology and viticulture, and job experience at Robert Mondavi, Geyser Peak, Stag's Leap Wine Cellars, and MacRostie, she moved back to her home state in 2000 to become an assistant winemaker at Chateau Ste. Michelle. While there she met her husband, Milum, and they embarked on their own winery adventure.

Tildio's first few vintages were a mixed bag that included small lots of rosé, pinot noir, zinfandel, sauvignon blanc, an Oregon sangiovese, a Red Mountain viognier, a tempranillo, a Meritage. More recently the 2,000-case winery is putting a focus on reds. There are proprietary wines such as El Buho (a cabernet-merlot-syrah blend), Robusto (a four-grape Bordeaux blend), SBW (a simple cab-merlot), and Profundo, a substantial, five-varietal Bordeaux blend.

Varietal bottlings include cabernet sauvignon, cabernet franc, malbec, and syrah. The first vintages of their estate-grown fruit went into a pleasant, off-dry riesling and a light, citrusy syrah. The star may prove to be the estate-grown tempranillo, but from grapes this young it's too soon to tell.

TL CELLARS

First vintage: 2004

www.TLCellars.com

Vintner-proprietor Troy Ledwick came up on the restaurant side of the wine business, working a range of jobs in Florida before packing up and moving to Walla Walla to study enology at the community college in 2002.

While still in school, he polished his craft during crush with short stints helping out at Basel Cellars, Forgeron, and Long Shadows. After graduating, he signed on as winemaker for Hence and started this project. TL Cellars currently makes just 250 cases annually (the goal is to top out at 2,000), using the Hence winery as a base. A 2005 cabernet sauvignon named simply Release Number Two showed impressive fruit and winemaking skills. With such limited production and so few wines, it's too soon to give a gold star to TL Cellars, but Ledwick is off to a fast start and has quickly impressed some of the national critics with these first efforts.

TRANCHE CELLARS

First vintage: 2004

www.tranchecellars.com

Tranche is a sister program to Corliss Estates. These are not a selection or second label; but they are offered at lower price points than the Corliss wines. The first four or five vintages of Tranche were made by (now departed) Corliss winemaker Kendall Mix at the Corliss winery in Walla Walla. As with Corliss, these wines have been held back an unusually long time; the premier release was not until May 2009.

Tranche is worth the wait. With a focus on chardonnay and Rhône varietals—and some Italian as well—it has a developing profile that sets it apart from Corliss. Corliss enologist Ali Mayfield became the Tranche winemaker in 2009, taking charge as the winery moved to a separate facility that formerly housed the Nicholas Cole winery. The nearby Blue Mountain vineyard will provide the fruit for the estate-focused Tranche reds. A total of 44 acres are planted to Bordeaux reds, syrah, sangiovese, and small amounts of grenache and mourvèdre.

Among the early releases, the chardonnay, from Celilo vineyard grapes, could honestly pass for a Chassagne-Montrachet. Flavors of apple, Asian pear, and melon, juicy acids, and just a bit of popcorn in the finish. A Rhône white—blending viognier and roussanne from the Evergreen and Sagemoor vineyards—is light and deft, with nicely defined streaks of melon, grapefruit, and orange peel.

Given Michael Corliss's vision and commitment to high quality, the advent of this more affordable lineup is especially welcome.

TRIO VINTNERS

First vintage: 2004

www.triovintners.com

In the autumn of 2006 the Port of Walla Walla opened five new incubator wineries at the eastern edge of the airport, and Trio Vintners was the first to move in. The owners are husband and wife Steve Michener and Denise Slattery, recent transplants from the Bay Area.

Though they both continue to hold day jobs, the winery has quickly found success with well-thought-out, brightly styled wines from excellent vineyards. I especially admired a pair of Lewis vineyard rieslings, but the owners are dropping riesling and most other white wines in favor of a creative lineup of reds, including a range of syrahs and zinfandels, along with very limited bottlings of sangiovese, tempranillo, carmenère, and mourvèdre.

Total production hit 1,200 cases in 2007, but Steve says that was because he can't say no to grapes; it was back down to 750 cases in 2008. Trio's first zinfandel won the notice of *Wine Business Monthly*, which named the tiny winery one of its ten "Hot Small Brands of 2008." Hot it was, at 16.2 percent alcohol, but the subsequent release, a 2007 zin from the Pheasant vineyard, retained the concentrated essence of raspberries and cherries, and swung less of a hammer, keeping the alcohol under 15 percent.

Good as the zins are, Trio's best wines are its sangioveses—the rare riserva bottling challenges Leonetti for best in the state—and its varietal mourvèdre. Prices are moderate, quantities limited, and the quality very high for such a young, bootstrap operation.

TRUST CELLARS

First vintage: 2005

www.trustcellars.com

Steve Brooks lived in Atlanta and for two decades worked at CNN as an editor. An exciting life, world travels, and the rest, but . . . Atlanta got more crowded and more like LA every day, he says, including smog, crime, and traffic. Midlife crisis time.

He and his producer-director wife started thinking about other things to do. They read a newspaper article about winemaking in far-off eastern Washington. "I had no winemaking background at all," he confesses, "but I told everyone I was going to go and start my own winery, so I couldn't back out. We opened the map and looked and saw that Walla Walla was in the middle of nowhere."

Nonetheless, they checked it out. "In 15 minutes," he says, "I knew it was the place." After taking some short courses in winemaking and volunteering at area wineries, Trust Cellars set up shop in the Va Piano incubator space, along with such noteworthy start-ups as Chateau Rollat, Gramercy Cellars, Otis Kenyon, and Tertulia. All have gone on to separate facilities and notable success.

Trust production is up to 1,500 cases annually, with slow growth expected from there. The first few released vintages have included some well-made wines, and some that have wobbled a bit. A beautiful riesling; nicely crafted syrahs; a very rich ice wine; an interesting, barrel-fermented rosé of cabernet franc; some lightly herbal reds—a search for direction. As is often the case with small start-ups, the most interesting wines are single-barrel, mailing list–only offerings: a Lewis vineyard syrah, a Champoux vineyard cabernet, and an elegant Bacchus vineyard cab franc.

TSILLAN CELLARS

First vintage: 2001

www.tsillancellarswines.com

By virtue of its stunning location, perched above the south shore of Lake Chelan, and its Tuscan villa–style architecture, Tsillan (pronounced "Chelan") Cellars has become the must-see destination winery in this new AVA. Owner Bob Jankelson is a trim man in his late sixties, with the butter-soft voice of an old-time radio guy. He earned a degree in dentistry and specialized in treating head and neck pain; that prior life included a lot of world travel. During dozens of teaching trips to Italy, he says, he "found the passion for what I've done subsequently. The Italians have perfected the art of living."

Jankelson owns 135 prime acres—mostly reclaimed orchard land—and a third of it is now planted to riesling, pinot gris, gewürztraminer, chardonnay ("an afterthought, for the tourists"), viognier, syrah, malbec, and experimental rows of sangiovese, barbera, and nebbiolo. The AVA application was driven largely by his sense of the uniqueness of the place, his time in Europe, and clearly his sense of urgency to get things done.

"Chelan is Mendoza with a big lake," he says. "It's at 1,100 feet. Stormy mountain, just six miles west, is 8,000 feet high. Syrah and malbec are the only two reds I want to deal with." The 2003 harvest was the first from estate vines; as of 2008, estate-grown fruit will be used exclusively. The winemaking and general manager positions at Tsillan have been a revolving door, which initially made for a hit-and-miss set of wines.

There's been some improvement recently, in both whites and reds, notably the estate chardonnay and the red blends Bellissima Rossa and Piccolo Rossa. A fourth winemaker—Shane Collins—is on board as of 2008. Tough gig: "I don't want winemakers," says Jankelson, "I want someone that can capture the vineyard and not get into the ego thing of making wine. I have enough confidence in that particular slope that the wines should show a sense of place. I want the wine clean, not manipulated, nor overworked, because what I'm trying to capture aromatically is what expressed itself in the tree fruit."

TULPEN CELLARS

First vintage: 2005

www.tulpencellars.com

Partners Ken Hart and Rick Trumbull have something like a half century of agriculture experience between them, Hart as a vineyard manager (for Abeja, Dunham Cellars, Walla Walla Vintners, àMaurice, and others), Trumbull as the king of composting for the entire Walla Walla Valley.

"I know where the good fruit's at and where to harvest it," says Hart. "I know the good rows, and I never take the whole row." Tulpen means "tulip," and tulips adorn the pretty labels for this boutique, whose production is just around 1,000 cases annually.

Using sustainably farmed fruit from choice vineyards in the Walla Walla and Columbia valleys, Hart crafts ripe, high-alcohol wines ready to drink upon release. The first vintage was made at Zerba: a pure cabernet sauvignon that opened into a beautiful nose, with clean, precise, supple, muscular fruit; a broad-shouldered merlot from Lewis and Gamache fruit, jammy and sweetly delicious; and a chewy, spicy syrah.

In subsequent years, the wines have been made at Artifex and include a potent sangiovese and a Bordeaux blend named Coalescence. If great wines are made in the vineyard—and they certainly are—Hart and Trumbull have the keys to the kingdom.

UPLAND ESTATES

First vintage: 2006

www.uplandwinery.com

Washington's tenth official AVA, Snipes Mountain, is home turf to this small winery. Owner Todd Newhouse is one of a family whose holdings total about 1,200 acres, 700 planted to vinifera, which represents more than three-quarters of the wine grapes grown on the mountain.

Newhouse, who was recently named president of the Washington Association of Wine Grape Growers, is a 1995 graduate of Whitman College, with a major in history and a minor in philosophy. He brings a dash of each to his work managing the family holdings. His tiny winery, named Upland Estates in honor of W. B. Bridgman's historic winery, reflects his dedication to preserving and promoting this unique region. Robert Smasne is the consulting winemaker.

Among the first releases is a remarkable muscat ice wine, made from vines that Bridgman planted on Snipes Mountain in 1917—surely the oldest bearing vinifera in Washington State. Moving forward a half century, there is a cabernet from a vineyard planted in 1973, a graceful wine with the brambly, wild fruit flavors of old vines. The white wines include a rich and fruity gewürztraminer, but the show-stopper is a stunning, supple, round and luscious, estate-grown, barrel-fermented sauvignon blanc.

WATERMILL

First vintage: 2005

www.watermillwinery.com

On the Oregon side of the Walla Walla Valley, many new vineyards are being planted where apple and cherry orchards once grew. Earl and Lorraine Brown settled in the region in 1957, and today the third generation has expanded the original farming enterprise to include vineyards, a winery, and the Blue Mountain cidery.

The Anna Marie vineyard was planted in 2001, followed by McClellan Estate in 2003, Watermill Estate in 2006, and Dugger Creek in 2009. Along with cabernet sauvignon, cabernet franc, merlot, and syrah, these vineyards include more unusual varietals: malbec, mourvèdre, petit verdot, barbera, nebbiolo, grenache, and tempranillo.

Watermill's first wines were made in 2005, under the guiding hand of consulting winemaker Rich Funk (Saviah Cellars). Andrew Brown is now credited as winemaker; in any event, the wines just keep on getting better and better. It's a challenge to differentiate yourself from the pack in Walla Walla, and Watermill is doing so by offering estate bottlings of cabernet franc, malbec and petit verdot (all outstanding), as well as a number of syrahs that are very K-like in their structure and supple energy.

The Praying Mantis syrah is the best yet, a tribute to the helpful insect whose cartoony label does not suggest the reserve-caliber wine in the bottle. The petit verdot keeps the tannins reined in and the nose loaded with violets, chocolate, and cassis. It's smooth and sexy and may be the best bottle of varietal PV I've ever had. A well-made viognier is the first white wine from Watermill, but it is the estate wines that best signal a bright future for this new winery.

WHIDBEY ISLAND

First vintage: 1991

www.whidbeyislandwinery.com

One of the first of the island wineries scattered throughout the Puget Sound AVA, Whidbey Island's owners planted their vineyard in 1986 and opened the winery six years later. Production has grown from just 400 cases to roughly 3,500 cases a year—half from estate-grown fruit, half from eastern Washington vineyards.

There have been some well-made wines over the years, though not without the occasional hiccup. The red wines in particular have been spotty, sometimes green and bitter, sometimes funky, sometimes simply unripe. Then a real success shows up, such as the Crawford vineyard syrah, and the sangiovese, with its delicate accents of black olive, smoke, and tobacco wrapped around strawberry fruit.

That said, the most interesting (and reliably well-made) wines from Whidbey Island continue to be the whites from estate-grown grapes. These cool-climate varietals include Madeleine angevine and siegerrebe—bracingly dry, citrusy, and quite low in alcohol.

A recent release of a Yakima Valley roussanne was a surprising standout—a refreshing mix of citrus rind, mineral, wet stone, and tangy lime. Prices are quite reasonable.

WILLIAM CHURCH

First vintage: 2005

www.williamchurchwinery.com

William Church remains a puzzling newcomer. The winery began with an all-star consulting winemaker (Matt Loso, formerly of Matthews Estate) and good contacts for its grapes. I've tasted most of its releases at least twice, sometimes at three separate intervals. What my notes consistently show is inconsistency.

The Conner Lee vineyard viognier can be tangy and refreshingly like a good gin and tonic, with citrus rind and grapefruit leading to a hint of quinine in the finish. Or then again, it can fall completely flat, with no midpalate. Bad bottle?

Similar inconsistency affects the syrahs and the malbecs. Stylistically the three vintages of syrah have been all over the map, from pruney in 2005 to rather puny in 2007. The blending of these wines seems a bit rote. And yet the potential remains for William Church to elevate itself to the top ranks of the Woodinville boutiques.

The recent addition of Marcus Rafanelli to the winery staff has brought stability to the day-to-day barrel management. Prices, which have been high, are coming down also—a pleasant red called Bishop's Blend was introduced in the spring of 2009 and has succeeded because it sells for less than $20 and delivers immediately accessible, fruit-driven flavors.

The commitment to quality is here—now this winery needs to find its stroke, and keep swinging.

WOODINVILLE WINE CELLARS

First vintage: 1999

www.woodinvillewinecellars.com

My tastings of Woodinville Wine Cellars releases over the first few vintages of this century suggested a winery struggling to find its way. Begun as an incubator facility at the old French Creek winery, the original Woodinville Wine Company released a 1999 Bear Creek syrah while serving as the first home for such rising star wineries as Gorman, Mark Ryan, Page, Red Sky, Ross Andrew, and Stevens.

Renamed Woodinville Wine Cellars, its own production plans grew and the co-op idea was abandoned. Sean Boyd (the son of wine writer Gerald Boyd) took over the winemaking in 2006, and his releases have been re-energizing the brand and drawing critical praise. About 3,000 cases are made annually, including 500 cases of a spicy and textural sauvignon blanc and another 500 of a value-priced red called Little Bear Creek.

As of 2006 the flagship wine, Ausonius, has been renamed Indomitable (the usual reason—threatened legal action over alleged trademark infringement). A vertical tasting of Ausonius/Indomitable releases from vintages 2002 through 2006 chronicled slow, steady improvement; the older wines started out well but finished poorly, while the most recent vintages were textural, loaded with fruit, and nicely balanced.

Boyd is offering a number of limited-production reds, including reserve syrahs and cabernets and a 100 percent malbec dubbed Last Man Standing. These are sold mostly to mailing list and tasting room customers. I am especially delighted with the winery's sauvignon blancs, using grapes from the Artz (Red Mountain) and Stillwater Creek

(Frenchman Hills) vineyards. If the red wines can rise to the same quality, Woodinville Wine Cellars will have successfully survived its self-described "trials and tribulations."

WOODHOUSE FAMILY CELLARS

First vintage: 1998

www.woodhouse-usa.com

Bijal Shah is the heart and soul of this expansive group of wineries, and one of the most generous men in the wine industry. A native of Kenya, Shah's successful business enterprises include a clothing company—Woodhouse apparel—and a software company based in India. His family winery includes five different labels, each with a separate name—a bit confusing.

The winery debuted with the release of the Darighe "Proprietor's Blend"—its flagship red, presented in heavy glass and priced at a premium. The Dussek Family Cellars label followed, used for cabernet sauvignon and syrah. The Maghee Cellars merlot was next to be introduced, a liquorous, chewy wine from Rattlesnake Hills fruit. Kennedy Shah, the fourth label, is sold only in the tasting room. At various times it has offered a chardonnay-chenin-viognier blend, a cabernet sauvignon, a cabernet franc, a malbec, a merlot, a petit verdot, a syrah, and a tempranillo, along with the occasional reserve and even an olive oil. And finally, Hudson•Shah has been added as the white wine label, including chardonnay, riesling, and viognier.

Plans are underway to build a separate production facility for Dussek and Maghee and to plant a sizable estate vineyard. Total production has jumped from 3,000 to 11,000 cases in just four years.

I have tasted dozens of Woodhouse wines over the years and found them challenging for my palate preferences. They tend to be full-blown, too ripe for my taste, and often quite oaky. Red wine tannins are sometimes rough; white wines can be soft and buttery. Winemaking has been exclusively the responsibility of a family member until recently, but in 2008 a Frenchman, Jean Claude Beck, joined the team. Beck's family estate, in Alsace, has been producing wine since the late 1500s. It is my sincere hope that he can fine-tune these Woodhouse Family wines so that I can give them all my wholehearted endorsement.

ZERBA CELLARS

First vintage: 2003

www.zerbacellars.com

Zerba is owned by Cecil and Marilyn Zerba, who for years operated Zerba Gardens, a plant nursery in Milton-Freewater (the Oregon side of the Walla Walla Valley).

The Zerbas planted their first vineyards in 2001 and 2003, only to be frozen out in 2004. Undaunted, they replanted with cuttings from Seven Hills. Their winery is a partnership with Mark and Dana Retz (Mark previously worked in sales and marketing for Oregon's Amity vineyards); and their new winemaker, Doug Nierman, brings with him excellent credentials. Early California winery experience led to a degree in enology and viticulture from UC Davis. That was followed by a move to Walla Walla and more work (at Long Shadows and Pepper Bridge) before joining Zerba Cellars.

While the new vineyards mature, the Zerbas have been relying mostly on purchased Columbia Valley fruit. The current lineup includes chardonnay, sémillon, viognier, cabernet sauvignon, cabernet franc, malbec, merlot, sangiovese, and syrah, along with the occasional reserve and some dessert wines.

Given the changes in winemakers during the first few vintages, the vineyard setbacks, and the changing fruit sources, it's too soon to pin any sort of a label on Zerba. But the most recent releases—a well-defined viognier, a tightly constructed syrah—show a winery on a path of steady improvement.

ZERO ONE VINTNERS

First vintage: 2007

www.zeroonevintners.com

Zero One is a project of Thomas Vogele—a veteran of wine sales who now works with Michael Mondavi's Folio wines—his wife, Kristin, and her sister Lynne Anderson, who is married to the winemaker for Northstar.

The first releases are a riesling named Golden Delicious and a cabernet sauvignon called The Wild Sky. The riesling, sourced from Gamache vineyard grapes, is generous and juicy, with lush and very ripe flavors of apples (duh!) and stone fruits. The cabernet, from Spofford Station grapes, is a chewy, dense, and meaty wine, beautifully proportioned with complex details of smoke, tar, and toasted grains.

The quality is not at all surprising considering that the wines are made at, and the fruit sourced through, the Wahluke Wine Company, under the supervision of Gordy Hill. With the marketing and sales expertise that Vogele brings to the project, it should continue to do well.

EPILOGUE
What's Next?

In the first edition of this book, I asked if Washington might be the Blanche Dubois of wine regions; its fortunes dependent on the kindness of strangers such as wine critics, wine buyers for influential restaurants, and judges at prestigious wine competitions.

Ten influential wine industry veterans, all with different perspectives and agendas, offered their comments, specifically addressing the most important criticisms and challenges facing Washington vintners. Let me quickly summarize their thoughts.

Myles Anderson, a partner in Walla Walla Vintners and the founding director of Walla Walla's Institute for Enology and Viticulture, noted the "collaborative spirit" of Washington winemakers and opined that the best Washington wines, rather than being too expensive, are undervalued. That said, Anderson criticized the "many wines that taste alike" and felt that "too many new wineries are being started by untrained owner-winemakers."

Ted Baseler, president and CEO of Ste. Michelle Wine Estates, cited the impressive growth of Washington wine sales, but pointed out two barriers to becoming more competitive: a lack of awareness that wines are made in Washington, and a paucity of tourists going to visit the vineyards.

Bob Betz, MW and the winemaker and owner of Betz Family winery, called the Columbia Valley "the hero of the story. The convergence of climate, soil, geography, and topography is unique and creates growing conditions that lead to high-quality fruit." But he also felt that "Washington's most glaring weakness is myopia: an unrealistic view of the wine world," as well as "a lack of understanding of the vinification fundamentals by some winemakers."

Andrew Browne, founder and CEO of Precept Brands, noted that Washington has not been forced into the competitive global marketplace on a large scale, because "the majority of wineries in the state are still focused on high quality, high price, and low production." The solution, said Browne, is to "expand our shelf or wine list presence in all channels by offering more wines at an everyday price point."

Steve Burns, the executive director of the Washington Wine Commission from 1996 to 2004, pointed to Japan as a "quality-conscious consumer product market" with a very favorable opinion of Washington wines. "Selling the brand that is Washington wine," Burns counseled, "is really no different than selling a brand like Columbia Crest or Woodward Canyon—it's hand-sold, one bottle at a time."

Tom Hedges, owner-founder of the state's largest family-owned winery, emphasized the importance of focusing marketing efforts on a single wine. "Our quality is there, but our message is not," he stated. "You can count on one hand all the wine regions in the world that are known for more than one wine. When you produce only two out of every 1,000 bottles of wine made in the world, for your message to stick, it must be real simple."

The late David Lake, MW and winemaker at Columbia winery (1979–2005), felt that to become more competitive globally, "Washington must emphasize the quality edge—we make no basic plonk, jug wine, vin ordinaire in Washington." Pointing to a "growing disenchantment with high-alcohol, superripe, overwrought reds from California," Lake advised that we "stress the drinkability and food compatibility of Washington wines."

Dan McCarthy, a founding partner in McCarthy & Schiering Wine Merchants, agrees that because most Washington wineries are tiny, "they don't have the production, marketing budget, or knowledge to actively establish national distribution, let alone an international reputation." Yet he felt that a more challenging problem was the lack of educational programs to turn potential winemakers into professional winemakers.

Robin Pollard, currently serving as the executive director of the Washington Wine Commission, was confident that "over time, our branded Washington wine industry message ["Washington State—The Perfect Climate for Wine"] will resonate with both trade and consumer audiences and increase Washington wine sales locally, nationally, and internationally."

Allen Shoup, the founder and CEO of Long Shadows Vintners and past CEO of Ste. Michelle Wine Estates, worried that "at the moment we are not on the radar screens of any of the important international markets." Worse still, "we still have not effectively developed the domestic market . . . for most unsophisticated consumers we are virtually unknown."

Looking back a few years later, my own impressions are that many of the issues discussed then, though still important, are well on their way to being addressed. Educational programs for would-be vintners are now being offered at several locations around the state, and the impact of their graduates can be easily seen in places such as Walla Walla, where most new wineries are owned by (or are hiring) Washington-trained winemakers.

The Wine Commission and other industry groups have been actively bringing in writers and sommeliers from around the world, showing them the AVAs, the vineyards, and the sheer beauty of Washington wine country, as well as educating them on the state's diverse wines.

The 2010 Bloggers Conference was held in Walla Walla—a clear sign that the young opinion makers who critique and evangelize wine in the so-called social media are especially interested in Washington. And after two years of the worst recession in memory, there have been slowdowns in planned growth, but no mass casualties or panic. In fact, the state's largest wine companies—Ste. Michelle Wine Estates and Precept Brands— have been adding wineries, brands, vineyards, and tasting rooms, not contracting or closing them.

The criticism that most of the best small Washington wineries do not own vineyards is no longer relevant. Many of the start-ups from the 1990s have begun to acquire and plant their own land. In the state's newest AVA, Lake Chelan, almost every winery has its own vineyard. The expansion of vineyards in the Rattlesnake Hills, on Red Mountain, in the Walla Walla Valley, the Horse Heaven Hills, the Wahluke Slope, the Columbia Gorge—virtually everywhere in the state—is testament to the importance being placed on owning, not just controlling, your grape sources.

The fact that the Wine Commission has made developing tourism such a high priority is also beginning to produce results. Ten years ago, visitors to Washington wine country might find a friendly tasting room here and there, but nothing comparable to the clusters of welcoming wineries now located throughout the state. Lake Chelan, Wenatchee, Leavenworth, Yakima, Prosser, the Tri-Cities, Walla Walla, the Rattlesnake Hills, the Columbia Gorge, and Woodinville all have concentrations of wineries and tasting rooms, wine festivals and special events, and other amenities that tourists require. Visiting Washington wine country has become a favorite pastime for residents of the big cities on the west side, as well as the locals who already live in eastern Washington and Oregon.

How dependent are wine sales on the scores and reviews from a handful of newsletters and wine magazines? That is difficult to gauge. Many sellers in the wine trade, especially distributors and independent retailers, still pound the drum every time one of their producers rings up a 90. But I suspect that consumers care less and less. The impact of even positive reviews is being diluted by score inflation, by reliance on judging panels rather than individual palates, by too many medal-awarding "competitions" designed chiefly to make money for the organizers, by trade publications that do not ever criticize.

Most important, young consumers and wine professionals are quite different today than in previous decades. They have grown up with wine, and they have often traveled to wine regions around the world by the time they can legally drink. It is older wine drinkers who are most likely to cling to the notion that massive flavors of oak and alcohol are the defining attributes of "fine wine." Younger, more educated palates increasingly favor wines with nuance, balance, terroir, individuality, finesse, aromatic complexity, and flavor complexity. They want wines that deliver all of the above qualities at moderate, food-friendly alcohol levels.

Washington still has its share of too-ripe, alcoholic wines, but most of the best winemakers and growers are striving for nuance and balance. They are finding new places to plant, different ways to regulate the vines, worrying less about sugar levels and more about skin and seed flavors at harvest. Climate change, if and when it affects Washington, is not likely to be a problem, given the vastness of the state, with many higher-elevation sites still unexplored. Water rights are hard to come by, so vineyards are now being dry-farmed in some emerging regions. Phylloxera may one day strike, so vintners are planting some new vineyards on grafted rootstock.

It is still, as I wrote a few years ago, "a delicious moment in time." But it is no longer a "who are we and where are we going?" moment. Washington's wine industry has moved through its uneasy adolescence into the first full bloom of glorious youth, with all of the energy, vitality, enthusiasm, and passion for discovery that implies. Those of us fortunate enough to live and work here invite the rest of you to come visit and see what all the excitement is about.

PAUL GREGUTT'S ANNUAL TOP 100 LISTS OF WASHINGTON STATE WINES

Two of the most eagerly awaited annual "Best of" lists are the year's Top 100 wines as profiled in *Wine Spectator* and *Wine Enthusiast* (for whose tasting panel I contribute wine reviews and scores). Washington does quite well in both of these publications, especially considering how truly small its wine industry is. But in 2006, while I was working on the first edition of this book, it occurred to me, why not do my own annual Top 100 Washington wine list? It remains the only such list focused exclusively on wines made with Washington grapes, and compiled by a single individual who lives and works here. It is published each December in my *Seattle Times* Wine Adviser column.

There are now more than 650 bonded wineries in the state. If they produce just 10 wines each annually (some less, some more), that's more than 6,500 wines. Do I taste them all? In my dreams! But I do taste a significant percentage of them, and that, along with frequent visits to wineries and vineyards, regular conversations and tastings with the winemakers themselves, and a depth of reference tastings reaching back a quarter century, all enter into these rankings.

With one or two exceptions, I list just one wine per winery, although many of the producers deliver a full lineup of outstanding wines. The wine named is the one that I felt was the best that each of them released in that year. Though the following lists are not compiled strictly by the wine scores, these are certainly all wines that score well. Consistency from year to year, overall style and quality, and relative value to comparably priced wines are some of the other important considerations when doing these rankings. Each list gives suggested retail prices at the time of the wine's release.

TOP 100 WINES FOR 2009

1. Wine of the Year: Charles Smith 2006 Royal City Syrah ($80)
2. Quilceda Creek 2006 Cabernet Sauvignon ($125)
3. Betz Family 2006 Père de Famille Cabernet Sauvignon ($58)

4. Abeja 2005 Reserve Cabernet Sauvignon ($80)
5. Leonetti Cellar 2006 Cabernet Sauvignon ($85)
6. Fielding Hills 2007 Riverbend Vineyard Cabernet Sauvignon ($38)
7. Owen Roe 2007 Lady Rosa Syrah ($45)
8. Andrew Will 2006 Ciel du Cheval Vineyard Red Wine ($55)
9. K Vintners 2006 En Chamberlin Roma Red ($60)
10. Sineann 2007 Block One Cabernet Sauvignon ($72)
11. Côte Bonneville 2005 DuBrul Vineyard Red ($125)
12. Poet's Leap 2008 Riesling ($20)
13. Buty 2007 70% Sémillon/26% Sauvignon/4% Muscadelle ($25)
14. Rôtie Cellars 2007 Southern Blend Red Wine ($35)
15. Rulo 2006 Cabernet Sauvignon ($40)
16. Gramercy Cellars 2006 Cabernet Sauvignon ($42)
17. Stevens 2006 XY Reserve Cabernet Sauvignon ($42)
18. Northstar 2006 Merlot ($50)
19. Corliss Estates 2004 Cabernet Sauvignon ($75)
20. Nicholas Cole Cellars 2005 Estate Reserve ($75)
21. Den Hoed 2006 Andreas Cabernet Sauvignon ($80)
22. Upland Estates 2007 Sauvignon Blanc ($18)
23. Novelty Hill 2007 Stillwater Creek Vineyard Viognier ($20)
24. Ardenvoir 2008 Artist Series Sémillon ($22)
25. Eroica 2008 Riesling ($24)
26. Beresan 2006 Cabernet Sauvignon ($29)
27. JM Cellars 2007 Chardonnay ($32)
28. Watermill 2006 Praying Mantis Syrah ($32)
29. Bunchgrass 2007 Frazier Bluff Vineyard Malbec ($32)
30. McCrea 2005 Boushey Grande Côte Vineyard Syrah ($36)
31. Balboa 2006 Sayulita Red ($40)
32. Woodward Canyon 2008 Chardonnay ($44)
33. Dunham 2006 Cabernet Sauvignon XII ($45)
34. Grand Rêve 2006 Collaboration Series III Ciel du Cheval Red ($45)
35. L'Ecole No 41 2006 Seven Hills Vineyard Perigee ($50)
36. Spring Valley Vineyard 2006 Uriah Red ($50)
37. Rasa Vineyards 2007 QED Syrah ($50)
38. Pepper Bridge 2006 Seven Hills Vineyard Red ($55)
39. Gorman 2007 The Evil Twin Syrah–Cabernet Sauvignon ($60)
40. DeLille Cellars 2006 Chaleur Estate Red Wine ($75)
41. J. Bookwalter 2006 Chapter Two Red ($78)
42. Boudreaux Cellars 2005 Reserve Cabernet Sauvignon ($100)
43. Whitman Cellars 2008 Riesling ($14)
44. Pacific Rim 2008 Organic Riesling ($14)

45. Amavi Cellars 2008 Sémillon ($20)

46. Syncline 2007 Syrah ($24)

47. Sleight of Hand 2007 The Enchantress Chardonnay ($24)

48. Darby 2008 Le Deuce Viognier 52%/Roussanne 48% ($24)

49. Barrister 2007 Cabernet Franc ($27)

50. Hestia Cellars 2006 Syrah ($32)

51. Tamarack Cellars 2006 DuBrul Vineyard Reserve Red ($45)

52. Arbor Crest 2005 Dionysus Red ($45)

53. Walla Walla Vintners 2006 Vineyard Select Cabernet Sauvignon ($48)

54. Doyenne 2006 Syrah ($49)

55. Cougar Crest 2005 Estate Grown Reserve Syrah ($55)

56. McKinley Springs 2007 Viognier ($14)

57. Merry Cellars 2008 Sauvignon Blanc ($14)

58. Trust 2008 Riesling ($16)

59. Nefarious Cellars 2008 Stone's Throw Vineyard Riesling ($18)

60. Gamache Vintners 2007 Estate Riesling ($18)

61. Gordon Brothers 2006 Syrah ($20)

62. Alexandria Nicole 2008 Crawford Viognier ($20)

63. Baer 2008 Shard ($21)

64. Waterbrook 2007 Reserve Syrah ($22)

65. Efesté 2006 Final-Final Cabernet-Syrah ($25)

66. Soos Creek 2007 Artist Series 7 Red Wine ($28)

67. Andrew Rich 2007 Ciel du Cheval Vineyard Roussanne ($28)

68. Olsen Estates 2007 Chardonnay ($28)

69. Basel Cellars 2006 Pheasant Run Vineyard Estate Merlot ($28)

70. Otis Kenyon 2006 Merlot ($30)

71. Tranche 2005 Chardonnay ($30)

72. Tulpen Cellars 2005 Merlot ($30)

73. Coeur d'Alene Cellars 2006 Boushey Vineyard Syrah ($36)

74. GLM 2005 Deluge Red ($40)

75. Forgeron 2004 Klipsun Vineyard Merlot ($46)

76. AlmaTerra 2006 Ciel du Cheval Vineyard Syrah ($50)

77. Reynvaan Family Vineyards 2007 The Contender Syrah ($55)

78. Col Solare 2006 Red Table Wine ($70)

79. Snoqualmie 2008 Naked Riesling ($12)

80. Hedges Family Estate 2008 CMS White–Sauvignon Blanc ($14)

81. Airfield Estates 2008 Riesling ($14)

82. Columbia Crest 2007 H3 Les Chevaux Red ($15)

83. Thurston Wolfe 2008 PGV ($16)

84. Woodinville Wine Cellars 2008 Sauvignon Blanc ($18)

85. SuLei Cellars 2007 Beet Red ($19)

86. Three Angels 2007 Coyote Canyon Vineyard Primitivo ($20)

87. Seven Hills 2007 Merlot ($22)

88. Cadaretta 2008 Sauvignon Blanc–Sémillon ($23)

89. Milbrandt Vineyards 2006 The Estates Cabernet Sauvignon ($25)

90. Isenhower 2006 River Beauty Syrah ($26)

91. Trio Vintners 2006 Morrison Lane Vineyard Sangiovese Riserva ($26)

92. Lullaby 2007 Viognier ($28)

93. Stephenson Cellars 2006 Syrah ($30)

94. Zerba Cellars 2006 Cabernet Sauvignon ($30)

95. Hard Row to Hoe 2006 Cabernet Franc ($32)

96. àMaurice 2006 Malbec ($34)

97. :Nota Bene 2006 Ciel du Cheval Vineyard Red ($35)

98. Tertulia Cellars 2006 Malbec ($35)

99. Va Piano 2006 Estate Cabernet Sauvignon ($48)

100. Bergevin Lane 2006 Intuition Reserve Red Wine ($55)

TOP 100 WINES FOR 2008

1. Wine of the Year: Betz Family 2005 Père de Famille Cabernet Sauvignon ($55)

2. Leonetti Cellar 2005 Reserve Red ($110)

3. Cayuse 2006 En Cerise Syrah ($65)

4. Quilceda Creek 2005 Cabernet Sauvignon ($115)

5. Woodward Canyon 2006 Estate Red ($60)

6. Poet's Leap 2007 Riesling ($20)

7. Thurston Wolfe 2004 JTW Reserve Dessert Wine ($20)

8. Stevens 2006 Black Tongue Syrah ($32)

9. Rulo 2005 Silo Red ($35)

10. Boudreaux Cellars 2005 Merlot ($40)

11. Fielding Hills 2006 Riverbend Vineyard Syrah ($40)

12. Owen Roe 2006 Lady Rosa Syrah ($45)

13. Sparkman 2006 Darkness Syrah ($50)

14. Chateau Rollat 2006 Edouard Cabernet Sauvignon ($65)

15. Gramercy Cellars 2006 John Lewis Syrah ($65)

16. DeLille Cellars 2005 Chaleur Estate Red ($72)

17. Sheridan Vineyard 2005 Reserve Cabernet Sauvignon ($75)

18. Dunham Cellars 2005 Lewis Vineyard Syrah ($75)

19. Gramercy Cellars/Waters 21 Grams 2005 Red Wine ($125)

20. Novelty Hill 2006 Stillwater Creek Viognier ($20)

21. Januik 2006 Elerding Vineyard Chardonnay ($25)

22. Pacific Rim 2007 Wallula Vineyard Biodynamic Riesling ($32)

23. JM Cellars 2006 Chardonnay ($32)

24. Buty 2006 Merlot-Cabernet Franc ($35)

25. Syncline 2006 Cuvée Elena Red ($35)

26. Beresan 2005 Stone River Red ($35)

27. Mark Ryan 2006 Chardonnay ($35)

28. Gorman 2007 Big Sissy Chardonnay ($38)

29. Soos Creek 2006 Ciel du Cheval Red ($40)

30. Abeja 2005 Cabernet Sauvignon ($42)

31. Bunnell Family 2006 Clifton Hill Syrah ($42)

32. Walla Walla Vintners 2005 Vineyard Select Cabernet Sauvignon ($48)

33. Pepper Bridge 2005 Cabernet Sauvignon ($55)

34. K Vintners 2006 Phil Lane Syrah ($70)

35. Doyenne 2005 Grand Ciel Syrah ($75)

36. Canoe Ridge 2007 Snipes Vineyard Dry Riesling ($17)

37. Andrew Rich 2006 Roussanne ($20)

38. Ardenvoir 2007 Sémillon ($22)

39. Dowsett Family 2007 Celilo Vineyard Gewurztraminer ($22)

40. Brian Carter Cellars 2006 Oriana White ($24)

41. Stephenson Cellars 2005 Cabernet Sauvignon ($30)

42. Reininger 2005 Helix Stillwater Creek Merlot ($30)

43. Forgeron Cellars 2003 Cabernet Sauvignon ($30)

44. Dumas Station 2005 Estate Syrah ($32)

45. JLC 2004 Spofford Station Estate Merlot ($36)

46. Waters 2006 Loess Vineyard Syrah ($40)

47. Chandler Reach 2004 Parris Estate Reserve Cabernet Sauvignon ($42)

48. Lachini 2005 Klipsun Vineyard La Bestia Cabernet Sauvignon ($45)

49. Sineann 2006 Cold Creek Cabernet Sauvignon ($48)

50. Browne Family Vineyards 2005 Cabernet Sauvignon ($50)

51. Cadence 2006 Cara Mia Vineyard Camerata Red ($55)

52. Col Solare 2005 Red ($75)

53. Chateau Ste. Michelle 2005 Canoe Ridge Estate Merlot ($22)

54. O•S Winery 2007 Champoux Vineyard Riesling ($22)

55. Barrister 2006 Merlot ($25)

56. McCrea Cellars 2007 Sirocco Blanc ($28)

57. Saviah 2007 Stillwater Creek Vineyard Chardonnay ($25)

58. Efesté 2005 Final-Final Cabernet-Syrah ($25)

59. Nefarious Cellars 2006 Cabernet Franc ($28)

60. Tamarack Cellars 2006 Cabernet Franc ($28)

61. Columbia 2003 Otis Vineyard Cabernet Sauvignon ($28)

62. Amavi 2006 Syrah ($28)

63. Matthews Estate 2005 Claret ($30)

64. SYZYGY 2005 Syrah ($30)

65. Adamant Cellars 2006 Winemaker's Select Red Blend ($30)

66. Ross Andrew 2006 Boushey Vineyard Syrah ($32)

67. :Nota Bene 2005 Conner Lee Red ($32)

68. Robert Karl 2005 Cabernet Sauvignon ($33)

69. L'Ecole No 41 2006 Seven Hills Estate Merlot ($37)

70. Va Piano 2006 Syrah ($38)

71. Balboa 2005 Mith Red ($40)

72. Northstar 2005 Columbia Valley Merlot ($41)

73. Dusted Valley 2006 Reserve Syrah ($45)

74. Seven Hills 2005 Pentad Red ($50)

75. Fidélitas 2005 Boushey Vineyard Red ($50)

76. Spring Valley Vineyard 2005 Derby Cabernet Sauvignon ($50)

77. Pedestal 2005 Merlot ($55)

78. Feather 2005 Cabernet Sauvignon ($60)

79. Nicholas Cole Cellars 2004 Reserve Red ($105)

80. Barnard Griffin 2007 White Riesling ($8)

81. Milbrandt Vineyards 2006 Traditions Merlot ($15)

82. Arbor Crest 2006 Merlot ($15)

83. Zero One Vintners 2007 Golden Delicious Riesling ($16)

84. Cadaretta 2007 sbs Sauvignon Blanc-Sémillon ($22)

85. Walter Dacon 2007 Viognier ($22)

86. Alexandria Nicole 2005 Destiny Ridge Merlot ($24)

87. Hedges Family 2006 Three Vineyards Red ($25)

88. Hestia 2006 Sémillon ($25)

89. Isenhower 2006 Red Paintbrush Red ($28)

90. Morrison Lane 2005 33⅓ Red ($33)

91. Columbia Crest 2005 Walter Clore Private Reserve Red ($34)

92. Tertulia Cellars 2006 Tempranillo ($35)

93. Tildio 2005 Profundo Red ($35)

94. Camaraderie 2004 Grâce Red ($35)

95. Guardian Cellars 2006 Chalk Line Red ($35)

96. Watermill 2005 Reserve Syrah ($35)

97. Three Rivers 2005 Meritage Red ($39)

98. Alder Ridge 2005 Cabernet Sauvignon ($40)

99. Gordon Brothers 2003 Tradition Red ($40)

100. Bergevin Lane 2005 Intuition Reserve Red ($55)

TOP 100 WINES FOR 2007

1. Wine of the Year: Leonetti Cellar 2004 Reserve ($110)

2. Chateau Ste. Michelle 2006 Ethos Late Harvest White Riesling ($40)

3. Quilceda Creek 2004 Galitzine Vineyard Cabernet Sauvignon ($95)

4. K Vintners 2005 The Beautiful Syrah ($50)

5. Sineann 2005 Block One Champoux Vineyard Cabernet Sauvignon ($65)

6. Cayuse 2005 Widowmaker Cabernet Sauvignon ($65)

7. JLC 2004 Spofford Station Estate Syrah ($32)

8. DeLille Cellars 2006 Chaleur Estate Blanc ($34)

9. Poet's Leap 2006 Riesling ($20)

10. Betz Family 2005 La Serenne Syrah ($50)

11. Dunham 2004 Lewis Vineyard Cabernet Sauvignon ($75)

12. Woodward Canyon 2004 Old Vines Cabernet Sauvignon ($75)

13. McCrea Cellars 2004 Cuvée Orleans Syrah ($60)

14. Chateau Rollat 2005 Edouard Cabernet Sauvignon ($62)

15. Andrew Will 2005 Sorella Red Wine ($65)

16. Matthews Estate 2003 Conner Lee Cabernet Franc Reserve ($110)

17. Robert Karl 2005 Syrah ($29)

18. Syncline 2005 Cuvée Elena Red Wine ($35)

19. Fielding Hills 2005 Cabernet Sauvignon ($38)

20. Walla Walla Vintners 2005 Sagemoor Vineyard Cabernet Sauvignon ($40)

21. Bunnell Family Cellar 2005 Boushey-McPherson Vineyard Syrah ($38)

22. Novelty Hill 2004 Stillwater Creek Vineyard Cabernet Sauvignon ($28)

23. Soos Creek 2005 Artist Series 5 Red Wine ($35)

24. Barnard Griffin 2004 Reserve Cabernet Sauvignon ($30)

25. Basel Cellars 2005 Syrah ($36)

26. Abeja 2004 Cabernet Sauvignon ($38)

27. Buty 2006 67% Sémillon/33% Sauvignon Blanc ($25)

28. Gorman Winery 2005 The Bully Cabernet Sauvignon ($40)

29. Mark Ryan 2006 Conner Lee Vineyard Viognier ($28)

30. Stevens 2004 XY Reserve Cabernet Sauvignon ($42)

31. Isenhower 2004 Bachelor's Button Cabernet Sauvignon ($32)

32. Nicholas Cole Cellars 2004 Camille ($48)

33. Pepper Bridge 2004 Cabernet Sauvignon ($50)

34. SYZYGY 2004 Cabernet Sauvignon ($32)

35. Northstar 2004 Merlot ($50)

36. Seven Hills Winery 2004 Syrah ($26)

37. :Nota Bene 2004 Syrah ($28)

38. Alexandria Nicole 2004 Destiny Ridge Vineyard Red Table Wine ($45)

39. Col Solare 2004 Red Table Wine ($75)

40. Smasne Cellars 2006 Smasne Vineyard Estate Dry Riesling ($22)

41. Beresan 2005 Merlot ($29)

42. Barrister 2005 Cabernet Franc ($25)

43. Januik 2004 Lewis Vineyard Syrah ($30)

44. O•S Winery 2005 Dineen Vineyard Syrah ($42)

45. Pedestal 2004 Merlot ($55)

46. Doyenne 2006 Roussanne ($32)

47. L'Ecole No 41 2006 Fries Vineyard Sémillon ($20)

48. Amavi Cellars 2006 Sémillon ($20)

49. Merry Cellars 2006 Stillwater Creek Vineyard Sémillon ($18)

50. Sparkman 2006 Lumière Chardonnay ($40)

51. Chateau Ste. Michelle 2005 Canoe Ridge Estate Chardonnay ($20)

52. Milbrandt Vineyards 2005 Legacy Syrah ($25)

53. Cadence 2005 Bel Canto Red Wine ($55)

54. Three Rivers 2004 Syrah ($24)

55. Forgeron 2003 Syrah ($30)

56. Otis Kenyon 2005 Seven Hills Vineyard Reserve Merlot ($40)

57. Va Piano 2005 Syrah ($38)

58. Walter Dacon 2005 C'est Syrah Magnifique ($38)

59. Canoe Ridge 2004 Block 1 Reserve Cabernet Sauvignon ($45)

60. Brian Carter Cellars 2004 L'Etalon ($30)

61. J. Bookwalter 2005 Merlot ($36)

62. Charles Smith Wines 2006 Kungfu Girl Riesling ($12)

63. Gamache Vintners 2004 GV Reserve Gamache. Champoux Vineyard Select Cabernet Sauvignon ($40)

64. Waters 2005 Columbia Valley Syrah ($25)

65. Saviah Cellars 2005 Une Vallée Red ($32)

66. Tertulia Cellars 2005 Syrah ($27)

67. Des Voigne Cellars 2005 Montreux Syrah ($27)

68. Seia 2005 Clifton Hill Vineyard Syrah ($30)

69. Cuillin Hills 2005 Syrah ($32)

70. Gordon Brothers 2006 Sauvignon Blanc ($13)

71. Animale 2005 Cabernet Sauvignon ($26)

72. Nelms Road 2005 Cabernet Sauvignon ($20)

73. Hedges 2004 Three Vineyards ($22)

74. Olsen Estates 2006 Chardonnay ($28)

75. Chatter Creek 2004 Clifton Hill Vineyard Syrah ($30)

76. Arbor Crest 2004 Wahluke Slope Vineyard Cabernet Sauvignon ($30)

77. Tamarack Cellars 2005 Cabernet Franc ($25)

78. Hightower Cellars 2004 Merlot ($28)

79. Ash Hollow 2006 Gewürztraminer ($19)

80. Hestia 2004 Red Wine ($20)

81. Apex 2006 Dry Riesling ($20)

82. Vin du Lac 2006 LEHM Estate Dry Riesling ($20)

83. Coeur d'Alene Cellars 2006 Chardonnay ($18)

84. Trust 2006 Sémillon Ice Wine ($40)

85. Cascadia Winery 2006 Riesling ($16)

86. Columbia Crest 2006 Two Vines Riesling ($8)

87. Snoqualmie 2006 Naked Riesling ($11)

88. Airfield Estates 2006 Pinot Gris ($16)

89. Lone Canary 2006 Sauvignon Blanc ($10)

90. Kestrel 2006 Estate Viognier ($20)

91. Bergevin Lane 2006 Viognier ($25)

92. Willow Crest 2005 Cabernet Franc ($16)

93. Wineglass Cellars 2005 Les Vignes de Marcoux Syrah ($35)

94. Thurston Wolfe 2005 Zephyr Ridge Petite Sirah ($20)

95. Woodinville Wine Cellars 2006 Sauvignon Blanc ($18)

96. Trio Vintners 2006 Lewis Vineyards Riesling ($12)

97. Waterbrook 2004 Merlot ($20)

98. Covey Run 2005 Quail Series Chenin Blanc ($8)

99. Dusted Valley 2005 Birch Creek Vineyard Chardonnay ($28)

100. San Juan Vineyards 2006 Madeleine Angevine ($14)

TOP 100 WINES FOR 2006

1. Wine of the Year: Quilceda Creek 2003 Cabernet Sauvignon ($95)

2. Cayuse 2003 Armada Syrah ($65)

3. Fielding Hills 2004 Cabernet Sauvignon ($30)

4. Betz Family Winery 2003 Père de Famille Cabernet Sauvignon ($45)

5. Cadence 2004 Camerata Red Wine ($50)

6. Andrew Will 2002 Annie Camarda Syrah ($58)

7. Mark Ryan 2004 Dead Horse Ciel du Cheval Vineyard ($42)

8. Columbia 2005 Gewürztraminer ($12)

9. Stephenson Cellars 2003 Syrah ($28)

10. Chateau Ste. Michelle 2003 Ethos Syrah ($29)

11. Soos Creek 2003 Champoux Vineyard Cabernet Sauvignon ($30)

12. Chaleur Estate 2005 Blanc ($33)

13. Abeja 2003 Cabernet Sauvignon ($35)

14. McCrea 2003 Boushey Grande Côte Syrah ($42)

15. Gorman 2004 The Evil Twin ($50)

16. Matthews 2004 Hedges Vineyard Syrah ($50)

17. Dunham 2004 Lewis Vineyard Syrah ($75)

18. Leonetti Cellar 2003 Reserve ($100)

19. Boudreaux Cellars 2003 Reserve Cabernet Sauvignon ($80)

20. J. Bookwalter 2005 Riesling ($16)

21. Syncline 2004 Milbrandt Vineyards Syrah ($22)

22. Owen Roe 2005 Sinister Hand Red ($24)

23. Buty 2005 Conner Lee Vineyard Chardonnay ($30)
24. Januik 2003 Syrah ($30)
25. Syncline 2004 Cuvée Elena Grenache-Mourvèdre-Syrah ($35)
26. Kestrel 2003 Cofermented Syrah ($37.50)
27. Spring Valley Vineyard 2004 Uriah ($40)
28. Basel Cellars 2004 Syrah ($42)
29. Pedestal 2003 Merlot ($45)
30. Robert Karl 2003 Inspiration Reserve Red ($45)
31. Bergevin Lane 2003 Jaden's Reserve Syrah ($55)
32. Woodward Canyon 2003 Old Vines Dedication Series 23 ($75)
33. Rulo 2004 Syrah ($19)
34. Morrison Lane 2003 Syrah ($35)
35. Chandler Reach 2003 Monte Regalo ($22)
36. Seia 2004 Clifton Hill Vineyard Syrah ($23)
37. McCrea 2004 Ciel du Cheval Mourvèdre ($28)
38. Latitude 46° N 2004 Syrah ($28)
39. Hightower 2003 Merlot ($28)
40. Baer 2003 Ursa ($29)
41. Novelty Hill 2003 Syrah ($29)
42. Sineann 2004 Cabernet Sauvignon ($30)
43. Alder Ridge 2002 Cabernet Sauvignon ($30)
44. James Leigh 2003 Spofford Station Merlot ($32)
45. Isenhower 2004 River Beauty Syrah ($32)
46. Bunnell Family Cellar 2004 Boushey-McPherson Vineyard Syrah ($33)
47. Stevens 2003 Reserve Cabernet Sauvignon ($35)
48. L'Ecole No 41 2004 Ferguson Commemorative Reserve Red ($45)
49. Walla Walla Vintners 2003 Vineyard Select Cabernet Sauvignon ($45)
50. K Vintners 2003 The Creator ($55)
51. Townshend 2004 Viognier ($10)
52. Canoe Ridge 2004 Oak Ridge Vineyard Gewürztraminer ($13)
53. Sagelands 2003 Merlot ($13)
54. Three Rivers 2005 Meritage White ($19)
55. Wineglass Cellars 2002 Boushey Vineyard Syrah ($23)
56. Seven Hills 2003 Syrah ($25)
57. Waters 2004 Interlude Red ($25)
58. :Nota Bene 2003 Miscela Red ($26)
59. Beresan 2004 Syrah ($29)
60. O•S Winery 2004 Champoux Vineyard Cabernet Franc ($30)
61. Saviah Cellars 2004 Une Vallée Red ($30)
62. Doyenne 2005 Roussanne ($31)
63. Woodinville Wine Cellars 2004 Ausonius ($35)

64. Sheridan 2003 Syrah ($38)

65. Walter Dacon 2004 C'est Syrah Magnifique ($38)

66. Northstar 2003 Syrah ($40)

67. Forgeron 2004 Boushey Vineyard Merlot ($46)

68. Fidélitas 2003 Champoux Vineyard Cabernet Sauvignon ($55)

69. Bonair 2005 Dry Gewürztraminer ($9)

70. Columbia Crest Grand Estates 2002 Shiraz ($11)

71. Arbor Crest 2003 Merlot ($15)

72. Alexandria Nicole 2005 Viognier ($16)

73. Chinook 2004 Sémillon ($17)

74. Cedergreen Cellars 2005 Sauvignon Blanc ($18)

75. Chatter Creek 2005 Viognier ($18)

76. San Juan Vineyards 2004 Celilo Vineyard Chardonnay ($19)

77. Andrew Rich 2004 Cabernet Franc ($20)

78. Helix by Reininger 2004 Syrah ($22)

79. Brian Carter Cellars 2004 Oriana White ($24)

80. Couvillion Winery 2004 Cabernet Sauvignon ($25)

81. Animale 2004 Cabernet Sauvignon ($26)

82. Harlequin 2003 Cuvée Alexander ($29)

83. Maryhill 2003 Proprietor's Reserve Cabernet Franc ($32)

84. C.R. Sandidge 2004 Stone Tree Red ($34)

85. Gamache Vintners 2003 GV Reserve Cabernet Sauvignon ($40)

86. Barons V 2003 Cabernet Sauvignon ($48)

87. Pepper Bridge 2003 Merlot ($50)

88. Barnard Griffin 2005 Rosé of Sangiovese ($8)

89. Balboa 2005 Cabernet Sauvignon ($16)

90. Willow Crest 2003 Syrah ($16)

91. JM Cellars 2005 Viognier ($20)

92. Vin du Lac 2005 LEHM Dry Riesling ($21)

93. Zerba Cellars 2004 Merlot ($28)

94. Maghee Cellars 2002 Merlot ($28)

95. Col Solare 2003 ($70)

96. Hedges 2005 CMS White ($11)

97. Apex II 2005 Sauvignon Blanc ($11)

98. Covey Run 2003 Merlot ($9)

99. Columbia Crest Two Vines 2003 Chardonnay ($8)

100. Snoqualmie Vineyards 2003 Syrah ($11)

INDEX

TEXT: 9.5/14 Scala
DISPLAY: Scala Sans
COMPOSITION: Michael Bass Associates
CARTOGRAPHER: Darmouth Publishing, Inc.
PRINTER AND BINDER: Thomson Shore, Inc.